Starting and Operating a Business in North Carolina

A Step-by-Step Guide

By Michael D. Jenkins and the
Entrepreneurial Services Group of Ernst & Young LLP

The Oasis Press® / PSI Research
Grants Pass, Oregon

98 AA / 94 A

Published by The Oasis Press®
© 1987, 1998 by Michael D. Jenkins
© 1987, 1994 by Ernst & Young LLP

This publication is designed to provide accurate and authoritative information
in regard to the subject matter covered. It is sold with the understanding that the
publisher is not engaged in rendering legal, accounting, or other professional
service. If legal advice or other expert assistance is required, the services of a
competent professional person should be sought.
— *from a declaration of principles jointly adopted by a committee of*
the American Bar Association and a committee of publishers.

The author of chapters 1–10 of the *Starting and Operating a Business* series is
Michael D. Jenkins. The author of the state chapter of *Starting and Operating a*
Business in North Carolina is James E. Scott of Ernst & Young LLP.

Series Editors: Linda Pinkham, Camille Akin, and Mary Lee Arthur
Designer: Constance C. Dickinson
Typographer: Jan Olsson
Series Managing Editor: Constance C. Dickinson

Please direct any comments, questions, or suggestions regarding this book to
The Oasis Press®/PSI Research:

Editorial Department
300 North Valley Drive
Grants Pass, OR 97526
(541) 479-9464

The Oasis Press® is a Registered Trademark of Publishing Services, Inc.,
an Oregon corporation doing business as PSI Research.

Library of Congress Catalog Card Number: 80-83053

ISBN 1-55571-267-3 (paperback)
ISBN 1-55571-266-5 (binder)

Printed in the United States of America
Third edition 10 9 8 7 6 5 4 3 2 1 0   Revision Code: 98 AA/94 A

 Printed on recycled paper when available.

Table of Contents

Part IV – State Laws & Related Resources

Notes to the State Chapter: What's New

Chapter 11. State Laws and Taxes

Index

Related Resources

Forms and Worksheets in this Book

Notes to Chapters 1–10

This update of chapters 1–10 features a number of major additions, including notable additions to the sections discussing limited liability companies and partnerships, blue sky laws, estate tax planning, and emerging trends and issues. The list below identifies the most significant changes and additions to the text and gives you the chapter–section number where you will find the discussion.

- All 50 states and the District of Columbia have enacted limited liability company laws. In addition, every state but Wyoming now also provides for limited liability partnerships – 2.3, 2.6
- Information on income tax and Social Security tax brackets have been updated to reflect 1997 changes – 2.6, 4.13
- New federal law has preempted most state "blue sky" law registration requirements for securities – 4.12
- Reduction of ERISA paperwork burden, including repeal of requirement to file summary plan descriptions and other reports with the Department of Labor, except on request – 5.5
- OSHA is now sending out employer surveys in an attempt to target companies most likely to be in violation of workplace safety and health regulations – 5.6
- New federal income tax break allows self-employed persons or small employers to set up Medical Savings Accounts – 8.3
- New SIMPLE retirement plans now allowed, similar to 401(k) deferral plans, but much simpler to establish and operate – 8.3
- Taxpayer Relief Act of 1997 created new backloaded Roth IRA, for which contributions are not deductible, but withdrawals are wholly tax-free – 8.3
- The tax break for educational assistance plans and the targeted jobs tax credit have been reinstated, but with some modifications – 8.3, 8.11
- Congress overrules Supreme Court *Soliman* decision, and eases requirements for claiming an office in the home deduction, starting in 1999 – 8.6
- The IRS increased the standard automobile mileage allowance to $0.315 (31.5 cents) a mile – 8.6
- New segment added regarding electronic data interchange (EDI), a capability that is becoming ever more important for small businesses that wish to be suppliers to large companies or government agencies – 9.14
- IRS adopts regulations which greatly simplify the tax treatment and reporting of various legal entities – 9.14
- Many new and useful Web site addresses of government agencies and private sources of small business information have been added, with descriptions of each – 10.12

The author of chapters 1–10 of the entire *Starting and Operating a Business in . . .* series, is Michael D. Jenkins. Mr. Jenkins, an attorney at law and a certified public accountant, is a graduate of Harvard Law School. He has worked in Los Angeles and San Francisco as an accountant and as an attorney with a prominent San Francisco firm well known in the venture capital arena. He is a member of the State Bar of California, the American Bar Association, the American Institute of Certified Public Accountants, the California Society of Certified Public Accountants, and the Washington Society of Certified Public Accountants.

How to Use This Book

0.1 Getting the Most Out of this Book

To most effectively use this book, become acquainted with the many helpful features it provides. Remember that each edition is updated regularly to provide you with the most current information available. To find the most recent changes made to federal laws, refer to the Notes to Chapters 1–10: What's New page. For similar state information, refer to the Notes to State Chapter: What's New page, which immediately precedes Chapter 11.

0.2 Numbered Section Heads Correspond to Table of Contents and Index

Text

Discussions range from explaining how to start and operate your business to examining such practical issues as insurance, marketing, cash-flow management, internal financial controls, and much more. This book also explains federal and state government requirements and tax laws, as well as a number of emerging trends and issues your business may face.

Topics Noted in Margins

To make the information in this workbook easily accessible to busy people, the primary topics discussed within each numbered section are identified by "sideheads" in the margin beside the text.

Smaller Heads for Subtopics

When subsections of primary topics are discussed, the sideheads are slightly smaller.

Lists

- This small bullet helps you easily locate lists of requirements, things to do, and aspects of a particular subject or law.

Checklists

☐ Small boxes encourage you to enter a check, so that you can clearly see those items you have considered and dealt with — and those left to do.

Worksheets

> **Where the Action Begins**
>
> A number of worksheets are provided for you to answer questions and fill in numbers that form the basis for action plans, self-evaluation, budgeting, personnel policies, marketing feasibility studies, and the like.
>
> The worksheets are set apart by boxes to clearly show where your interaction is required to focus your thoughts, to record information, and to create the plans and reports that will help you establish and guide your business.

Resources

Sources and Data	Resources are set in tabular form to highlight the many agencies and companies listed to assist you.	**Contacts** Addresses Phone and fax numbers E-mail and Internet addresses

Table of Contents

The detailed Table of Contents will help you quickly find any specific section of the book you wish to refer to. The first digit of the chapter–section number indicates the chapter, followed by a period and the section number.

Endnotes

The endnotes follow each chapter and are provided to assist you with accessing specific statutes, cases, regulations, and publications, allowing you to use this book as a starting place for legal research.

Index

The subject-matter index, organized alphabetically with cross-referenced entries, provides an exhaustive list of topics, indexed not only by the terms actually used in the entries but also by various other terms you might think of instead. The index entries are referenced by the chapter–section number, not by page number, to help you find the corresponding discussions in the text.

Related Resources

At the back of this book, you will find a compendium of additional resources that will save you valuable research time and money.

Appendix

The Appendix features a checklist of tax and various other major requirements for most businesses and a checklist of official government posters and notices required to be displayed by a business.

Forms

Since many business requirements depend on submitting specific forms to various government agencies, some samples of these forms are included for your reference and listed in the Table of Contents.

Post Cards

At the back of this book, you will also find post cards preaddressed to government agencies and other sources so you can request additional **information, posters, and forms.**

Preface

Anyone who runs a small business today, or who is thinking about starting one, knows that he or she faces serious and growing challenges. The hurdles one must get over to start or continue to operate a business seem to have grown a little higher each year since this series of books was first introduced in 1981. In particular, the government has shifted more and more responsibilities onto the shoulders of employers in recent years, a trend that seems likely to continue.

Despite the growing complexities of running a business and the fact that according to Dun & Bradstreet, more than 420,000 businesses failed in the last decade, small businesspeople have not been deterred. Quite to the contrary — business start ups are flourishing in this tough environment. According to *Investor's Business Daily*, for every business that failed in the "wave of creative destruction" in the 1980s, at least 15 new businesses sprang up to take its place. While many in the mass media have bemoaned the rash of takeovers, leveraged buyouts, mass layoffs, downsizing, corporate restructuring, and other wrenching changes in the 1980s and early 1990s, all this ferment seems to have provided fertile ground for new, small, and nimble businesses.

In fact, according to Dun & Bradstreet, the number of "total concerns in business" almost tripled in the 1980s to more than eight million by 1990. That compares very favorably to the 1970s, when the total number of businesses increased by just 13.8%, to 2.8 million by the end of that decade. The desire of Americans, especially many recent immigrants from all corners of the world, to start and run their own businesses seems indomitable, obstacles or no.

The publisher and I would like to think this 51-book *Starting and Operating a Business in* series — which features a book for each state and the District of Columbia — might have played a significant part in empowering many of the millions of people who have started their own businesses since our first edition in 1981. A more modest view would suggest that we were merely on the leading edge of change, part of a huge expansion in the resources that have arisen in recent years to provide help to new and small firms.

We must confess, however, to being very pleased when, in April 1994, *Inc.* magazine chose the *Starting and Operating a Business in . . .* series as one of the best small business books available. After an exhaustive survey of hundreds of small business self-help books, *Inc.* chose our book (series) as one of the six overall winners. Similarly, a November, 1996, article in *Forbes* concluded that most small business self-help books are not worth the paper they are printed on, but mentioned four such books which they did find to be very useful, one of which was this *Starting and Operating a Business in ...* series. We are also pleased with the award we received from the U.S. Small Business Administration "in recognition of significant contributions to the nation's small business." In fact, the *Starting and Operating a Business in ...* series is featured in the SBA's Business Information Centers (BICs) located throughout the United States.

When the series was introduced, only a few useful small business self-help books were available, and relatively few government resources were devoted to helping new enterprises get off the ground. Today, however, there are books and software programs offering assistance on almost every aspect of running a large, small, or medium-sized business. In fact, this book series is now only part of a much larger series of business self-help books on a wide array of subjects offered by the publisher, The Oasis Press. In addition, Small Business Development Centers (SBDCs) and "one-stop" business permit offices are now located in almost every state, and while state governments are cutting services left and right, most are expected to maintain or even increase their business services and economic development and other assistance to small businesses.

Why the turnaround? State governments recognize that new and existing small businesses are the backbone of their economies and the only sector of the economy that is currently providing growth in jobs for their residents. Thus, it should not be surprising that the states are doing as much as possible to encourage business growth, expansion, and relocation.

I became involved in this trend after advising small and large businesses over the years — first as an economic and management consultant; then later, as a tax attorney; and more recently, as a certified public accountant. After years of helping many small businesses and venture capital start ups get off the ground, I had become increasingly aware of the need for a single, authoritative, and practical guide that would serve people starting and operating a business in a particular state — and acutely aware that no such guides existed, except in a few states.

Thus, in 1980, I was particularly receptive when my neighbor and publisher, Emmett Ramey, approached me with the idea of writing a nuts-and-bolts guidebook for the state of California that would assist a small businessperson or entrepreneur through the maze of red tape at both the federal and state levels of government, as well as provide the basic steps and advice needed to get a new business off the ground.

We decided to create an operating manual that would draw together — in a readable, usable, and nontechnical format — the practical facts of life a person needed to know when establishing a business in California. Since first publishing that California edition, we have enlisted local experts in each of the other states to work with us and coauthor the books for their states.

By and large, tax, legal, and business information is useless when it is out of date. As a result, we update the federal section (chapters 1–10) in this series each year and each state chapter (Chapter 11) on a regular basis.

So, if you want an up-to-date guide to the basic financial, legal, and tax ground rules that apply to most businesses operating in your state, the *Starting and Operating a Business in ...* series has been designed with you in mind as a self-help tool. It is also intended to be a useful (and end-noted) reference source to the attorney who has only a limited knowledge of business taxation and the basic regulatory requirements of a large number of federal, state, and local government agencies. Accountants will also find this series a useful resource for understanding the broad scope of government regulations that affect their small business clients.

While the *Starting and Operating a Business in ...* books provide an authoritative discussion of many legal and tax matters regarding small business, they are not intended to be a substitute for professional legal or tax advice. On the contrary, they are designed to help you focus on key points to explore in greater depth with your attorney, accountant, benefits consultant, or other adviser. By being better informed, you can use your professional advisers' time more efficiently.

Many of the items covered in this book have been added at the request of readers who have written to us with their suggestions. This series is not a "finished" project, but is under constant revision. Accordingly, as the principal author, I invite and welcome your feedback or suggestions as to improvements we might make. Your letters should be addressed either to me or my coauthor for the state chapter of this edition, in care of the publisher.

This book is dedicated to America's entrepreneurs — tenacious, courageous men and women — whose contribution to the variety, richness, and quality of our lives is immeasurable.

MICHAEL D. JENKINS

January 1998

Preliminary Considerations

Part I

Chapter 1

Making the Decision to Go into Business

Entrepreneurship is the last refuge of the troublemaking individual.

— James K. Glassman

1.1 Introduction

No book can tell you whether or not you should take the plunge and go into business for yourself. You alone must make that difficult decision. Before you make the decision, carefully consider some of the key points discussed in this chapter. Some of the points discussed you may not have considered yet, while others may assist you in dealing successfully with some initial problems you may face.

One of the first points to consider when starting your business is the major financial risk you will be taking. Once you have committed yourself financially, it will not be a simple or easy thing to change your mind and back out.

In addition, be aware there is a substantial failure rate among new businesses. Don't assume just because you are an expert in your field, you will be an automatic success. You will need to have strengths in other areas as well. In fact, statistics show that a very high percentage of those business failures result from poor management. Poor or ineffective management is usually a lack of balanced experience and competence in three areas:

- Marketing strategies. Know what kind of product or service to sell, how to target and reach your customers, and how to sell your product or service at a price that maximizes your profits.
- Technical ability. Be able to get the work done and do it right, so you will have satisfied customers. If you are going into the auto repair business, for example, you ought to know a great deal about how to keep autos running right, or you will not be in business very long.

- Financial knowledge. While you do not necessarily have to be a financial wizard, you do need to know how to plan and control your business' cash flow, raise or borrow the money you will need to start your business, and get through tight periods without being caught short of cash. A certain amount of financial sophistication is becoming more and more important in today's increasingly complex financial world, even for the small business owner.

If you lack experience or knowledge in one or more of these three critical areas, you greatly reduce the odds of your business succeeding.

This chapter engages you in the process of realistically evaluating your entrepreneurial strengths and weaknesses. It is also intended to cause you to focus on some of the typical start-up problems and choices you are likely to face, as well as assist you with dealing effectively and rationally with those issues.

Worksheets are provided at the end of the chapter to help you evaluate yourself. While reading the text, write in your responses when appropriate. Often, the simple process of writing down your thoughts on specific problem areas may provide significant new insights.

1.2 Advantages and Disadvantages of Owning Your Own Business

Have you realistically considered both the advantages and the disadvantages of owning and operating your own business? If not, the time to do so is before, not after, you have committed yourself.

Advantages

If you are actively considering going into business for yourself, you most likely have already thought about the potential advantages, such as:

- Being your own boss and not having to report to a superior;
- Having the independence and authority to make your own business decisions;
- Direct contact with customers, employees, suppliers, and others;
- The personal satisfaction and sense of achievement that comes with being a success, plus the recognition that goes with it;
- The opportunity to create substantial wealth and job security for you and your family;
- The opportunity to be creative and to develop your own idea, product, or service;
- The chance to make a living doing something you truly enjoy; and
- Doing something that contributes to others, whether by providing an excellent product or service, providing employment, paying dividends to stockholders, or doing something else that is useful or that creates value.

If you are like most people, you may not have thought much about the downside of going into business; however, awareness of the potential disadvantages should not discourage you from your goal of going into business for yourself if you have a strong commitment to that goal.

Seriously consider whether you and your family are prepared to handle the disadvantages that often come with being an entrepreneur.

Disadvantages

- In many ways, you are still not your own boss. Instead of having one boss, you will have many — your customers, the government agencies to whom you must report, and in some cases, your key suppliers.

- You are taking a large financial risk. The failure rate is relatively high in new businesses, and you may lose not only your own money, but also that of your friends and relatives who may have bankrolled you.

- The hours are long and hard. When you start your business, you will no longer be working 9 to 5. Count on working 10 to 12 or even 15 hours a day, often six or seven days a week.

- You will not have much spare time for family or social life. And you can forget about taking any long vacations for the first few years since the business is unlikely to run itself without your presence for any extended length of time.

- Your income may not be steady like a salary. You may make more or less than you could working for someone else, but in either case, your income may fluctuate up and down from month to month.

- The buck stops with you. If a problem arises, there is no boss you can take it to and say: "What do we do about this?" You are the boss and all the responsibility is yours. If anything goes wrong, the cost comes out of your pocket.

- You may be stuck for years doing work you do not like. Unlike an employee, you cannot simply quit and look for a better job. It may take you years to sell the business or find some other way to get out of it without a major financial loss.

- As a business grows, the amount of activity not associated with the primary business objective will increase. You will spend more time on personnel, administrative, and legal matters and less doing what you may have wanted most to do in your business.

- Increasingly intrusive government regulation and private litigation make owning a business very risky. You can work a lifetime to build a business only to have it lost because of a lawsuit or a new law or regulation.

1.3 Typical Characteristics of the Successful Entrepreneur

A good deal is known about what it takes to be a successful entrepreneur. For the most part, it seems the one overriding factor is a tremendous need to achieve. In short, attitude seems to have almost everything to do with success in business, while factors, such as intelligence, education, physical appearance, and a pleasing personality, are much less important. Characteristics of typical successful entrepreneurs include:

- An overpowering need to achieve, as opposed to a need to be liked or to exercise power; the form in which different individuals measure their achievement varies widely, ranging from amassing wealth to building a larger organization to creating a better mousetrap than anyone else;
- The trait of following through on a commitment, not quitting halfway through when the going gets tough: in short, perseverance;
- A positive mental attitude or the ability to remain optimistic in new and unfamiliar situations, which essentially grows out of being self-confident about one's abilities;
- Objectivity — the ability to accurately weigh and assess risks associated with a particular course of action, as well as being realistic about one's own abilities and limitations;
- A respectful attitude toward money, but a tendency to look upon money as a means for accomplishing things, or a way of keeping score in the game of business, rather than as a thing to be sought as an end in itself;
- The tendency to anticipate developments and to make things happen rather than constantly reacting to problems as they arise;
- Resourcefulness — the ability to solve unique problems in unique ways and to be able to handle things that come up for which the entrepreneur has no previous experience to rely on as a guide;
- Strong personal relations skills — the characteristics of being cheerful and cooperative, and usually getting along well with, without necessarily being close to, employees and associates;
- Well-developed communication skills, both in oral and written presentations; and
- Well-rounded technical knowledge with emphasis on the knowledge about the physical process of producing goods and services.

How do your personal characteristics stack up against the foregoing profile of the typical successful entrepreneur? If that profile doesn't sound very much like you, maybe you had better give some long, hard thought as to whether you are cut out for making it as a business owner.

Running a business is not like working for someone else. No one is there to tell you what to do when something goes wrong. You are responsible for everything.

Are you capable of handling that kind of total responsibility? Are you a self-starter, capable of planning, organizing, and carrying out projects on your own? If not, you may find that starting and running a successful business is not for you.

Running a business demands a great deal in the way of initiative, hard work, self-discipline, and resourcefulness. On the other hand, solving the problems that arise from day to day and making it all work out can be a source of immense satisfaction, as well as be financially rewarding.

Before reading further, complete Worksheet 1, which is a useful questionnaire that may help you to get a better idea of your suitability for playing the role of entrepreneur in the real world. Worksheet 1 is located at the end of this chapter.

1.4 Knowing Your Market

One of the most important questions you should ask yourself is whether you feel that you know and understand the market for the particular kind of products or services you intend to sell. Do you know who your competition is and whether the particular market you intend to appeal to is large enough for both you and the existing competition? Also, how will your products or services measure up against those of your competitors in terms of quality and price?

If your product or service is something new or unusual, you need to have a sense of whether you will be selling an item that is wanted and needed in the marketplace. Or, even if you intend to sell a product or service that you know there is a need for, you should be satisfied in your own mind that you are going to be making it available at the right place at the right time.

Few sights are sadder than the boarded-up mom-and-pop store or restaurant — in which the owners have sunk their life savings — that never got off the ground for some obvious reason, such as lack of visibility from the street, lack of substantial foot traffic by its doors, or some other fatal flaw the inexperienced owners overlooked.

To succeed, you must find the right business opportunity. If you do not have a clear idea of what business you want to go into and where you want to operate it, you will need to do some intelligent investigation of all possible opportunities that might be suitable for you.

If you already have a concept of what you want to do, you will still need to do a great deal of investigating to make sure it is as good an opportunity as it appears to be. In either case, a lot of initial research and footwork is advisable, unless you want to close your eyes and indulge in wishful thinking.

In other words, to quote a well-known brokerage firm: "Investigate before you invest." This often entails doing your own marketing feasibility study before committing yourself to opening a new business.

Determining Market Feasibility

A marketing feasibility study is simply a systematic analysis of any information you can obtain about the potential market for your product or service. This information can include the competition you face, the amount of sales you can reasonably expect to obtain in that particular market, and whether that level of sales will be adequate for your business to operate at a reasonable profit. For example, if you are planning to build homes in a small community where there is only a demand for five homes a year, and you need to build and sell ten homes a year to survive, doing a marketing feasibility study might help you realize your proposed business venture is not feasible, even if you were to capture 100% of the local housing market. Investigate first, then invest.

Alternatively, if you have several thousand dollars to spend and a well-defined idea of what it is you want to do, you can hire a professional economist or marketing consultant to do a feasibility study. In every major city, there are several firms that can do a thorough marketing and demographic study for you. Such a feasibility study can be quite valuable, but it will also be fairly expensive. Most people starting a new business tend to do their own marketing feasibility study, which is usually done very informally, if at all. The exception would be for people who create a formal, written business plan to obtain financing, for example. A thorough analysis of the market for a new business' product or service is always a key portion of any business plan. The Oasis Press publishes books and software that can assist you with creating a written business plan. See the list of publications in the back of this book for ordering information.

Before doing a marketing feasibility study, you obviously need to know what business you want to go into. When choosing your type of business, keep these thoughts in mind:

- If you see that a particular business is doing quite well and you want to compete head-to-head with it, don't make the mistake of adopting a me-too approach and assume you can take away a lot of its business by competing only on a price basis. You need several other good reasons — besides price — for why you think another business' customers will switch over to you, such as having a distinctly better product, service, or location.
- Keep your eyes open for developing social, economic, and technological trends that will create new markets you can move into at an early stage. It will help if you are a voracious reader of magazines such as *Time* and *Newsweek* (social trends); *Forbes* and *Business Week* (economic trends); or *Omni* or *Discover* (technological innovations).

An example of how observing social trends can translate into profits — in this instance, stock market profits — is the case of an investment analyst in the 60s who noticed the trend toward mini-skirts and correctly anticipated that the spread of mini-skirts among women would create a boom market for pantyhose. The analyst made a killing by buying shares of pantyhose stock.

So how do you analyze the market for your product or service once you have focused on a particular business you might want to start? Worksheet 2 — located at the end of this chapter — will help you pinpoint the kind of information you need to develop for satisfying yourself that a good market exists for whatever it is you are planning to sell. Before you read any further, spend some time writing down your responses to each of the items on Worksheet 2.

Market Data Resources

Once you have identified your most likely potential customers, find out how to locate your business or structure and to direct your advertising and promotional efforts so that you most efficiently reach them. Fortunately, there is a great deal of published data you can use if you need to do this type of research. One of the best sources is *Sales and Marketing Management* magazine, which publishes *Survey of Buying Power* each year. This survey provides breakdowns of population, households, retail sales by type of business, and total purchasing dollars for each county in the United States and for cities with a population of more than 10,000. To request information about *Survey of Buying Power*, see Statistical Information in Section 10.4.

Some of the printed sources of market information you can use in your research are:

- A.C. Nielsen market studies;
- *National Trade and Professional Association (NTPA) Directory*;
- Newspapers;
- Statistical abstracts; and
- Trade magazines.

Many of these items can be found in your local business or university library. The *NTPA Directory* can be ordered from:

National Trade and Professional Association Directory
Columbia Books
Washington, DC
(202) 898-0662

Various industry and government sources of information to consider are:

- Trade associations;
- U.S. Chamber of Commerce;
- U.S. Department of Commerce; and
- U.S. Small Business Administration.

Another excellent source is the 1990 U.S. census data, which gives vast amounts of detailed information on the U.S. population and its buying habits by individual census tract. You may want to obtain a couple of useful pamphlets from your nearest U.S. Small Business Administration field office. Ask for the pamphlet entitled, *Researching Your Market*, for guidance on how to do your own market research.

If you have a computer modem and access to the Internet, a mother lode of census demographic information is also available through the Census Bureau's home page on the Worldwide Web. A slick and easy-to-navigate series of screens with mouse-driven menus will allow you to pick a geographical area — ranging from the entire country to a small town — and review detailed demographic information about it. Click SUBMIT, to get a report on anything from commuting time to home values, and much more. The Census Bureau's electronic address is:

Census Bureau
http://www.census.gov/

Finding the Optimum Site

Finding the best location for your business is a very important part of any market research project. Depending on your type of business, you will want to investigate future and current projections for city population, income trends, and economic outlooks. You may also be interested in information on available transportation and freight services, the local labor force, and public utilities in a particular area to ensure the location has the resources to meet your retail, service, or manufacturing needs. If finding an optimum site to locate your business is important to your marketing effort, do the following:

- Talk to a knowledgeable person at your local chamber of commerce or economic development organization about business and other trends in the area you are considering for the location of your business.
- Talk to a staff person at your local planning commission about census tract projections of future population growth, income trends, and economic development in the area you are considering. Also, they — or some other local agency, such as a traffic or road department — will usually have done traffic counts showing how many cars pass certain points every day. This information can be very useful if you are opening a retail business.
- Consult any trade association that serves your business and may have available information tailored to your needs.
- Obtain a copy of the U.S. Small Business Administration's publication, *Choosing a Retail Location* if your business will be a retail store.

For a complete guide to specifying, ranking, and evaluating the factors you must consider when choosing an optimum site for your new or relocating business, obtain a copy of *Location, Location, Location: How to Select the Best Site for Your Business*. This handbook features tables and checklists to consider before you decide to rent, build, or lease. Get your copy through your local book source or:

The Oasis Press
(800) 228-2275

1.5 Knowing the Business

Do you have any experience in the area of business in which you will be engaged? Of course, it is possible to learn while doing, but it helps a great deal to know a business before you start. Often, the most successful businesses are started by people who have worked in a particular line of business for years and who finally decide that they know the ropes well enough to leave their employer and start their own similar operation.

It helps to have experience in the particular business you propose to enter, but in most cases, your experience working in some other line of business will also have considerable carryover value. If you have neither type of experience, you may find you have much to learn once you begin the business.

A major management weakness that causes businesses to fail is the inability to get the job done and to do it right, on time, and efficiently enough to charge a competitive price for the product or service and still make a profit. For example, with the tremendous proliferation of personal computers, you may have decided to go into business repairing small computers. You may be absolutely right, but unless you have the technical capability to do such repairs, or the ability to properly select and hire employees who can do the job, you had better look for some other kind of business.

In many cases, if you know you lack the technical experience you need to open a particular kind of business, your best approach will be to get a job in that industry and work for someone else for a few years until you learn what you need to know. This may require patience, but it is definitely preferable to getting into a business you do not know well and losing your shirt in the process.

1.6 Knowing How Much Money It Will Take to Succeed

Can you afford to start a full-time business if it will mean giving up your current employment and income? Many small businesses never really have a chance to succeed because the owners run out of money before the business becomes a viable operation. As a result, the owners often wind up having to go back to work for someone else again, disappointed and broke.

Carefully calculating and scheduling out, in as much detail as possible, the income and expenses you can reasonably expect for at least the first year of operation, as well as your living expenses and a reserve for emergencies, is a helpful step when determining how much money it will take to start and maintain your business. Remember, you will have many expenses involved for starting up almost any kind of business, and most businesses start out operating in the red for a time.

Consequently, you will obviously want to budget and make projections of your start-up income and expenses so you make it through any rough times and get your business to the point where it can support you and your family.

To help you plan your cash flow for the crucial first year of business, complete worksheets 3 through 5. Worksheet 3 will help you to project your monthly sales revenue in terms of actual cash to be received. Worksheet 4 projects your monthly operating expenses for the first year of business, plus one-time, start-up expenses. Worksheet 5 is a schedule of your estimated personal living expenses during the first year.

Once you have completed worksheets 3 through 5, enter the monthly totals from the bottom line of each onto Worksheet 6, which is a summary of your cash needs. This will show you how much cash you will have to put into the business each month — and on a cumulative basis — during the first year of business. Once you have completed Worksheet 6, you will have a pretty good handle on how much money it is going to take to get your business started and approximately when you will need it.

If, under your most realistic projections, you are still running a deficit in cash flow each month at the end of the first year, you may want to do a similar projection out into the second year of operation. If it appears you will need to borrow or raise money to keep the business operating until it gets into the black, find out well in advance how much you will be able to raise and whether or not you will be able to get that amount.

If you plan to borrow, do you know how to put together a strong financing proposal so the prospective lender understands how you will be able to repay the loan? If not, see Section 9.7 and Chapter 10 for sources of information and help on obtaining financing for a small business. In addition, *Raising Capital: How to Write a Financing Proposal* can help you raise larger amounts of money for both equity and debt financing. Two new books, *The Insider's Guide to Small Business Loans* and *The Small Business Insider's Guide to Bankers* are easy-to-follow guidebooks for preparing a successful loan application. For more information on these and other books for small businesses, call:

The Oasis Press
(800) 228-2275

1.7 Signing a Lease

If you will need to lease space for your business location, have you located a suitable place that is available? If so, there are a number of critical points you need to consider before you sign a lease with a landlord.

Remember that a lease is a binding legal contract, and if you agree to pay rent of $2,500 a month for two years, you are on the hook for $60,000, unless you can sublease or assign the lease to someone else, which could be difficult or impossible to do, depending on the terms of the lease. Key points to consider when signing a lease agreement include:

- What are the terms of the lease? Most businesses tend to start off by either growing rapidly or folding quickly. Thus, except in a retail or service business, you will probably be better off initially leasing on a month-to-month basis or for as short a lease term as you can get, such as three or six months, even if the monthly rent is higher than for a longer lease. You will already have enough financial problems if your business fails, without being saddled with a long-term lease obligation.

- Can you put up the kind of sign you must have on the building? A business like a restaurant can be devastated if the landlord doesn't permit a sign that is sufficiently visible to passersby.

- Will the landlord permit you to make necessary improvements and alterations to the leased premises?

- Will the local health department, fire and police departments, air pollution control authorities, and zoning rules permit operation of your particular type of business at the location you have chosen?

- Is your location in a high-crime area that will require expensive burglary insurance and security precautions?

- Is there enough parking nearby or good public transit access for customers?

- Is the location appropriate for the kind of business you will conduct? There is usually no need to locate a manufacturing operation in a busy, high-traffic area. On the other hand, retail businesses are usually heavily dependent on the number of people passing nearby on foot or by car.

- Does the lease provide you with an option to renew — and at what rental price — after the initial term expires?

- If the lease is for more than just a few months, do you have the right to sublease or assign the lease? If so, under what conditions or restrictions?

1.8 Will You Hire Employees?

In certain kinds of businesses, during the initial start-up phases — and perhaps even afterwards — you may be able to operate without employees by either doing all the work yourself, with the help of family members, or by contracting out certain functions to independent, outside contractors. To the extent you can do so, you may find your life is much simpler by doing it yourself or with independent contractors.

Once you hire even one employee, you take on a great many responsibilities as an employer, over and above meeting a payroll every week or two. These responsibilities include paying and filing tax returns for federal and state unemployment taxes, Social Security taxes, and income tax withholding from wages. In addition, you will need to comply with workers' compensation laws, employee health and safety laws, anti-discrimination laws, U.S. immigration law restrictions on hiring, and a variety of other federal and state labor laws and regulations that may apply once you hire employees. These and other employer requirements are discussed in Chapter 5.

This section reviews some of the legal restrictions on your hiring practices and provides you with a working outline of what you will need to consider in the way of personnel policies once your business reaches the point where you will have to hire employees.

Hiring Practices

Hiring personnel can be complicated because of the broad array of state and federal laws designed to prevent an employer from hiring on the basis of discriminatory factors, such as age, sex, race, disability, or religion. Most of these laws affect all but the smallest employers, so you will have to be alert to most of these rules to avoid even the appearance of discrimination in your hiring practices.

While anti-discrimination rules apply to promotions, job assignments, firing, and other aspects of the employment relationship as well as to hiring, the focus here is mainly on hiring practices. This is the area where most small business owners are likely to stumble into trouble, even when they have no intention to discriminate.

Things Not to Do

All questions or information you express should relate to job qualifications only and not to extraneous factors, such as age, race, sex, or physical size or condition. If your business has special occupational requirements — for example, hard physical labor that might preclude hiring certain disabled individuals — be sure to carefully document such unusual situations or requirements.

Help Wanted Ads

Use the list below to guide you when writing a help wanted advertisement.

- Do not mention race or national origin or any attribute of national origin, such as native language.
- Do not refer to sex classifications, such as "girl wanted."
- Avoid any type of reference to age, such as "young boy" or "recent high school graduate."

Job Application Forms

Your employment application forms should avoid any questions or information on these topics:

- Arrest record;
- Whether the applicant has ever filed for unemployment benefits;
- Place of birth or where parents were born;
- Physical characteristics, such as height or weight;
- Social Security number;
- Marital status;
- Labor union affiliation;
- Request for photograph;
- Religious affiliation;
- Mode of transportation to work;
- Sex;
- Race or national origin;
- Clubs or organizations, unless you instruct the applicant not to list organizations that indicate race or national origin; and
- Native language or how the applicant learned a foreign language.

A sample employment application form is provided for your review at the end of this chapter. If you wish to add additional questions to it, be careful not to indirectly request anything that would reflect on the applicant's race, religion, sex, age, marital status, national origin, or physical condition. Because state laws differ, check with your legal adviser or state employment department before preparing your employment application.

Employment Interviews

During interviews with potential employees, refrain from asking questions, such as:

- Are you a U.S. citizen?
- When did you attend grade school, high school, or college?
- Do you have children, and who will care for them while you are working?
- Do you have any physical or mental disabilities?
- What does your spouse do for a living, and are you likely to move elsewhere?
- Would your religion prevent you from working on holidays or certain days of the week?

Federal law generally bans the use of any kind of lie detector tests in most private employment situations, except for drug manufacturers and distributors and certain security firms.[1] Many state laws are even more stringent. In addition, questions on possible felony convictions, previous military service, and drug or alcohol addiction are not necessarily illegal in all cases, but they may entail difficulties and probably should be avoided.

Checking References

As a general rule, former employers have no legal obligation to give you any information about a former employee. As a practical matter, however, most former employers will at least verify the former employee's employment and the date of employment. Since a former employer can get into trouble for giving you negative information that they cannot substantiate, don't expect them to volunteer much information or to put anything negative in writing. For that reason, you should generally do reference checks by phone. Acceptable questions would include:

- Verifying information given by the applicant;
- Asking about the applicant's principal strong points, weak points, and degree of supervision needed;
- Asking about the applicant's attitude;
- Asking how the applicant's performance compared with others; and
- Asking if the applicant would be rehired.

Personnel Policies

Even before you hire your first employee, you will need to outline some basic personnel policies. If you write down your policies on matters such as hours, vacation time, and sick leave, and give these written policies to new employees, it will help clarify the employment relationship. Perhaps it will even prevent a misunderstanding that could lead to legal action by an employee against you. Worksheet 7 provides a series of questions that will help you focus on different personnel policies that are typical in a small to medium-sized business. For a more thorough treatment of this area, and if you wish to develop a personnel policy manual for your business, you may want to obtain a copy of *A Company Policy and Personnel Workbook* from The Oasis Press.

Related Information

To supplement the information you have just read in this chapter, you may want to read the following sections, which discuss more related information:

- Employee or Independent Contractor? – Section 9.11
- Fair Employment Practices – Section 5.8
- Immigration Law Restrictions on Hiring – Section 5.9
- Hiring a Spouse as an Employee – Section 8.12
- Employee Wage-Hour and Child Labor Laws – Section 5.7
- The Americans with Disabilities Act – Section 5.11
- Mandatory Family and Medical Leave Requirements – Section 5.12

In addition, to get an overview of other legal obligations that come with the territory when you have employees, scan through Chapter 5.

1.9 Other Questions You Need to Ask

- Will or should you advertise? If you do, you need to decide what kind of advertising will be the most cost effective for your business, whether it is newspaper ads, direct mail, radio, posters, handbills, or other forms of advertising and promotion.
- Do you understand what will be involved in purchasing, managing, and restocking your inventory of goods?
- How will you go about selling? Will you hire sales clerks or outside salespeople, or will you do most of the selling yourself?
- Will you sell to customers on credit? If so, how will you protect yourself from bad credit risks and outright deadbeats?
- How much of your personal savings are you putting at risk by going into business? Are you willing to risk losing it all if the business is a failure?
- Can you run the business alone — or with help from family members — or would you do better with one or more partners or business associates to provide additional capital and skills and to divide up some of the responsibilities of running the business?

Again, the questions posed in this chapter are not intended to discourage you from going ahead with starting your business. Chances are you have already considered most of the points raised in this chapter and are reasonably confident that you will be able to do what is necessary to make your business work. If so, many of the questions raised above probably seem rather elementary and obvious to you, as they will to most individuals seriously considering going into business, and you will now want to proceed to the discussions in the remainder of this book.

If you have not previously given serious thought to most of the above points that are relevant to the type of business you are planning to start, now is the time to take a long, hard look at whether you are adequately prepared to embark upon such a venture.

1.10 How Likely Are You to Succeed?

One of the chief deterrents to starting your own business is the fear of failure. This fear has long been enforced by scary statistics that state approximately four out of five new businesses fail after only a short period of time. Given those kinds of frightening odds, it is surprising that anyone is brave enough to start a business.

However, a recent in-depth study of business failure rates done at the New Jersey Institute of Technology (NJIT) suggests the grim statistics on new firm failures may be little more than myth. According to the study, no more than 18% of new firms fail during the first eight years of being in business. More than half (54%) of all start ups survive more than eight years with either their original owners (28%) or with a change in ownership (26%). The other 28% of new firms voluntarily terminate operations without losses to creditors.

The author of the study, Bruce A. Kirchoff, professor of entrepreneurship at NJIT and former chief economist for the U.S. Small Business Administration, states, "I suspect entrepreneurs have known the truth about survival and success for some time. While economists argue that entrepreneurs are foolish to start new businesses because the risk of failure is so high, 400,000 or more new firms are formed every year in the United States. All these entrepreneurs cannot be stupid; they look around and talk to others and realize that their chances of survival and success are far better than academic economists have estimated. It's the economists that look foolish."[2]

According to Kirchoff, the greater survival rate is consistent with the evidence that small firms are the primary job creators in the U.S. economy. While other, even more recent, studies have suggested that most *net* new jobs are created by mid-sized businesses, rather than by either small or large businesses, a 1994 Dun & Bradstreet (D&B) study strongly backs Kirchoff's conclusion that the failure rate for new businesses is much lower than previously believed. The D&B study of 249,768 businesses that started up in 1985 showed that 177,133 (about 71%) were still going strong in early 1994.[3] The Kirchoff and D&B studies are not reasons to become foolhardy or overconfident about your prospects for success. On the other hand, they do indicate that starting your own business may not be the five-to-one long shot gamble you may have been told it was.

Endnotes

1. The Employee Polygraph Protection Act, 29 U.S.C. 2001, *et seq.*

2. Kirchoff, Bruce A., Ph.D. *Assessing Firm Failure Fictions*. New Jersey Institute of Technology, 1993.

3. *Forbes,* June 6, 1994.

Worksheet 1 – Self-Evaluation Checklist for Going into Business

Under each question, check the answer that says what you feel or comes closest to it. Be honest with yourself.

Are you a self-starter?

☐ I do things on my own. Nobody has to tell me to get going.

☐ If someone gets me started, I keep going all right.

☐ Easy does it. I don't put myself out until I have to.

How do you feel about other people?

☐ I like people. I can get along with just about anybody.

☐ I have plenty of friends; I don't need anyone else.

☐ Most people irritate me.

Can you lead others?

☐ I can get most people to go along when I start something.

☐ I can give the orders if someone tells me what we should do.

☐ I let someone else get things moving; then I go along if I feel like it.

Can you take responsibility?

☐ I like to take charge of things and see them through.

☐ I will take over if I have to, but I would rather let someone else be responsible.

☐ There are always some eager beavers around wanting to show how smart they are. I say let them take the responsibility.

How good of an organizer are you?

☐ I like to have a plan before I start. I am usually the one to get things lined up when the group wants to do something.

☐ I do all right unless things get too confusing; then I quit.

☐ Just when I am all set, something comes along and presents too many problems, so I just take things as they come.

How good of a worker are you?

☐ I can keep going as long as I need to. I don't mind working hard for something I want.

☐ I will work hard for awhile, but when I have had enough, that is it.

☐ I can't see that hard work gets me anywhere.

Worksheet 1 – Self-Evaluation Checklist for Going into Business (continued)

Can you stick with it?

☐   If I make up my mind to do something, I don't let anything stop me.

☐   I usually finish what I start if it goes well.

☐   If it doesn't go right away, I quit. Why beat my brains out?

How good is your health?

☐   I never get run down.

☐   I have enough energy for most things I want to do.

☐   I run out of energy sooner than most of my friends seem to.

Count the checks you made.

How many checks are beside the first answer to each question? _____

How many checks are beside the second answer to each question? _____

How many checks are beside the third answer to each question? _____

If most of your checks are beside the first answers, you probably have what it takes to run a business. If not, you are likely to have more trouble than you can handle by yourself. You may want to find a partner who is strong on the points you are weak on. If many checks are beside the third answer, not even a good partner will be able to shore you up.

Source: U.S. Small Business Administration.

Worksheet 2 – Marketing Feasibility Study Checklist for Your Product or Service

Your Product

Briefly describe the nature of the product or service you will offer.

_____

_____

_____

Most products or services have a life cycle, beginning with very rapid growth in the introductory stage, which slows down in the maturity stage, flattens out in the saturation stage, and finally begins shrinking in the declining stage. Which stage of its market cycle do you believe your product or service is in?

- ☐ introductory ☐ saturation
- ☐ maturity ☐ declining

If you believe your product is in one of the earlier, faster-growing stages of its life cycle, what edge do you believe your product will have over similar products that may be introduced by new competitors who may come into the field?

_____

_____

_____

If you are entering at a fairly late stage of the product marketing cycle, why is it you believe that you can succeed in taking away others' market share with your product or service?

_____

_____

_____

How is your product or service different in terms of quality and price from what is already on the market?

_____

_____

_____

Is there good reason to believe that your customers will recognize the difference? _____ If so, why?

_____

_____

_____

What is different about your marketing strategy or distribution strategy that will enable your product or service to succeed in a market where there is little, if any, growth?

_____

_____

_____

Worksheet 2 – Marketing Feasibility Study Checklist for Your Product or Service (continued)

Your Potential Customers

Not everyone is a potential customer. Certain age groups, income levels, geographic areas, ethnic groups, and educational levels will be more likely than others to be your customers. You need to focus on who will need your product and be most likely to buy it, and then decide where to locate your business or how to structure your marketing approach to reach those segments of the market that you are most interested in reaching. Spell out below, as clearly as you can, who your customers are most likely to be.

The particular geographic area from which I will be able to draw most of my customers is:

_____

_____

_____

_____

In addition, I should draw a significant number of customers from the following geographic area or areas:

_____

_____

_____

My plan or strategy for reaching potential customers in the above areas can be summarized as follows:

_____

_____

_____

_____

The target market for my product or service, in terms of demographics, should be among the following persons: (Describe your ideal customer's age, gender, educational level, and geographical location.)

_____

_____

_____

_____

In terms of income groups, my particular product or service should appeal primarily to people in the following income levels:

- ☐ Under $25,000 a year household income
- ☐ $25,000 – $35,000 a year
- ☐ $35,000 – $50,000 a year
- ☐ $50,000 – $75,000 a year
- ☐ $75,000 – $100,000 a year
- ☐ More than $100,000 a year

My product or service is likely to be more in demand by certain social, cultural, and ethnic groups than others. The groups that are most likely to be customers, if any, are:

_____
_____
_____
_____
_____
_____
_____

The groups that are least likely to be customers are:

_____
_____
_____
_____
_____
_____

Your Competition

Even though you may have done a great job pinpointing and studying your market segment, the job isn't done until you have considered your competition.

Main competitors in my market area are: (List firms by name.)

1. _____
_____
2. _____
_____
3. _____
_____
4. _____
_____
5. _____
_____
6. _____
_____

Worksheet 2 – Marketing Feasibility Study Checklist for Your Product or Service (continued)

Based on my market research of statistical data, such as *Sales Marketing and Management* magazine, the amount of buying power per business represented in my area is $ _____.

If I can generate that amount of sales, it: will ☐, will not ☐ be sufficient for me to operate successfully.

Five reasons why customers would buy from me rather than my competitors are:

1. _____
2. _____
3. _____
4. _____
5. _____   _____

Five weaknesses my business will have when compared to my competitors are:

1. _____
2. _____
3. _____
4. _____
5. _____

To overcome these weaknesses, I will:

_____
_____
_____
_____
_____
_____
_____
_____
_____
_____
_____
_____
_____
_____
_____

Worksheet 3 – Estimated Cash Inflow from Sales for Year _____

	Jan.	Feb.	Mar.	Apr.	4-month Total
Gross sales for month					
Less: Credit sales made					
Subtotal: Cash sales					
Plus: Collections on prior credit sales					
Less: Bad debts*					
Total: Net cash flow from monthly sales					

	May	June	July	Aug.	4-month Total
Gross sales for month					
Less: Credit sales made					
Subtotal: Cash sales					
Plus: Collections on prior credit sales					
Less: Bad debts*					
Total: Net cash flow from monthly sales					

	Sept.	Oct.	Nov.	Dec.	4-month Total
Gross sales for month					
Less: Credit sales made					
Subtotal: Cash sales					
Plus: Collections on prior credit sales					
Less: Bad debts*					
Total: Net cash flow from monthly sales					

Total net cash flow from monthly sales for year $ _____

* Consider using some percentage, say 1 or 2% of credit sale collections, to estimate your uncollectible debts.

Worksheet 4 – Estimated Business Cash Outlays for Year _____

	Jan.	Feb.	Mar.	Apr.	May
Monthly Expenses					
Rent					
Salaries and wages (except owner)					
Payroll taxes					
Advertising and promotion					
Insurance					
Federal estimated income tax					
State estimated income tax					
Owner's FICA or SE tax					
Telephone and utilities					
Inventory replacement purchase					
Interest on loans					
Maintenance					
Legal and accounting fees					
Office supplies					
Delivery expense					
Miscellaneous					
One-Time Expenses					
Fixtures and equipment					
Decorating and remodeling					
Initial stock of inventory					
Utility and lease deposits					
Licenses and permits					
Other					
Total Expenses for Month					
Plus: Loan principal payment					
Less: Purchases on credit					
Plus: Payment on prior credit					
Net Monthly Cash Outlay					

June	July	Aug.	Sept.	Oct.	Nov.	Dec.	Annual Totals

Worksheet 5 – Estimated Personal and Living Expenses for Year _____

	Jan.	Feb.	Mar.	Apr.	May
Regular Payments					
Rent or house payment					
Property taxes					
Condo owner's dues					
Car payments					
Furniture and appliance payments					
Loan payments					
Health insurance					
Other insurance					
Household Expenses					
Food – restaurants					
Food – at home					
Telephone and utilities					
Water					
Personal Expenses					
Clothing and laundry					
Medical, dental, and drugs					
Education					
Dues and subscriptions					
Gifts and charity					
Gasoline and auto					
Entertainment and travel					
Miscellaneous spending					
Total Personal Expenses (Draw Required)					

June	July	Aug.	Sept.	Oct.	Nov.	Dec.	Annual Totals

Worksheet 6 – Summary of Estimated Cash Requirements for Year _____

	Jan.	Feb.	Mar.	Apr.	4-month Total
Net cash for month from sales – Worksheet 3					
Less: Net monthly cash outlay – Worksheet 4					
Subtotal: Net operating cash flow (or deficit)					
Less: Owner's draw for living and personal expenses – Worksheet 5					
Add: Money borrowed					
Add (or subtract): Equity capital paid in (or withdrawn) from the business					
Total: Net cash flow (or deficit) for month					
Cumulative* cash flow (or deficit)					

	May	June	July	Aug.	4-month Total
Net cash for month from sales – Worksheet 3					
Less: Net monthly cash outlay – Worksheet 4					
Subtotal: Net operating cash flow (or deficit)					
Less: Owner's draw for living and personal expenses – Worksheet 5					
Add: Money borrowed					
Add (or subtract): Equity capital paid in (or withdrawn) from the business					
Total: Net cash flow (or deficit) for month					
Cumulative* cash flow (or deficit)					

	Sept.	Oct.	Nov.	Dec.	4-month Total
Net cash for month from sales – Worksheet 3					
Less: Net monthly cash outlay – Worksheet 4					
Subtotal: Net operating cash flow (or deficit)					
Less: Owner's draw for living and personal expenses – Worksheet 5					
Add: Money borrowed					
Add (or subtract): Equity capital paid in (or withdrawn) from the business					
Total: Net cash flow (or deficit) for month					
Cumulative* cash flow (or deficit)					

* Add each month's net cash flow to the previous month's cumulative total.

Annual totals: To get your total figures for the list below, add the three, four-month totals together for each item.

Net cash for month from sales – Worksheet 3 _____

Less: Net monthly cash outlay – Worksheet 4 _____

Subtotal: Net operating cash flow (or deficit) _____

Less: Owner's draw for living and personal
expenses – Worksheet 5 _____

Add: Money borrowed _____

Add (or subtract): Equity capital paid in (or
withdrawn) from the business _____

Annual cumulative cash flow (or deficit) _____

Sample Employment Application Form

Employment Application

Personal Data

Name: _____
          (last)   (first)   (middle)

Present address: _____
                        (street address)   (city)   (state)   (zip)

Telephone numbers: _____ _____
                              (home)   (work)

Education

High school: _____ Graduated? Yes ☐ No ☐ Location: _____

College or University: _____ Graduated? Yes ☐ No ☐ Degree(s): _____

Other (specify type): _____ Graduated? Yes ☐ No ☐ Certificate(s): _____

_____ Graduated? Yes ☐ No ☐ Certificate(s): _____

Work Experience

List below all present and previous employment, starting with the most recent.

Company name: _____ From (mo/yr): _____ Type of work: _____

Address: _____ To (mo/yr): _____ Name of supervisor: _____

_____ Reason you left: _____

Company name: _____ From (mo/yr): _____ Type of work: _____

Address: _____ To (mo/yr): _____ Name of supervisor: _____

_____ Reason you left: _____

Company name: _____ From (mo/yr): _____ Type of work: _____

Address: _____ To (mo/yr): _____ Name of supervisor: _____

_____ Reason you left: _____

Company name: _____ From (mo/yr): _____ Type of work: _____

Address: _____ To (mo/yr): _____ Name of supervisor: _____

_____ Reason you left: _____

May we contact the employers above? Yes ☐ No ☐ If yes, list any employers you do not wish us to contact:

_____

_____

Remarks: _____

_____

_____

Worksheet 7 – Defining Your Company's Personnel Policies

Working Hours

Describe briefly the policy you will set for working hours, including:

Starting time: _____

_____

How much time will be allowed for lunch: _____

_____

Quitting time: _____

_____

Which days of the week employees will be expected to work: _____

_____

If, like many companies these days, you will adopt some kind of "flex-time" system, spell out how it will work.

_____

_____

_____

_____

Overtime

Outline your policy on overtime work. Refer to Section 5.7 of this book for legal requirements for paying overtime premiums. See also Section 11.5 regarding state wage laws. Points to consider here include:

Will you pay exempt employees (administrative or professional) overtime if they work extra hours? _____

_____

Will you require employees to obtain permission to work overtime? _____

_____

Compensation

Make a list of the job positions in the company other than your own and the compensation level for each. On a separate piece of paper, write out a specific job description for each position, outlining duties and responsibilities. Refer to sections 5.7 and 11.5 of this book for a description of hourly minimum wage requirements.

Position	Hourly Wage	Salary	Total Monthly Pay
_____	_____	_____	_____
_____	_____	_____	_____
_____	_____	_____	_____
_____	_____	_____	_____
_____	_____	_____	_____

Worksheet 7 – Defining Your Company's Personnel Policies (continued)

Vacation Policy

Describe how much paid vacation employees will have and how this may increase after a certain number of years of service. _____

_____

Will vacation time and sick leave time off be combined into a single category for employees (as some companies now do to reward employees who do not abuse sick leave and to discourage others from using sick leave as additional vacation by playing hooky)? _____

_____

Will you pay employees who terminate for unused vacation? (The laws of many states require you to do so.)

_____

_____

Family and Medical Leave Policy

Outline your policy for both paid and unpaid sick leave and family and medical leave. (If you have more than 50 employees, the federal Family and Medical Leave Act may apply to you. See Section 5.12.)

Sick leave: _____

_____

Family/medical leave: _____

_____

Birth or adoption of a child: _____

_____

Leaves of Absence

What will your policy be towards employees who request unpaid leaves of absence? _____

_____

_____

Time Off with Pay

Will you provide other time off with pay for such eventualities as funerals, jury duty, and training?

Funerals or family emergencies: _____

_____

Jury duty: _____

_____

Attend work-related seminars and training sessions: _____

_____

Promotions and Evaluations

Outline your policy for evaluating employees' performance and determining when promotions will be made.

_____

_____

_____

_____

_____

Fringe Benefits

Consider which employee fringe benefits you will provide and specify your policy for each.

Medical insurance: _____

_____

Long-term disability insurance: _____

_____

Life insurance: _____

_____

Dental insurance: _____

_____

Medical expense reimbursement: _____

_____

Child care benefits: _____

_____

Maternity benefits: _____

_____

Pension or profit-sharing plans: _____

_____

Paid holidays: _____

_____

Automobiles or allowances: _____

_____

Expense accounts: _____

_____

Worksheet 7 – Defining Your Company's Personnel Policies (continued)

Fringe Benefits (continued)

Education assistance programs: _____

_____

_____

_____

Employee discounts on purchases: _____

_____

Stock options (if incorporated): _____

____   _____

Incentive bonus plan: _____

_____

Other: _____

_____

_____

_____

Placement Fees

If you hire employees through a personnel agency or "headhunting" firm, will you pay the placement fee?

_____

_____

Other Company Policies

_____

_____

_____

_____

_____

_____

_____

_____

_____

_____

_____

Chapter 2

Choosing the Legal Form of the Business

The hardest thing in the world to understand is Income Tax.

— Albert Einstein

2.1 General Considerations

A business venture can generally be structured into one of three legal forms — the sole proprietorship, the partnership, or the corporation. There are also certain variations on some of these basic legal forms, such as the S corporation and the limited partnership. In addition, the limited liability company (LLC), a relatively new form of business organization, has gained legal status in all 50 states and the District of Columbia. See Section 2.6 for more on LLCs.

If you are planning to start a business, consider the following questions when deciding your business' legal form:

- Will someone else share in ownership of the business? If so, it will not be a sole proprietorship. The choice will be between a partnership arrangement and a corporation, or possibly an LLC.
- How important is it to limit personal liability for debts or claims against the business? If this is a major consideration, incorporating the business would generally be the best means of limiting your liability.
- Which form of business organization will result in the least taxes? While there is no universal answer to this question, the rest of this chapter explains when it is and isn't beneficial to incorporate for tax reasons.

Tax Election on Form 8832

Since new IRS regulations went into effect on January 1, 1997, the task of achieving the desired type of tax treatment of an entity, where you wish to avoid treatment as a corporation, has been greatly simplified. The new IRS "check-the-box" regulations provide new and simplified default rules for domestic companies:

- A corporation will be taxable as a corporation.
- An unincorporated entity will be taxed as a partnership or, if it has only one owner, will be disregarded for tax purposes (i.e., treated as a sole proprietorship of the owner).

Under these default classification rules, it is no longer necessary, in the case of a limited partnership or limited liability company, to meet numerous complex rules regarding centralized management, transferability of interests, and the like, in order to avoid corporate tax classification. The IRS also provides a new tax election form, *Form 8832, Entity Classification Election*, for certain foreign entities and for domestic entities that wish to elect tax treatment other than as provided under the default rules. In most cases, unless you wish to do something out of the ordinary, such as electing corporate tax treatment for an LLC, or changing the current tax classification of your business, it will not be necessary to make a *Form 8832* election.

Changing Legal Forms

Before choosing the legal form of your business, it is important to realize that you may need to change to a different form at some time in the future. Changing legal forms is easier to do with some forms of business than with others. As a broad generalization, it is usually a simpler matter to change from a sole proprietorship to a partnership, or to change from a sole proprietorship or partnership to a corporation, than it is to move in the opposite direction. An LLC is usually treated like a partnership.

For example, converting a corporation into a sole proprietorship or partnership may result in substantial individual and corporate-level taxes when the corporation is liquidated. This would occur if the value of the business, when transferred to the stockholders of the corporation, was greater than the cost or tax basis for their stock, resulting in taxable gains to the stockholders. If some of the corporate assets have value in excess of their tax basis, the corporation will also have taxable gains and will pay a corporate tax on such gains when it transfers the assets to its stockholders.

While there are almost always some expenses and complications in changing the legal form of a business, such changes are quite routine transactions. Many businesses start off as sole proprietorships, develop into partnerships, and later incorporate if tax and other considerations indicate that it no longer makes good business sense not to be incorporated. Thus, the choice of one legal form over another when starting a business should not be considered a final choice.

To get a brief overview of the various legal forms of doing business, refer to the summary table at the end of this chapter, which lists the key characteristics of sole proprietorships, partnerships, corporations, and limited liability companies.

2.2 Advantages and Disadvantages of Sole Proprietorships

A sole proprietorship is one of the most common ways in which to organize a new start up. For example, many self-employed individuals, home-based businesses, and small cottage industries operate as sole proprietorships. The list can go on, but generally, sole proprietorships are one- or two-person businesses. As a sole proprietor, you are the sole owner of your business. If married, however, your spouse will usually have a one-half interest in the business if you live in a state that has community property laws. It is an exciting, independent way to operate a business, and it has its own unique set of advantages and disadvantages.

Advantages

To give you a better perspective on why a sole proprietorship is a popular legal form of doing business, consider the benefits listed below. Not only is a sole proprietorship easy to start, but everyone likes the idea of receiving all the profits from the business, saving on unemployment taxes, and having more freedom to withdraw assets.

Easy to Organize

The great advantage of operating a new business as a sole proprietorship is that it is simple and does not require any formal action to set it up. You can start your business today as a sole proprietorship — there is no need to wait for an attorney to draft and file documents or for the government to approve them. Of course, you will need a business license, and a growing number of states require you to register to do business.

Profit (or Loss) Is Yours

All of the profit or loss from your business belongs to you and must be reported on your federal income tax return, *Schedule C, Income (or Loss) from a Business or Profession*, on *Form 1040*. This can either be an advantage or a disadvantage for income tax purposes, depending on the circumstances.

If operating the business results in losses or significant tax credits, you may be able to use the tax losses or tax credits to reduce taxes on income from other sources. Or, if your sole proprietorship generates modest profits — but not more than about $60,000 to $75,000 a year — overall taxes may be less than if incorporated, assuming you need most of the income to live on.

Unemployment Tax Savings

As a sole proprietor, you are not considered an employee of your business. As a result, you will avoid having to pay unemployment taxes on your earnings from the business. Both the state and federal governments impose unemployment taxes on wages or salaries, but not on self-employment income. Note that a corporation would normally get an income tax deduction for the unemployment tax it paid on your salary, so that the actual after-tax savings from operating as a sole proprietorship would be somewhat less than the unemployment taxes you would avoid paying. Refer to sections 5.3 and 11.5 regarding the unemployment taxes you must pay for each employee.

Withdraw Assets Tax Free

Another advantage of a sole proprietorship is that you can shift funds in and out of your business account or withdraw assets from the business with few tax, legal, or other limitations. In a partnership or a limited liability company, you can generally withdraw funds only by agreement and, in the case of a corporation, a withdrawal of funds or property will usually be taxable as a dividend or capital gain and may violate some states' corporation laws.

Disadvantages

As with any decision, you must always look at the downside of a situation or opportunity so you not only make a more informed decision, but you also realize what to expect in a negative sense, once you decide to move ahead. Sole proprietorships have several advantages, but be sure to consider some important disadvantages.

Personal Liability

As the owner of the sole proprietorship, you will be personally liable for any debts or taxes of the business or other claims, such as legal damages resulting from a lawsuit. This is one reason why many entrepreneurs prefer to use a corporation rather than a sole proprietorship. Unlimited personal liability is perhaps the major disadvantage of operating a business in the form of a sole proprietorship.

Limited Tax Savings for Fringe Benefits

A major disadvantage of sole proprietorships (and partnerships) is they cannot obtain a number of significant tax benefits regarding group-term life insurance benefits, long-term disability insurance coverage, and medical insurance or medical expense reimbursements. To qualify for favorable tax treatment regarding these fringe benefit plans, you need to incorporate. A self-employed individual is allowed to deduct 30% of his or her health insurance when computing adjusted gross income.[1] Beginning January 1, 1997 the deduction rises to 40% and will continue to gradually increase to 80% over a period of several years.

The special advantages of corporate pension and profit-sharing plans have largely been eliminated. There are now virtually no differences in the tax treatment of self-employed (Keogh) plans of sole proprietorships and partnerships, as compared with corporate retirement plans. See Section 8.3.

2.3 Advantages and Disadvantages of Partnerships

In general, any two or more individuals or entities who agree to contribute money, labor, property, or skill to a business and who agree to share in its profits, losses, and management are considered to have a partnership. You can choose to have a general partnership or a limited partnership, or in a growing number of states, a limited liability partnership in lieu of a professional corporation.

Creating a general partnership can be a very simple matter since the law does not require any official written documents or other formalities for most partnerships. As a practical matter, however, it is much sounder business practice for partners in a business to have a written partnership agreement that, at a minimum, spells out their agreement on basic issues such as:

- How much and what kind of property each partner will contribute to the venture;
- What value will be placed on the contributed property;
- How profits and losses will be divided among the partners;
- When and how profits will be withdrawn;
- Whether or how certain partners will be compensated for their services to the partnership or for making capital available to the partnership; and
- How changes in ownership of interests in the partnership will be handled.

A written partnership agreement should be prepared by an attorney and, if possible, should be reviewed by a tax accountant before it is put into effect. Partnerships are a bit like marriages; they usually start out with a great deal of trust but have a high break-up rate. Be advised that partnerships are easy to get into, require a lot of patience and understanding to live with, and are often costly and painful to get out of.

If you are considering having a partner or partners in your new venture, you will be interested in the discussion below, which features some reasons why having a partnership can be advantageous.

- Complete control over operations. As a partner, you are an agent for the partnership and can do anything necessary to operate the business, such as hire employees, borrow money, or enter into contracts on behalf of the partnership.
- Flexibility in withdrawing assets. Taking money or other assets out of a partnership is slightly more complicated than with a sole proprietorship, but you have much more flexibility than in the case of a corporation, and usually no serious tax or legal consequences result from withdrawing assets out of a partnership — provided you don't violate the terms of your partnership agreement.
- Favorable taxation on income for partners. Like a sole proprietor, a partner is not generally considered an employee of the partnership for income tax and payroll tax purposes. The income tax advantages and disadvantages of a sole proprietorship are equally applicable to a partnership since a partner's share of income from a partnership is treated essentially the same as income from a sole proprietorship. For example, your income from a partnership may be subject to federal self-employment tax but not to federal and state unemployment taxes, as discussed in Section 2.2.
- Partnership pays no income tax. While a partnership must file federal and usually state information returns — *Form 1065* is the federal form — it generally pays no income tax. Instead, the partnership reports each partner's share of income or loss on the information return, and each

General Partnerships

Advantages

partner reports the income or loss on *Schedule E* of his or her individual income tax return, *Form 1040*. In addition, partnerships are required to file a special report, *Form 8308*, with the IRS each time a sale or exchange of an interest in the partnership occurs.[2]

- Assistance in operations. One less appealing aspect of starting your own business is the long hours and extra duties you will take on as owner/manager. If you have a trustworthy, conscientious partner by your side, you will be in a better position to have competent assistance with the day-to-day operations of running your partnership. Your chances of catching a mistake, meeting a particular deadline, or improving product quality and overall service will be increased. In addition, a potential partner could bring an expertise into the business that otherwise would have to be brought in by hiring an employee or outside consultant. Having a diverse partnership, with each partner using his or her strengths to improve operations, will only prove worthwhile in the long run.

Disadvantages

Knowing some of the positive aspects of organizing a partnership gives you a chance to better weigh the negative aspects, such as disagreements, taxable year, unlimited personal liability for the partnership's debts, and uncertainty in the event one of the partners dies.

- Dissension among partners. While a good relationship between partners can make for a strong business team, the downside risk is that you and your partner or partners may not get along. You and one or more of your partners may, in fact, have totally different views about how the business is to be run, which can lead to dissension, acrimony, deadlock, and in some cases, dissolution of the partnership or even lawsuits.

- Taxable year issue. Unlike C corporations, partnerships are generally not allowed to use a fiscal year for tax purposes. Instead, they must report on a calendar-year basis. Those partnerships that are allowed to use a fiscal tax year are required to report and pay income taxes directly if the use of a fiscal year would otherwise result in a tax-deferral benefit to its partners.[3]

- Liability of partners. You and each of your partners — except for a limited partner in a limited partnership — have personal liability for the debts, taxes, and other claims against the partnership. If the partnership's assets are not sufficient to pay creditors, the creditors can satisfy their claims out of your personal assets. In addition, when any partner fails to pay personal debts, the partnership's business may be disrupted if his or her creditors proceed to satisfy their claims out of his or her interest in the partnership by seeking what is called a charging order against partnership assets.

- No perpetual existence. Unless a partnership agreement provides otherwise, a partnership usually terminates when any partner dies or withdraws from the partnership. This is in contrast to a corporation, which theoretically, has perpetual existence. Under the laws of most states, bankruptcy of a partner or the partnership itself will cause the dissolution of the partnership, regardless of any agreement.

Limited Partnerships

In contrast to the general partnership, which has unlimited personal liability for all of its partners, the limited partnership allows investors who will not be actively involved in the partnership's operations to become partners without being exposed to unlimited liability for the business' debts if it should go out of business.

A limited partner risks only his or her investment but must allow one or more general partners to exercise control over the business. In fact, if the limited partner becomes involved in the partnership's operations, he or she may lose his or her protected status as a limited partner. The general partners in a limited partnership are fully liable for the partnership's debts. Every limited partnership must have one or more general partners, as well as one or more limited partners. Besides enjoying all the benefits derived from limited personal liability, a limited partner's share of the partnership's income is not subject to the self-employment tax.[4]

State law requires certain formalities in the case of a limited partnership that are not required for other partnerships. To qualify for their special status, limited partnerships must usually file a certificate of limited partnership with the secretary of state or other state and county offices. Establishing a limited partnership also requires a written partnership agreement. See Section 11.2 regarding special filing requirements for partnerships under state law.

Limited Liability Partnerships

All 50 states — plus the District of Columbia — have enacted limited liability company (LLC) laws and every state but Wyoming has also enacted additional provisions for another new entity, the limited liability partnership (LLP). See Section 2.6. In general, the LLP is simply a regular general partnership that is granted limited liability — like a corporation or LLC — if it files a required form or statement with the state.

LLPs vary considerably from state to state. In some states, they are allowed only for certain professional service firms, as an alternative to professional corporations, while in others an LLP may engage in any lawful business. In most states, an LLP does not provide the full liability protection afforded by a corporation or LLC. Instead, most state LLP laws provide liability protection only for certain defined types of misdeeds of another partner, such as malpractice, intentional misconduct, or negligence, and do not offer any limitation of liability from general trade creditors of the partnership, in the event the LLP's business simply fails. Also, no liability protection is offered in any state to an individual partner for his or her own wrongdoing (such as malpractice) — a partner is protected only from liability for acts of the other partners. Thus, an LLP should not be considered as the equivalent of a partnership or LLC, with regard to limiting the liability of the owners of a business.

Generally, where allowable for professional service firms, LLPs provide only the same, partial limitation of liability as do professional corporations — that is, they do not offer any limitation on personal liability for malpractice of an individual practitioner of a profession such as law or medicine, but do protect the practitioner from personal liability for the malpractice of a partner.

Advantages

While LLPs have not garnered the degree of attention recently focused on LLCs, they have a number of advantages over LLCs, corporations, or other partnerships.

- Like LLCs or S corporations, LLPs have the tax advantage of flow-through tax treatment — that is, they will generally qualify for partnership tax treatment for federal income tax purposes. In addition, most states treat LLPs as partnerships for tax purposes, which is usually advantageous. Even states that treat LLCs less favorably for tax purposes, such as California, tend to grant more favorable tax treatment to LLPs.

- Like LLCs, they are not subject to the numerous limitations that apply to S corporations with regard to ownership, capital structure, and division of profits.

- LLPs have the advantages of simplicity and familiarity, as compared with LLCs. In most cases, an existing partnership can simply elect to become an LLP by filing a specified form or document and paying the applicable fee. There is usually no need to draw up a new governing document, such as articles of incorporation or articles of organization, as for a corporation or LLC. The existing partnership agreement can generally continue to serve as the governing document when a regular partnership becomes an LLP.

Disadvantages

Despite the obvious advantages of LLPs, do not be in too great a rush to set one up, even if you are located in one of the states that has adopted a limited liability partnership law. Keep in mind several disadvantages of operating your business as an LLP.

- You may not actually have limited liability if you conduct business in a state that does not yet have an LLP law or in a state like California or New York that allows LLPs only for certain kinds of professional partnerships. Creditors in any of those states would be free to go after your personal assets if the business failed.

- Even if your home state and the other states in which you do business all have LLP laws, some of those state laws provide that if you fail to properly register as a foreign LLP, or forget to make annual filings required of both domestic and foreign LLPs, your LLP status may be lost and your partnership will revert to plain vanilla, general partnership status by operation of state law.

- Except in a few states, LLPs do not provide liability protection for the individual partner's own acts of malpractice or other wrongdoings, and do not provide any shield from ordinary trade creditors in the event the partnership business fails.

- Sole owners will not be able to establish LLPs since, as a partnership, an LLP must have at least two partners to exist.
- The self-employment tax treatment of partners in an LLP is uncertain at present. While limited partners in a limited partnership are not subject to self-employment tax on their share of the partnership income, and IRS proposed regulations would also exempt nonmanagerial partners in some LLCs from self-employment taxation, there is no existing or proposed similar exemption for any partners in an LLP.

2.4 Advantages and Disadvantages of Corporations

When you are considering which legal entity to choose for your business, you will want to carefully consider the pros and cons of the corporation. A corporation is unlike any other form of doing business because it is considered by federal and state law to be an artificial legal entity that exists separately from the people who own, manage, control, and operate it. It can make contracts, pay taxes, and is liable for debts. Corporations exist only because state statutory laws allow them to be created. Deciding whether to incorporate in this state or elsewhere is discussed in Section 9.12.

A business corporation issues shares of its stock, as evidence of ownership, to the person or persons who contribute the money or business assets that the corporation will use to conduct its business. Thus, the stockholders or shareholders are the owners of the corporation, and they are entitled to any dividends the corporation pays and to all corporation assets — after all creditors have been paid — if the corporation is liquidated.

Corporations can exist in many different forms. For example, there is the regular C corporation, which is the main focus of this section; the S corporation, which is discussed in Section 2.5; and the personal service corporation, which is mentioned briefly at the end of this section.

Before getting into the general advantages and disadvantages of incorporating, you need to know that to set up a corporation, you must file articles of incorporation with the state office that grants and approves corporate charters. See Section 11.2 for more information on state incorporation requirements. In addition to the requirements for establishing a corporation, there will be recurring costs, often including annual franchise or corporate income taxes.

Corporate Taxes

Since many of the advantages associated with incorporating involve how a corporation is taxed on its income, it is important that you understand corporate tax rates and how your income from the corporation is viewed by the IRS. Corporations filing their income tax returns on *Form 1120-A* or *Form 1120* will be taxed at different rates depending on the amount of their taxable income. The following table lists the current federal corporate income tax rates, which are 39% in the highest bracket.

Taxable Income	Tax Rate
Not more than $50,000	15%
$50,000 to $75,000	25
$75,000 to $100,000	34
$100,000 to $335,000	39
$335,000 to $10 million	34
$10 million to $15 million	35
$15 million to $18,333,333	38
More than $18,333,333	35

As a corporate shareholder/owner, you will be considered an employee and most likely draw a salary from your corporation. This salary will be subject to personal income tax, FICA (Social Security) taxes, and state and federal unemployment taxes. FICA taxes are generally the same (in total) on the wages of a corporate employee/owner as would be the self-employment tax on the same amount of business income if you were a sole proprietor or a partner.

Advantages

Some of the tax advantages of a corporation include income splitting, fringe benefit plan tax deductions, the dividends received deduction, and the tax break for investing in small business stock. In addition to these tax advantages, there is also the benefit of limited personal liability and continuous existence.

Income Splitting

By using a corporation, it may be possible to split your overall profit between two or more taxpayers so that none of the income gets taxed in the highest tax brackets. Thus, the total tax paid by the two taxpayers — you and your corporation — may be less than if all of the income were taxed to you, as in a sole proprietorship. See Section 8.2 for a more detailed discussion of how income splitting can help reduce your income and estate taxes.

Fringe Benefit Plan Deductions

Federal and state tax laws permit you, as a corporate employer, to provide a number of different fringe benefits to shareholders/employees on a tax-favored basis. These tax-favored fringe benefits include medical insurance plans, self-insured medical reimbursement plans, disability insurance, and group-term life insurance. An unincorporated business receives the same tax treatment for its employees, but not for its owners. In addition, a corporation — other than an S corporation — can generally deduct medical insurance premiums it makes on behalf of an employee, who is an owner of the business, and the employee is not taxed on the value of the benefit provided. This is far more favorable than payments of salary to an employee, which are fully taxable. So the tax benefits of employee fringe benefits are another reason for incorporating your business and becoming an employee of the corporation.

Major types of fringe benefits that allow for tax deductions to the corporation and no taxable income to the employee are discussed in more detail in Section 8.3.

Another important tax advantage of a C corporation is that, in general, it can deduct 70% of the dividends it receives from stock investments from its federal taxable income.[5] This tax benefit, called the dividends received deduction, is discussed more in Section 8.2.

Tax Break for Dividends Received by a Corporation

The tax law provides major tax incentives for investing in the stock of certain small corporations. This incentive is not available for investments in unincorporated businesses or in stock of S corporations.

Tax Break for Investing in Small Business Stock

A noncorporate investor who purchases "qualified small business stock" after August 10, 1993 and holds it for five years or more will be allowed to exclude from his or her taxable income up to 50% of any capital gain reported on the sale of stock.[6] At the current maximum tax rate on such capital gains of 28%, this translates into a very low effective tax rate of only 14% on gains from qualified small business stock.

In addition, even if such stock is sold before the five-year holding requirement is met, the 1997 tax law allows the seller to "roll over" the gain by reinvesting the proceeds within 60 days in another qualifying company's stock, with no tax incurred if the entire proceeds of sale are reinvested.[7] Better yet, the period in which the first company's stock was held can be counted towards the five-year holding period requirement if the second company's stock is later sold for a gain.

Qualified small business stock is stock of a C corporation that meets an active business test during the period the stock is held. To meet the active business test, a corporation must use at least 80% of its assets in the conduct of one or more qualified trades or businesses. Personal service firms, banks, finance or investment businesses, insurance companies, and farming businesses are not considered qualified trades or businesses; neither are companies in certain extractive industries, or in the hotel, motel, or restaurant businesses. In addition, the corporation must not have more than $50 million in gross assets before or immediately after the stock is issued to the investor. Stock in a special entity, such as a Domestic International Sales Corporation (DISC), regulated investment company, or a real estate investment trust, is also considered ineligible for this tax incentive.

The main reason most businesses incorporate is to limit owner liability to the amount invested in the business. Generally, stockholders in a corporation are not personally liable for claims against the corporation and are, therefore, at risk only to the extent of their investment in the corporation. Likewise, the officers and directors of a corporation are not normally liable for the corporation's debts, although in some cases, an officer whose duty it is to withhold federal income tax from employees' wages may be liable to the IRS if the taxes are not withheld and paid over to the IRS as required.

Limited Personal Liability

Being incorporated can also protect you from personal liability regarding lawsuit damages not covered by your corporation's liability insurance policies; for example, someone slips on a banana peel in your store and sues the corporation for ten million dollars. When you incorporate, however, you need to follow several corporate formalities and requirements to protect your limited liability benefit. For example, don't start a corporation on a shoestring. If your corporation is capitalized too thinly with equity capital (your money) as compared to debt capital (borrowed money), the courts may determine that your corporation is a thin corporation and hold you and your stockholders directly liable to creditors.

Failure to observe corporate formalities, such as the election of directors by shareholders and appointment of officers by action of the board of directors, and the separate legal existence of the corporation can have a similar result. This is called "piercing the corporate veil" by the courts, and means if a corporation is not adequately capitalized and properly operated to protect the interests of creditors, the courts can take away the veil of limited liability that normally protects the stockholders. Piercing the corporate veil is relatively uncommon. A much more frequent problem is that many banks and other lenders will not loan money to a small incorporated business unless someone, usually the stockholders of the corporation, personally guarantees repayment of the loan.

Despite this common business practice, the limited liability feature can still be an important protection from personal liability for other debts, such as accounts payable to suppliers and others who sell goods or services to the corporation on credit, typically without requiring any personal guarantee of payment by the owners. Even this partial protection is a significant advantage of incorporating for most small business owners. To help you avoid personal liability for corporate acts, consult your attorney and keep thorough and specific records of your corporation's operations, policies, and meetings.

Continuous Existence

Unlike a sole proprietorship or partnership, a corporation has continuous existence and does not terminate upon the death of a stockholder or a change of ownership of some or all of its stock. Creditors, suppliers, and customers, therefore, often prefer to deal with an incorporated business because of this greater continuity. Naturally, a corporation can be terminated by mutual consent of the owners or even by one stockholder in some instances.

Disadvantages

In addition to having much more paperwork and recordkeeping requirements — in order to maintain the corporate veil of limited liability — corporations must ensure they meet all annual report filings and SEC requirements as well. Incorporation takes a lot of organization and maintenance, and you will want to know all you can about its operations and costs.

Cost of Incorporating

Besides the usual filing fees that are required by state agencies for articles of incorporation, name reservation, and issuing stock, legal fees usually run between $500 and $1,000, even for a simple incorporation. And if it is necessary to obtain a permit from the state to issue stock or securities, legal fees can be much more. Thus, one of the disadvantages of incorporating is the cost involved, which will be substantial even for the simplest incorporation.

Double Taxation

While this section has outlined a number of important tax advantages of incorporating a business, the picture is not all that one-sided. Regular corporations have one major potential disadvantage that usually does not exist for other legal forms of doing business — the problem of potential double taxation of the earnings of the corporation. This problem arises because a C corporation must pay corporate income taxes on its taxable income. Then, the after-tax earnings may be subject to a second tax on either the individual stockholders, if the earnings are distributed as dividends, or as a corporate penalty tax if the earnings are not distributed as dividends.

The main ways in which a corporation's earnings can be subject to double taxation are:

- Payment of taxable dividends
- Penalty tax on corporate accumulated earnings
- Penalty tax on personal holding company income

See Section 8.9 for a discussion of these and other various tax-planning techniques that will permit you to avoid the problems of potential double taxation listed above. Most of those disadvantages are not applicable if you elect S corporation status.

Personal Service Corporations

Certain kinds of corporations, called qualified personal service corporations (QPSCs), are taxed at a flat rate of 35%, instead of the graduated tax rates listed in the corporate tax rate table featured earlier in this section.[8] While it may not always be clear whether an incorporated service business is a QPSC, the IRS defines a QPSC by these characteristics:

- At least 95% of the value of its stock is held by employees or their estates or beneficiaries; and
- The employees perform services at least 95% of the time in the following fields: health, law, engineering, architecture, accounting, actuarial science, performing arts, or consulting.

2.5 Advantages and Disadvantages of S Corporations

The first thing to understand about S corporations — formerly referred to as Subchapter S corporations — is they are just like any other corporation in terms of corporate law requirements, limited liability of shareholders, and all other corporate aspects; however, they are treated differently when it comes to how they are taxed. An S corporation is simply a regular corporation that meets certain requirements and has elected to be treated somewhat like a partnership for federal income tax purposes. Most, but not all, states also allow this special tax treatment for S corporations. See Section 11.2 for a discussion of how S corporations are treated for tax purposes in this state.

S Corporation Requirements

To qualify for S corporation treatment, your corporation must meet the following requirements:

- It must be a domestic corporation — that is, incorporated in the United States.[9]
- No shareholder can be a nonresident alien individual.[10]
- All of its shareholders must generally be individuals, although certain trusts, called Qualified Subchapter S Trusts and Grantor Trusts, may hold stock under certain circumstances. No shareholder can be a corporation or a partnership.[11]
- The corporation can have only one class of common stock and no preferred stock.[12]
- There cannot be more than 75 shareholders.[13] For this purpose, a husband and wife who are both stockholders will be counted as only one stockholder, whether or not they hold the stock in joint ownership.[14]
- The corporation cannot be a member of an affiliated group of corporations.[15] If it owns stock in a subsidiary that is considered an affiliate, it may not be able to qualify under the S corporation provisions.
- Less than 25% of the corporation's gross receipts must be from passive sources, such as interest income, dividends, rent, royalties, or proceeds from the sale of securities. If this test is failed in three successive tax years, S corporation status will be terminated.[16] The passive income limit does not apply at all for a brand new corporation or an existing corporation that has no accumulated earnings and profits when it elects S corporation status.[17]

See Section 9.14 for a summary of S Corporation and other changes under the Small Business Job Protection Act of 1996.

Electing S Corporation Status

To become an S corporation, your company must meet the above requirements and file an election on *Form 2553* with the IRS. For your convenience, a sample of *Form 2553, Election by a Small Business Corporation*, is provided at the end of this chapter. The election must be signed by all of the corporation's shareholders,[18] including your spouse, who may have a community property interest in stock that is in your name. The S corporation election must be filed during the first two months and 15 days of the corporation's tax year for which the election is to go into effect or at any time during the preceding tax year.[19]

Since a newly formed corporation that wants to start out as an S corporation does not have a preceding tax year, it has to file an election in the two-month and 15-day period after it is considered to have begun its first tax year. Its first tax year is considered to start when it issues stock to shareholders, acquires assets, or begins to do business, whichever occurs first. Filing of articles of incorporation with the secretary of state usually does not begin the first taxable year.

Care must be taken to file the election at the right time, which can be tricky, since it is sometimes difficult to determine when a corporation first begins to do business. There can be some horrendous tax consequences if you operate the corporation as though it were an S corporation, and the election is later determined to have been filed too early or too late.

Extreme care must also be taken if a regular C corporation elects to change over to S corporation status; this should not be done without consulting a competent tax adviser. A regular corporation that elects to become an S corporation will generally be subject to an eventual corporate-level tax on any built-in gains on its assets — assets with a value greater than their tax basis — if assets are sold for a gain within ten years.

Once a corporation has made an election with the IRS to be treated as an S corporation, its shareholders will generally report their share of the corporation's taxable income or loss on their individual tax returns. That is, the corporation "passes through" its income or loss and tax credits to the shareholders in proportion to their stock holdings in the corporation, much like a partnership.

Federal Tax Treatment of S Corporations

The S corporation does not usually pay tax on any of its income. Any domestic S corporation, however, must file *Form 1120S, U.S. Income Tax Return for an S Corporation*, regardless of any tax due. *Form 1120S* must be filed by March 15, if filing under a calendar-year basis, or the 15th day of the third month following the close of a fiscal year.

An S corporation must furnish a copy of *Schedule K-1, Shareholder's Share of Income, Credits, Deductions* to each shareholder. By not providing *Schedule K-1* before filing *Form 1120S*, the S corporation could incur penalties.

Profits of an S corporation are deemed to be distributed to its shareholders on the last day of the corporation's tax year, whether or not the profits are actually distributed.[20] Thus, if profits of an S corporation are distributed as dividends, the distribution itself is ordinarily not taxable, so there is no double taxation of distributed profits.

Until the 1993 tax law changes, S corporations enjoyed a clear tax advantage over regular corporations because the maximum tax rate on S corporation income taxed to shareholders was significantly below the top regular corporation tax rate. However, now that the top individual rate is 39.6% on S corporation shareholders, and the top corporation rate is generally 34.0% or 35.0%, S corporations don't necessarily offer an advantage over regular corporations. They may even be at a tax disadvantage in the case of high-income S corporation shareholders who are in the 39.6% bracket — those with taxable incomes of more than 250 million dollars.

**Terminating an
S Corporation Election**

If it becomes desirable to revoke or terminate S corporation status after a few years, as is often the case, this can be done if shareholders owning more than half the stock sign and file a revocation form.[21] A revocation is effective for the tax year it is filed if it is filed during the first two months and 15 days of that tax year.[22] If it is filed later in the year, it does not become effective until the next tax year.[23]

Doing anything, however, that causes the corporation to cease to qualify as an S corporation — such as selling stock to a corporate shareholder — will also terminate the election, effective on the first day after the corporation ceases to qualify as an S corporation. In that case, the company must file two short-period tax returns for the year, the first — up to the date it ceased to qualify — as an S corporation, the second as a regular taxable corporation.

Once a corporation terminates an S corporation election, it cannot re-elect S corporation status for five years, unless it obtains the consent of the IRS.[24]

For a corporation, electing S corporation status can be very advantageous in some instances, and less so, or even disadvantageous in other situations. An S corporation election should not be made without the advice and assistance of a tax professional, since it is a very complex and technical area of the tax law.

Electing S corporation treatment for a corporation is usually most favorable in these types of situations:

- Where it is expected that the corporation will experience losses for the initial year or years of doing business and where the shareholders will have income from other sources that the "passed through" losses can shelter from tax. If S corporation losses are passive losses — such as losses from real estate investments — they can only be used to offset other passive activity income, except for certain shareholders who are real estate professionals.

- Where, because of the low tax brackets the shareholders are in, there will be tax savings if the anticipated profits of the corporation are passed through to them rather than being taxed at corporate tax rates.

- Where, particularly in the case of a new business, the risk of failure makes the limited liability feature of a corporation important, and where flow-through tax treatment of losses or income is desired. A regular corporation provides limited liability, but not flow-through tax treatment. A sole proprietorship or partnership provides the latter, but not limited liability. While it is true that both flow-through tax treatment and limited liability can be obtained in most states by creating a limited liability company (LLC), an LLC must have at least two owners, unlike an S corporation, which can be owned entirely by one person.

- Where the nature of the corporation's business is such that the corporation does not need to retain a major portion of profits in the business.

In this case, all or most of the profits can be distributed as dividends without the double taxation that would occur if no S corporation election were in effect.

- Where a corporation is in danger of incurring an accumulated earnings penalty tax for failure to pay out its profits as dividends.

Disadvantages

While there are some significant advantages to operating as an S corporation, the S corporation election is frequently not advisable under some circumstances. Some of the possible disadvantages of operating your business in the form of an S corporation are:

- The change to S corporation status may eventually result in a large corporate-level tax on built-in gains or an immediate last in, first out (LIFO) recapture tax.

- The tax law regarding S corporations is very complex and you should expect to pay fairly substantial additional legal or accounting fees to your tax adviser, compared to what would be necessary with a regular corporation.

- S corporations are now treated almost exactly like regular corporations with respect to pension and profit-sharing plans. One important difference remains; any employee who owns 5% or more of the stock and participates in the S corporation's pension or profit-sharing plan is prohibited from borrowing from the plan, unlike a participant in a regular corporation's retirement plan.[25]

- Certain built-in gains of an S corporation may be taxed to the corporation and the shareholder for federal tax purposes.[26] Built-in gains are untaxed gains on the assets of a corporation that would have been recognized as taxable if the assets had been sold at fair market value on the day a corporation became an S corporation. In addition, capital gains on sale of the stock of an S corporation will not qualify for the new 50% capital gain exclusion that is discussed in Section 2.4 under "Tax Break for Investing in Small Business Stock."

- Fringe benefit payments for medical, disability, and group-term life insurance for 2% shareholders are deductible, to the corporation, but are taxable to the shareholder/employee.[27] An exception to this partnership treatment of S corporation shareholders is for medical insurance premiums paid on their behalf, which can be deducted by the S corporation. However, the amount deducted by the corporation for medical insurance must be reported as taxable compensation income on the shareholder/employee's *Form W-2*, for income tax purposes,[28] but not for FICA (Social Security) tax purposes if the insurance plan covers employees generally.[29]

- S corporations cannot benefit from the corporate dividends received deduction that is discussed in further detail in Section 8.2.

- Unlike many regular corporations, very few newly electing S corporations may now have a fiscal tax year that ends earlier than September.[30]

2.6 Advantages and Disadvantages of Limited Liability Companies

The S corporation and the limited partnership may soon become endangered species due to the appearance of a new form of legal entity that has a number of advantages over both and that is proliferating across the country. This new type of entity is called a limited liability company (LLC). An LLC closely resembles and is taxed as a partnership, but it offers the benefit of limited liability, just like corporations. It is also similar to a limited partnership, except that in an LLC, all partners have the benefit of limited liability.

In 1988, the IRS concluded in Revenue Ruling 88-76 that a Wyoming limited liability company could be classified as a partnership for federal income tax purposes, despite its limited liability, because it lacked continuity of life. This ruling was highly favorable, from a taxpayer's standpoint, because it held that an LLC, which offers the corporate benefits of limited liability, could qualify for the flexible flow-through tax treatment of a partnership. Because this favorable IRS ruling opened the floodgates, the District of Columbia and all 50 states have followed Wyoming's lead in adopting similar LLC laws.

Advantages

Doing business as an LLC has a number of benefits over any other form of business organization, which accounts for the sudden popularity of this new type of business entity. Advantages of the LLC include the following:

- It combines the limited liability features of a corporation and the flow-through tax treatment of income and losses of a partnership.
- It provides the simplicity of a sole proprietorship, for a one-owner business, but with the limited liability features of a corporation. Under IRS regulations effective January 1, 1997, a sole proprietorship can be set up as, or converted to, a one-person LLC with no federal tax consequences.
- Unlike a general partnership, owners of an LLC have limited liability, and, unlike limited partners in a limited partnership, they do not lose their limited liability if they actively participate in management.
- While its flow-through tax advantages are generally only slightly superior to those of an S corporation, an LLC is not subject to the numerous technical rules that apply to S corporations. Thus, for example, an LLC can have more than 75 shareholders; have foreign owners ("members"); have owners that are corporations, partnerships, trusts, or other LLCs; own 80% or more of the stock of an affiliated corporation; derive a large portion of its revenue from certain net passive income sources; and issue more than one class of stock.

  Violation of any one of these technical restrictions may disqualify an S corporation.
- For certain leveraged real estate investments, LLCs have significant advantages over either partnerships or S corporations with regard to the ability of the owners to take tax losses, under technical tax rules having to do with "tax basis."

Despite the obvious advantages of LLCs, do not be in too great a rush to set one up. Some of the disadvantages of operating your business as an LLC are as follows:

Disadvantages

- LLC laws are very new and untested, unlike the corporation and partnership laws, which have evolved over very long periods of time. As such, your lawyer may not be able to give you clear advice on a number of legal questions that may arise in the course of operating an LLC, which could lead to some unpleasant surprises.

- Sole owners are not able to establish LLCs under the laws of many states. However, now that the IRS has changed its policy, and will allow LLCs to be treated as sole proprietorships for tax purposes — rather than taxed as corporations, as previously — it is expected that most or all states will change their LLC laws to permit one-owner LLCs. Until your state does so, one way to get around this problem would be to make your spouse a second member of the LLC.

- Before 1997, one of the problems associated with setting up an LLC was the tax complexity of properly structuring an LLC so that it would not be considered a corporation for tax purposes by the Internal Revenue Service. However, under new IRS regulations that went into effect in 1997, a new LLC will now automatically be considered to be a partnership if it has more than one member, or, if it has only one member, will be treated as a sole proprietorship and thus disregarded as an entity for all tax purposes.

- A significant disadvantage of an LLC, compared to a limited partnership, is that limited partners in a limited partnership are not subject to the self-employment tax on their distributive share of the partnership's profits.[31] No such exemption is currently available for an LLC that is treated as a partnership for tax purposes.

   However, IRS Proposed Regulations, if they go into effect, will treat certain nonmanaging members of an LLC like limited partners, thus exempting them from self-employment tax on their share of an LLC's earnings in states where state law permits designation of certain members of an LLC as managers and others as nonmanagers.[32] For now, Congress has ordered the IRS to refrain from implementing the proposed regulations at any time before July 1, 1998, while Congress seeks to develop a legislative solution to this issue.

- While most states will follow federal tax treatment of an LLC where it is taxable as a partnership for federal income tax purposes, a few states, for example, Texas, Pennsylvania, and Florida, impose a corporate income or franchise tax on LLCs.

- Perhaps unintentionally, a partnership tax law provision in the Revenue Reconciliation Act of 1993 will adversely impact some professional service firms that are organized as LLCs, rather than as partnerships. Under the 1993 tax law amendments, certain payments made by partnerships to outgoing partners, for goodwill or unrealized receivables, are no longer deductible to the partnership, unless they are made to a general partner in a service partnership, such as a law or medical partnership.[33]

Since LLCs, if properly organized, are treated as partnerships for income tax purposes, this new law will apply equally to professional service firms that are either LLCs or partnerships — with one important Catch-22. Since an LLC has no general partners (all of its partners have limited liability, like limited partners), then no payments by an LLC to buy out one of its members will qualify as deductible under the new tax law. This can be a serious tax disadvantage for a professional service firm that operates as an LLC rather than as a partnership.

- Although LLCs can engage in most businesses that are permissible for a corporation to engage in, certain states do not yet allow for professional service firms, such as law firms, physicians, or other professionals, to operate in LLC form.

- Finally, some states have a built-in requirement that an LLC must terminate within 30 years, which is not required of other kinds of business entities. However, many states have recently repealed such requirements.

In Revenue Ruling 95-37, the IRS ruled favorably that an existing partnership may generally be converted, tax-free, to an LLC if the LLC qualifies for partnership tax treatment. In fact, this conversion can be done without terminating the partnership's taxable year — the LLC is simply treated as a continuation partnership — and without obtaining a new federal employer identification number for the LLC.

In contrast, be aware there is no tax-free way to convert a corporation to an LLC. The conversion of an existing incorporated business to an LLC is likely to have severe tax consequences, including:

- Recognition of gain or loss by the corporation upon distribution or transfer of its assets; and

- Recognition of gain or loss by the shareholders upon liquidation of their stock in exchange for the corporation's assets.

Accordingly, extreme caution is advised before adopting LLC status. Consult a good tax adviser before you even consider setting up an LLC, despite its obvious attractions. See Chapter 11 for more specific information on LLCs in this state.

Endnotes

1. I.R.C. § 162(l).
2. I.R.C. § 6050K.
3. I.R.C. §§ 444 and 7519.
4. I.R.C. § 1402(a)(13).
5. I.R.C. § 243(a).
6. I.R.C. § 1202.
7. I.R.C. § 1045.
8. I.R.C. § 11(b)(2).
9. I.R.C. § 1361(b).
10. I.R.C. § 1361(b)(1)(C).
11. I.R.C. § 1361(b)(1)(B).
12. I.R.C. § 1361(b)(1)(D).
13. I.R.C. § 1361(b)(1)(A).
14. I.R.C. § 1361(c).
15. I.R.C. § 1361(b)(2)(A).
16. I.R.C. § 1362(d)(3).
17. I.R.C. § 1362(d)(3)(B).
18. I.R.C. § 1362(a)(2).
19. I.R.C. § 1362(b).
20. I.R.C. § 1366.
21. I.R.C. § 1362(d)(1)(B).
22. I.R.C. § 1362(d)(1)(C)(i).
23. I.R.C. § 1362(d)(i)(C)(ii).
24. I.R.C. § 1362(g).
25. I.R.C. § 4975(d).
26. I.R.C. § 1374(a).
27. Rev. Rul. 91-26, 1991-1 C.B. 184.
28. Id.
29. I.R.S. Ann. 92-16, 1992-5 I.R.B. 53.
30. I.R.C. § 1378(a).
31. I.R.C. § 1402(a)(13).
32. Prop. Reg. § 1.1402(a)-18.
33. I.R.C. § 736(b)(3).

Key Characteristics of the Various Legal Forms of Business Organization – Summary

	Proprietorship	General or Limited Partnership
Simplicity in Operation and Formation	Simplest to establish and operate.	Relatively simple and informal, except that a limited partnership must have a written agreement.
Liability for Debts, Taxes, and Other Claims	Owner has unlimited personal liability.	General partners have unlimited personal liability; limited partners are only at risk to the extent of their investment.
Federal Income Taxation of Business Profits	Taxed to the owner at individual tax rates of up to 39.6% or more, depending on exemptions and deductions which may phase out.	Taxed to partners at their individual tax rates.
Double Taxation if Profits Withdrawn from Business	No.	No.
Deduction of Losses by Owners	Yes. May be subject to "passive loss" restrictions.	Yes. But limited partner's deductions cannot exceed amount invested as a limited partner — except for real estate, in some instances. Losses are generally restricted by the "passive loss" rules.
Social Security Tax on Earnings of Owner from Business	15.3% of owner's self-employment earnings in 1997 on first $65,400 of income, plus 2.9% on earnings of more than $65,400, half of which is now deductible for income tax purposes.	15.3% of each partner's share of self-employment earnings from the business in 1997 on up to $65,400 in earnings are taxed, plus 2.9% tax on earnings over $65,400. Half of tax is deductible for income tax. Limited partners are generally not subject to self-employment tax.
Unemployment Taxes on Earnings of Owner from Business	None.	None.
Retirement Plans	Keogh plan. Deductions, other features now generally the same as for corporate pension and profit-sharing plans. But proprietor cannot borrow from Keogh Plan.	Keogh plan. Same as for proprietorships. A 10% partner cannot borrow from Keogh Plan.
Tax Treatment of Medical, Disability, and Group-Term Life Insurance on Owners	Not deductible, except part of medical expenses may be an itemized deduction on owner's tax return, including medical insurance premiums. However, 40% of medical insurance on an owner is allowed as a deduction from adjusted gross income. This deduction increases to 45% for 1998 and 1999.	Not deductible, except part of medical expenses may be an itemized deduction on owner's tax return, including medical insurance premiums. However, 40% of medical insurance on an owner is allowed as a deduction from adjusted gross income. This deduction increases to 45% for 1998 and 1999.
Taxation of Dividends Received on Investments	Dividends received on stock investments are fully taxable to owner.	Dividends taxable to individual partners. See proprietorship.

Limited Liability Company	Regular Corporation	S Corporation
Generally similar to a partnership, but required to file articles of organization.	Requires most formality in establishment and operation.	Same as a regular corporation but requires close oversight by a tax adviser (an additional cost).
Members are generally not liable for an LLC's debts, but they often have to guarantee loans, as a practical matter, which is similar to a corporation.	Stockholders are not generally liable for corporate debts, but often have to guarantee loans, as a practical matter, if the corporation borrows money. Also, corporate officers may be liable to the IRS for failure to withhold and pay withholding taxes on employees' wages.	Stockholders are not generally liable for corporate debts, but often have to guarantee loans, as a practical matter, if the corporation borrows money. Also, corporate officers may be liable to the IRS for failure to withhold and pay withholding taxes on employees' wages.
Taxed to owners at their individual tax rates, unless the IRS treats the LLC as a corporation.	Taxed to the corporation, at rates higher than those of individuals — maximum of 34% or 39% in 1995, except for very large corporations.	Taxed to individual owners at their individual rates — certain gains are taxable to the corporation as well.
No, unless the LLC is treated as a corporation.	Yes, but not on reasonable compensation paid to owners who are employees of the corporation.	No, in general.
Yes, generally, if treated as a partnership by IRS. No, if treated as a corporation by IRS.	No. Corporation must carry over initial losses to offset future profits, if any.	Yes, in general, for federal tax purposes. But not for state tax purposes in all states. Loss for a shareholder limited to investment in stock plus amount loaned to the corporation. Losses may be subject to "passive loss" restrictions.
Not clear yet. Probably same as for a partnership, if treated as partnership by IRS. Same as a corporation, if the LLC is treated as a corporation. If treated as a partnership, some owners may be treated like "limited partners" (not taxed).	Owner/employee of corporation pays 7.65% on his or her salary and corporation pays 7.65%. Total Social Security (FICA) tax on employer and employee is 15.3% of employee's first $65,400 of wages (in 1997). Employee and corporation each pay 1.45% on wages above $65,400.	Owner/employee of corporation pays 7.65% on his or her salary and corporation pays 7.65%. Total Social Security (FICA) tax on employer and employee is 15.3% of employee's first $65,400 of wages (in 1997). Employee and corporation each pay 1.45% on wages above $65,400.
Not clear yet, but probably none, if treated as a partnership for income tax purposes by IRS.	Yes. State and federal unemployment taxes apply to salaries paid to owners.	Yes. State and federal unemployment taxes apply to salaries paid to owners.
Not clear yet, but probably same as a partnership, if treated as a partnership by IRS.	Corporate retirement plans are no longer significantly better than Keogh plans. Deduction limits are same now as for Keogh, but participants can borrow from plan.	Plans now essentially identical to regular corporate retirement plans, except that shareholder/employee (5% shareholder) of S corporation cannot borrow from plan.
Not clear yet, but probably same as a partnership, if treated as a partnership by IRS.	Corporations may be allowed to deduct corporation medical insurance premium or reimbursements paid under medical reimbursement plan. Generally not taxable to the employee, even if employee is an owner. Similar treatment for disability and group-term life insurance plans.	Fringe benefits for 2% shareholders are deductible by corporation, but must be included in income of the shareholder, who may be allowed to deduct 40% of medical insurance from adjusted gross income. This deduction increases to 45% for 1998 and 1999.
Dividends taxable to individual members, if the LLC is treated as a partnership.	Dividends are taxable to the corporation. However, 70% of the dividends received are generally free of federal income tax (unless stock is purchased with borrowed money), an important tax advantage.	Dividends taxable to individual shareholders of the S corporation, as in the case of a partnership.

Instructions for Form 2553: Sample

Instructions for Form 2553
(Revised September 1997)
Election by a Small Business Corporation

 Department of the Treasury
Internal Revenue Service

Section references are to the Internal Revenue Code unless otherwise noted.

General Instructions

Purpose.— To elect to be an S corporation, a corporation must file Form 2553. The election permits the income of the S corporation to be taxed to the shareholders of the corporation rather than to the corporation itself, except as noted below under **Taxes an S Corporation May Owe.**

Who May Elect.— A corporation may elect to be an S corporation only if it meets all of the following tests:

1. It is a domestic corporation.

2. It has no more than 75 shareholders. A husband and wife (and their estates) are treated as one shareholder for this requirement. All other persons are treated as separate shareholders.

3. Its only shareholders are individuals, estates, certain trusts described in section 1361(c)(2)(A), or, for tax years beginning after 1997, exempt organizations described in section 401(a) or 501(c)(3). Trustees of trusts that want to make the election under section 1361(e)(3) to be an electing small business trust should see Notice 97-12, 1997-3 I.R.B. 11.

Note: *See the instructions for Part III regarding qualified subchapter S trusts.*

4. It has no nonresident alien shareholders.

5. It has only one class of stock (disregarding differences in voting rights). Generally, a corporation is treated as having only one class of stock if all outstanding shares of the corporation's stock confer identical rights to distribution and liquidation proceeds. See Regulations section 1.1361-1(1) for more details.

6. It is not one of the following ineligible corporations:

   a. A bank or thrift institution that uses the reserve method of accounting for bad debts under section 585;

   b. An insurance company subject to tax under the rules of subchapter L of the Code;

   c. A corporation that has elected to be treated as a possessions corporation under section 936; or

   d. A domestic international sales corporation (DISC) or former DISC.

7. It has a permitted tax year as required by section 1378 or makes a section 444 election to have a tax year other than a permitted tax year. Section 1378 defines a permitted tax year as a tax year ending December 31, or any other tax year for which the corporation establishes a business purpose to the satisfaction of the IRS. See Part II for details on requesting a fiscal tax year based on a business purpose or on making a section 444 election.

8. Each shareholder consents as explained in the instructions for column K.

See sections 1361, 1362, and 1378 for additional information on the above tests.

An election can be made by a parent S corporation to treat the assets, liabilities, and items of income, deduction, and credit of an eligible wholly-owned subsidiary as those of the parent. For details, see Notice 97-4, 1997-2 I.R.B. 24.

Taxes an S Corporation May Owe.— An S corporation may owe income tax in the following instances:

1. If, at the end of any tax year, the corporation had accumulated earnings and profits, and its passive investment income under section 1362(d)(3) is more than 25% of its gross receipts, the corporation may owe tax on its excess net passive income.

2. A corporation with net recognized built-in gain (as defined in section 1374(d)(2)) may owe tax on its built-in gains.

3. A corporation that claimed investment credit before its first year as an S corporation will be liable for any investment credit recapture tax.

4. A corporation that used the LIFO inventory method for the year immediately preceding its first year as an S corporation may owe an additional tax due to LIFO recapture.

For more details on these taxes, see the Instructions for Form 1120S.

Where To File.— File this election with the Internal Revenue Service Center listed below.

If the corporation's principal business, office, or agency is located in	Use the following Internal Revenue Service Center address
New Jersey, New York (New York City and counties of Nassau, Rockland, Suffolk, and Westchester)	Holtsville, NY 00501
New York (all other counties), Connecticut, Maine, Massachusetts, New Hampshire, Rhode Island, Vermont	Andover, MA 05501
Florida, Georgia, South Carolina	Atlanta, GA 39901
Indiana, Kentucky, Michigan, Ohio, West Virginia	Cincinnati, OH 45999
Kansas, New Mexico, Oklahoma, Texas	Austin, TX 73301
Alaska, Arizona, California (counties of Alpine, Amador, Butte, Calaveras, Colusa, Contra Costa, Del Norte, El Dorado, Glenn, Humboldt, Lake, Lassen, Marin, Mendocino, Modoc, Napa, Nevada, Placer, Plumas, Sacramento, San Joaquin, Shasta, Sierra, Siskiyou, Solano, Sonoma, Sutter, Tehama, Trinity, Yolo, and Yuba), Colorado, Idaho, Montana, Nebraska, Nevada, North Dakota, Oregon, South Dakota, Utah, Washington, Wyoming	Ogden, UT 84201
California (all other counties), Hawaii	Fresno, CA 93888
Illinois, Iowa, Minnesota, Missouri, Wisconsin	Kansas City, MO 64999
Alabama, Arkansas, Louisiana, Mississippi, North Carolina, Tennessee	Memphis, TN 37501
Delaware, District of Columbia, Maryland, Pennsylvania, Virginia	Philadelphia, PA 19255

When To Make the Election.— Complete and file Form 2553 (a) at any time before the 16th day of the 3rd month of the tax year, if filed during the tax year the election is to take effect, or (b) at any time during the preceding tax year. An election made no later than 2 months and 15 days after the beginning of a tax year that is less than 2½ months long is treated as timely made for that tax year. An election made after the 15th day of the 3rd month but before the end of the tax year is effective for the next year. For example, if a calendar tax year

corporation makes the election in April 1998, it is effective for the corporation's 1999 calendar tax year.

However, an election made after the due date will be accepted as timely filed if the corporation can show that the failure to file on time was due to reasonable cause. To request relief for a late election, the corporation generally must request a private letter ruling and pay a user fee in accordance with Rev. Proc. 97-1, 1997-1 I.R.B. 11 (or its successor). But if the election is filed within 6 months of its due date and the original due date for filing the corporation's initial Form 1120S has not passed, the ruling and user fee requirements do not apply. To request relief in this case, write "FILED PURSUANT TO REV. PROC. 97-40" at the top of page 1 of Form 2553, attach a statement explaining the reason for failing to file the election on time, and file Form 2553 as otherwise instructed. See Rev. Proc. 97-40, 1997-33 I.R.B. 50, for more details.

See Regulations section 1.1362-6(b)(3)(iii) for how to obtain relief for an inadvertent invalid election if the corporation filed a timely election, but one or more shareholders did not file a timely consent.

Acceptance or Nonacceptance of Election.— The service center will notify the corporation if its election is accepted and when it will take effect. The corporation will also be notified if its election is not accepted. The corporation should generally receive a determination on its election within 60 days after it has filed Form 2553. If box Q1 in Part II is checked on page 2, the corporation will receive a ruling letter from the IRS in Washington, DC, that either approves or denies the selected tax year. When box Q1 is checked, it will generally take an additional 90 days for the Form 2553 to be accepted.

Do not file Form 1120S for any tax year before the year the election takes effect. If the corporation is now required to file Form 1120, U.S. Corporation Income Tax Return, or any other applicable tax return, continue filing it until the election takes effect.

Care should be exercised to ensure that the IRS receives the election. If the corporation is not notified of acceptance or nonacceptance of its election within 3 months of date of filing (date mailed), or within 6 months if box Q1 is checked, take follow-up action by corresponding with the service center where the corporation filed the election. If the IRS questions whether Form 2553 was filed, an acceptable proof of filing is (a) certified or registered mail receipt (timely filed) from the U.S. Postal Service or its equivalent from a designated private delivery service (see Notice 97-26, 1997-17 I.R.B. 6); (b) Form 2553 with accepted stamp; (c) Form 2553 with stamped IRS received date; or (d) IRS letter stating that Form 2553 has been accepted.

End of Election.— Once the election is made, it stays in effect until it is terminated. If the election is terminated in a tax year beginning after 1996, the corporation (or a successor corporation) can make another election on Form 2553 only with IRS consent for any tax year before the 5th tax year after the first tax year in which the termination took effect. See Regulations section 1.1362-5 for more details.

Cat. No. 49978N

Instructions for Form 2553: Sample (continued)

Specific Instructions

Part I

Note: *All corporations must complete Part I.*

Name and Address of Corporation.— Enter the true corporate name as stated in the corporate charter or other legal document creating it. If the corporation's mailing address is the same as someone else's, such as a shareholder's, enter "c/o" and this person's name following the name of the corporation. Include the suite, room, or other unit number after the street address. If the Post Office does not deliver to the street address and the corporation has a P.O. box, show the box number instead of the street address. If the corporation changed its name or address after applying for its employer identification number, be sure to check the box in item G of Part I.

Item A. Employer Identification Number (EIN).— If the corporation has applied for an EIN but has not received it, enter "applied for." If the corporation does not have an EIN, it should apply for one on Form SS-4, Application for Employer Identification Number. You can order Form SS-4 by calling 1-800-TAX-FORM (1-800-829-3676).

Item D. Effective Date of Election.— Enter the beginning effective date (month, day, year) of the tax year requested for the S corporation. Generally, this will be the beginning date of the tax year for which the ending effective date is required to be shown in Item I, Part I. For a new corporation (first year the corporation exists) it will generally be the date required to be shown in item H, Part I. The tax year of a new corporation starts on the date that it has shareholders, acquires assets, or begins doing business, whichever happens first. If the effective date for item D for a newly formed corporation is later than the date in item H, the corporation should file Form 1120 or Form 1120-A for the tax period between these dates.

Column K. Shareholders' Consent Statement.— Each shareholder who owns (or is deemed to own) stock at the time the election is made must consent to the election. If the election is made during the corporation's tax year for which it first takes effect, any person who held stock at any time during the part of that year that occurs before the election is made, must consent to the election, even though the person may have sold or transferred his or her stock before the election is made.

An election made during the first 2½ months of the tax year is effective for the following tax year if any person who held stock in the corporation during the part of the tax year before the election was made, and who did not hold stock at the time the election was made, did not consent to the election.

Each shareholder consents by signing and dating in column K or signing and dating a separate consent statement described below. The following special rules apply in determining who must sign the consent statement.

• If a husband and wife have a community interest in the stock or in the income from it, both must consent.

• Each tenant in common, joint tenant, and tenant by the entirety must consent.

• A minor's consent is made by the minor, legal representative of the minor, or a natural or adoptive parent of the minor if no legal representative has been appointed.

• The consent of an estate is made by the executor or administrator.

• The consent of an electing small business trust is made by the trustee.

• If the stock is owned by a trust (other than an electing small business trust), the deemed owner of the trust must consent. See section 1361(c)(2) for details regarding trusts that are permitted to be shareholders and rules for determining who is the deemed owner.

Continuation sheet or separate consent statement.— If you need a continuation sheet or use a separate consent statement, attach it to Form 2553. The separate consent statement must contain the name, address, and EIN of the corporation and the shareholder information requested in columns J through N of Part I. If you want, you may combine all the shareholders' consents in one statement.

Column L.— Enter the number of shares of stock each shareholder owns and the dates the stock was acquired. If the election is made during the corporation's tax year for which it first takes effect, do not list the shares of stock for those shareholders who sold or transferred all of their stock before the election was made. However, these shareholders must still consent to the election for it to be effective for the tax year.

Column M.— Enter the social security number of each shareholder who is an individual. Enter the EIN of each shareholder that is an estate, a qualified trust, or an exempt organization.

Column N.— Enter the month and day that each shareholder's tax year ends. If a shareholder is changing his or her tax year, enter the tax year the shareholder is changing to, and attach an explanation indicating the present tax year and the basis for the change (e.g., automatic revenue procedure or letter ruling request).

Signature.— Form 2553 must be signed by the president, treasurer, assistant treasurer, chief accounting officer, or other corporate officer (such as tax officer) authorized to sign.

Part II

Complete Part II if you selected a tax year ending on any date other than December 31 (other than a 52-53-week tax year ending with reference to the month of December).

Box P1.— Attach a statement showing separately for each month the amount of gross receipts for the most recent 47 months as required by section 4.03(3) of Rev. Proc. 87-32, 1987-2 C.B. 396. A corporation that does not have a 47-month period of gross receipts cannot establish a natural business year under section 4.01(1).

Box Q1.— For examples of an acceptable business purpose for requesting a fiscal tax year, see Rev. Rul. 87-57, 1987-2 C.B. 117.

In addition to a statement showing the business purpose for the requested fiscal year, you must attach the other information necessary to meet the ruling request requirements of Rev. Proc. 97-1 (or its successor). Also attach a statement that shows separately the amount of gross receipts from sales or services (and inventory costs, if applicable) for each of the 36 months preceding the effective date of the election to be an S corporation. If the corporation has been in existence for fewer than 36 months, submit figures for the period of existence.

If you check box Q1, you will be charged a $250 user fee (subject to change). Do not pay the fee when filing Form 2553. The service center will send Form 2553 to the IRS in Washington, DC, who, in turn, will notify the corporation that the fee is due.

Box Q2.— If the corporation makes a back-up section 444 election for which it is qualified, then the election will take effect in the event the business purpose request is not approved. In some cases, the tax year requested under the back-up section 444 election may be different than the tax year requested under business purpose. See **Form 8716**, Election To Have a Tax Year Other Than a Required Tax Year, for details on making a back-up section 444 election.

Boxes Q2 and R2.— If the corporation is not qualified to make the section 444 election after making the item Q2 back-up section 444 election or indicating its intention to make the election in item R1, and therefore it later files a calendar year return, it should write "Section 444 Election Not Made" in the top left corner of the first calendar year Form 1120S it files.

Part III

Certain qualified subchapter S trusts (QSSTs) may make the QSST election required by section 1361(d)(2) in Part III. Part III may be used to make the QSST election only if corporate stock has been transferred to the trust on or before the date on which the corporation makes its election to be an S corporation. However, a statement can be used instead of Part III to make the election.

Note: *Use Part III only if you make the election in Part I (i.e., Form 2553 cannot be filed with only Part III completed).*

The deemed owner of the QSST must also consent to the S corporation election in column K, page 1, of Form 2553. See section 1361 (c)(2).

Paperwork Reduction Act Notice.— We ask for the information on this form to carry out the Internal Revenue laws of the United States. You are required to give us the information. We need it to ensure that you are complying with these laws and to allow us to figure and collect the right amount of tax.

You are not required to provide the information requested on a form that is subject to the Paperwork Reduction Act unless the form displays a valid OMB control number. Books or records relating to a form or its instructions must be retained as long as their contents may become material in the administration of any Internal Revenue law. Generally, tax returns and return information are confidential, as required by section 6103.

The time needed to complete and file this form will depend on individual circumstances. The estimated average time is:

Recordkeeping	6 hr., 26 min.
Learning about the law or the form	3 hr., 41 min.
Preparing, copying, assembling, and sending the form to the IRS	3 hr., 56 min.

If you have comments concerning the accuracy of these time estimates or suggestions for making this form simpler, we would be happy to hear from you. You can write to the Tax Forms Committee, Western Area Distribution Center, Rancho Cordova, CA 95743-0001. **DO NOT** send the form to this address. Instead, see **Where To File** on page 1.

Form 2553 – Election by a Small Business Corporation: Sample

Form **2553** (Rev. September 1997) Department of the Treasury Internal Revenue Service	**Election by a Small Business Corporation** (Under section 1362 of the Internal Revenue Code) ▶ For Paperwork Reduction Act Notice, see page 2 of instructions. ▶ See separate instructions.	OMB No. 1545-0146

Notes: 1. This election to be an S corporation can be accepted only if all the tests are met under **Who May Elect** on page 1 of the instructions; all signatures in Parts I and III are originals (no photocopies); and the exact name and address of the corporation and other required form information are provided.

2. Do not file **Form 1120S**, U.S. Income Tax Return for an S Corporation, for any tax year before the year the election takes effect.

3. If the corporation was in existence before the effective date of this election, see **Taxes an S Corporation May Owe** on page 1 of the instructions.

Part I Election Information

Please Type or Print	Name of corporation (see instructions)	A Employer identification number
	Number, street, and room or suite no. (If a P.O. box, see instructions.)	B Date incorporated
	City or town, state, and ZIP code	C State of incorporation

D Election is to be effective for tax year beginning (month, day, year) . . . . ▶   /   /

E Name and title of officer or legal representative who the IRS may call for more information | F Telephone number of officer or legal representative (   )

G If the corporation changed its name or address after applying for the EIN shown in A above, check this box . . . . ▶ ☐

H If this election takes effect for the first tax year the corporation exists, enter month, day, and year of the **earliest** of the following: (1) date the corporation first had shareholders, (2) date the corporation first had assets, or (3) date the corporation began doing business . . . . ▶   /   /

I Selected tax year: Annual return will be filed for tax year ending (month and day) ▶ _____

If the tax year ends on any date other than December 31, except for an automatic 52-53-week tax year ending with reference to the month of December, you must complete Part II on the back. If the date you enter is the ending date of an automatic 52-53-week tax year, write "52-53-week year" to the right of the date. See Temporary Regulations section 1.441-2T(e)(3).

J Name and address of each shareholder; shareholder's spouse having a community property interest in the corporation's stock; and each tenant in common, joint tenant, and tenant by the entirety. (A husband and wife (and their estates) are counted as one shareholder in determining the number of shareholders without regard to the manner in which the stock is owned.)	K Shareholders' Consent Statement. Under penalties of perjury, we declare that we consent to the election of the above-named corporation to be an S corporation under section 1362(a) and that we have examined this consent statement, including accompanying schedules and statements, and to the best of our knowledge and belief, it is true, correct, and complete. We understand our consent is binding and may not be withdrawn after the corporation has made a valid election. (Shareholders sign and date below.)		L Stock owned		M Social security number or employer identification number (see instructions)	N Share-holder's tax year ends (month and day)
	Signature	Date	Number of shares	Dates acquired		

Under penalties of perjury, I declare that I have examined this election, including accompanying schedules and statements, and to the best of my knowledge and belief, it is true, correct, and complete.

Signature of officer ▶ _____   Title ▶ _____   Date ▶ _____

See Parts II and III on back.   Cat. No. 18629R   Form **2553** (Rev. 9-97)

Form 2553 – Election by a Small Business Corporation: Sample (continued)

Form 2553 (Rev. 9-97)   Page **2**

Selection of Fiscal Tax Year (All corporations using this part must complete item O and item P, Q, or R.)

O   Check the applicable box to indicate whether the corporation is:

   1. ☐ A new corporation adopting the tax year entered in item I, Part I.

   2. ☐ An existing corporation retaining the tax year entered in item I, Part I.

   3. ☐ An existing corporation changing to the tax year entered in item I, Part I.

P   Complete item P if the corporation is using the expeditious approval provisions of Rev. Proc. 87-32, 1987-2 C.B. 396, to request **(1)** a natural business year (as defined in section 4.01(1) of Rev. Proc. 87-32) or **(2)** a year that satisfies the ownership tax year test in section 4.01(2) of Rev. Proc. 87-32. Check the applicable box below to indicate the representation statement the corporation is making as required under section 4 of Rev. Proc. 87-32.

   1. Natural Business Year ► ☐ I represent that the corporation is retaining or changing to a tax year that coincides with its natural business year as defined in section 4.01(1) of Rev. Proc. 87-32 and as verified by its satisfaction of the requirements of section 4.02(1) of Rev. Proc. 87-32. In addition, if the corporation is changing to a natural business year as defined in section 4.01(1), I further represent that such tax year results in less deferral of income to the owners than the corporation's present tax year. I also represent that the corporation is not described in section 3.01(2) of Rev. Proc. 87-32. (See instructions for additional information that must be attached.)

   2. Ownership Tax Year ► ☐ I represent that shareholders holding more than half of the shares of the stock (as of the first day of the tax year to which the request relates) of the corporation have the same tax year or are concurrently changing to the tax year that the corporation adopts, retains, or changes to per item I, Part I. I also represent that the corporation is not described in section 3.01(2) of Rev. Proc. 87-32.

Note: *If you do not use item P and the corporation wants a fiscal tax year, complete either item Q or R below. Item Q is used to request a fiscal tax year based on a business purpose and to make a back-up section 444 election. Item R is used to make a regular section 444 election.*

Q   Business Purpose—To request a fiscal tax year based on a business purpose, you must check box Q1 and pay a user fee. See instructions for details. You may also check box Q2 and/or box Q3.

   1. Check here ► ☐ if the fiscal year entered in item I, Part I, is requested under the provisions of section 6.03 of Rev. Proc. 87-32. Attach to Form 2553 a statement showing the business purpose for the requested fiscal year. See instructions for additional information that must be attached.

   2. Check here ► ☐ to show that the corporation intends to make a back-up section 444 election in the event the corporation's business purpose request is not approved by the IRS. (See instructions for more information.)

   3. Check here ► ☐ to show that the corporation agrees to adopt or change to a tax year ending December 31 if necessary for the IRS to accept this election for S corporation status in the event (1) the corporation's business purpose request is not approved and the corporation makes a back-up section 444 election, but is ultimately not qualified to make a section 444 election, or (2) the corporation's business purpose request is not approved and the corporation did not make a back-up section 444 election.

R   Section 444 Election—To make a section 444 election, you must check box R1 and you may also check box R2.

   1. Check here ► ☐ to show the corporation will make, if qualified, a section 444 election to have the fiscal tax year shown in item I, Part I. To make the election, you must complete **Form 8716**, Election To Have a Tax Year Other Than a Required Tax Year, and either attach it to Form 2553 or file it separately.

   2. Check here ► ☐ to show that the corporation agrees to adopt or change to a tax year ending December 31 if necessary for the IRS to accept this election for S corporation status in the event the corporation is ultimately not qualified to make a section 444 election.

Qualified Subchapter S Trust (QSST) Election Under Section 1361(d)(2)*

Income beneficiary's name and address	Social security number
Trust's name and address	Employer identification number

Date on which stock of the corporation was transferred to the trust (month, day, year) . . . . ►   /   /

In order for the trust named above to be a QSST and thus a qualifying shareholder of the S corporation for which this Form 2553 is filed, I hereby make the election under section 1361(d)(2). Under penalties of perjury, I certify that the trust meets the definitional requirements of section 1361(d)(3) and that all other information provided in Part III is true, correct, and complete.

_____   _____

Signature of income beneficiary or signature and title of legal representative or other qualified person making the election   Date

*Use Part III to make the QSST election only if stock of the corporation has been transferred to the trust on or before the date on which the corporation makes its election to be an S corporation. The QSST election must be made and filed separately if stock of the corporation is transferred to the trust after the date on which the corporation makes the S election.

Form 8832 – Entity Classification Election: Sample

Form **8832** (December 1996) Department of the Treasury Internal Revenue Service	**Entity Classification Election**	OMB No. 1545-1516

Please Type or Print	Name of entity	Employer identification number (EIN)
	Number, street, and room or suite no. If a P.O. box, see instructions.	
	City or town, state, and ZIP code. If a foreign address, enter city, province or state, postal code and country.	

1 Type of election (see instructions):

a ☐ Initial classification by a newly-formed entity (or change in current classification of an existing entity to take effect on January 1, 1997)

b ☐ Change in current classification (to take effect later than January 1, 1997)

2 Form of entity (see instructions):

a ☐ A domestic eligible entity electing to be classified as an association taxable as a corporation.

b ☐ A domestic eligible entity electing to be classified as a partnership.

c ☐ A domestic eligible entity with a single owner electing to be disregarded as a separate entity.

d ☐ A foreign eligible entity electing to be classified as an association taxable as a corporation.

e ☐ A foreign eligible entity electing to be classified as a partnership.

f ☐ A foreign eligible entity with a single owner electing to be disregarded as a separate entity.

3 Election is to be effective beginning (month, day, year) (see instructions) . . . . ▶ ___/___/___

4 Name and title of person whom the IRS may call for more information	**5** That person's telephone number

Consent Statement and Signature(s) (see instructions)

Under penalties of perjury, I (we) declare that I (we) consent to the election of the above-named entity to be classified as indicated above, and that I (we) have examined this consent statement, and to the best of my (our) knowledge and belief, it is true, correct, and complete. If I am an officer, manager, or member signing for all members of the entity, I further declare that I am authorized to execute this consent statement on their behalf.

Signature(s)	Date	Title

For Paperwork Reduction Act Notice, see page 2.   Cat. No. 22598R   Form **8832** (12-96)

Chapter 3

Buying an Existing Business

Trust everyone, but brand your cattle.

— Hallie Stillwell

3.1 General Considerations

Obviously, it may not be necessary for you to build your business from the ground up. If you wish to go into a particular type of business, you may find an appropriate existing business that is for sale. Buying an existing business can have considerable advantages over starting one from scratch, one of the most important of which is the chance to start out with an established customer base. It is also sometimes possible to have the seller stay on as an employee or consultant for a transitional period to help you become familiar with the operation of the business.

Other advantages of purchasing a going business include:

- You may be able to take a regular draw or salary right from the start if it is a profitable operation. This is usually not the case in a start-up operation, which typically starts off losing money.

- Your risk is frequently less when you buy an established, profitable business. You know that it has a viable market if it is already profitable. Your main risk would be that something would change after you acquire the business, such as new competition or product obsolescence, and this would adversely affect your business. Another risk is that you will mismanage the business, destroying its value.

- Getting started is simpler. By buying an established business, you can focus your attention on giving good service and operating profitably. Since most facilities, operating systems, and employees will already be in place, your efforts will not be diluted by remodeling the premises, trying to hire employees, setting up accounting systems, acquiring initial inventory, and the like. In most cases, you should be able to step right into an operation that has already been established by someone else.

While there are some definite advantages to buying an established business, as compared to starting a new business, it can also be much more complicated and involves many potential pitfalls that you must avoid. The watchword in buying any kind of business should be *caveat emptor* — let the buyer beware.

Because the process of buying and selling businesses is very complicated even for experts, do not attempt it without retaining the services of a reliable attorney and, usually, a good accountant. Even skilled professionals, however, can generally only protect you from certain legal, financial, or tax pitfalls that arise in connection with the purchase of a business. Many of the potential problems that would not become obvious until it is too late can only be spotted in advance, if at all, by the exercise of your good judgment and as a result of your doing the necessary homework. Important pitfalls you should look out for in connection with buying an existing business are discussed in Section 3.3.

3.2 Finding a Business for Sale

How do you go about finding a business that is for sale? You have a number of ways to approach the problem, none of which are ideal, so you will probably want to use two or more of the approaches discussed below to find and buy an existing business.

Advertisements

The business opportunities section of your local newspaper, regional magazine, or trade association journal can be a major source of leads to businesses that are for sale. These ads often do not tell you very much about the nature of the business, but at least they can be a starting point in your search. In many cases, the ads will have been placed by a business broker rather than the owner. The business broker represents people who are seeking to sell their businesses.

Business Brokers and Realtors

Business brokers and realtors can be excellent sources in your search for a business that is for sale. The main drawback of going through a business broker or realtor is that his or her fee (paid by the seller) is usually a percentage, often 10%, of the sales price of the business; so the broker or realtor, like the seller, is trying to get the highest possible price for the business. At the same time, the seller will usually want more than he or she would if the sale were made without a broker, since he or she knows that the broker will take a healthy commission out of the negotiated sales price.

Your local chamber of commerce can usually tell you a great deal about the local business community and also provide you with leads to firms that are for sale.

Local Chambers of Commerce

Professionals, such as accountants, attorneys, and bankers, can often provide leads regarding good businesses even before they are on the market. Frequently, a business client will tell his or her accountant, attorney, or banker that he or she is planning to sell out or retire, long before making any formal attempt to put the business up for sale. So, if you have friends who are accountants, attorneys, or bankers, take them to lunch and tell them what you have in mind. Typically, they will have a vested interest in finding a friendly buyer for a retiring client's business, since they may lose that account if the firm is sold to buyers who have their own professional advisers.

Accountants, Attorneys, and Bankers

Certified public accountants (CPAs) can be excellent sources of leads. Not only will they usually not charge you any kind of finder's fee, but they usually know which of their clients' businesses are little gold mines. In some cases, a CPA who has a very profitable client who wishes to sell out may even want to go into the business with you as a financial partner, leaving the day-to-day operations to you. In these cases, you can generally be sure that if the CPA is putting up his or her money, he or she has studied the client's business carefully and feels that it is a real moneymaker. In short, the CPA will have already done much of the prescreening for you.

Often, if you see a small business you think you might like to buy, the simplest approach will be to talk to the owner and see if he or she is interested in selling. While an owner may have had no serious thoughts about selling the business before, the appearance of an interested potential buyer is not only somewhat flattering, but it may even cause him or her to decide to sell out to you. Many businesses are bought and sold by someone simply asking the right question at the right time.

The Direct Approach

3.3 What to Look for Before You Leap

One of the first questions you may want to ask is: "Why are you selling your business?" Often, the response will be the owner wants to retire or is in poor health. While an explanation like this may be true in many cases, it is also quite likely to be a well-rehearsed cover story. The real reason may be the business is in a declining neighborhood and the owner has been robbed several times recently and wants out. Or, the owners of a profitable little corner grocery store may be anxious to sell out while they can because they have learned that a major chain-store supermarket will

Why Is the Business for Sale?

be opening in the neighborhood in a few months. Another common reason behind a planned sale is that the business is either losing money or is not sufficiently profitable to make continuing worthwhile.

Whatever the real reason behind the owner's attempt to sell the business, you are unlikely to discover it without rolling up your sleeves and doing some independent and in-depth investigation. Perhaps the best way to find that needle in the haystack is to talk to a number of other businesspeople in the vicinity of the business you are investigating, particularly competitors in the same business. The business' suppliers can also be a source of important information.

Even if you are very diligent and thorough, you may not be able to discover the hidden reason — if there is one — underlying an owner's desire to sell out. You may simply have to rely on your intuition in deciding whether the seller's reason for getting out of the business is the real reason. Just remember that in most cases a good and profitable small business is not something that most people walk away from, unless there is a very good reason to do so, or the price offered is too good to turn down.

What Kind of Reputation Does the Business Have?

One of the great advantages of taking over an existing business can be the opportunity to enjoy the reputation and goodwill that the existing owner has built up with customers and suppliers over the years. On the other hand, you may be much better off starting your own business from scratch than acquiring a business that has a poor reputation because of inferior work or merchandise or inferior service. It could take you years of hard work and reduced profits to overcome a former owner's poor reputation.

Even if the present owner has an excellent business reputation, you will want to know whether or not that goodwill is based on personal relationships built up between the owner and customers. These types of relationships aren't easily transferable. If the business relies heavily on a few key customers with whom the owner has very favorable business arrangements based on personal relationships, you may find those business arrangements could be lost when you attempt to take the owner's place. In short, satisfy yourself the goodwill you are buying is not based solely on personal relationships.

How Profitable Is the Business Now?

Unless you have some very good reasons to believe that you can operate the business more profitably than the current owner, you should not purchase a going business that does not produce a satisfactory profit under its current ownership. Thus, it is extremely important to find out how the business has fared financially for the last few years. This is where the services of a good accountant, who has knowledge of the particular type of business, will be invaluable.

Insist on having the seller make the business' financial and business records available to your accountant. Be particularly wary of a business that keeps poor records. Often, the most reliable sources of financial information can be the owner's income tax and sales tax returns, since it is not very likely that a business owner will report more income than was actually earned for tax purposes. Be sure to ask the seller to have his or her outside accounting firm send you a copy of these tax returns, verifying they are true copies of the actual returns that were filed. Some unscrupulous sellers are not above filling out two tax returns — one version showing low income to file with the taxing authorities and another showing much higher income to present to a potential buyer of their business.

If the owner is not willing to make financial records available, make it clear that you are not willing to negotiate any further. Buying a business is much like buying a used car; you want to make sure it runs before you pay for it.

Assets and Liabilities

You will need to review both the tangible and intangible assets of the business to see if they are worth the price you will pay and also to determine just what assets you will acquire under the sales agreement.

Personally inspect the business premises and look for things like obsolete or unsalable inventory, out-of-date or rundown equipment, or furniture or fixtures that you may have to repair or replace. Also, determine whether the business is able to expand at its present location or if it is already too cramped. What you determine might require you to buy or lease additional facilities if you wish to expand.

Review the terms of any leases. Some businesses close because of the imminent expiration of a favorable long-term lease or because the landlord plans to either raise the rent drastically or not renew the lease at all when the current lease expires.

If you will be acquiring the accounts receivable of the business, review them in detail. An aging of the accounts should be performed to determine how long various receivables have been outstanding. As a general rule, the longer a given receivable has been outstanding, the more likely it will prove to be uncollectible.

If a few large accounts of credit customers make up a significant portion of the receivables, you will want to particularly focus on those accounts and perhaps even have credit checks run on those customers. The bankruptcy of a major credit customer can ruin an otherwise successful business.

Part of your job in investigating a business that you want to buy is to find out what makes it tick — and make sure you will be getting whatever it is. For example, a business that has well-developed customer or mailing lists should ordinarily include those lists in the sales agreement. If there is a favorable lease, make sure it can and will be assigned to you. If patents, trademarks, trade names, or certain skilled employees are vital to the business, be sure that you will get them as part of the package.

You also need to be aware of potential problems with the government that the seller is experiencing or expects to experience in the near future, such as zoning problems or new environmental restrictions that may hamper the business' profitability.

Hidden Liabilities

Liabilities of the business may not always show up on its accounting records. There may be any number of hidden claims against the business, such as security agreements encumbering the accounts receivable, inventory, or equipment; unpaid back taxes of various kinds; undisclosed lawsuits or potential lawsuits; or simply unpaid bills.

If you are going to assume the liabilities of the business, the written agreement of sale should specify exactly which liabilities are being assumed and the dollar amount of each.

Other examples of hidden liabilities to look out for are:

- Pension liabilities. You may be taking on significant termination liability as a successor employer if the seller maintains or contributes to a pension fund and has unfunded pension fund liabilities.

- Vacation liabilities. If you are a successor employer, you may be liable for accrued but unpaid vacation leave of employees, which can be a significant hidden liability in some cases.

- Environmental liabilities. In many instances, environmental law imposes liability for past environmental abuses on current land owners or lessors. Many banks and savings and loans have recently learned about this the hard way, after foreclosing on land, which had been contaminated over the years by toxic substances, and being held liable for clean-up costs as the contamination problems came to light.

  Many companies, when buying land or other companies that own land, now require the sellers to make detailed representations and warranties concerning environmental matters and to undertake extensive and costly environmental audits as a condition to buying a business. See Section 9.9 for a more detailed discussion of these issues.

If you intend to buy a corporation, you will be well advised to buy the business assets from the corporation rather than purchase its stock. The latter approach will subject the business to all hidden or contingent liabilities of the old corporation, whether or not you have agreed to pay for any liabilities of the corporation that predated the sale.

One exception to this general rule would be for a corporation that had substantial tax loss or tax credit carryovers that you might be able to use if you bought the stock of the corporation rather than the assets. Be aware, however, the tax law is a minefield when it comes to taking over someone else's tax loss or credit carryovers. So before you do so, seek good advice from a tax attorney or tax accountant. If you don't, you may find that the carryovers you thought you were acquiring have evaporated like a mirage.

A change in ownership of more than 50% of the stock of a corporation in a three-year period will generally result in a severe restriction on the amount of its prior net operating losses that can be deducted in any subsequent taxable year.

For more helpful tips on what to beware of when buying a business, obtain a copy of *The Secrets to Buying and Selling a Business*, available from The Oasis Press or your local bookstore.

3.4 Should You Consider a Franchise Operation?

Many small businesses, particularly fast food restaurants and print shops, are operated under franchises from a large national company (a franchisor). There can be substantial advantages to operating a franchised business, such as the benefits of national advertising, training programs, and assistance in setting up and running the business. If you are investigating a franchise, determine whether the franchise can be transferred to you, and if so, provide for the transfer as part of the sale in the sales agreement.

Keep in mind, if you acquire a franchise, either from the franchisor or as a transfer from another franchisee, you may be able to amortize (write off) the cost of acquiring the franchise, under certain circumstances, for federal income tax purposes. Consult your tax adviser as to whether or not this will be possible in your case. If it is amortizable, you may want to allocate a significant part of the purchase price for the business to the cost of the franchise, which could save you major tax dollars in the long run.

Review Franchise Agreement and Disclosures

Carefully review the franchise agreement with the help of your attorney to determine whether the franchisor must approve the transfer, what the costs of operating are under the franchise, and the other terms of the agreement.

The Federal Trade Commission (FTC) and a number of states provide franchising laws and regulations that offer you protection. These laws and regulations mandate the timing and content of the various disclosures that the franchisor must make to you, as the potential franchisee. Make sure you or your attorney asks for all of these disclosures on a timely basis, and be wary of any franchisor who does not provide these disclosures to you unless you ask for them. In January 1995, the FTC's new requirements regarding disclosure statements went into effect. Ensure your attorney is familiar with these new requirements.

Investigate Franchise Reputation

If the franchisor is not a well-known and respected company, contact your local Better Business Bureau or an appropriate state agency to see if they have any information regarding the history, ethics, and reputation of the franchisor. You do not want to sign on with one of the less-than-reputable franchising operations that charge substantial franchising fees for very little in the way of useful services.

Helpful Resources

Recently updated to include information on the new FTC disclosure requirements, *Franchise Bible* is a very helpful book for anyone interested in buying a franchise or franchising his or her business. This book explains what the franchise system entails and presents how both the franchisor and the franchisee should approach a franchising venture or opportunity.

For more information on additional franchise publications and how to order *Franchise Bible*, refer to Section 10.11. Once you have focused on a particular franchise opportunity, you will find the checklist located at the end of this chapter very useful for evaluating the franchise operation.

3.5 Negotiating the Purchase

The Purchase Price

No book can tell you how much you should pay for the business you are planning to buy. You are on your own on that one. If, however, you have done your homework thoroughly in investigating the business in question and have talked to bankers and other businesspeople about what the normal purchase price for a business of that type and size should be, you will have a fairly good basis for determining whether the purchase price is a reasonable one.

For example, you may find that small businesses of the type you are considering generally sell for about one and one-half times their annual gross sales. That could be very important to know if the seller is asking three times last year's gross sales.

Even if you conclude the purchase price is a fair one, or even a bargain, you still must decide whether the price is one you can afford. Assuming that you can get the purchase price together, will it so deplete your liquid resources that you will not have enough working capital to make the business go, or put you in a bind if income from the business drops off while you are at the learning stage? Or, if you are financing a substantial part of the purchase price, will your operating budget be able to stand the cost of making the payments on the debt and still leave enough for you to live on?

Remember, just because you can get the purchase price or down payment together does not necessarily mean that you can afford to buy a particular business even when the price is right.

Disclosure of Financial Information

At an early stage in the negotiations, specify that you want access to tax returns, books of account, and other financial records of the business, and make it clear that you have no interest in continuing the negotiations unless the seller cooperates fully in this respect.

Additionally, be sure this condition is expressed in any informal "memorandum of understanding" or letter of agreement between you and the seller that is written up before the final contract of sale.

Allocation of Purchase Price

One very important item that is often omitted in business sales agreements, perhaps because it is not absolutely necessary, is a provision in the agreement that shows how the parties agree to allocate the purchase price between the various assets that are being acquired. For tax purposes, however, it is often very important to both you, as the purchaser, and the seller to have a written allocation agreement.

In most cases, whatever value of an asset you and the seller agree on is binding for tax purposes. So, it is very important from a tax standpoint to negotiate the best possible allocation of the purchase price among the assets you acquire and have that allocation reflected in the contract of sale.[1]

Since you and the seller usually have opposing interests in making an agreed allocation, the courts and IRS have generally been willing to accept any allocation agreement between the parties.

1993 Tax Law Simplified Allocations

The passage of the Revenue Reconciliation Act of 1993 greatly simplified the allocation process and made it easier, on an after-tax basis, to acquire a business when a significant portion of its assets are intangibles.[2]

Under the 1993 tax law, a broad new category of amortizable assets, called "Section 197 Intangibles," was created. Section 197 Intangibles may be amortized over a 15-year period for assets purchased after August 10, 1993. Before passage of this law, a business buyer would seek to allocate as much of the purchase price as possible to depreciable tangible assets and amortizable intangible assets, such as technical know-how, customer lists, or covenants not to compete. In addition, buyers usually sought to minimize the portion of the purchase price allocated to other intangible items, such as goodwill or going concern value, which could never be amortized.

However, there was often little choice but to allocate most of the purchase price to intangibles because the value of tangible assets, such as office equipment and furniture and a few supplies, made up only a small portion of the purchase price. Since the IRS clearly would not accept a purchase price allocation that put a $50,000 value on $5 worth of paper clips, buyers were forced to become creative and try to define some asset, such as a customer base or insurance renewals list, and allocate some part of the purchase price to that asset.

Thankfully, the new law should put an end to most of these disputes with the IRS over intangible assets. For the first time ever, the tax law allows goodwill and the going-concern value to be amortized as Section 197 Intangibles over 15 years. Included in the definition of Section 197 Intangibles are:

- Workforce in place;
- Information base;
- Any license, permit, or other right granted by a governmental unit or agency;
- Know-how, such as patents, copyrights, formulas, designs, patterns, or similar items — special rules apply to computer software and interests in films, tapes, books, and videos;
- Any customer-based intangible, such as customer lists, depositor lists, subscribers, and insurance expirations;
- Any supplier-based intangible, such as favorable supplier contracts;

- Covenants not to compete; and
- Any franchise, trademark, or trade name.

Computer software is considered an intangible asset, but it is generally not subject to the 15-year amortization requirement of Section 197. Software that is readily available for purchase by the general public is not considered a Section 197 Intangible asset and can now be amortized over three years.[3] Other computer software is a Section 197 Intangible asset only if acquired in a transaction that involves the purchase of a whole business or a substantial portion of a business.

Section 197 will benefit most business buyers by preventing many disputes with the IRS regarding the purchase price of a business and by allowing amortization of the cost of intangible assets that were not deductible in the past. The new law, however, is not entirely favorable. Previously, business buyers who were allowed to amortize certain intangibles were often able to do so over a period of only a few years, which was far better than the new 15-year amortization requirement.

Allocation Agreements Are Still Important

Do not assume that the new law makes a purchase price allocation agreement unnecessary or unimportant. Certain assets that might be acquired in a business purchase, such as land, are still not depreciable or amortizable, so it will be advisable to try to allocate as little as possible to the cost of land in a purchase price allocation agreement. Also, it will still be advantageous to allocate as much as possible of the purchase price to inventories or depreciable assets whose costs can be written off in a time frame shorter than the 15-year amortization period for Section 197 Intangibles.

A tax deduction you can take today or in the near future is almost always worth a great deal more than a tax deduction 15 years from now.

3.6 Closing the Deal

Legal Steps in Buying a Business

The legal and recommended procedures involved in buying an existing business are rather complex. To ensure you are protected as fully as possible from liabilities you have not agreed to assume, have your attorney take the steps described below.

File Bulk Transfer Notice if Still Applicable

In the past, all states required that a purchaser of a retail or wholesale establishment or certain other types of businesses had to prepare a notice to creditors of bulk transfer, file it in counties where the business operated, and also publish this notice in a general circulation newspaper before the purchase of the business. If this was not properly done, the seller's unsecured creditors could place a lien or security on the property that the purchaser thought he or she was buying free and clear. This filing was the requirement of bulk sale or bulk transfer laws.

In 1988 and 1989, the National Conference of Commissioners on Uniform State Laws and the American Law Institute, respectively, recommended that states abolish or repeal their bulk sale or bulk transfer laws. Both of these prestigious organizations concluded that bulk sale laws no longer serve any useful purpose, but are instead a significant burden upon persons buying existing businesses. Since these recommendations were made, most states have repealed or amended and simplified their bulk sale laws. This trend is likely to continue in the next few years. For information on whether your state still has a bulk sale law in effect, contact your state's secretary of state's office or your attorney, or refer to Section 11.3.

Check Security Interests

Before closing the purchase, your attorney should check with the secretary of state's office to determine whether anyone has recorded a security interest — a lien or chattel mortgage — against the personal property of the seller's business. Naturally, if the transaction involves a purchase of real property, you should also have a title search performed to see if the seller has good title and if there are any recorded mortgages or other claims against the property that the seller has not disclosed to you. For a fee, the secretary of state's office — or its equivalent — will provide a listing of any security interests that have been recorded as a lien against the assets of the business you are buying.

Get Tax Releases

As a condition of the sale, have the seller obtain the necessary form that certifies all state employment taxes have been paid by the seller from the appropriate state agency. If you fail to withhold enough of the purchase price to cover any of the seller's unpaid employment taxes, you may be liable to the state for those taxes. See Section 11.3 for specifics on state requirements. Similarly, require the seller to obtain and provide you with a sales and use tax certification showing that all outstanding sales and use tax payments due have been made by the seller. You do not want to end up paying for the seller's unpaid sales or use taxes.

File with the IRS

Tax regulations require both you and the seller to file *Form 8594* with the IRS any time a business is bought or sold.[4] *Form 8594* reports certain information about the purchase price allocation. Penalties for failure to file this form can be extremely large. Needless to say, the information on your *Form 8594* and that of the seller's should be identical, or you both will be inviting IRS audits.

Retain a Lawyer

Do not attempt to buy or sell a business without the assistance of an attorney to review and structure the deal. Preferably, the attorney should be one who specializes in business law practice rather than a lawyer who is a litigation specialist or general practitioner. Obtain competent tax advice, either from your attorney or from an accountant, when negotiating and structuring aspects of the deal, such as the allocation of the purchase price and the disposition of any employee benefit plans carried on by the seller for the employees of the business.

Use an Escrow

In general, both you and the seller will be protected — from the time the sales agreement is signed until the deal closes — if an escrow is used to handle the sale of the business. The escrow holder, which is usually an escrow company or escrow department of a financial institution, will hold the agreement, escrow instructions, funds, and important documents until all conditions for closing the deal or releasing the funds or documents are fulfilled.

When the deal closes, the escrow holder will disburse the funds to the seller and deliver the documents of title to you. If the deal is not completed, the escrow instructions will specify how the items held in escrow are to be distributed to the parties.

Your attorney or the seller's attorney may also act as escrow holder, but you probably will not want the seller's attorney to act in that role in most cases, for obvious reasons.

Build in Holdbacks

If the seller has made misrepresentations to you in the contract of sale regarding assets that do not exist, or the like, you may always seek satisfaction by suing for damages. In view of the cost, delay, and uncertainty in bringing a lawsuit, however, you would generally be far better off if there were some simple way you could merely offset any such overstated asset or understated liability against the purchase price, retroactively.

To make this possible, seek to structure the deal so part of the purchase price is held back for some period, say a year, just in case such a contingency arises. Then, if you discover false representations as to assets or liabilities, it will be relatively simple — compared to bringing a lawsuit against a seller who may have skipped town — to have your claim deducted from the amount held back.

Discuss with your attorney the possibilities of structuring the transaction so you either:

- Give the seller a note as part of the purchase price, with a right to reduce the principal amount of the note if certain contingencies occur; or
- Have part of the cash payment price held in escrow for six months or more after the sale occurs.

3.7 Summary Checklist for Buying an Existing Business

Investigation

☐ Find out why the present owner wants to sell the business.

☐ Determine whether the reputation of the business will help or harm you once you take over the business.

☐ Obtain tax returns, bank deposit records, and other financial records to see if the business is viable. You may need the help of an accountant or other experts to do this.

☐ If the business is not currently very profitable, list the reasons why you think you can run it more profitably than the present owner.

☐ Review or have reviewed the provisions of key contracts, leases, franchise agreements, or any other legal arrangements that have a significant effect on the business. Be sure you are not assuming an unfavorable lease or contract or losing the benefits of a favorable one.

☐ Make sure that the purchase price is fair. Even if it is, be sure you can afford it. Will you have enough working capital to run the business properly after you pay the purchase price?

Negotiations

☐ Insist on getting accurate financial information and access to the supporting data, early in the negotiations.

☐ Push for an allocation of the purchase price to specific assets in the sales agreement. Seek to maximize the amounts allocable to depreciable assets and inventory. Seek to minimize allocations to goodwill or land purchased, or to real estate improvements.

☐ Look for hidden liabilities, such as pending lawsuits, accrued vacation liabilities, unfunded pension plan liabilities, or potential exposure to environmental clean-up costs.

☐ Retain an attorney to participate in drawing up the sales agreement.

Closing the Transaction

☐ If your state still has a bulk sale law, comply with the requirements of the law if it applies to the particular type of business being acquired.

☐ Be sure that the acquired property is not subject to any recorded security interests or other liens beyond those disclosed by the seller.

☐ Have·the seller obtain and furnish a certification that all employment taxes due have been paid.

☐ Have the seller obtain and furnish a certification that all sales and use taxes due have been paid.

☐ Seek to hold back part of the purchase price as security to reimburse yourself for any misrepresentations as to assets or liabilities by the seller.

☐ Prepare *Form 8594*, and file it with the IRS.

☐ See Section 11.3 for state law considerations.

☐ Determine whether the sale of the business will result in a sales tax liability with respect to part or all of the purchase price. If so, is there a way to reshape the transaction to reduce or avoid sales tax? For example, allocate more of the purchase price to assets not subject to sales tax and less to assets that are.

Other Tax Considerations

☐ If you are buying a corporation that has not been paying income taxes because it has carryovers of net operating losses or investment tax credits, be aware you may be able to use only a small portion of those carryovers to shelter the income of the business once you become the owner.

☐ If the seller has a favorable experience rating for unemployment tax purposes, make sure you act promptly so that you can succeed to that rating as a successor employer.

☐ Under recent tax legislation, if you are acquiring intangible assets, including previously non-deductible intangibles, such as goodwill or going concern value, you may now amortize the cost of most such intangible assets over 15 years.

Endnotes

1. I.R.C. § 1060(a).

2. I.R.C. § 197.

3. I.R.C. § 167(f)(1).

4. Temp. Treas. Regs. 1.1060-1T(h)(2).

Checklist for Evaluating a Franchise

The Franchise

YES NO

☐ ☐ After studying it paragraph by paragraph, did your lawyer approve the franchise contract you are considering?

☐ ☐ Does the franchise call upon you to take any steps that are, according to your lawyer, unwise or illegal in your state, county, or city? If yes, what are the steps? _____

_____

_____

☐ ☐ Does the franchise give you an exclusive territory for the length of the franchise? or

☐ ☐ Can the franchisor sell a second or third franchise in your territory?

☐ ☐ Is the franchisor connected in any way with another franchise company handling similar merchandise or services? If yes, what is your protection against this second franchisor organization?

_____

_____

☐ ☐ Can you terminate the franchise contract? Under what circumstances can you do it and at what cost to you if you decide for any reason at all that you wish to cancel it?

_____

_____

☐ ☐ If you sell your franchise, will you be compensated for the goodwill you have built into the business?

The Franchisor

How many years has the firm offering you a franchise been in operation? _____

☐ ☐ Does the firm have a reputation for honesty and fair dealing among the local firms holding its franchise?

☐ ☐ Has the franchisor shown you any certified figures indicating exact net profits of one or more going firms?

☐ ☐ Have you personally checked these certified figures with the franchisor?

☐ ☐ Will the firm assist you in the following areas?

YES NO   YES NO

☐ ☐ A management training program   ☐ ☐ Capital

☐ ☐ An employee training program   ☐ ☐ Credit

☐ ☐ A public relations program   ☐ ☐ Merchandising ideas

☐ ☐ Will the firm help you find a good location for your new business?

☐ ☐ Is the franchising firm adequately financed so it can carry out its stated plan of financial assistance and expansion?

Checklist for Evaluating a Franchise (continued)

YES NO

☐ ☐ Is the franchisor a one-person company? or

☐ ☐ Is the franchisor a corporation with experienced management, trained in-depth (so that there would always be an experienced person at its head)?

Exactly what can the franchisor do for you that you cannot do for yourself? _____

_____

_____

_____

☐ ☐ Has the franchisor investigated you carefully enough to assure itself that you can successfully operate one of the franchises at a profit both to the franchisor and to you?

☐ ☐ Does your state have a law regulating the sale of franchises? and

☐ ☐ Has the franchisor complied with that law?

You – The Franchisee

How much equity capital will you need to have to purchase the franchise and operate it until your income equals your expenses? _____

Where are you going to get the capital? _____

_____

☐ ☐ Are you prepared to give up some independence of action to secure the advantages offered by the franchise?

☐ ☐ Do you believe you have the innate ability, training, and experience to work smoothly and profitably with the franchisor, your employees, and your customers?

☐ ☐ Are you ready to spend much or all of the remainder of your business life with this franchisor, offering its product or service to your public?

Your Market

☐ ☐ Have you made any study to determine whether the product or service that you propose to sell under franchise has a market in your territory at the prices you will have to charge?

Will the population in your territory increase ☐, remain static ☐, or decrease ☐ over the next five years?

Will the product or service you are considering be in greater demand ☐, about the same ☐, or in less demand ☐ five years from today?

What competition already exists in your territory for the product or service you contemplate selling:

From nonfranchise firms? _____

From franchise firms? _____

Starting the Business

Part II

Chapter 4

A Trip through the Red Tape Jungle: Requirements that Apply to Nearly All New Businesses

*If you think health care is expensive now, wait until you
see what it costs when it's free.*

— P. J. O'Rourke

4.1 General Considerations

This chapter outlines the most common governmental requirements and
other red tape that virtually everyone starting a new business or buying
an existing business must attend to. Specifically, this chapter focuses on
the necessary requirements that apply to nearly all businesses, regardless
if they have employees. If you expect to have one or more employees, a
large number of additional legal requirements will affect your business
immediately. Chapter 5 covers the additional requirements that apply to
businesses that have employees. This chapter does not discuss the special
licenses that many types of businesses are required to have. If you do not
know whether the type of business you are considering going into requires
a special license or licenses from federal, state, or local government agencies, refer to Chapter 6 and Section 11.6.

4.2 Choosing a Name for the Business

The name you choose for your business can be important from a business
image standpoint and also for communicating to the public what you
have to offer. Most small businesses should select a name that, at least in

part, clearly describes the product or service provided. If you ignore this basic common-sense rule, you run the risk of losing many potential customers for the simple reason they will pass right by without realizing what you do. A fanciful or whimsical name is fine from an image standpoint, but it should also give the public a clear idea of what it is your business provides in the way of goods or services. For example, if you call your restaurant, "The Comestible Emporium," a lot of hungry people will probably drive right by without realizing that you serve food.

However, in order to protect your business' name as a trademark or service mark under federal and state laws, it makes sense for you to adopt a name that is partly arbitrary or nondescriptive and partly descriptive of the services or goods provided, such as the "21 Club Restaurant." The reason you should select a name that is at least partially whimsical or arbitrary is because names that are merely descriptive of the goods or services cannot be legally protected from use by others, unless you can prove that the name has acquired a secondary meaning — which is very difficult for a new or small business to establish.[1]

You also need to think of the possible consequences of putting your name out before the public. You may want to consider using some sort of fictitious name (see Section 4.10) for your business, rather than your name. There is nothing illegal or shady about using a fictitious business name. If you put your name on the business and the venture goes belly up, as some new businesses do, many people in the community will automatically associate your name with the defunct or bankrupt business. This may make it very difficult if you try to start another business or to obtain credit in the same community in the future.

Once you have settled on a name for your business, you or preferably your attorney, should find out whether the same name, or a confusingly similar name, has already been preempted by someone else. This involves making an inquiry with the state's secretary of state's office to find out whether the name is already being used in the state. Inquiry should also be made of the county clerk, in each county where you will do business, to see if another business is already using the same or a confusingly similar name in the county and has filed a fictitious business name statement. If so, you may have to choose a different name. See Section 9.5 for more information on trademark protection.

4.3 Local Business Licenses

Almost every business will need city or county business licenses, or both. These licenses can be obtained at the local city hall or county offices. Failure to obtain a license when you start business will usually result in a penalty when the local government eventually catches up with you; therefore, obtaining the necessary licenses should be among the first steps taken when you start a business.

Some cities and counties impose a gross receipts, income, or payroll tax on businesses. Certain types of businesses, such as restaurants, may also be required to obtain special permits from local health authorities and fire or police departments. If you will construct your own business building, consult your local city or county zoning ordinances to obtain any necessary building permits. Most local governments require permits for both new construction and remodeling.

In addition, whether or not you plan to carry on any construction activity or do any remodeling, you will need to make certain that the business activity you intend to carry on does not violate any zoning regulations or any ordinances regarding hazardous activities. You may also be required to obtain a use permit from the city or county planning commission.

4.4 State Licenses

Most states impose license fees or taxes on a wide range of businesses, occupations, and professions. The fees often vary widely among the different types of businesses and occupations, ranging from relatively nominal to substantial amounts or rates, depending upon the activity. The many different types of licenses and permits are usually granted based on some combination of requirements such as registration, bonding, education, experience, and passage of licensing examinations.

Since you may not legally operate any of these regulated businesses or professions without being licensed, you should find out whether there is a state licensing requirement for the business you plan to start. If so, determine whether and how you will be able to comply with the licensing requirements.

See Section 11.6 for a partial listing of businesses, occupations, and professions that must be licensed under the laws of this state.

4.5 Federal Licenses

Most new small businesses will not require any type of federal permit or license to operate, unless they are engaged in rendering investment advice, making alcohol or tobacco products, preparing meat products, or making or dealing in firearms. Federal permits or licenses would also be necessary to commence certain large-scale operations, such as a radio or television station or a common carrier and the production of drugs or biological products. If you wish to engage in any of the foregoing activities, all of which are heavily regulated, consult an attorney regarding regulatory requirements well in advance.

4.6 Estimated Income Taxes

Individual

As a sole proprietor or partner in a partnership, you will have to make advance payments of estimated federal — and possibly state — income taxes and federal self-employment tax once your business begins to turn a taxable profit. Individual estimated tax payments are due in four annual installments on April 15, June 15, September 15, and January 15 of the following year for an individual whose tax year is the calendar year. Any remaining unpaid federal tax is due with your tax return on April 15 of the following year — which is also the date when the first estimated tax installment is due for that year. You will file *Form 1040-ES* with your federal estimated tax payments. During a year, you must make estimated tax payments equal to 90% of the current year's tax or 100% of the prior year's tax, whichever is less.

Certain high-income taxpayers — with more than $150,000 of adjusted gross income in the prior year — are not allowed to base their payments on the prior year's tax. However, they may base their payments on 105% (100% in 1998) of the previous year's tax.[2]

Corporate

If your business is incorporated, the corporation will generally have to make corporate estimated tax payments as early as the fourth month of its first tax year if it has taxable income. Your corporation must pay estimated tax equal to 100% of its current year tax or 100% of its tax for the prior year, whichever is less. A large corporation — one which had one million dollars or more of taxable income in one of the three preceding years — may not base its estimates on the prior year's tax. Estimated tax installments are due on April 15, June 15, September 15, and December 15, for a corporation using a calendar year for its taxable year.

Federal estimated tax payments should be computed on *Form 1120-W* — which can be obtained, along with other federal tax forms, from any IRS office — and must be deposited in a bank that is authorized to accept federal tax deposits. The corporate estimated tax deposits must be accompanied by federal tax deposit coupons. Your corporation will be issued one coupon book that contains coupons with your corporate tax identification number already preprinted on them. These coupons can be used for deposits of all types of federal taxes. On each coupon, you must indicate, by checking the applicable box, the kind of tax being deposited and the calendar quarter to which payroll tax deposits are to be applied. The boxes on the coupon indicate the form name for the type of tax being paid.

Federal Tax Deposits

Type of Tax	Box to Darken on Coupon
Payroll tax deposits	941
Federal unemployment tax	940 (or 940-EZ)
Corporate income tax estimates (and year-end payments)	1120

Coupon books will be sent to you automatically when you file *Form SS-4*, which requests a tax identification number for the corporation. When you receive your coupon book, a reorder form, *Form 8109A*, will be provided so you can request additional coupon books for the current year, if needed.

A penalty may be imposed for failure to make deposits directly to an authorized government depository bank. In the past, when tax deposit cards were unavailable, it was common practice to mail payments to the Internal Revenue Service accompanied by a letter indicating the nature of the tax payment and requesting additional tax deposit cards. This method of paying business taxes is no longer acceptable. Thus, it is important to mail the reorder form in time to receive additional coupon books before you run out; however, the IRS will sometimes send you blank coupons for temporary use. Refer to Section 11.4 regarding state filing requirements for individual and corporate estimated income taxes.

4.7 Miscellaneous Tax Information Returns

Reporting Payments to Individuals

As a general rule, every person engaged in a trade or business must report to the IRS any payments of $600 or more made to any person during the calendar year, for items such as rent, compensation for services, commissions, interest, and annuities, plus other items of fixed or determinable income.[3] To make these filings, you will use a series of 1099 forms. A number of additional tax reporting requirements are listed below. Be aware there are stiff penalties for failure to comply with them.

Obtaining Social Security Numbers

It is necessary to obtain the name and Social Security number or other tax identification number of any person to whom you make payments of $600 or more. There is a $50 penalty for failure to obtain their tax identification number — unless you have a reasonable excuse, such as their refusal to give you the number.[4] If they do refuse to give you the number, you must withhold 31% of whatever amount you owe them and deposit it with the IRS, or you will be subject to a penalty for failure to withhold.[5]

Reporting Sales to Direct Sellers

In addition, you must report sales of $5,000 or more of consumer products to any individual who is engaged in direct selling — that is, selling in any way other than through a permanent retail establishment.[6] This will mainly apply to sales made to people in direct sales organizations, such as Tupperware, Amway, or Shaklee. It would also apply in many other situations, such as where the person you sell to resells the goods by mail order. Use *Form 1099-MISC* to report these sales.

1099 Forms

Reportable payments you make that are in excess of $600 per year are usually filed for each payee on *Form 1099-MISC* (information return) or

Form 1099-INT (for interest); a duplicate must be sent to the payee. In addition, you must prepare and file a *Form 1096* return summarizing all the information on the 1099-MISC forms and on the other forms in the 1099 series. Each of these forms is due by February 28 each year, for the prior calendar year, and a copy must also be sent to the recipient of the payment by January 31.

Be aware that instructions for *Form 1099* say that you should use your personal Social Security number rather than your business' employer identification number on the form. Putting down the wrong taxpayer identification number in such a case will subject you to a penalty.

Compensation payments in excess of $600 made to nonemployees — independent contractors — are also reported on *Form 1099-MISC*. Businesses must also report royalty payments of $10 or more made to any person.

Penalties

There are stiff IRS penalties for not filing the above 1099 forms. The penalty for not filing or not giving a 1099 to a payee is $50 per failure. Since there is a separate penalty for not giving a copy of the 1099 to the payee, as well as for not filing a copy with the IRS, it can cost you $100 for each person for whom you fail to prepare 1099s.[7] The $50 penalty for late-filed 1099s, and certain other information returns, can be reduced to $30 if you file more than 30 days late but before August 1 of the year the filing is due. Or, if you file within 30 days after the due date, the penalty can be reduced to only $15.

In addition, if you erroneously, but in good faith, treat a person as an independent contractor, and it is later shown that the person was actually an employee, you will only be liable as an employer for 20% of the employee's Social Security tax that should have been withheld. You will also be held liable for income tax withholding equal to 1.5% of what you paid the individual provided that you properly filed *Form 1099-MISC* with the IRS.[8] If you failed to file *Form 1099-MISC* for that person, the amount of withholding tax you are liable for is doubled.[9]

Exemptions for 1099 Filings

Fortunately, a number of important exemptions from the 1099 filing requirements will eliminate most of the people or companies to whom you are likely to make payments of $600 or more. You do not have to report:

- Payments to corporations — except certain corporations in the medical field, and for payments made after 1997, gross amounts paid to law corporations for legal services;[10]
- Payments of compensation to employees that are already reported on their W-2s;[11]
- Payments of bills for merchandise, telegrams, telephone, freight, storage, and similar charges;[12]
- Payments of rent made to real estate agents;[13]
- Expense advances or reimbursements to employees that the employees must account to you (the employer) for;[14] and
- Payments to a governmental unit.[15]

If your business is incorporated, your corporation will have to file a *Form 1099-DIV* for each person to whom it pays dividends of $10 or more each year.[16] You must also file *Form 1099-INT* for each person to whom you pay $10 or more in interest on bonds, debentures, or notes issued by the corporation in registered form.[17] *Form 1099-DIV* or *Form 1099-INT* is also required for any other payment of dividends or interest on which you are required to withhold tax. Payments reported on *Form 1099-DIV* and *Form 1099-INT* must also be reported on the *Form 1096* summary. *Form 1099-S* must be given to recipients of the proceeds from the sales of real estate, in general.

Reporting Dividends and Interest

Any business that receives a payment of more than $10,000 in cash, in cash equivalents — such as cashier's checks or traveler's checks — or in foreign currency in one transaction, or in two or more related transactions, is required to report the details of the transactions within 15 days to the IRS.[18] In addition, the business must furnish a similar statement to the payor by January 31 of the following year.[19] *Form 8300* is used for reporting such "suitcase" transactions.

Reporting Large Cash Transactions

The penalties for noncompliance are generally the same as for not filing 1099s, except that in cases of intentional failure to file, there is an additional penalty equal to the higher of $25,000 or the amount of the cash or cash equivalent received in the transaction, up to $100,000.[20] In addition to the requirement that you file 1099s with the IRS, you may have to file similar forms with the state.

Federal law requires that you give *Form 1098* to any individual from whom you receive $600 or more in mortgage interest during the year, in the course of your trade or business. *Form 1098* has the same filing requirements as *Form 1099*.[21]

Reporting Mortgage Interest Received

The IRS now permits you to file *Form 1098* and *Form 1099*, as well as certain other information returns, electronically or on magnetic media (computer tapes or disks) rather than the actual paper forms, if very specific formats for the computer tape or disk are met. The IRS requires that certain information returns be filed electronically or on magnetic media if your business files 250 or more such returns for a calendar year.[22] These include *Form 1098*, all of the 1099 series and W-2 series of information returns, and various others, such as *Form 5498* and *Form 8027*.

Reporting on Magnetic Media

A "hardship waiver" to excuse you from having to file in electronic or magnetic media format may be granted under certain circumstances if you file a request on *Form 8508* at least 90 days in advance of the due date.

Failure to file an information return electronically or on magnetic media — or on a machine-readable form where magnetic media filing is not required — when required to do so is treated as a failure to file and can result in penalties, as noted earlier.

If your business finds it will be required to file information returns electronically or on magnetic media, there are many data processing firms and computer programs you can buy that will encode the data for you, at a relatively small cost, in a way that meets the IRS's highly technical specifications.

4.8 Sales and Use Tax Permits

With a limited number of exceptions, every business that sells tangible personal property, such as merchandise, to customers must obtain a seller's permit from the state sales tax agency. Usually, a separate permit must be obtained for each place of business where property subject to tax is sold. See Section 11.4 for a discussion of the state's sales and use tax laws and permit requirements. Some states have a gross income or a gross receipts tax rather than a sales tax. A few states have neither.

In general, as a wholesaler or manufacturer, you will not have to collect sales tax on goods you sell to a retailer for resale if the retailer holds a valid seller's permit and provides you with a resale certificate in connection with the transaction. Likewise, if your business, as a retailer, buys goods for resale, you need not pay sales tax to the wholesalers if you provide them with resale certificates. You may buy blank resale certificate forms at most stationery stores in states where such certificates are required.

The sales and use tax laws typically require a business that sells or leases tangible personal property to keep complete records of the gross receipts from sales or rentals, whether or not the receipts are believed to be taxable. You must also keep adequate and complete records to substantiate all deductions claimed on sales and use tax returns and of the total purchase price of all tangible personal property bought for sale, lease, or consumption in the state.

4.9 Real Estate Taxes

Property Taxes

As a rule, you do not need to worry about contacting the county tax assessor's office regarding payment of any real property taxes on real property acquired for your business. They will usually contact you by mailing a property tax bill to the owner of record. See Section 11.4 for a general description of how state or local real property and personal property taxes are assessed and collected.

FIRPTA Withholding Tax on Purchase of Real Property

In addition to local property taxes, U.S. citizens and residents who acquire U.S. real estate from foreign persons — including partnership interests or stock in certain firms owning U.S. real property — must withhold up to

10% of the purchase price and remit it to the IRS under the Foreign Investment in Real Property Tax Act (FIRPTA). If you fail to withhold the tax, you are liable for it. This is a potentially dangerous tax trap for unsuspecting American buyers of real estate, since it is often difficult to determine whether a seller is a foreign person.

While there is an exception for residences costing $300,000 or less — if you will live in it for at least 50% of the time for two years — it is far safer to obtain a certificate of nonforeign status from the seller if there is any possibility that the seller is a nonresident alien or a foreign company.

To protect yourself when purchasing real estate — or your client if you are in the real estate business — you should require, as a condition of closing the transaction, that the seller provide you with an affidavit certifying whether or not the seller is a nonresident alien or a foreign company.

If the seller refuses to sign the affidavit and provide the required information, you should withhold 10% of the gross purchase price and transmit it to the IRS within ten days of the sale along with IRS *Form 8288* and *Form 8288-A*. This can be a real problem in a highly leveraged deal where less than 10% of the purchase price is paid in cash at the closing.

Some states have adopted similar withholding provisions with regard to purchases of real estate within those states and where the seller is a nonresident of the state.

In short, if the seller is a foreign person, you will owe the IRS 10% of the purchase price if you fail to withhold the tax, unless you received a certificate of nonforeign status from the seller.

4.10 Fictitious Business Name Statement

Almost every state has laws that require any person — including a partnership, LLC, or corporation — who regularly transacts business in the state for profit under a fictitious or assumed business name to file or register that fictitious or assumed business name. This filing is usually done with either the state or county offices, or both. Some states also require publication of the fictitious name for a specified period in a newspaper. There is nothing illegal or unethical about using a fictitious name, as long as you register it and — if required by state law — publish it. In fact, you may have no choice but to use a fictitious name if you wish to do business in another state and the real name of your business is already being used by someone else in that state.

In most states, the only penalty for not registering a fictitious business name is that you can't start a lawsuit in the state courts until you file the fictitious name statement or registration. However, a more practical reason to register or file your fictitious business name is that most banks will not let you open a business account with them until you show them proof you have done so.

For a sole proprietorship or partnership, a business name is generally considered fictitious unless it contains the surname of the owner or all of the general partners and does not suggest the existence of additional owners. Use of a name that includes words like "company," "associates," "group," "brothers," or "sons" will suggest additional owners and will make it necessary for a business to file and publish a fictitious business name statement.

Putting a name that would be considered fictitious on your company letterhead, on your business cards, in advertising, or on your products will be considered a use of the name.

Many newspapers will provide the form for filing, publish the notice, and file the required affidavit. See Section 11.4 regarding specific requirements for filing a fictitious business name statement in this state.

4.11 Insurance — A Practical Necessity for Businesses

Insurance, like death and taxes, is an inevitable necessity for the owner of any small business. For almost any business, even one that has no employees, insurance coverage for general liability, product liability, fire and similar disasters, robbery, theft, and interruption of business should be considered.

If your business will have employees, workers' compensation insurance is usually mandatory under state law. Employee life, health, and disability insurance have also become virtual necessities in many businesses and professions if you wish to be competitive with other firms in hiring and retaining capable employees.

Fidelity bonding should be considered for employees who will have access to the cash receipts or other funds of the business. If you have an employee pension or profit-sharing plan subject to the Employee Retirement Income Security Act of 1974 (ERISA), employees involved in administering the plan or handling its funds are required to be covered by a fidelity bond.[23] See Section 5.5 for further information.

Insurance Agents

Since it isn't realistic to expect you to become a sophisticated comparison shopper for insurance while you are trying to get a business off the ground, seek out a good insurance agent whom you can trust and rely upon to give you good advice. There is no easy way to find such an agent, just as there is no sure way of finding a good lawyer or accountant. In general, the best approach will be to ask friends, lawyers, accountants, or other businesspeople you know to refer you to a topflight insurance agent.

Agents who have earned the Chartered Life Underwriter (CLU) designation will, as a rule, be more experienced and capable than those without the CLU credential. This can be an additional factor to consider when selecting your insurance agent.

Agents who deal primarily in property and casualty insurance will not usually have CLU on their business cards. Instead, they may have the initials CPCU — Chartered Property/Casualty Underwriter — after their name, which is a similar mark of distinction in the field of property/casualty insurance.

Another good tip in finding an insurance agent is to analyze your own insurance needs. There are several how-to books that can help you analyze your risks and compare insurance prices. One such book is *The Buyer's Guide to Business Insurance*. The book and its companion software, *The Insurance Assistant*, are available from The Oasis Press.

Insurance Consultants

If you cannot find an agent with whom you feel comfortable, call an insurance consultant. Be sure the consultant is a member of the Society of Risk Management Consultants. To belong to the group, the individual or firm cannot be an insurance broker. These consultants are insurance experts and can give you an objective analysis on risk management and insurance.

Society of Risk Management Consultants
300 Park Avenue
New York, NY 10022
(800) 765-SRMC (Nationwide)

The usual hourly fees may seem high, but most new businesses probably will not need an excessive amount of time. Most will bill in quarter-hour increments.

You will probably recoup the consultant's fee several times over in premium savings in just the first year alone. Be wary, however, of a consultant who wants to increase the number of hours by offering to create specifications and provide additional services.

Once you have met with an independent consultant and know what is needed, shop for the insurance you need from insurance brokers. Don't let them bid up the amount of coverage or add on additional types of insurance.

Use the insurance consultant as you would an attorney or physician — follow his or her advice.

4.12 Securities Laws

Inherent in the choice of the legal form of the business is the potential application of federal and state securities laws if the new business is to have more than one owner or it becomes necessary to raise capital for an existing business. Because of the potentially dire consequences of violating federal or state securities laws, consult with your attorney as early as possible when considering issuing or transferring a security. Corporate stock and limited partnership interests generally are considered securities, and even a general partnership interest can be a security in appropriate circumstances, as can certain types of debt instruments.

Registration of Securities

Since the Securities Act of 1933, federal law has required registration as a prior condition to the issuance or transfer of securities. The law exempts various types of securities and certain types of transactions. The most important of these exemptions for small businesses have been the exemption for securities sold to persons residing within a single state and transactions by an issuer not deemed to involve any public offering. The Securities and Exchange Commission (SEC) from time to time has issued regulations exempting small securities issues, attempting to balance the needs of small businesses to raise capital against the public policy of protecting investors. In 1982, the commission adopted Regulation D as its primary method of regulation of securities offerings by small businesses, although not to the exclusion of other exemptions that might apply.

Rule 504 Exemption

If your company's issuance of stock or other securities meets the requirements of Rule 504 under Regulation D, you will be exempted from having to register the offering of securities with the SEC. This exemption is available to any company that offers its securities for sale if the total offering price of all the exempt securities sold by the company during a twelve-month period is one million dollars or less — but remember that no more than $500,000 of securities can be sold without registration under some states' securities laws.[24]

The shares of stock or other securities you may sell under this exemption cannot be offered or sold by any form of public solicitation or general advertising, and no one who buys the securities can resell them without registration, unless they also qualify for an exemption from registration.

Rule 504 does not require that you give any specific information to the purchasers of the securities; however, since the anti-fraud provisions of the securities laws apply even to a transaction that is exempt from registration, it is advisable and customary to give purchasers a written summary of material information about the offering.

Rule 505 Exemption

Rule 505 exempts offers and sales of securities from registration if the total price of all exempt securities your company sold over a twelve-month period is five million dollars or less.[25] While this exemption allows you to do larger offerings, in dollar terms, than under the Rule 504 exemption, there is an additional restriction: You must not issue the securities to more than 35 purchasers. However, any sales of securities to sophisticated "accredited investors" need not be counted when determining whether you have sold to more than 35 investors.[26]

Examples of accredited investors include banks, insurance companies, an individual whose net worth at the time of purchase exceeds one million dollars, or an individual who has individual income in excess of $200,000 — or

$300,000 jointly with a spouse — in each of the two most recent years and expects the same in the current year.

Exceptions are also made for certain large investors, including corporations, partnerships, or business trusts with total assets in excess of five million dollars, unless formed for the specific purpose of acquiring the securities.

For purposes of Rule 505, the issuer must furnish extensive information and certified financial statements to the investors, unless securities were sold only to accredited investors. The prohibition against advertising and solicitation applies to this rule, as do the anti-fraud provisions of the securities laws.

Rule 506 Exemption

Rule 506 provides exemptions similar to those under Rule 505, including the 35-purchaser limitation, with the same exception for accredited investors described above.[27] However, Rule 506 requires that an issuer of securities must reasonably believe, immediately before making a sale to a nonaccredited investor, that the investor is sufficiently knowledgeable to adequately evaluate the merits and risks of the investment. Alternatively, the issuer can rely on the knowledge and experience of a person who represents the investor.

The other main difference between Rule 505 and Rule 506 is that there is no five million dollar or other maximum size limitation on the amount of securities that can be issued in a Rule 506 offering.

Regulation D Filing Requirements

Issuers using any of the above exemptions must file *Form D* with the SEC generally no later than 15 days after the first sale of securities and at other specified times thereafter. Rule 507 disqualifies any issuer found to have violated the *Form D* filing requirement from future use of the Regulation D exemptions if the issuer has been enjoined by a court for violating the notice filing requirement — but apparently this does not disqualify prior issuances of securities merely due to failure to file *Form D*.[28]

The exemptions available under the federal securities laws are more liberal than those available under the securities laws of many states. In connection with any issuance or transfer of securities, it is necessary to consider the possible application of securities laws in the state where the business entity is established or operates, and, if different, the states where purchasers of the securities live. See Section 11.2 for further information concerning state securities laws.

Rule 147 – Intrastate Offering Exemption

Rule 147, under the Securities Act of 1933, exempts from registration a sale of securities solely to persons resident in one state, where the issuer has at least 80% of its assets in that state, and uses at least 80% of the proceeds of the sale within the state.[29] Resales of such securities may be made only to persons within the state during the period of the offering and for nine months thereafter. No SEC filing is required under a Rule 147 offering.

Regulation A Exemption

Yet another possible exemption is under Regulation A, which allows an issuer — that is not a "public" company immediately before the offering — to sell up to $5 million of securities within a one-year period without registration.[30] No limits are placed on the number of offerees, or their degree of financial sophistication. However, purchasers must be given an offering circular, and a copy of the offering circular must also be filed with the SEC. Financial statements included in the offering circular need not be audited statements.

A *Form 1-A* offering statement must be filed with the SEC, followed by a 20-day waiting period, before sales may commence.

Public Companies

A company whose equity securities are considered to be publicly traded must be registered with the SEC under the Securities Exchange Act of 1934. Any such "public" companies are subject to a host of costly reporting requirements, including:

- Filing an annual report, *Form 10-K*, which includes audited financial statements;
- Filing quarterly (unaudited) *Form 10-Q* reports; and
- Filing *Form 8-K* monthly reports, which must be filed when a "material event" occurs.

Issuers who must register their securities under the 1934 Act include:

- A company that has any security (stock, bonds, or other) that is traded on a national security exchange; or
- A company with total assets in excess of $5 million if it has a class of equity securities held by 500 or more shareholders and is traded in interstate commerce.

Going Public Easier for Small Businesses

Through its 1993 Regulation S-B, the SEC provided a new set of rules designed to make it easier and simpler for small businesses to raise capital in the public market. Regulation S-B is an integrated system of rules, forms, and reporting requirements designed especially for small firms, which have traditionally found the costs and complexity of "going public" to be prohibitive.

To make a public offering of securities that qualifies under the streamlined procedures of Regulation S-B, an issuing company must meet all the following requirements:

- A company must be a U.S. or Canadian company and cannot be an investment company.
- A company's revenues must be less than $25 million per year.
- The total value of a company's outstanding securities — not counting those held by affiliated companies or persons — must not exceed $25 million.
- If the issuer is a majority-owned subsidiary of another corporation, the parent company must also meet the above criteria.[31]

State Blue Sky Laws

In addition to federal regulations, each state has its own set of securities laws, generally referred to as blue sky laws. The exemptions available under the federal securities laws are generally more liberal than those available under the securities laws of many states.

Even where a federal securities law exemption applies in connection with any issuance or transfer of securities, it is necessary to consider the possible application of securities laws in the state where the business entity is established or operates. If potential purchasers of the securities live in other states, it is also necessary to consider the possible application of securities laws of those states. State requirements may consist of extensive registration procedures or simpler notice filings, where a business is only required to file a notice and pay a fee to the state agency that regulates securities.

Although most state blue sky laws are based on the Uniform Securities Act, the laws of each state — even the interpretation from state to state of identical laws — can differ. Fortunately, a large number of states have adopted the SEC regulations and rely on the SEC to enforce the securities laws within these states. For example, many states provide for transactional exemptions for Regulation D securities offerings if there is full compliance with SEC Rules 501 through 503. Transactions in exchange-listed securities are also exempt under state laws.

Federal Preemption of Blue Sky Laws

A major change in the state regulation of securities has occurred. The National Securities Markets Improvement Act of 1996, was enacted by Congress in Fall 1996. A key feature of the act is the repeal of Section 18 of the Securities Act of 1933, which authorized states to regulate most sales of securities. The repeal of this section has preempted many state security registration and qualification requirements under their blue sky laws, although the new law still allows states to continue to enforce antifraud laws in connection with the issuance of securities.

However, this preemption mostly benefits large issuers of securities — such as investment companies registered with the SEC and companies that issue securities listed on stock exchanges and with NASDAC. Also exempted are sales to certain qualified purchasers, private placements under Rule 506, and sales to qualified institutional buyers under SEC Rule 144A. In some cases, these transactions may still be subject to state notice-filing requirements and payment of applicable filing fees.

Most small businesses will still have to be concerned with state securities regulations, as the states retain the right to regulate penny stocks, certain small and intrastate offerings, and some offerings of securities exempt under federal laws. While the new law simplifies securities law compliance requirements for many companies, its benefits for small, nonpublicly traded companies will be minimal or nonexistent.

Consult a business attorney who is familiar with the blue sky law requirements of the state or states in which you operate, before you issue any stock or other securities.

4.13 Requirements Specific to the Legal Form of the Business

Each legal form of doing business has its own set of requirements. This section briefly mentions them to help you understand your new business' potential "to-do" list. To make this list more complete, read Section 11.4, which discusses state-specific requirements for each legal form, and refer to the checklist at the end of that section. Section 11.2 also discusses state-specific filing and income tax requirements for each legal form of doing business.

Sole Proprietorships

No significant government regulatory requirements apply specifically to sole proprietorships; although, as a sole proprietor of a business, you will need to attach a form *Schedule C* to your individual federal tax return, on which you will report the income or loss from your business.

If your sole proprietorship shows a profit, you will usually have to pay a self-employment tax equal to 15.3% of your net self-employment income from the business, or at least on the first $65,400 of such income, plus an additional 2.9% on self-employment income of more than $65,400 in 1997.

The self-employment tax is a Social Security and Medicare tax for those who work for themselves. The tax is computed on *Schedule SE*, which must also be attached to your federal income tax return.

Partnerships

Like a sole proprietor, as a partner, you will have to pay a self-employment tax on your share of your partnership's net self-employment income. Net self-employment income usually includes all partnership income less all partnership deductions allowed for income tax purposes. Some types of income, such as interest, may or may not be considered self-employment income.

The source of your income and your involvement in the activity from which your income is received will determine whether it is self-employment income. Limited partners in a limited partnership are generally not subject to the self-employment tax.

If your earnings from self-employment are $400 or more for the year, you will have to figure self-employment tax on *Schedule SE* of your federal *Form 1040*. *Schedule E* of your federal *Form 1040* deals with your personal income tax and includes all other taxable income, such as royalties, rentals, and interest. You report your share of partnership ordinary income or loss on *Schedule E*.

In addition, your partnership must file a partnership information return, federal *Form 1065*, reporting the partnership's income and each partner's share of income and other items. The partnership must also file *Form SS-4* with the IRS to obtain a federal employer identification number, even if it has no employees. A sample *Form SS-4* is provided at the end of this chapter.

When a partner buys, sells, or exchanges a partnership interest, the partnership must file *Form 8308*, which is a special information return, if the partnership's assets include unrealized receivables or substantially appreciated inventory that might cause the seller to have ordinary gain, rather than all capital gain, on the sale or exchange.[32] Statements also have to be sent to the partners involved in the transaction.[33] A limited partnership, to qualify as such, is usually required to file a certificate of limited partnership with the secretary of state or other state agency. In most states, a limited partnership should also file certified copies in each county where it does business or owns real estate.

Corporations

As mentioned in Chapter 2, corporations are a more complicated form of doing business, and as a result, have several requirements specific only to that form. Here is a brief listing of some of these requirements.

- Filing articles of incorporation with the appropriate state agency;
- Adopting a set of bylaws;
- Observing necessary corporate formalities on a regular basis;
- Filing federal income tax returns on *Form 1120* — or *Form 1120-S* for an S corporation — and state income or franchise tax returns in most states where they do business;
- Reporting certain information relating to the transfer of tax-free property under Internal Revenue Code Section 351 on the corporation's income tax return for that year;[34]
- Filing *Form SS-4* with the IRS to obtain an employer identification number, even if there are no employees; and
- Qualifying with the secretary of state to do business if the corporation was organized under the laws of another state.

Limited Liability Companies

A limited liability company (LLC) must file articles of organization — similar to articles of incorporation — with the secretary of state or other appropriate state agency, and pay any applicable filing fees. Tax treatment of an LLC will generally be the same as a partnership or, if the LLC has only one owner, it will be treated as a sole proprietorship (that is, its existence will be disregarded for tax purposes). Or, should you so choose, an LLC can elect to be taxed like a corporation by filing *Form 8832*.

4.14 Checklist of Requirements for Nearly All New Businesses

Since there are so many requirements to remember, this checklist may come in handy.

- ☐ Obtain local business licenses.
- ☐ Check on local zoning ordinances, regulations, and other land use restrictions.

☐ Determine if your particular business requires a state license to operate.

☐ Determine whether any type of federal permit or license is required.

☐ Be prepared to make estimated income tax payments almost immediately after starting business or incorporating.

☐ Apply for a sales and use tax seller's permit if you will sell tangible personal property.

☐ File sales and use tax returns if you must collect sales or use tax.

☐ File with the county clerk, and publish a fictitious business name statement if the business operates under a fictitious name, and then file an affidavit of publication with the county clerk (in some states).

☐ Locate a good insurance agent or retain and meet with an insurance consultant regarding fire, accident, liability, theft, and other types of commercial insurance coverage. Then, obtain the necessary insurance coverage.

☐ If you purchase real estate, you must withhold up to 10% of the purchase price and remit it to the IRS if the seller is a foreign individual or foreign-owned company, under the Foreign Investment in Real Property Tax Act.[35] Otherwise, you should insist upon receiving an affidavit that the seller is not a nonresident alien, with his or her taxpayer identification number, unless you are certain that he or she is a U.S. citizen or resident.

☐ For a sole proprietorship, report any self-employment income on *Schedule SE* of federal *Form 1040*, and report income or loss on *Schedule C* of *Form 1040*.

☐ A partnership files *Form 1065* reporting partnership income. Each partner reports his or her share of self-employment income on *Schedule SE* of *Form 1040* and income or loss from partnership operations on *Schedule E* of *Form 1040*.

☐ For a limited partnership, file a certificate of limited partnership with the secretary of state and copies in counties where the partnership has places of business or real estate (in most states).

☐ For an LLC, file articles of organization and, if treated as a partnership, file partnership tax returns and report each owner's share of income or loss on the owners' tax returns. If treated as a corporation, comply with all corporate tax filing requirements.

☐ For a corporation, file articles of incorporation, adopt bylaws, and observe necessary corporate formalities. File federal income tax return *Form 1120*; *Form 1120-S* for an S corporation. If property is transferred to the corporation tax-free under Internal Revenue Code Section 351, report required information relating to the transfer on the corporation's income tax return for that year.

☐ For a corporation, limited liability company, or a partnership, apply for a federal employer identification number on *Form SS-4*, even if the business has no employees.

☐ File annual tax information returns, *Form 1096* and the *Form 1099* series, for payments of $600 or more for items such as rent, interest, and compensation for services, and send 1099s to the payees.

☐ File *Form 1098* for mortgage interest of $600 or more your business receives in a year from an individual.

☐ Report any cash payments or cash equivalents of more than $10,000 that you receive to the IRS within 15 days. Such filing may have to be done on computer-readable magnetic media.

☐ If your business is a corporation, be sure to obtain an adequate supply of federal tax deposit coupons in time to make your corporate estimated tax payments.

☐ Comply with the public accommodations provisions of the Americans with Disabilities Act. See Section 5.11.

The above requirements apply to any business, whether it has employees or not. There are many additional requirements for businesses that do have employees, and these are covered in the next chapter. See Section 11.4 for a checklist of additional state law requirements that apply to nearly all new businesses.

Endnotes

1. *Armstrong Paint and Varnish Works v. New and U-Enamel Corp.* 305 U.S. 315 (1938); *Carter-Wallace, Inc. v. Proctor and Gamble Co.* 434 F.2d 794 (9th Cir. 1970). The author wishes to acknowledge Henry C. Bunsow, esq. of the San Francisco patent and trademark law firm of Keker & Van Nest LLP, for alerting him to this important point.

2. I.R.C. § 6654.

3. I.R.C. § 6041(a).

4. I.R.C. § 6724(d)(3).

5. I.R.C. § 3406(a).

6. I.R.C. § 6041A(b).

7. I.R.C. §§ 6721–6722.

8. I.R.C. § 3509(a).

9. I.R.C. § 3509(b).

10. Treas. Regs. § 1.6041-3(c) and I.R.C. § 6045(f).

11. Treas. Regs. § 1.6041-3(a).

12. Treas. Regs. § 1.6041-3(d).

13. Treas. Regs. § 1.6041-3(e).

14. Treas. Regs. § 1.6041-3(i).

15. I.R.C. § 6041(a) requires filing of information returns for payments made to another "person." Person, as defined in IRC § 7701(a)(1), does not include governmental bodies.

16. I.R.C. § 6042(a).

17. I.R.C. § 6049(a).

18. I.R.C. § 6050I.

19. I.R.C. § 6722.

20. I.R.C. § 6721.

21. I.R.C. § 6050H.

22. Rev. Proc. 46-42, 1996-32 I.R.B. 14.

23. 29 U.S.C. § 1112 (§ 412 of ERISA).

24. 17 C.F.R. § 230.504.

25. 17 C.F.R. § 230.505.

26. 17 C.F.R. § 230.501(e)(1)(iv).

27. 17 C.F.R. § 230.506.

28. Rule 507, as interpreted in Securities Act Release No. 6825, March 14, 1989 (17 C.F.R. § 230.507).

29. 17 C.F.R. § 230.147.

30. 17 C.F.R. § 230.251 *et seq.*

31. 17 C.F.R. § 228.10 *et seq.*

32. I.R.C. § 6050K(a).

33. I.R.C. § 6050K(b).

34. Treas. Regs. § 1.351-3.

35. I.R.C. § 1445(a).

Form SS-4 – Application for Employer Identification Number: Sample

Form **SS-4**	**Application for Employer Identification Number**	EIN
(Rev. December 1995)	(For use by employers, corporations, partnerships, trusts, estates, churches, government agencies, certain Individuals, and others. See instructions.)	
Department of the Treasury Internal Revenue Service	▶ Keep a copy for your records.	OMB No. 1545-0003

Please type or print clearly.

1 Name of applicant (Legal name) (See instructions.)

2 Trade name of business (if different from name on line 1)	**3** Executor, trustee, "care of" name
4a Mailing address (street address) (room, apt., or suite no.)	**5a** Business address (if different from address on lines 4a and 4b)
4b City, state, and ZIP code	**5b** City, state, and ZIP code

6 County and state where principal business is located

7 Name of principal officer, general partner, grantor, owner, or trustor—SSN required (See instructions.) ▶

8a Type of entity (Check only one box.) (See instructions.)
- ☐ Sole proprietor (SSN) _____
- ☐ Partnership   ☐ Personal service corp.
- ☐ REMIC   ☐ Limited liability co.
- ☐ State/local government   ☐ National Guard
- ☐ Other nonprofit organization (specify) ▶ _____ (enter GEN if applicable) _____
- ☐ Other (specify) ▶
- ☐ Estate (SSN of decedent) _____
- ☐ Plan administrator-SSN _____
- ☐ Other corporation (specify) ▶
- ☐ Trust   ☐ Farmers' cooperative
- ☐ Federal Government/military   ☐ Church or church-controlled organization

8b If a corporation, name the state or foreign country (if applicable) where incorporated | State | Foreign country

9 Reason for applying (Check only one box.)
- ☐ Started new business (specify) ▶ _____
- ☐ Hired employees
- ☐ Created a pension plan (specify type) ▶
- ☐ Banking purpose (specify) ▶ _____
- ☐ Changed type of organization (specify) ▶ _____
- ☐ Purchased going business
- ☐ Created a trust (specify) ▶ _____
- ☐ Other (specify) ▶

10 Date business started or acquired (Mo., day, year) (See instructions.) | **11** Closing month of accounting year (See instructions.)

12 First date wages or annuities were paid or will be paid (Mo., day, year). **Note:** *If applicant is a withholding agent, enter date income will first be paid to nonresident alien. (Mo., day, year)* ▶

13 Highest number of employees expected in the next 12 months. **Note:** *If the applicant does not expect to have any employees during the period, enter -0-. (See instructions.)* ▶ | Nonagricultural | Agricultural | Household

14 Principal activity (See instructions.) ▶

15 Is the principal business activity manufacturing? . . . . ☐ Yes ☐ No
If "Yes," principal product and raw material used ▶

16 To whom are most of the products or services sold? Please check the appropriate box. ☐ Business (wholesale)
☐ Public (retail)   ☐ Other (specify) ▶   ☐ N/A

17a Has the applicant ever applied for an identification number for this or any other business? . . . . . ☐ Yes ☐ No
Note: *If "Yes," please complete lines 17b and 17c.*

17b If you checked "Yes" on line 17a, give applicant's legal name and trade name shown on prior application, if different from line 1 or 2 above.
Legal name ▶   Trade name ▶

17c Approximate date when and city and state where the application was filed. Enter previous employer identification number if known.
Approximate date when filed (Mo., day, year) | City and state where filed | Previous EIN

Under penalties of perjury, I declare that I have examined this application, and to the best of my knowledge and belief, it is true, correct, and complete. | Business telephone number (include area code)

Fax telephone number (include area code)

Name and title (Please type or print clearly.) ▶

Signature ▶   Date ▶

Note: *Do not write below this line. For official use only.*

Please leave blank ▶	Geo.	Ind.	Class	Size	Reason for applying

For Paperwork Reduction Act Notice, see page 4. | Cat. No. 16055N | Form **SS-4** (Rev. 12-95)

Instructions for Form SS-4: Sample

General Instructions

Section references are to the Internal Revenue Code unless otherwise noted.

Purpose of Form

Use Form SS-4 to apply for an employer identification number (EIN). An EIN is a nine-digit number (for example, 12-3456789) assigned to sole proprietors, corporations, partnerships, estates, trusts, and other entities for filing and reporting purposes. The information you provide on this form will establish your filing and reporting requirements.

Who Must File

You must file this form if you have not obtained an EIN before and:

• You pay wages to one or more employees including household employees.

• You are required to have an EIN to use on any return, statement, or other document, even if you are not an employer.

• You are a withholding agent required to withhold taxes on income, other than wages, paid to a nonresident alien (individual, corporation, partnership, etc.). A withholding agent may be an agent, broker, fiduciary, manager, tenant, or spouse, and is required to file **Form 1042**, Annual Withholding Tax Return for U.S. Source Income of Foreign Persons.

• You file **Schedule C**, Profit or Loss From Business, or **Schedule F**, Profit or Loss From Farming, of **Form 1040**, U.S. Individual Income Tax Return, and have a Keogh plan or are required to file excise, employment, information, or alcohol, tobacco, or firearms returns.

The following must use EINs even if they do not have any employees:

• State and local agencies who serve as tax reporting agents for public assistance recipients, under Rev. Proc. 80-4, 1980-1 C.B. 581, should obtain a separate EIN for this reporting. See **Household employer** on page 3.

• Trusts, except the following:

1. Certain grantor-owned revocable trusts. (See the **Instructions for Form 1041**.)

2. Individual Retirement Arrangement (IRA) trusts, unless the trust has to file **Form 990-T**, Exempt Organization Business Income Tax Return. (See the **Instructions for Form 990-T**.)

3. Certain trusts that are considered household employers can use the trust EIN to report and pay the social security and Medicare taxes, Federal unemployment tax (FUTA) and withheld Federal income tax. A separate EIN is not necessary.

• Estates

• Partnerships

• REMICs (real estate mortgage investment conduits) (See the **Instructions for Form 1066**, U.S. Real Estate Mortgage Investment Conduit Income Tax Return.)

• Corporations

• Nonprofit organizations (churches, clubs, etc.)

• Farmers' cooperatives

• Plan administrators (A plan administrator is the person or group of persons specified as the administrator by the instrument under which the plan is operated.)

When To Apply for a New EIN

New Business.—If you become the new owner of an existing business, **do not** use the EIN of the former owner. IF YOU ALREADY HAVE AN EIN, USE THAT NUMBER. If you do not have an EIN, apply for one on this form. If you become the "owner" of a corporation by acquiring its stock, use the corporation's EIN.

Changes in Organization or Ownership.—If you already have an EIN, you may need to get a new one if either the organization or ownership of your business changes. If you incorporate a sole proprietorship or form a partnership, you must get a new EIN. However, **do not** apply for a new EIN if you change only the name of your business.

Note: *If you are electing to be an "S corporation," be sure you file* **Form 2553,** *Election by a Small Business Corporation.*

File Only One Form SS-4.—File only one Form SS-4, regardless of the number of businesses operated or trade names under which a business operates. However, each corporation in an affiliated group must file a separate application.

EIN Applied For, But Not Received.—If you do not have an EIN by the time a return is due, write "Applied for" and the date you applied in the space shown for the number. **Do not** show your social security number as an EIN on returns.

If you do not have an EIN by the time a tax deposit is due, send your payment to the Internal Revenue Service Center for your filing area. (See **Where To Apply** below.) Make your check or money order payable to Internal Revenue Service and show your name (as shown on Form SS-4), address, type of tax, period covered, and date you applied for an EIN. Send an explanation with the deposit.

For more information about EINs, see **Pub. 583**, Starting a Business and Keeping Records, and **Pub. 1635**, Understanding Your EIN.

How To Apply

You can apply for an EIN either by mail or by telephone. You can get an EIN immediately by calling the Tele-TIN phone number for the service center for your state, or you can send the completed Form SS-4 directly to the service center to receive your EIN in the mail.

Application by Tele-TIN.—Under the Tele-TIN program, you can receive your EIN over the telephone and use it immediately to file a return or make a payment. To receive an EIN by phone, complete Form SS-4, then call the Tele-TIN phone number listed for your state under **Where To Apply.** The person making the call must be authorized to sign the form. (See **Signature block** on page 4.)

An IRS representative will use the information from the Form SS-4 to establish your account and assign you an EIN. Write the number you are given on the upper right-hand corner of the form, sign and date it.

Mail or FAX the signed SS-4 **within 24 hours** *to the Tele-TIN Unit at the service center address for your state.* The IRS representative will give you the FAX number. The FAX numbers are also listed in Pub. 1635.

Taxpayer representatives can receive their client's EIN by phone if they first send a facsimile (FAX) of a completed **Form 2848**, Power of Attorney and Declaration of Representative, or **Form 8821**, Tax Information Authorization, to the Tele-TIN unit. The Form 2848 or Form 8821 will be used solely to release the EIN to the representative authorized on the form.

Application by Mail.—Complete Form SS-4 at least 4 to 5 weeks before you will need an EIN. Sign and date the application and mail it to the service center address for your state. You will receive your EIN in the mail in approximately 4 weeks.

Where To Apply

The Tele-TIN phone numbers listed below will involve a long-distance charge to callers outside of the local calling area and can be used only to apply for an EIN. THE NUMBERS MAY CHANGE WITHOUT NOTICE. Use 1-800-829-1040 to verify a number or to ask about an application by mail or other Federal tax matters.

If your principal business, office or agency, or legal residence in the case of an individual, is located in:	Call the Tele-TIN phone number shown or file with the Internal Revenue Service Center at:
Florida, Georgia, South Carolina	Attn: Entity Control Atlanta, GA 39901 (404) 455-2360
New Jersey, New York City and counties of Nassau, Rockland, Suffolk, and Westchester	Attn: Entity Control Holtsville, NY 00501 (516) 447-4955
New York (all other counties), Connecticut, Maine, Massachusetts, New Hampshire, Rhode Island, Vermont	Attn: Entity Control Andover, MA 05501 (508) 474-9717
Illinois, Iowa, Minnesota, Missouri, Wisconsin	Attn: Entity Control Stop 57A 2306 E. Bannister Rd. Kansas City, MO 64131 (816) 926-5999
Delaware, District of Columbia, Maryland, Pennsylvania, Virginia	Attn: Entity Control Philadelphia, PA 19255 (215) 574-2400
Indiana, Kentucky, Michigan, Ohio, West Virginia	Attn: Entity Control Cincinnati, OH 45999 (606) 292-5467
Kansas, New Mexico, Oklahoma, Texas	Attn: Entity Control Austin, TX 73301 (512) 460-7843

Instructions for Form SS-4: Sample (continued)

Form SS-4 (Rev. 12-95)   Page **3**

Alaska, Arizona, California
(counties of Alpine, Amador,
Butte, Calaveras, Colusa, Contra
Costa, Del Norte, El Dorado,
Glenn, Humboldt, Lake, Lassen,
Marin, Mendocino, Modoc,   Attn: Entity Control
Napa, Nevada, Placer, Plumas,   Mail Stop 6271-T
Sacramento, San Joaquin,   P.O. Box 9950
Shasta, Sierra, Siskiyou, Solano,   Ogden, UT 84409
Sonoma, Sutter, Tehama, Trinity,   (801) 620-7645
Yolo, and Yuba), Colorado,
Idaho, Montana, Nebraska,
Nevada, North Dakota, Oregon,
South Dakota, Utah,
Washington, Wyoming

California (all other   Attn: Entity Control
counties), Hawaii   Fresno, CA 93888
                                                     (209) 452-4010

Alabama, Arkansas,   Attn: Entity Control
Louisiana, Mississippi,   Memphis, TN 37501
North Carolina, Tennessee   (901) 365-5970

If you have no legal residence, principal place of business, or principal office or agency in any state, file your form with the Internal Revenue Service Center, Philadelphia, PA 19255 or call 215-574-2400.

Specific Instructions

The instructions that follow are for those items that are not self-explanatory. Enter N/A (nonapplicable) on the lines that do not apply.

Line 1.—Enter the legal name of the entity applying for the EIN exactly as it appears on the social security card, charter, or other applicable legal document.

Individuals.—Enter the first name, middle initial, and last name. If you are a sole proprietor, enter your individual name, not your business name. Do not use abbreviations or nicknames.

Trusts.—Enter the name of the trust.

Estate of a decedent.—Enter the name of the estate.

Partnerships.—Enter the legal name of the partnership as it appears in the partnership agreement. **Do not** list the names of the partners on line 1. See the specific instructions for line 7.

Corporations.—Enter the corporate name as it appears in the corporation charter or other legal document creating it.

Plan administrators.—Enter the name of the plan administrator. A plan administrator who already has an EIN should use that number.

Line 2.—Enter the trade name of the business if different from the legal name. The trade name is the "doing business as" name.

Note: *Use the full legal name on line 1 on all tax returns filed for the entity. However, if you enter a trade name on line 2 and choose to use the trade name instead of the legal name, enter the trade name on all returns you file. To prevent processing delays and errors,* **always** *use either the legal name only or the trade name only on all tax returns.*

Line 3.—Trusts enter the name of the trustee. Estates enter the name of the executor, administrator, or other fiduciary. If the entity applying has a designated person to receive tax information, enter that person's name as the "care of"

person. Print or type the first name, middle initial, and last name.

Line 7.—Enter the first name, middle initial, last name, and social security number (SSN) of a principal officer if the business is a corporation; of a general partner if a partnership; or of a grantor, owner, or trustor if a trust.

Line 8a.—Check the box that best describes the type of entity applying for the EIN. If not specifically mentioned, check the "Other" box and enter the type of entity. Do not enter N/A.

Sole proprietor.—Check this box if you file Schedule C or F (Form 1040) and have a Keogh plan, or are required to file excise, employment, information, or alcohol, tobacco, or firearms returns. Enter your SSN in the space provided.

REMIC.—Check this box if the entity has elected to be treated as a real estate mortgage investment conduit (REMIC). See the **Instructions for Form 1066** for more information.

Other nonprofit organization.—Check this box if the nonprofit organization is other than a church or church-controlled organization and specify the type of nonprofit organization (for example, an educational organization).

If the organization also seeks tax-exempt status, you must file either **Package 1023** or **Package 1024,** Application for Recognition of Exemption. Get **Pub. 557,** Tax-Exempt Status for Your Organization, for more information.

Group exemption number (GEN).—If the organization is covered by a group exemption letter, enter the four-digit GEN. (Do not confuse the GEN with the nine-digit EIN.) If you do not know the GEN, contact the parent organization. Get Pub. 557 for more information about group exemption numbers.

Withholding agent.—If you are a withholding agent required to file Form 1042, check the "Other" box and enter "Withholding agent."

Personal service corporation.—Check this box if the entity is a personal service corporation. An entity is a personal service corporation for a tax year only if:

● The principal activity of the entity during the testing period (prior tax year) for the tax year is the performance of personal services substantially by employee-owners, and

● The employee-owners own 10% of the fair market value of the outstanding stock in the entity on the last day of the testing period.

Personal services include performance of services in such fields as health, law, accounting, or consulting. For more information about personal service corporations, see the **Instructions for Form 1120,** U.S. Corporation Income Tax Return, and **Pub. 542,** Tax Information on Corporations.

Limited liability co.—See the definition of limited liability company in the **Instructions for Form 1065.** If you are classified as a partnership for Federal income tax

purposes, mark the "Limited liability co." checkbox. If you are classified as a corporation for Federal income tax purposes, mark the "Other corporation" checkbox and write "Limited liability co." in the space provided.

Plan administrator.—If the plan administrator is an individual, enter the plan administrator's SSN in the space provided.

Other corporation.—This box is for any corporation other than a personal service corporation. If you check this box, enter the type of corporation (such as insurance company) in the space provided.

Household employer.—If you are an individual, check the "Other" box and enter "Household employer" and your SSN. If you are a state or local agency serving as a tax reporting agent for public assistance recipients who become household employers, check the "Other" box and enter "Household employer agent." If you are a trust that qualifies as a household employer, you do not need a separate EIN for reporting tax information relating to household employees; use the EIN of the trust.

Line 9.—Check only **one** box. Do not enter N/A.

Started new business.—Check this box if you are starting a new business that requires an EIN. If you check this box, enter the type of business being started. **Do not** apply if you already have an EIN and are only adding another place of business.

Hired employees.—Check this box if the existing business is requesting an EIN because it has hired or is hiring employees and is therefore required to file employment tax returns. **Do not** apply if you already have an EIN and are only hiring employees. For information on the applicable employment taxes for family members, see **Circular E,** Employer's Tax Guide (Publication 15).

Created a pension plan.—Check this box if you have created a pension plan and need this number for reporting purposes. Also, enter the type of plan created.

Banking purpose.—Check this box if you are requesting an EIN for banking purposes only, and enter the banking purpose (for example, a bowling league for depositing dues or an investment club for dividend and interest reporting).

Changed type of organization.—Check this box if the business is changing its type of organization, for example, if the business was a sole proprietorship and has been incorporated or has become a partnership. If you check this box, specify in the space provided the type of change made, for example, "from sole proprietorship to partnership."

Purchased going business.—Check this box if you purchased an existing business. **Do not** use the former owner's EIN. **Do not** apply for a new EIN if you already have one. Use your own EIN.

Created a trust.—Check this box if you created a trust, and enter the type of trust created.

Instructions for Form SS-4: Sample (continued)

Note: *Do not file this form if you are the grantor/owner of certain revocable trusts. You must use your SSN for the trust. See the Instructions for Form 1041.*

Other (specify).—Check this box if you are requesting an EIN for any reason other than those for which there are checkboxes, and enter the reason.

Line 10.—If you are starting a new business, enter the starting date of the business. If the business you acquired is already operating, enter the date you acquired the business. Trusts should enter the date the trust was legally created. Estates should enter the date of death of the decedent whose name appears on line 1 or the date when the estate was legally funded.

Line 11.—Enter the last month of your accounting year or tax year. An accounting or tax year is usually 12 consecutive months, either a calendar year or a fiscal year (including a period of 52 or 53 weeks). A calendar year is 12 consecutive months ending on December 31. A fiscal year is either 12 consecutive months ending on the last day of any month other than December or a 52-53 week year. For more information on accounting periods, see **Pub. 538**, Accounting Periods and Methods.

Individuals.—Your tax year generally will be a calendar year.

Partnerships.—Partnerships generally must adopt the tax year of either (a) the majority partners; (b) the principal partners; (c) the tax year that results in the least aggregate (total) deferral of income; or (d) some other tax year. (See the **Instructions for Form 1065**, U.S. Partnership Return of Income, for more information.)

REMIC.—REMICs must have a calendar year as their tax year.

Personal service corporations.—A personal service corporation generally must adopt a calendar year unless:

● It can establish a business purpose for having a different tax year, or
● It elects under section 444 to have a tax year other than a calendar year.

Trusts.—Generally, a trust must adopt a calendar year except for the following:

● Tax-exempt trusts,
● Charitable trusts, and
● Grantor-owned trusts.

Line 12.—If the business has or will have employees, enter the date on which the business began or will begin to pay wages. If the business does not plan to have employees, enter N/A.

Withholding agent.—Enter the date you began or will begin to pay income to a nonresident alien. This also applies to individuals who are required to file Form 1042 to report alimony paid to a nonresident alien.

Line 13.—For a definition of agricultural labor (farmworker), see **Circular A**, Agricultural Employer's Tax Guide (Publication 51).

Line 14.—Generally, enter the exact type of business being operated (for example, advertising agency, farm, food or beverage establishment, labor union, real estate agency, steam laundry, rental of coin-operated vending machine, or investment club). Also state if the business will involve the sale or distribution of alcoholic beverages.

Governmental.—Enter the type of organization (state, county, school district, municipality, etc.).

Nonprofit organization (other than governmental).—Enter whether organized for religious, educational, or humane purposes, and the principal activity (for example, religious organization—hospital, charitable).

Mining and quarrying.—Specify the process and the principal product (for example, mining bituminous coal, contract drilling for oil, or quarrying dimension stone).

Contract construction.—Specify whether general contracting or special trade contracting. Also, show the type of work normally performed (for example, general contractor for residential buildings or electrical subcontractor).

Food or beverage establishments.—Specify the type of establishment and state whether you employ workers who receive tips (for example, lounge—yes).

Trade.—Specify the type of sales and the principal line of goods sold (for example, wholesale dairy products, manufacturer's representative for mining machinery, or retail hardware).

Manufacturing.—Specify the type of establishment operated (for example, sawmill or vegetable cannery).

Signature block.—The application must be signed by (a) the individual, if the applicant is an individual, (b) the president, vice president, or other principal officer, if the applicant is a corporation, (c) a responsible and duly authorized member or officer having knowledge of its affairs, if the applicant is a partnership or other unincorporated organization, or (d) the fiduciary, if the applicant is a trust or estate.

Some Useful Publications

You may get the following publications for additional information on the subjects covered on this form. To get these and other free forms and publications, call 1-800-TAX-FORM (1-800-829-3676). You should receive your order or notification of its status within 7 to 15 workdays of your call.

Use your computer.—If you subscribe to an on-line service, ask if IRS information is available and, if so, how to access it. You can also get information through IRIS, the Internal Revenue Information Services, on FedWorld, a government bulletin board. Tax forms, instructions, publications, and other IRS information, are available through IRIS.

IRIS is accessible directly by calling 703-321-8020. On the Internet, you can telnet to fedworld.gov. or, for file transfer protocol services, connect to ftp.fedworld.gov. If you are using the WorldWide Web, connect to http://www.ustreas.gov

FedWorld's help desk offers technical assistance on accessing IRIS (not tax help) during regular business hours at 703-487-4608. The IRIS menus offer information on available file formats and software needed to read and print files. You must print the forms to use them; the forms are not designed to be filled out on-screen.

Tax forms, instructions, and publications are also available on CD-ROM, including prior-year forms starting with the 1991 tax year. For ordering information and software requirements, contact the Government Printing Office's Superintendent of Documents (202-512-1800) or Federal Bulletin Board (202-512-1387).

Pub. 1635, Understanding Your EIN

Pub. 15, Employer's Tax Guide

Pub. 15-A, Employer's Supplemental Tax Guide

Pub. 538, Accounting Periods and Methods

Pub. 541, Tax Information on Partnerships

Pub. 542, Tax Information on Corporations

Pub. 557, Tax-Exempt Status for Your Organization

Pub. 583, Starting a Business and Keeping Records

Package 1023, Application for Recognition of Exemption

Package 1024, Application for Recognition of Exemption Under Section 501(a) or for Determination Under Section 120

Paperwork Reduction Act Notice

We ask for the information on this form to carry out the Internal Revenue laws of the United States. You are required to give us the information. We need it to ensure that you are complying with these laws and to allow us to figure and collect the right amount of tax.

The time needed to complete and file this form will vary depending on individual circumstances. The estimated average time is:

Recordkeeping . . . . . . 7 min.
Learning about the law or the form . . . . . . 18 min.
Preparing the form . . . . . 45 min.
Copying, assembling, and sending the form to the IRS . 20 min.

If you have comments concerning the accuracy of these time estimates or suggestions for making this form simpler, we would be happy to hear from you. You can write to the Tax Forms Committee, Western Area Distribution Center, Rancho Cordova, CA 95743-0001. **Do not send this form to this address. Instead, see Where To Apply** on page 2.

*U.S. Government Printing Office: 1996 - 405-493/40061

Chapter 5

The Thicket Thickens: Additional Requirements for Businesses with Employees

*Man is a thinking animal, a talking animal, a tool-making animal,
a building animal, a political animal, a fantasizing animal. But in
the twilight of a civilization, he is chiefly a taxpaying animal.*

— Hugh MacLennan

5.1 General Considerations

As the previous chapter indicated, there is a considerable amount of governmental red tape involved in starting almost any new business. If your business will have any employees — even if it is incorporated and you are the only employee — the level of government regulation and red tape will multiply several times over in a typical case. This chapter outlines the bases you must cover, in addition to those described in Chapter 4, if you start a business that will have employees.

5.2 Social Security and Income Tax Withholding

Once you go into business and begin paying salary or wages to employees, you will find that you have been appointed, as an agent of the government, to collect taxes from your employees. In addition to paying various payroll taxes, you will also be required to collect income taxes and Social Security (FICA) tax, which includes the Medicare tax, from employees' wages.

The first order of business is to apply for a federal employer identification number (EIN) with the IRS. This number will be used to identify

Employer Identification Number

your business on payroll and income tax returns and for most other federal tax purposes. To apply for an EIN number, file a completed *Form SS-4* at the earliest possible time, especially if you have employees. This ensures you will receive tax deposit coupons in time for depositing federal payroll taxes or corporate income tax. Corporations and partnerships must file *Form SS-4* even if they have no employees. A sample of this form is located at the end of Chapter 4.

The IRS can provide you with a business tax kit that is specifically put together for new employers. You can also obtain *Circular E, Employer's Tax Guide*, an IRS publication that explains federal income tax withholding and Social Security tax requirements for employers. *Circular E* contains up-to-date withholding tables that you must use to determine how much federal income tax and Social Security tax is to be withheld from each employee's paycheck.

Employer Social Security Tax

In addition to withholding Social Security tax from an employee's paycheck — at the rate of 7.65% on gross wages up to $65,400, 1.45% on wages in excess of $65,400 in 1997 — the employer must also pay an equal amount of employer's Social Security tax. The withheld federal income tax, withheld employee Social Security tax, and employer's Social Security tax are lumped together and paid to the IRS at the same time. In some cases, these taxes can simply be mailed in with your payroll tax return (*Form 941* series) at the end of the calendar quarter or year; however, if you have significant amounts of these taxes to pay, you will generally be required to deposit the taxes with a federal tax deposit form, a precoded coupon, at an authorized commercial bank or a federal reserve bank. As a rule, the greater the amount of taxes due, the sooner they must be paid.

The complex tax deposit deadlines of previous years have been totally revised and considerably simplified and revised under recent IRS regulations. Rules for how and when federal income and Social Security taxes are to be mailed in or deposited are summarized briefly as follows:

Type of Depositor	Deadline
Small depositor — An employer with less than $500 of combined income and Social Security taxes for the calendar quarter.[1]	Deposit by last day of month following the end of the quarter, or mail with *Form 941* return by then.
Monthly depositor — An employer, who for the 12-month period ending June 30th of the preceding calendar year, reported $50,000 or less of employment taxes.[2]	Deposit by 15th day of the following month.
Semi-weekly depositor — All other employers:[3] For Wednesday–Friday semi-weekly period: For Saturday–Tuesday semi-weekly period:	Deposit on or before next Wednesday. Deposit on or before next Friday.

Some exceptions to the above tax deposit schedules do exist. For example, any employer with $100,000 of employment taxes accumulated at the end of any day — for the current month or semi-weekly period only, whichever applies — must deposit those taxes in an authorized bank by the end of the next banking day, subsequently becoming a semi-weekly depositor.[4] Shortfalls in required deposits will result in underpayment penalties. No penalty, however, will be imposed if the shortfall does not exceed 2% of the required deposit (or $100, if greater) provided the shortfall is made up within specified periods. For a more detailed explanation of federal tax deposits, see IRS *Notice 109*. Deposits of payroll and withholding taxes may be mailed to a depository bank if postmarked at least two days before the tax deposit due date. But tax deposits of $20,000 or more by employers making more than one deposit a month must reach the bank by the due date, regardless of the postmark date.[5]

Electronic Funds Transfers

The IRS is gradually shifting over to electronic funds transfers (EFTs) as a mode of payment, in place of the tax deposit system described above. Taxpayers will eventually be required to remit withholding, payroll, excise, corporate income, and certain other taxes by EFT payment, either directly, or by means of an intermediary, third-party bulk data processor. The EFT payment requirements began phasing in on January 1, 1995, for certain large employers. Smaller employers, who are not yet required to make EFT remittances, do have the option of making EFT payments.

The applicable effective dates for phase-in of EFT requirements are as follows, based on the "threshold amount" of combined FICA and income tax withholding in the "determination period":

Threshold Amount	Determination Period	Applicable Effective Date
$78 million	1-1-93 to 12-31-93	Jan. 1, 1995
47 million	1-1-93 to 12-31-93	Jan. 1, 1996
47 million	1-1-94 to 12-31-94	Jan. 1, 1996
50 thousand	1-1-95 to 12-31-95	July 1, 1998
50 thousand	1-1-96 to 12-31-96	July 1, 1998
20 thousand	1-1-97 to 12-31-97	Jan. 1, 1999[6]

Employers with less than $20,000 of annual FICA and federal income tax wage withholding will apparently not be required to make EFT payments.

To implement the new EFT system, the IRS has developed the Taxlink system, which uses the same Automated Clearing House (ACH) network that was already in place for such items as Social Security and veterans benefits payments and automatic loan payments. Since all but the smallest employers will be required to participate in the EFT payment system by 1999, you may want to sign up and participate in Taxlink voluntarily, before you are required to do so.

Taxlink permits EFT payments to be made directly from a taxpayer's bank account to the U.S. Treasury's general account, either by telephone or computer, using one of two payment options: ACH debit or ACH credit. Both payment options require payments to be made one day before the tax payment due date. The ACH debit option allows you to pay either by voice response, voice operator, personal computer, or point-of-sale equipment. The ACH credit option allows you to pay by arranging with your bank or other financial institution to initiate an ACH credit to the IRS.

To enroll in Taxlink, request enrollment forms by writing to:

IRS Atlanta Service Center
Cash Management Site Office – Stop 295
P.O. Box 47669
Doraville, GA 30362

New Employees

When a new employee is hired, give the employee a federal *Form W-4*. He or she must then complete and return the form to you. When completed, *Form W-4* provides the employee's Social Security number and the number of withholding exemptions the employee is claiming.

The number of exemptions is used to determine how much income tax you must withhold from his or her wages. You keep *Form W-4*. Neither it nor the information on it is filed with the IRS, except in the case of an employee who claims more than ten withholding exemptions, or who claims exemption from income tax withholding.

By January 31 of each year, you must furnish each employee with copies of *Form W-2, Annual Wage and Tax Statement*, showing the taxable wages paid to an employee during the preceding calendar year and the taxes withheld, including state income tax. By February 28, the original of *Form W-2* and a summary form, *Form W-3*, should be filed with the IRS.

Nonpayroll Withholding

In addition to FICA and income tax withholding from wages that are required of employers, businesses are sometimes required to withhold income taxes with regard to nonpayroll payments, such as:

- Withholding on certain gambling winnings;
- Withholding on annuities, pensions, IRAs, and certain other payments of deferred income; and
- Backup withholding on certain reportable payments, when required by the IRS.[7]

The time for depositing these taxes is based on your status as a monthly or semi-weekly depositor under the payroll tax rules. However, a "small depositor" for payroll taxes is treated as a monthly depositor for nonpayroll taxes withheld. Beginning in 1996, deposits of nonpayroll taxes are required monthly if the amount of such withheld tax in the second preceding year (1994, in the case of 1996) was $50,000 or less. Otherwise, such taxes must generally be deposited on a semi-weekly basis in 1996 and subsequent years.

Taxpayers required to withhold nonpayroll income taxes must now report this withholding on IRS *Form 945, Annual Return of Withheld Income Tax*, rather than on the *Form 941* that is used to report payroll tax withholding.

Independent Contractors

A person who performs services for your business does not necessarily have to be your employee. In many cases, you can structure your legal relationships with persons who provide services to you so they are considered independent contractors for tax and other legal purposes. From an employer standpoint, it is preferable to treat someone as an independent contractor rather than as an employee of your business because you do not have to pay Social Security tax or federal or state unemployment taxes on his or her compensation. An independent contractor is considered to be self-employed for tax purposes and pays self-employment tax.

In addition, you don't have to withhold income and payroll taxes from compensation paid to independent contractors or file payroll tax returns with respect to their compensation. You must, however, file a *Form 1099-MISC* for each independent contractor to whom you make payments of $600 or more during a calendar year (with certain exceptions) or, in the case of a direct seller of consumer goods, for each such direct seller to whom you sell $5,000 of goods during a year.

Because of the obvious advantages employers obtain by treating their employees as independent contractors, the IRS has been very aggressive in attempting to reclassify so-called independent contractors as employees where they perform functions in a manner that is more typical of an employer/employee relationship. Requiring businesses to file *Form 1099-MISC* is an attempt by the IRS to identify those businesses that may be improperly treating employees as independent contractors.

Before you decide to treat anyone who works for you as an independent contractor, consult your tax adviser because there can be serious consequences if those individuals are reclassified as employees by the IRS. See Section 9.11 for a discussion of the risks involved.

Each state has its own withholding taxes. For information on the withholding tax requirements for this state, refer to your accountant.

5.3 Unemployment Taxes

With relatively few exceptions, all businesses with employees must pay both federal and state unemployment taxes. These taxes are imposed entirely on you, the employer. Theoretically, the federal unemployment tax is 6.2% of the first $7,000 of annual wages per employee.[8] In actuality, however, the rate is usually only 0.8% because a credit for up to 5.4% is given for state unemployment taxes paid and for a favorable experience rating for state unemployment tax purposes.[9]

The state unemployment tax rate for an employer can be either more or less than the standard new employer rate, depending upon the amount of unemployment claims by former employees. The more unemployment benefits your former employees claim, the higher your unemployment tax rate will be, within certain limits.

Federal Unemployment Tax

Your business will be required to pay federal unemployment tax (FUTA) for any calendar year in which it pays wages of $1,500 or more[10] or if it has one or more employees for at least a portion of the day during any 20 calendar weeks during the year.[11] Needless to say, this will cover almost any business that has one employee, even if that employee is part-time.

If the FUTA liability during any of the first three calendar quarters is more than $100, you must deposit the tax with a federal tax deposit coupon, *Form 8109*, at an authorized bank during the month following the end of the quarter. If the tax is $100 or less, you are not required to make a deposit, but you must add it to the taxes for the next quarter. For the fourth quarter, if the undeposited FUTA tax for the year is more than $100, deposit the tax with a tax deposit coupon at an authorized bank by January 31. If the balance due is $100 or less, either deposit it with the coupon or mail it to the IRS with your federal unemployment tax return, *Form 940*, by January 31. *Form 940* is not due until February 10 if all of the FUTA tax for the prior year has already been deposited when due.

**Simplified Filing for
Small Employers**

The IRS also provides *Form 940-EZ*, a greatly simplified FUTA return for certain small employers. In general, the small employers who can use *Form 940-EZ* are those:

- Who pay unemployment tax to only one state;
- Who pay state unemployment taxes by the *Form 940-EZ* due date; and
- Whose wages subject to FUTA are also taxable for state unemployment tax purposes.

The state also imposes an unemployment tax that meshes closely with the federal unemployment tax. Refer to Section 11.5 for details on state unemployment taxes, rates, returns, and registration as an employer.

5.4 Workers' Compensation Insurance

A business is generally required by state law to obtain workers' compensation insurance for its employees. This means that you, as an employer, may have to immediately seek out and obtain a workers' compensation insurance policy covering all your employees, or you will be subject to possible legal sanctions. Workers' compensation insurance coverage provides various benefits to an employee who suffers a job-related injury or illness.

Many insurance companies offer workers' compensation coverage, though many may be reluctant to write a policy that covers only one or a few employees, unless it is tied to other types of insurance policies. See Section 11.5 for a description of other formal requirements applicable to employers under the workers' compensation laws in this state.

5.5 Compliance with ERISA — Employee Benefit Plans

If you have employees and provide them with fringe benefits, such as group insurance — other than workers' compensation — or other types of employee welfare plan benefits, or if you adopt a pension or profit-sharing retirement plan, you will almost certainly have to comply with at least some aspects of the Employee Retirement Income Security Act of 1974 (ERISA). There are criminal penalties for willful failure to comply with two types of ERISA requirements: 1) reporting to government agencies, and 2) disclosure to employees.[12] In addition, a number of different types of civil penalties apply, which are incredibly numerous and complex, for unintentional failures to comply with ERISA requirements.[13] In short, compliance with ERISA is not a simple matter.

This section lays down some relatively simple and straightforward guidelines you, as a layperson, can follow in trying to recognize when you might have an ERISA compliance obligation. If you recognize your need to be in compliance, call your attorney, accountant, or benefit consultant for help. ERISA deals with two kinds of employee benefit plans: pension plans and welfare plans.

Pension Plans

Pension plans under ERISA are pretty much what you might expect — tax qualified retirement plans, including both pension and profit-sharing plans (including Keogh plans), plus other types of benefit programs that defer payments until after employment has terminated.[14]

Because these compliance requirements are so very complex and are constantly in a state of flux, no attempt to spell them out in detail is made here. Instead, the basic ERISA compliance requirements for most pension and profit-sharing plans are summarized in the table located at the end of this chapter.

If your business maintains a pension or profit-sharing plan, it should be obvious from this summary of basic ERISA compliance requirements that you need some expert help from an attorney, accountant, or pension consulting firm — or all of them — if you are going to be able to properly comply with the requirements of ERISA and avoid potential fines and other civil and criminal penalties.

The cost of maintaining these plans has unfortunately multiplied several times over since the passage of ERISA in 1974, followed by a labyrinth of ERISA regulations issued by several different federal agencies. In short, unless you make substantial contributions to and obtain significant tax savings from an employee retirement plan, it may not be worth having because of the heavy costs of compliance with ERISA.

Welfare Plans

Welfare plans under ERISA include most other types of employee benefit plans that are not considered pension plans.[15] These include typical fringe benefit plans adopted by small firms, such as health insurance, long-term disability, group-term life insurance, and accidental death insurance plans. ERISA compliance for welfare plans is usually less of a burden than for pension plans, but is required for almost every business that provides any kind of benefits for employees of the type mentioned above.

A number of so-called fringe benefits that are in the nature of payroll practices, such as paid holidays, vacation pay, bonuses, overtime premium pay, and most kinds of severance pay arrangements, are usually not considered to be either pension or welfare plans under ERISA.[16] Thus, these kinds of payroll practices are not subject to ERISA at all. Compliance requirements for reporting and disclosure under ERISA are briefly discussed below.

Summary Plan Descriptions

The one ERISA compliance requirement that applies to most small businesses is the requirement for you to prepare a summary plan description (SPD) for distribution to all employees covered by any type of welfare plan you sponsor, such as typical health, accident, life, or disability insurance plans.[17] An SPD must contain more than 20 specific items of information listed in the U.S. Department of Labor Regulations,[18] including an ERISA rights statement, which must be copied more or less verbatim from the regulations.

An SPD must be prepared for each plan and distributed to covered employees within 120 days after the plan is first adopted.[19] Each new employee must be given a copy of the SPD within 90 days after becoming a participant in the plan.[20] Since an SPD must be prepared for each employee plan subject to ERISA, even a very small business may find that it has to produce three or four of these documents, each of which must meet detailed technical requirements.

One important consideration in taking out insurance coverage for employees should be a firm commitment from the insurance company or brokers that they will prepare the necessary SPDs for the insurance plans they are selling you. Otherwise, you may need to have your attorney or benefit consultant prepare the SPDs, which can result in substantial professional fees.

Other than the need for you to prepare SPDs and distribute them to employees, there are no significant ERISA requirements that apply to most kinds of insured-type welfare plans that cover fewer than 100 employees.[21] You must, however, make available the insurance policies and other plan documents for inspection by your employees and you must furnish copies to them upon request.[22]

Additional ERISA Requirements

If your business should grow to have 100 or more employees who are covered by a plan, or if you adopt any type of uninsured funded welfare plan, you will suddenly become subject to a whole array of additional ERISA requirements, including:

- Providing to the U.S. Department of Labor, upon request (within 30 days), a copy of the SPD and, if any, a summary of material modifications to the plan;[23]
- Filing an annual return/report or registration (*Form 5500* series) with the IRS each year;[24]

- Preparing and distributing a summary annual report to covered employees each year;[25]
- Preparing a summary of material modifications of the plan if necessary, and distributing it to covered employees;[26] and
- Filing a terminal report if the plan is terminated.[27]

Besides the ERISA reporting and disclosure requirements listed in the summary at the end of this chapter, you should be aware of two other points regarding ERISA: the bonding requirement and withholding requirements on pension or profit-sharing plan distributions. If any of your employees are deemed to handle assets of an employee benefit plan that is subject to ERISA, they must be covered by a fidelity bond.[28] Consult your attorney or benefit consultant to determine if you must cover your employees with a fidelity bond in regard to any benefit plans you maintain for your employees. This is particularly important if you have a pension or profit-sharing plan.

Withholding is mandatory on distributions of pension, profit-sharing, and IRA benefits.[29] However, there is an exception for certain periodic distributions on which the recipient elects, in advance, not to have any tax withheld.

In addition to reporting and disclosure requirements under ERISA, there are other federal reporting and recordkeeping requirements for certain types of fringe benefit plans.[30] For example, employers maintaining educational assistance programs and so-called cafeteria plans will be required to file annual reports with the IRS — once the IRS prescribes the forms — and, if needed, to maintain records to show that those plans qualified for tax purposes for each year after 1984.[31]

5.6 Employee Safety and Health Regulations

As has been discussed in Section 5.4, employers are required by state law in many states to carry workers' compensation insurance for the protection of employees who develop job-related illnesses or who are injured on the job. In addition, comprehensive and far-reaching federal laws set safety standards designed to prevent injuries arising from unsafe or unhealthy working conditions. The primary federal law regulating job safety, the Occupational Safety and Health Act of 1970 (OSHA), imposes several reporting and recordkeeping obligations for employers.

Over the years, the Occupational Safety and Health Administration has issued reams of regulations and standards for workplace safety. If you have employees, you will need to consult an attorney, preferably one with OSHA expertise, to determine what, if any, steps you must take to comply with federal and state safety standards at your place of business.

Otherwise, you may be subject to fines and other legal sanctions if any employee is injured on the job or OSHA inspectors find that you are not in compliance with applicable safety standards at your place of business. OSHA has recently begun sending out mandatory employer surveys to help target high-risk employers for inspections.

You can also contact the nearest regional U.S. Department of Labor – OSHA office to request information on any free consultative services or publications the office may have available. Many state occupational safety and health agencies provide confidential, on-site consultations for no charge. These consultations point out state compliance issues at your place of business without fining or penalizing you for any discovered violations. You may also request a federal OSHA consultation, but you will be cited for any violations.

Notice to Employees

OSHA requires that you post a permanent notice to employees regarding job safety.[32]

Recordkeeping Requirements

Under OSHA, it is necessary to keep a log of industrial injuries and illnesses.[33] Records maintained under an approved state OSHA plan can be used to satisfy this federal requirement.[34] The information in the log must also be summarized and posted prominently in your workplace from February 1 to March 1.[35] This requirement has been eliminated for most retail, financial, insurance, and service firms,[36] but not for:

- Building material and garden supply stores;
- General merchandise stores;
- Food stores;
- Hotels and other lodging places;
- Repair, amusement, and recreation services; and
- Health services.[37]

Under OSHA, a supplementary record must be prepared after a recordable injury or illness occurs, using federal *Form 101* or any of the substitutes state law permits to be used for this purpose.[38] These recordkeeping forms are not ordinarily filed with the government, but these records must be retained and kept available for inspection for five years.[39] In addition, special recordkeeping requirements will generally apply if your employees are exposed to toxic substances, asbestos, radiation, or carcinogens on the job.

You can obtain more detailed information on OSHA recordkeeping requirements by calling the nearest OSHA office — usually listed in the phone book under U. S. Government – Department of Labor — and asking for the booklet entitled, *Recordkeeping Requirements for Occupational Injuries and Illnesses*.

Exemption from Recordkeeping

OSHA exempts any employer with ten or fewer employees from most of its reporting and recordkeeping requirements; however, these small employers are not exempt from keeping a log of all injuries and accidents or reporting job-related fatalities and multiple injuries.[40]

Federal OSHA reporting requirements include:

Reporting Requirements

- The Bureau of Labor Statistics may require certain selected employers, including small employers, to report certain summary information on job-related injuries and illnesses annually on an occupational injuries and illness survey form.[41]
- In the event of a fatality or an accident resulting in the hospitalization of three or more employees, you must notify the area OSHA director within eight hours, describing the circumstances of the accident, the extent of any injuries, the number of fatalities, and other information.[42] There are penalties in the event you fail to give notice as required.[43]

See Section 11.5 for a discussion of laws this state may have that govern employee safety and health.

5.7 Employee Wage-Hour and Child Labor Laws

Not all businesses nor all employees of a given business are covered by federal and state wage-hour and child labor laws. The coverage of these laws is a crazy quilt patchwork of exceptions. Thus, there is no simple way to tell you whether your business will be subject to one or more of the federal and state laws relating to minimum wage, overtime pay, and child labor, or, if it is, which employees are covered and which are not.

To find out which laws apply to your business, contact your attorney or the local wage-hour office.

The Federal Fair Labor Standards Act (FLSA) includes a number of requirements regarding compensation of employees covered under the act. There are two major requirements you need to know about — the minimum wage and overtime pay requirements.

Federal Wage-Hour Laws

The minimum wage provisions of the FLSA set an hourly minimum wage that you must pay to an employee. The current federal minimum wage has been increased from $4.75 to $5.15 an hour on September 1, 1997.[44] An employer may continue to pay new employees under age 20 at a rate of $4.25 an hour for the first 90 days of employment.

Minimum Wage Requirement

Certain states provide for a minimum wage in excess of the federal requirement while other states have either no minimum wage or a rate that is less than the federal standard. Exemptions vary from state to state. Refer to Section 11.5 for the requirements in this state.

Overtime Pay Requirement

The overtime pay requirement rule states you must pay a covered employee at one and one-half times the employee's regular hourly rate for any hours worked in excess of 40 in a week.[45] The regular hourly rate cannot be less than the minimum wage.

For the overtime pay requirement, the FLSA takes a single workweek as its measuring period and does not permit averaging of hours over two or more weeks. For example, if an employee works 30 hours one week and 50 hours during the next, he or she must receive overtime compensation (time and one-half) for the 10 overtime hours worked in the second week, even though the average number of hours worked during each of the two weeks is 40.

Note that the FLSA only requires overtime pay based on the number of hours worked during a week and not just for working long hours on a particular day.

The above rules generally apply to salaried workers as well as to those paid on an hourly basis. To determine the regular hourly rate for a salaried employee, it is necessary to divide the employee's weekly salary by the number of hours in his or her regular workweek (40 or less).

Employee Exemptions

Executives, administrators, professionals, and outside salespeople are not covered by federal wage-hour laws and thus are not entitled by law to a minimum wage or to any pay for overtime hours worked. A 1996 law has also exempted certain skilled computer works, including systems analysts, programmers, and software engineers.[46] The theory behind this exemption is apparently the view that these types of employees are independent and sophisticated enough to take care of themselves and do not need to be protected by the government from possible exploitation by their employers.

Under the Department of Labor Regulations, an employee qualifying for the exemption as an outside salesperson must meet the two requirements listed below.

- The employee customarily and regularly works away from the employer's place of business while making sales or obtaining orders or contracts for services or for the use of facilities for which a consideration will be paid by the client or customer.
- The employee cannot do any other kind of work for the company, besides that of selling, for more than 20% of the usual workweek put in by the company's nonexempt employees; for example, the outside salesperson or exempted employee could do receptionist work for only 8 hours of each 40-hour workweek.[47]

Various indicators of an employee's bona fide status as an outside salesperson include:

- A contractual designation or job title that reflects involvement in sales;
- Significant compensation on a commission basis;
- Special sales training; and
- Little or no direct or constant supervision in carrying out daily tasks.

Under 1996 legislation, certain computer professionals are added to the list of classes of employees who are exempted from the wage-hour law requirements. This includes computer professionals paid on an hourly basis, if paid at least $27.63 an hour.

The coverage of the federal wage-hour laws, as interpreted by the Department of Labor and the courts, is very broad. Employees who are considered to be engaged in interstate "commerce," except for exempted classes of employees such as executives and administrators, will be subject to the minimum wage and overtime requirements, even if employed by the smallest of firms and, in many cases, even if engaged in what you might consider to be purely local activities.

Covered Employees and Businesses

Thus, in most cases, all of your employees except the exempted classes discussed above are likely to be subject to the federal wage-hour laws, although it is possible that some of your employees will be covered and others will not. In rare cases, none of your employees will be covered.

The legal niceties of whether a particular employee can be considered to be engaged in work that affects interstate commerce are, unfortunately, far too technical to explain here in a meaningful way. However, suffice it to say that the courts have tended to bend over backwards in wage-hour cases to find some way that a particular employee or firm can be deemed to be engaged in activities that affect interstate commerce and thus are covered by the FLSA wage-hour laws.

The law also provides that all the employees of an "enterprise engaged in commerce" are covered, except those who are members of exempted classes, if the firm has any "employees engaged in commerce or in the production of goods for commerce, or that has employees handling, selling, or otherwise working on goods or materials that have been moved in commerce or produced for commerce by any person," and if it "is an enterprise whose annual gross volume of sales made or business done is not less than $500,000." [48]

All of which means that if your firm does a half million or more in sales a year, then all but the exempted classes of employees will be covered by the wage-hour laws, even if only one or a few of your employees are actually engaged in interstate commerce. [49]

Even if it is determined that your employees are not engaged in interstate commerce and they are not subject to the FLSA wage-hour rules, state wage-hour laws may apply. State requirements may be more stringent than federal laws in many states.

Numerous other exemptions from the wage-hour laws are based on the type of business, the nature of the work performed by the employee, where the work is done, and other factors. [50] Before you assume your employees are covered by the FLSA, consult your attorney, or at least call the local wage-hour office on an anonymous basis and ask for an informal and nonbinding opinion over the phone.

Detailed Records Required

Possibly, the most important thing you should be aware of, if you have employees subject to FLSA standards, is the need to keep detailed records of hours worked, the type of work, and wages or salary paid.

Under the law, if an employee files a claim against you for alleged failure to pay required wages in the past, you will need to be able to produce proof that you met the statutory requirements. Keeping detailed pay and work records for each employee is the only way to protect yourself against such claims for back pay. In addition, the FLSA requires employers to preserve these records for up to three years.

Poster Requirement

If you have employees whose wages, hours, and working conditions are subject to FLSA regulations, you will need to post the official wage-hour poster that is provided by the U.S. Department of Labor. In addition, you will most likely be required to post an official wage-hour poster for this state. For a discussion of the basic wage-hour and other significant labor law requirements under this state's law, refer to Section 11.5.

Child Labor Laws

Both the FLSA and various state laws regulate or prohibit the employment of children in businesses, with very few exceptions. If you intend to hire children to work in your business — other than hiring your own children, which is usually permitted, except in hazardous situations — you need to be aware of the following basic child labor law provisions.

As a general rule, the FLSA prohibits the employment of children under 16 years of age;[51] however, there are a number of exceptions to this rule.[52] In addition, all children under age 18 are excluded from certain occupations that are designated as hazardous by the secretary of labor.[53] Children under 16 years of age cannot be hired under any of the following circumstances:

- To work in any workplace where mining, manufacturing, or processing operations take place;
- To operate power machinery, other than office equipment;
- To operate or serve as a helper on motor vehicles — with certain exceptions for vehicles not exceeding 6,000 pounds gross weight, during daylight hours;
- To work in public messenger services; and
- To work in the following occupations: transportation, warehousing or storage, communications or public utilities, or construction — except in sales or office work.[54]

Children 14 or 15 years of age can be hired in other occupations not considered to be hazardous, but there are numerous limitations on the hours and times when they may work, particularly when schools are in session.

A few occupations, such as delivering newspapers and doing theatrical work, are exempt from the federal child labor laws, even for children under 14 years of age.[55]

Most states also strictly regulate the employment of children. See Section 11.5 regarding state child labor laws in this state. Thus, if you intend to employ children under 18 years of age in a business, you will probably need legal guidance as to the conditions under which they may work, if at all, under federal and state child labor laws.

5.8 Fair Employment Practices

As an employer, you will also need to be alert to your obligations under a number of federal and state laws that prohibit discrimination in employment on the basis of sex, age, race, color, national origin, religion, or on account of mental or physical disabilities. These anti-discrimination laws are not just limited to hiring practices, but relate to almost every aspect of the relationship between an employer and employee, including compensation, promotions, type of work assigned, and working conditions.

In addition to outlawing discrimination in employment, companies contracting for business with the federal government are generally required to adopt affirmative action programs in the employment of minorities, women, people with disabilities, and Vietnam veterans.

Affirmative action programs are employment programs that go beyond elimination of discrimination. Under such programs, employers consciously make an effort to hire more women and minority group members and to upgrade the pay and responsibility levels of women and other groups that have historically been subject to patterns of discrimination.

Affirmative action programs are generally required for businesses that are government contractors. On the other hand, most other businesses are only required to refrain from discrimination in their employment practices.

Anti-Discrimination Laws

If your small business employs fewer than 15 employees and is not working on government contracts or subcontracts, the federal anti-discrimination laws listed below will generally not apply to you. The one exception to this would be the Equal Pay Act of 1963, which requires equal pay for equal work for women and men. This act is applicable to employers with two or more employees. Employers violating any of the laws below may be sued by either the complaining individuals or by various government enforcement agencies, or both.

Employers Subject to Federal Anti-Discrimination Laws

Name of Law	Employers Who Are Covered	What the Law Requires
Title VII of the Civil Rights Act of 1964 and Americans with Disabilities Act (ADA)	Employers with 15 or more employees during 20 weeks of a calendar year	No discrimination in employment practices based on race, religion, disability or national origin

(continued)

Employers Subject to Federal Anti-Discrimination Laws (continued)

Name of Law	Employers Who Are Covered	What the Law Requires
Pregnancy Discrimination Act	Same as for Title VII above	Equal treatment for pregnant women and new mothers for all employment-related purposes, including fringe benefits
Executive Order 11246 as amended	Employers with federal contracts or subcontracts of $10,000 or more	No discrimination in employment practices based on race, sex, color, religion, or national origin
Equal Pay Act of 1963	Nearly all employers with two or more employees	Equal pay for women and men doing similar work
Age Discrimination in Employment Act of 1967, as amended	Employers with 20 or more employees during 20 or more weeks in a calendar year.	No discrimination in hiring or firing on account of age, for persons age 40 or older
Rehabilitation Act of 1973	Employers with federal contracts or subcontracts of $2,500 or more	No discrimination in employment practices on account of mental health or physical disabilities
Vietnam-Era Veteran Readjustment Assistance Act of 1974	Employers with federal contracts or subcontracts of $10,000 or more	Affirmative action programs for certain disabled veterans
Americans with Disabilities Act of 1990	Employers with 15 or more employees during 20 weeks of a calendar year	No discrimination in employment based on disability, plus required special accommodations for disabled employees.
Veterans Reemployment Rights Act of 1994	All employers	No discrimination on account of military service; provide certain benefits during absence; reemployment required after periods of military service of up to five years.[56]

Formal Compliance Requirements

Small businesses are not required to do great amounts of paperwork or filling out of forms when it comes to federal anti-discrimination laws. If you are an employer with more than 100 employees, however, you must file *Form EEO-1* with the Equal Employment Opportunity Commission (EEOC) each year.[57]

As an employer, you are required to keep detailed records — and should, for your own protection — as to the reasons for hiring or not hiring, promoting or not promoting, any employee or job applicant. In the event it is ever necessary to demonstrate that your firm has not discriminated against any group or individual member of a group in violation of federal laws, these records will provide the needed documentation.

Besides the requirements already mentioned, there are a number of official posters you may need to post in your place of business. The table on the next page describes some of the posters you may be required to display to meet EEOC requirements.

Display Posters

Type of Poster	Who Must Post	Source of Poster
Civil rights poster regarding sexual, racial, religious, and ethnic discrimination or because of physical or mental disability (*WH Publication 1088*)	Employers with 15 or more employees during 20 weeks of the year or with federal contracts or subcontracts of $10,000 or more [58]	EEOC offices, the nearest Office of Compliance
Age discrimination poster	Employers with 20 or more employees who work 20 or more weeks a year [59]	EEOC offices
Notice to employees working on government contracts (*WH Publication 1313*)	Any employer performing government contract work subject to the Service Contract Act or the Public Contracts Act	U.S. Department of Labor, Employment Standards Division
Poster required under the Vietnam-Era Veterans Readjustment Assistance Act	Employers with federal contracts or subcontracts of $10,000 or more	From the federal contracting officer administering the contract
Poster explaining the Family and Medical Leave Act of 1993	Employers with 50 or more employees during 20 weeks of the year	U.S. Department of Labor, Wage and Hour Division

To obtain these posters, contact each of the appropriate federal agencies and request a copy of their required poster.

Veterans Reemployment Rights Act

The Veterans Reemployment Rights Act, which went into effect in October 1994, prohibits employment discrimination against any person who serves in or applies to serve in the uniformed military services.[60] The new law also requires you, in most cases, to reemploy any employees who leave your employ to serve in the military, unless they are absent on account of military service for more than five years. In many cases, you may not only be required to rehire returning reservists and veterans, but you also will be required to reinstate them at the job level, pay status, and seniority they would have attained if they had remained in your employment.

In addition, you may also be responsible for having to offer job training or retraining to the returning reservist and to make reasonable efforts for two years to accommodate the returning former employee who has been disabled as a result of military service. In effect, this requires you, as an employer, to bear some of the costs of a person who is disabled while in the military. This new mandate is an unprecedented shift of responsibility for veterans' benefits from the federal government to civilian employers, and it may place an unbearable financial burden on some small employers in the future.

Other provisions of this new law require the U.S. Department of Labor to provide military reservists with lawyers, or pay reasonable lawyers' fees on their behalf, when reservists take legal action against their former civilian employers to enforce their rights under this new legislation. In addition, an employer must continue a reservist's health insurance during deployments of less than 31 days and give the reservist the option to continue coverage at his or her own cost for up to 18 months.

Sexual Harassment

You need to be keenly aware of your potential liability for sexual harassment in the workplace, another increasingly significant area of the anti-discrimination laws under Title VII of the Civil Rights Act. While the federal Civil Rights Act does not specifically refer to sexual harassment as a form of discrimination, the courts and the EEOC have long accepted it as such. There are two types of sexual harassment under Title VII, as it has been interpreted over the years.

One type of sexual harassment is where tangible job benefits are granted or withheld based on an employee's receptiveness to unwelcome requests or conduct. For example, a male supervisor tells a female employee to meet him in the hot tub of his mountain chalet on a Saturday afternoon to discuss a business contract. She refuses to meet him at his place and later receives a bad rating from him for a "poor attitude and unwillingness to work overtime," which costs her a raise or promotion. The female employee in such a case has been denied a tangible job benefit due to sexual harassment.

The second type of sexual harassment involves a hostile work environment — that is, a situation in which the work environment is oppressive and hostile to members of one sex. This occurs when the harassment either unreasonably interferes with the individual's work performance or creates an intimidating, hostile, or offensive environment. This type of harassment may not have any economic effects on the individual, and management or supervisory personnel may not be involved. Nevertheless, an employer who allows a hostile environment to persist may still be liable, especially if the employer was aware of the harassment by co-workers — or even by customers — and failed to take appropriate actions to remedy the situation.

Merely having a company policy that prohibits sexual harassment at your company won't automatically stop the behavior or protect the firm from liability if harassment occurs. But the absence of a sexual harassment policy makes such conduct somewhat more likely and will also tend to strengthen an employee's claim against you if your firm is sued for allowing sexual harassment to occur.

Adopt a sexual harassment policy that not only prohibits such conduct, but that also sets up a grievance mechanism for employees who are victims of any harassment, and communicate this company policy strongly and clearly to your employees. For help with defining your company policy on sexual harassment, obtain the book, *Draw the Line: A Sexual Harassment-Free Workplace*, available at your local bookstore or from The Oasis Press.

In addition to federal civil rights case law, the statutes of many states, or the regulations of many state civil rights commissions, now specifically prohibit sexual harassment in the workplace. Some of these laws go well beyond the protections afforded under federal law. For more information about anti-discrimination laws in this state, refer to Section 11.5.

5.9 Immigration Law Restrictions on Hiring

The Immigration Reform and Control Act of 1986 represents a major governmental requirement regarding the relationship between an employer and employee.[61] Under this law, you are prohibited from hiring illegal aliens, and depending on the number of any prior violations, you are subject to fines of $250 to $20,000 for each illegal alien hired after November 6, 1986. At the same time, the act also prohibits employment discrimination on the basis of citizenship status and national origin; you may not fire or fail to hire anyone on the basis of foreign appearance, language, or name.

For all employees hired after November 6, 1986, you are required to verify their eligibility for employment within three business days of each new hire. As an employer, you will need to fill out and retain *Form I-9*. The employee fills out the top portion of the form, indicating whether he or she is a citizen or national of the United States; an alien lawfully admitted for permanent residence; or an alien authorized by the U.S. Immigration and Naturalization Service (INS) to work in the United States.

On the back portion of *Form I-9*, there are three separate lists of various forms of identification and employment eligibility documents the employee must provide for you. In Section 2 of the form, you must record the documents you have examined, such as a passport or certificate of naturalization. These papers must include either one document in List A or one each in lists B and C. Both you and the employee must sign the form under penalty of perjury, and you must retain the completed form and make it available if the INS or U.S. Department of Labor requests it during an inspection. You may obtain copies of *Form I-9* and a related *Employer's Handbook* from the nearest office of the U.S. Immigration and Naturalization Service. A sample *Form I-9* is also included at the end of this chapter. For more information on employer responsibilities, call:

U.S. Immigration and Naturalization Service
(800) 755-0777 (Nationwide)

The U.S. Department of Justice also has a hotline number you can call to hear prerecorded taped messages regarding the type of documents you can request to establish identity and work eligibility. The messages also offer tips on how to avoid discrimination when completing *Form I-9*. To hear these messages, call:

Office of Special Counsel for Immigration-Related Unfair Employment Practices (OSC)
U.S. Department of Justice
(800) 255-8155 (Nationwide)

5.10 Restrictions on Layoffs of Employees

The WARN Act

If your business grows to where you have 100 or more full-time employees — or the equivalent, based on 40-hour workweeks — at a single location, you may be subject to the potentially onerous provisions of the plant closing law called the Worker Adjustment and Retraining Notification Act, or WARN Act.[62] This act would affect you if you laid off 50 or more employees, or one-third of the workforce, in a 30-day period. It applies to virtually any plant closing or major layoff for any reason, with a few obvious exceptions, such as due to an earthquake or flood, or due to a labor dispute, such as a strike or lockout for which no notice need be given. A "layoff" under this act includes any of the following:

- A permanent termination of employment;
- A layoff of an employee for more than six months; or
- A loss of half the employees' working hours for six consecutive months.

In case of any major layoff or shutdown, the law requires you to give at least 60 days advance notice. If you give less than that, you are required to pay the laid-off workers for 60 days minus the actual number of days' notice you gave. The law requires you to notify the labor union that represents the employees, or, if none, the individual employees by mailing the notice to their last known address or including it in their pay envelope. You must also notify the local city or county government and state labor agency of the planned shutdown or cutback.

The WARN Act generally does not prohibit a company from making layoffs or shutting down a money-losing plant, but it makes it more costly for the employer to do so, and also gives local unions and politicians time to find some way to attempt to coerce or persuade a company into maintaining its operations, even if it is no longer economically viable.

The WARN law does impose stiff restrictions on a firm's ability to sell off, reorganize, merge, or consolidate operations if such a decision would adversely affect the jobs of 50 or more employees. In other words, if foreign competition renders your plant obsolete, you will not be allowed to sell it to a competitor if doing so would cost 50 or more employees their jobs. There is considerable litigation over what does and does not constitute a mass layoff or shutdown under the WARN Act.

5.11 The Americans with Disabilities Act

In 1990, Congress enacted a revolutionary and wide-reaching piece of legislation, the Americans with Disabilities Act (ADA), which is designed to make both the workplace and most public facilities much more accessible to disabled persons.

The ADA and related regulations are having a significant impact on a great many businesses, both in terms of employment practices and in terms of removing architectural barriers and other physical features that have limiting effects on the lives of disabled persons.[63]

Anti-Discrimination Rules for People with Disabilities

Title I of the ADA prohibits discrimination against any "qualified individual with a disability" in all aspects of employment, including hiring and discharging of workers, compensation, and benefits. Title I applies to employers who employ 15 or more employees during 20 weeks of any calendar year. In addition, you must reasonably accommodate employees' or applicants' disabilities, which may mean modifying facilities, restructuring work schedules, or transferring disabled workers to vacant positions for which they are qualified, in appropriate circumstances. You are not required to accommodate a disabled worker, however, if doing so would impose an "undue hardship" on your business.

Medical Screening Tests

One area that is now significantly affected in the hiring process is the limitation on medical screening of applicants. Under the ADA, companies can no longer screen out prospective employees with disabilities because the applicant has an elevated risk of an on-the-job injury or a medical condition that might be aggravated because of job demands. The law specifically bans questions about a job applicant's physical or mental condition either on an employment application form or during a job interview. This would include general questions such as, "Do you have any mental or physical conditions that would prevent you from performing your job functions?"

Medical exams are still allowed, but they are greatly restricted. Pre-offer exams are prohibited, but an offer may be conditioned upon the satisfactory results of a medical examination. Results, however, cannot be used to withdraw an offer, unless they show that the individual in question is not able to perform the tasks required by the position.

The definition of "disabled" under the ADA includes people with AIDS, those who test positive for the HIV virus, and rehabilitated drug abusers and alcoholics; however, the ADA does not:

- Prohibit voluntary tests, such as employer-sponsored cholesterol or blood pressure tests; or
- Require employers to hire persons who are drug users or who have contagious diseases.

The ADA is neutral on the issue of drug testing of employees, in effect leaving that up to regulation by the states.

Accommodations for People with Disabilities

Title III of the ADA requires practically all businesses to make their facilities accessible to disabled employees and customers. Examples of various accessibility requirements with regard to public accommodations include:

- Specified numbers of designated parking spaces for the disabled must be provided, based on the total number of parking spaces.
- Hotels and motels must have specified percentages of their rooms accessible to wheelchairs, and other rooms must be equipped with various devices that assist those with certain disabilities, such as visual alarms for the hearing-impaired.
- Access ramps must be in place where the floor level changes more than certain specified amounts.
- Elevators must be provided in three-story or taller buildings and in those with more than 3,000 square feet per story.
- In retail or grocery stores, checkout aisles must be wide enough for wheelchairs.
- Theaters and similar places of assembly must have specified numbers of wheelchair spaces dispersed throughout the seating area.

Tax Incentives

Companies spending money to remove architectural and transportation barriers to the disabled can deduct up to $15,000 a year of such expenses.[64] In addition, small firms — those with gross receipts under one million dollars or fewer than 30 full-time employees — who spend between $250 and $10,250 a year on access for the disabled, can claim a tax credit for up to 50% of the cost of such expenditures, a maximum annual credit of $5,000.[65]

For more information on the ADA, contact:

Equal Employment Opportunity Commission or
1801 L Street, NW
Washington, DC 20507
(202) 663-4900 or
(800) 669-4000 (Information)
(800) 669-3362 (Publications)

Civil Rights Division
U.S. Department of Justice
(800) 514-0301 (Nationwide)

5.12 Mandatory Family and Medical Leave Requirements

The Family and Medical Leave Act of 1993 applies to all companies — as well as nonprofit entities — that have 50 or more employees during 20 or more calendar workweeks during the current or preceding calendar year.[66] As a result, many companies, which employ roughly half of all employees in the United States, are now subject to the family leave law's requirements.

The new act requires covered employers to:

- Offer their employees twelve weeks of unpaid leave after the birth or adoption of a child; to care for a seriously ill child, spouse, or parent; or for an employee's own serious illness;
- Maintain a written family leave policy;

- Give employees a handout, explaining their rights;
- Maintain health care coverage for an employee who is on a leave of absence as described above;
- Guarantee that employees will be able to return to either the same job or to a comparable position after the leave; and
- Post the notice, which may be obtained from the U.S. Department of Labor – Wage and Hour Division, explaining the rights of employees under the Family and Medical Leave Act of 1993.[67]

A serious illness must be verified by a physician's certification, and as the employer, you may require a second medical opinion if desired. An employee is required to provide you with 30 days notice for foreseeable leaves of absence for a birth, adoption, or planned medical treatment.

One major exception to the law's coverage is a provision that exempts certain "key employees" from coverage. Key employees are defined as the highest-paid 10% of the employer's workforce and those whose leave of absence would cause significant economic harm to the employer. Also exempted from the law's provisions are employees who haven't worked at least one year for the employer and who haven't worked at least 1,250 hours, or 25 hours a week, in the preceding twelve months. In addition, you are given the option of substituting an employee's accrued paid leave, if any, for any part of the twelve-week period of family leave.

A number of states, such as California and Hawaii, have also enacted similar family leave laws. Refer to Chapter 11 for information on any such laws that have been adopted in this state.

Endnotes

1. Treas. Regs. §31.6302-1(f)(4).
2. Treas. Regs. §31.6302-1(b)(2).
3. Treas. Regs. §31.6302-1(b)(3).
4. Treas. Regs. §31.6302-1(c)(3).
5. I.R.C. §7502(e)(3).
6. Treas. Temp. Regs. §31.6302-1(h)(2).
7. Treas. Regs. §31.6302-4.
8. I.R.C. §§3301(1) and 3306(b)(1).
9. I.R.C. §§3301(1) and 3302(b).
10. I.R.C. §3306(a)(1)(A).
11. I.R.C. §3306(a)(1)(B).
12. 29 U.S.C. §1131.
13. 29 U.S.C. §1132; I.R.C. §§4971, 4975, 6057–6059, and 6652.
14. 29 U.S.C. §1002(2); 29 C.F.R. §2510.3-2.
15. 29 U.S.C. §1002(1); 29 C.F.R. §2510.3-1.
16. 29 C.F.R. §2510.3-1(b); 29 C.F.R. §2510.3-2(b).
17. 29 C.F.R. §2520.104b-2.
18. 29 C.F.R. §2520.102-3.
19. 29 C.F.R. §2520.104b-2(a)(2).
20. 29 C.F.R. §2520.104b-2(a)(1).
21. 29 C.F.R. §2520.104-20.
22. 29 U.S.C. §1024(b)(4); 29 C.F.R. §2520.104b-1.
23. 29 U.S.C. §1024(a)(6).
24. 29 C.F.R. §2520.104a-5.
25. 29 C.F.R. §2520.104b-10.
26. 29 C.F.R. §2520.104b-3.
27. 29 U.S.C. §1021(c).
28. 29 U.S.C. §1112.
29. I.R.C. §3405(a).
30. I.R.C. §6039 D.
31. Announcement 86-20, 1986-87 I.R.B. 34.
32. 29 C.F.R. §1903.2.
33. 29 C.F.R. §1904.2.
34. 29 C.F.R. §1904.10.
35. 29 C.F.R. §1904.5.
36. 29 C.F.R. §1904.16.
37. 29 C.F.R. §1904.12.
38. 29 C.F.R. §1904.4.
39. 29 C.F.R. §1904.6.
40. 29 C.F.R. §1904.15.
41. 29 C.F.R. §§1904.15 and 1904.21.
42. 29 C.F.R. §1904.8.
43. 29 C.F.R. §1904.9.
44. 29 U.S.C. §206(a)(1).
45. 29 U.S.C. §207(a)(1).
46. 29 U.S.C. §213(a)(1).
47. 29 C.F.R. §541.5.
48. 29 U.S.C. §203(s).
49. 29 U.S.C. §207(a)(1).
50. 29 U.S.C. §213.
51. 29 U.S.C. §§203(1) and 212.
52. 29 U.S.C. §213(c) and (d).
53. 29 C.F.R. §570.50–570.71.
54. 29 C.F.R. §570.33.
55. 29 U.S.C. §213(c) and (d).
56. 38 U.S.C. §§4301 *et seq.*
57. 29 C.F.R. §1602.7.
58. 29 C.F.R. §1601.30.
59. 29 U.S.C. §627 and 29 C.F.R. §1627.10.
60. 38 U.S.C. §§4301 *et seq.*
61. 8 U.S.C. §1324a(b).
62. 29 U.S.C. §§2101–2109.
63. 42 U.S.C. §§12101 *et seq.* and 29 C.F.R. §1630.
64. I.R.C. §190.
65. I.R.C. §44.
66. 29 C.F.R. §825.104(a).
67. 29 C.F.R. §825.300(a).

Summary of Basic ERISA Compliance Requirements for Pension Plans

Item	Provided to
Summary plan description.	U.S. Department of Labor; participants; beneficiaries
Annual return/report (*Form 5500, 5500-EZ,* or *5500-C/R*).	IRS (now required even for a simple one-person Keogh plan)
Schedule A, Form 5500 series (insurance information).	IRS
Schedule B, Form 5500 series (actuarial information prepared and signed by an enrolled actuary for "defined benefit" plans only).	IRS
Schedule SSA, Form 5500 series (registration statement).	IRS
Form W-2P (report of periodic plan benefit payments made during the year).	IRS; recipient of distribution
Form 1099-R (report of total distribution of benefits during the year).	IRS; recipient of distribution
Form W-3 or *W-3G* (transmittal of *Form W-2P* and *Form 1099-R*).	IRS
Form PBGC-1 (premium payment of required plan termination insurance — for "defined benefit" plans only).	Pension Benefit Guaranty Corporation (a government agency that insures pension plans of corporate employers)
Summary annual report.	Participants; beneficiaries
Individual deferred vested benefit statement to separated employee.	Former participant in plan
Summary of material modifications to a plan.	U.S. Department of Labor; participants; beneficiaries
Terminal report (when plan is terminated).	U.S. Department of Labor; participants; beneficiaries
Written explanation of joint and survivor annuity and financial effect of not electing to receive it (if plan provides benefits in the form of an annuity).	Participants
Written explanation of reasons for denying benefit claim and description of appeal procedures.	Person claiming entitlement to plan benefits
Various documents and information to be provided on request.	U.S. Department of Labor; participants
Various formal notices upon occurrence of certain events.	IRS; U.S. Department of Labor; Pension Benefit Guaranty Corporation; participants

Form I-9 – Instructions

U.S. Department of Justice
Immigration and Naturalization Service

OMB No. 1115-0136

Employment Eligibility Verification

INSTRUCTIONS
PLEASE READ ALL INSTRUCTIONS CAREFULLY BEFORE COMPLETING THIS FORM.

Anti-Discrimination Notice. It is illegal to discriminate against any individual (other than an alien not authorized to work in the U.S.) in hiring, discharging, or recruiting or referring for a fee because of that individual's national origin or citizenship status. It is illegal to discriminate against work eligible individuals. Employers **CANNOT** specify which document(s) they will accept from an employee. The refusal to hire an individual because of a future expiration date may also constitute illegal discrimination.

Section 1 - Employee. All employees, citizens and noncitizens, hired after November 6, 1986, must complete Section 1 of this form at the time of hire, which is the actual beginning of employment. **The employer is responsible for ensuring that Section 1 is timely and properly completed.**

Preparer/Translator Certification. The Preparer/Translator Certification must be completed if Section 1 is prepared by a person other than the employee. A preparer/translator may be used only when the employee is unable to complete Section 1 on his/her own. However, the employee must still sign Section 1 personally.

Section 2 - Employer. For the purpose of completing this form, the term "employer" includes those recruiters and referrers for a fee who are agricultural associations, agricultural employers, or farm labor contractors.

Employers must complete Section 2 by examining evidence of identity and employment eligibility within three (3) business days of the date employment begins. If employees are authorized to work, but are unable to present the required document(s) within three business days, they must present a receipt for the application of the document(s) within three business days and the actual document(s) within ninety (90) days. However, if employers hire individuals for a duration of less than three business days, Section 2 must be completed at the time employment begins. **Employers must record: 1)** document title; **2)** issuing authority; **3)** document number, **4)** expiration date, if any; and **5)** the date employment begins. Employers must sign and date the certification. Employees must present original documents. Employers may, but are not required to, photocopy the document(s) presented. These photocopies may only be used for the verification process and must be retained with the I-9. **However, employers are still responsible for completing the I-9.**

Section 3 - Updating and Reverification. Employers must complete Section 3 when updating and/or reverifying the I-9. Employers must reverify employment eligibility of their employees on or before the expiration date recorded in Section 1. Employers **CANNOT** specify which document(s) they will accept from an employee.

- If an employee's name has changed at the time this form is being updated/ reverified, complete Block A.

- If an employee is rehired within three (3) years of the date this form was originally completed and the employee is still eligible to be employed on the same basis as previously indicated on this form (updating), complete Block B and the signature block.

- If an employee is rehired within three (3) years of the date this form was originally completed and the employee's work authorization has expired **or** if a current employee's work authorization is about to expire (reverification), complete Block B and:
  - examine any document that reflects that the employee is authorized to work in the U.S. (see List A **or** C),
  - record the document title, document number and expiration date (if any) in Block C, and
  - complete the signature block.

Photocopying and Retaining Form I-9. A blank I-9 may be reproduced provided both sides are copied. The instructions must be available to all employees completing this form. Employers must retain completed I-9s for three (3) years after the date of hire **or** one (1) year after the date employment ends, whichever is later.

For more detailed information, you may refer to the INS Handbook for Employers, (Form M-274). You may obtain the handbook at your local INS office.

Privacy Act Notice. The authority for collecting this information is the Immigration Reform and Control Act of 1986, Pub. L. 99-603 (8 U.S.C. 1324a).

This information is for employers to verify the eligibility of individuals for employment to preclude the unlawful hiring, or recruiting or referring for a fee, of aliens who are not authorized to work in the United States.

This information will be used by employers as a record of their basis for determining eligibility of an employee to work in the United States. The form will be kept by the employer and made available for inspection by officials of the U.S. Immigration and Naturalization Service, the Department of Labor, and the Office of Special Counsel for Immigration Related Unfair Employment Practices.

Submission of the information required in this form is voluntary. However, an individual may not begin employment unless this form is completed since employers are subject to civil or criminal penalties if they do not comply with the Immigration Reform and Control Act of 1986.

Reporting Burden. We try to create forms and instructions that are accurate, can be easily understood, and which impose the least possible burden on you to provide us with information. Often this is difficult because some immigration laws are very complex. Accordingly, the reporting burden for this collection of information is computed as follows: 1) learning about this form, 5 minutes; 2) completing the form, 5 minutes; and 3) assembling and filing (recordkeeping) the form, 5 minutes, for an average of 15 minutes per response. If you have comments regarding the accuracy of this burden estimate, or suggestions for making this form simpler, you can write to both the Immigration and Naturalization Service, 425 I Street, N.W., Room 5304, Washington, D. C. 20536; and the Office of Management and Budget, Paperwork Reduction Project, OMB No. 1115-0136, Washington, D.C. 20503.

Form I-9 (Rev. 11-21-91) N

EMPLOYERS MUST RETAIN COMPLETED I-9
PLEASE DO NOT MAIL COMPLETED I-9 TO INS

Form I-9 – Employment Eligibility Verification: Sample

U.S. Department of Justice
Immigration and Naturalization Service

OMB No. 1115-0136
Employment Eligibility Verification

Please read instructions carefully before completing this form. The instructions must be available during completion of this form. ANTI-DISCRIMINATION NOTICE. It is illegal to discriminate against work eligible individuals. Employers CANNOT specify which document(s) they will accept from an employee. The refusal to hire an individual because of a future expiration date may also constitute illegal discrimination.

Section 1. Employee Information and Verification. To be completed and signed by employee at the time employment begins

Print Name: Last	First	Middle Initial	Maiden Name

Address *(Street Name and Number)*	Apt. #	Date of Birth *(month/day/year)*

City	State	Zip Code	Social Security #

I am aware that federal law provides for imprisonment and/or fines for false statements or use of false documents in connection with the completion of this form.

I attest, under penalty of perjury, that I am (check one of the following):
☐ A citizen or national of the United States
☐ A Lawful Permanent Resident (Alien # A_____)
☐ An alien authorized to work until ____/____/____
(Alien # or Admission #_____)

Employee's Signature	Date *(month/day/year)*

Preparer and/or Translator Certification. *(To be completed and signed if Section 1 is prepared by a person other than the employee.) I attest, under penalty of perjury, that I have assisted in the completion of this form and that to the best of my knowledge the information is true and correct.*

Preparer's/Translator's Signature	Print Name

Address (Street Name and Number, City, State, Zip Code)	Date *(month/day/year)*

Section 2. Employer Review and Verification. To be completed and signed by employer. **Examine one document from List A OR examine one document from List B and one from List C** as listed on the reverse of this form and record the title, number and expiration date, if any, of the document(s)

List A	OR	List B	AND	List C
Document title: ____		____		____
Issuing authority: ____		____		____
Document #: ____		____		____
Expiration Date *(if any)*: ___/___/___		___/___/___		___/___/___
Document #: ____				
Expiration Date *(if any)*: ___/___/___				

CERTIFICATION - I attest, under penalty of perjury, that I have examined the document(s) presented by the above-named employee, that the above-listed document(s) appear to be genuine and to relate to the employee named, that the employee began employment on *(month/day/year)* ____/____/____ and that to the best of my knowledge the employee is eligible to work in the United States. (State employment agencies may omit the date the employee began employment).

Signature of Employer or Authorized Representative	Print Name	Title

Business or Organization Name	Address *(Street Name and Number, City, State, Zip Code)*	Date *(month/day/year)*

Section 3. Updating and Reverification. To be completed and signed by employer

A. New Name *(if applicable)*	B. Date of rehire *(month/day/year) (if applicable)*

C. If employee's previous grant of work authorization has expired, provide the information below for the document that establishes current employment eligibility.

Document Title:_____ Document #:_____ Expiration Date (if any): ___/___/___

I attest, under penalty of perjury, that to the best of my knowledge, this employee is eligible to work in the United States, and if the employee presented document(s), the document(s) I have examined appear to be genuine and to relate to the individual.

Signature of Employer or Authorized Representative	Date *(month/day/year)*

Form I-9 (Rev. 11-21-91) N

Form I-9 – Employment Eligibility Verification: Sample (continued)

LISTS OF ACCEPTABLE DOCUMENTS

LIST A	LIST B	LIST C
Documents that Establish Both Identity and Employment Eligibility	Documents that Establish Identity	Documents that Establish Employment Eligibility

OR ... **AND**

LIST A — Documents that Establish Both Identity and Employment Eligibility

1. U.S. Passport (unexpired or expired)

2. Certificate of U.S. Citizenship (INS Form N-560 or N-561)

3. Certificate of Naturalization (INS Form N-550 or N-570)

4. Unexpired foreign passport, with I-551 stamp or attached INS Form I-94 indicating unexpired employment authorization

5. Alien Registration Receipt Card with photograph (INS Form I-151 or I-551)

6. Unexpired Temporary Resident Card (INS Form I-688)

7. Unexpired Employment Authorization Card (INS Form I-688A)

8. Unexpired Reentry Permit (INS Form I-327)

9. Unexpired Refugee Travel Document (INS Form I-571)

10. Unexpired Employment Authorization Document issued by the INS which contains a photograph (INS Form I-688B)

LIST B — Documents that Establish Identity

1. Driver's license or ID card issued by a state or outlying possession of the United States provided it contains a photograph or information such as name, date of birth, sex, height, eye color, and address

2. ID card issued by federal, state, or local government agencies or entities provided it contains a photograph or information such as name, date of birth, sex, height, eye color, and address

3. School ID card with a photograph

4. Voter's registration card

5. U.S. Military card or draft record

6. Military dependent's ID card

7. U.S. Coast Guard Merchant Mariner Card

8. Native American tribal document

9. Driver's license issued by a Canadian government authority

For persons under age 18 who are unable to present a document listed above:

10. School record or report card

11. Clinic, doctor, or hospital record

12. Day-care or nursery school record

LIST C — Documents that Establish Employment Eligibility

1. U.S. social security card issued by the Social Security Administration (other than a card stating it is not valid for employment)

2. Certification of Birth Abroad issued by the Department of State (Form FS-545 or Form DS-1350)

3. Original or certified copy of a birth certificate issued by a state, county, municipal authority or outlying possession of the United States bearing an official seal

4. Native American tribal document

5. U.S. Citizen ID Card (INS Form I-197)

6. ID Card for use of Resident Citizen in the United States (INS Form I-179)

7. Unexpired employment authorization document issued by the INS (other than those listed under List A)

Illustrations of many of these documents appear in Part 8 of the Handbook for Employers (M-274)

Form I-9 (Rev. 11-21-91) N

Chapter 6

Businesses that Require Licenses to Operate

*The bureaucrat who smiles when something serious has gone wrong
has already found someone to blame it on.*

— Anonymous

6.1 General Licensing

Almost any kind of business activity you engage in will require a city or
county business license, which is usually fairly simple to obtain. For example, if you will be in the food business, you may have to get a license
from the county health department; or, if your business would like to do
any construction or remodeling, you might have to get approval from
your local planning commission. In addition to local licenses, some types
of businesses will have to obtain licenses from the federal government to
operate, while other businesses, occupations, and professions are also
licensed and regulated by the state.

Even though there are tremendous variations regarding the requirements
for obtaining necessary federal and state licenses, these requirements
generally relate to educational attainments, experience in the particular
field, passage of examinations, submission of detailed applications, meeting financial or bonding requirements, or some combination of the foregoing, plus payment of a licensing fee or tax.

Before you begin to operate any kind of business, find out whether you
will be required to obtain any special government licenses or permits. In
most cases, you will be required to obtain the particular license before
opening your doors for business.

This chapter and Section 11.6, respectively, provide a partial listing of the
federal and state licensing requirements you most likely will encounter as

a small business owner. Because the number of activities that may require federal or state licenses is so large, no attempt has been made to try to list all of them in this book.

Thus, the lists of licensing agencies and businesses that require licenses found in this chapter and in Chapter 11 should be helpful in alerting you, as a small business owner, to possible licensing needs. Remember, however, that these lists are not complete and you will need to confirm through the appropriate agencies, or your attorney, whether you have all the necessary permits and licenses.

6.2 Federal Licenses

If you are starting a small business, it is relatively unlikely that you will need any type of license or permit from the federal government; however, the following is a list of the federal licensing requirements you might possibly encounter:

For a partial listing of businesses and professions required to be licensed in this state, see Section 11.6.

Federal Licensing Requirements

Activity	Federal Agency
Rendering investment advice	Securities and Exchange Commission
Providing ground transportation as a common carrier	Interstate Commerce Commission
Preparation of meat products	Food and Drug Administration
Production of drugs or biological products	Food and Drug Administration
Making tobacco products or alcohol	Treasury Department, Bureau of Alcohol, Tobacco, and Firearms
Making or dealing in firearms	Treasury Department, Bureau of Alcohol, Tobacco, and Firearms
Radio or television broadcasting	Federal Communications Commission

Operating the Business

Part III

Chapter 7

Excise Taxes

Taxation without representation is tyranny.

— Patrick Henry

Taxation with representation is worse.

— Will Rogers

7.1 General Considerations

Both federal and state tax laws impose excise or similar taxes on a number of different types of businesses, products, services, and occupations. These taxes are usually imposed without any assessment or notice to the taxpayer. Thus, it is up to you to find out if you are subject to any of these taxes and, if so, to obtain the proper tax return forms and pay the tax on time.

It is not uncommon for a small business to operate for several years without the owner ever being aware of the need to pay excise taxes. Then comes the day of reckoning, when a formal notice is received from the government demanding immediate payment of several years' worth of back taxes on some particular item subject to excise tax, plus interest and penalties for not filing the returns and not paying the tax. This can be a disastrous surprise, especially since the business owner has not factored the cost of paying the excise into the price of his or her goods or services.

This chapter is designed to alert you in advance to the types of federal and state excise — and similar — taxes that you may need to know about. Some excise taxes, such as those on telephone service and insurance companies, are not discussed below since they are passed along or absorbed by the telephone company, insurance company, or other large institution with which your business may deal, and you have no obligation to file any returns or make any direct payment to the government of such taxes.

See Section 11.7 for a summary of various state excise taxes that may affect your business.

7.2 Federal Excise Taxes

Federal excise taxes on many products and transactions have been repealed over the last 20 years, so these taxes are much less pervasive now than in the past. The excise tax that the largest number of small businesses are likely to be subject to is the motor vehicle highway use tax on vehicles of more than 55,000 pounds gross weight.[1] *Form 2290* must be filed by owners of trucks and buses subject to the highway use tax. If you want information about the highway use tax, request a copy of IRS *Publication 349* from any IRS office.

The federal government imposes a number of excise taxes on various types of business activities. Some excise taxes are on the production or sale of certain goods. Some are on services or the use of certain products or facilities. Still others are imposed on businesses of a certain type.

Most federal excise taxes are reported on *Form 720, Quarterly Federal Excise Tax Return*, the most common excise tax form. Environmental taxes on petroleum and 42 designated chemical substances are reported on *Form 6627* and attached to *Form 720*. Federal excise taxes can be broken down into several major categories:

- The motor vehicle highway use tax. This tax is imposed on vehicles of more than 55,000 pounds gross weight.[2]
- Retailer taxes on certain fuels.[3] The federal gasoline tax is $0.183 (18.3 cents) per gallon on gasoline, and the tax on diesel is $0.243 (24.3 cents) per gallon. An additional fuel tax of 0.1 cent per gallon, for cleanup of leaking underground storage tanks, applies after September 30, 1997. A reduced fuel tax rate applies to qualified methane and ethanol fuel.

Other retail excise taxes are imposed on sales of:
- Heavy trucks and trailers;[4]
- Tires and tubes;[5]
- Recreation equipment, such as bows, arrows, fishing rods, reels, lures, and creels;[6] and
- Firearms and ammunition.[7]

Other excise taxes exist on the following as well:

- Air transportation. If you are in the business of transporting people by air, you may have to collect an excise tax — although this tax expired January 1, 1996, it has been reinstated until 2007;[8]
- Telephone and teletype services;[9]
- Wagering;[10]
- Coal mined in the United States;[11]
- Alcohol and tobacco products;[12] and
- Manufacturers of certain vaccines. Certain vaccines manufactured or imported into the United States are subject to an excise tax in order to create a Vaccine Injury Compensation Trust Fund, a no-fault program for compensating persons who are injured by, or die from, certain vaccines.[13]

There are also several environmental excise taxes, such as:

- An excise tax on ozone-depleting chemicals;[14]
- A hazardous substance Superfund tax on oil of $0.097 (9.7 cents);[15] and
- Environmental taxes on various chemicals and hazardous wastes.[16]

Luxury Taxes

A luxury tax applies to retail purchases of passenger automobiles costing more than $30,000.[17] The tax is equal to 10% of the amount by which the purchase price exceeds $30,000. For example, the luxury tax on a new $35,000 automobile would be 10% of $5,000 — the excess of $35,000 over $30,000, or $500. The $30,000 threshold amount has been indexed for inflation that has occurred since December 31, 1990, and is set at $36,000 in 1997. The tax rate is 8% in 1997 and is scheduled to be phased out completely over the next several years.

The luxury tax does not apply to:

- Vehicles of more than 6,000 pounds unloaded gross weight; or
- Any vehicle, such as a taxicab, that is used exclusively in the active conduct of a trade or business of transporting people or property for compensation or hire.

The luxury tax on automobiles is collected by the retailer who sells the item. This luxury tax only applies to the first retail sale of an item. For example, if you buy a used $50,000 automobile, there is no luxury tax on the purchase.

For further information on excise taxes and other federal taxes, you may wish to obtain IRS *Publication 334, Tax Guide for Small Business*, or for more detailed information on excise taxes, IRS *Publication 510, Excise Taxes.*

Endnotes

1. I.R.C. § 4481(a).
2. Id.
3. I.R.C. § 4081(a)(2)(A).
4. I.R.C. § 4051.
5. I.R.C. § 4071(a).
6. I.R.C. § 4161(a) and (b).
7. I.R.C. § 4181.
8. I.R.C. §§ 4261(a) and 4271(a).
9. I.R.C. § 4251.
10. I.R.C. §§ 4401 and 4411.
11. I.R.C. § 4121(a).
12. I.R.C. §§ 5001, 5041(a), and 5701.
13. I.R.C. §§ 4131–4132.
14. I.R.C. § 4681.
15. I.R.C. § 4611(c)(1)(A).
16. I.R.C. § 4661.
17. I.R.C. § 4001(a).

Chapter 8

Planning for Tax Savings in a Business

*The words of such an act as the income tax merely dance before
my eyes in a meaningless procession: cross-reference to cross-
reference, exception upon exception — couched in abstract terms
that offer no handle to seize hold of — leave in my mind only
a confused sense of some vitally important, but successfully
concealed, purport, which it is my duty to extract, but which
is within my power, if at all, only after the most inordinate
expenditure of time. I know that these monsters are the result of
fabulous industry and ingenuity, plugging up this hole and
casting out that net against all possible evasion; yet at times
I cannot help recalling a saying of William James' about certain
passages of Hegel: that they were no doubt written with a
passion of rationality; but that one cannot help wondering
whether to the reader they have any significance save that the
words are strung together with syntactical correctness.*
— Judge Learned Hand

referring to the 1939 Internal Revenue Code, a statute that was almost
childlike in its simplicity compared to our current tax law.

8.1 General Considerations

One of the most shocking and unpleasant realizations of many successful
small business owners comes when they realize they have acquired an
unwanted silent partner — a partner who contributes nothing to the business
but who often lays claim to half or more of the owner's hard-earned profits.
That silent partner, of course, is the government income tax collector, and
this chapter is a summary of many of the best and most effective legal ways
to reduce that silent partner's share of the profits from your business.

This chapter is not intended to be a substitute for professional tax advice regarding your individual situation. Because the tax laws are so enormously complex, a technique that may work brilliantly in most cases might be useless or even disastrous in your particular tax situation. This chapter will provide you with a working understanding of some of the key ways to plan for tax savings and to avoid tax pitfalls in your business.

After you have read this chapter, you may want to talk to your tax adviser about one or more of the ideas discussed if you feel they might be useful for your business. Your tax adviser should be able to tell you whether a particular idea will work in your situation. If it will, he or she can help you implement it.

Tax attorneys and accountants often have a very heavy workload and a large number of clients to serve. An unfortunate result of this situation is your tax adviser may tend to spend most of the time responding to inquiries by clients and meeting tax deadlines rather than taking the initiative in seeking out ways to minimize your taxes. Thus, by having some understanding of what you would like to do in the way of reducing taxes on your business income, you can propose ideas to your tax advisers and maximize the effectiveness of their expert knowledge and advice. In tax planning, as in so many areas of life, it pays to be assertive. "The squeaky wheel gets the grease."

8.2 Using a Corporation as a Tax Shelter

One of the most effective ways to reduce your taxes, in many cases, is to incorporate your business. Incorporation is most likely to be advantageous if the business is generating about $75,000 or less in annual profits and salary for the owner — or per owner if more than one. In addition to adopting employee fringe benefit plans, your corporation can help reduce your taxes on business income by:

- Leaving profits in the corporation;
- Income-splitting; and
- Investing in stock and taking advantage of the dividends received deduction.

Leaving Profits in the Corporation

If you are able to leave your first $75,000 of annual profits in your corporation, the profits will generally be taxed at corporate rates, which are lower than your individual income tax rates. This provides a strong incentive for you to leave at least that much taxable income in the corporation rather than pay it all out to yourself as salary. At taxable income levels above $75,000, corporate income is taxed at roughly the same rates as individual income, except at very high income levels of $335,000 or more. Refer to the table of corporate income tax rates in Section 2.4 and compare those rates with the personal income tax rates for your filing status. Be careful about leaving too much profit in your corporation. Sections 8.5 and 8.9 discuss the potential benefits and risks of having your profits accumulate in your corporation.

Income Splitting

By using a corporation, it is also possible to split your overall profit between two or more taxpayers, so that none of the income gets taxed in the highest tax brackets. For example, with an overall economic profit of $100,000, an incorporated business may be able to reduce its taxable income to $50,000 by paying (and deducting) a $50,000 salary to its owner, as an officer/ employee of the corporation. The corporation would pay tax only on the remaining $50,000 profit, at a maximum federal tax rate of only 15%, while the owner would pay tax on the $50,000 salary received.

Because of the progressive tax rate structure under the federal income tax laws, the tax on the $100,000 income divided between the owner and his or her corporation would typically be much less than if the whole $100,000 were taxable to the owner. In 1997, for example, a single individual would pay $26,003 in federal income taxes on $100,000 of taxable income, while, if the income were split evenly between the owner and his or her corporation, the corporation's tax would be $7,500 and the owner's $10,796, a savings of $7,707 — assuming the corporation is not a personal services corporation subject to a 35% flat rate of tax.

Another way to split the income of a business between multiple taxpayers is for you to make your children part owners of the business. Ideally, the children should be given an interest in the business when it is started, since the value of the gifts to them will often be minimal for gift tax purposes at that time.

It is frequently more feasible to split corporate income with your children by giving them some of the corporation's stock. This approach, however, will work only if your corporation has filed for an S corporation election on *Form 2553* with the IRS. The taxable income of a corporation that qualifies as an S corporation is taxable to its shareholders — in proportion to the stock they own in the corporation — and is generally not taxed to the corporation.

By giving a number of shares of stock in an S corporation to one or more of your children, part of the taxable income of the business can often be shifted to the children and taxed at their low tax brackets — assuming, as is usually the case, that the children do not have a lot of taxable income from other sources. If, however, the parents attempt to shift too much income to the children by drawing no salary or too little salary from the corporation, the IRS has the power to reallocate the corporation's income to the parents to reflect the value of services rendered to the corporation.[1] Shifting significant income to your children will not work if the children are under 14 years of age.[2]

Dividends Received Deduction

By investing accumulated corporate funds in dividend-paying stocks of other corporations, you can take advantage of the 70% deduction that corporations are entitled to on the dividends they receive.[3] Because this special deduction makes most dividends received by a corporation — other than those received by an S corporation — practically tax-free to the recipient corporation, your incorporated business can be an excellent place to hold stocks you wish to invest in if you do not need the dividend income to live on.

Before you get too excited about putting your whole stock portfolio into your incorporated business, take these potential drawbacks into account:

- If you decide to later withdraw your corporate dividends or the stocks themselves, the withdrawal will usually be taxable to you as ordinary income[4] or perhaps, if you liquidate the corporation, as capital gains.[5] Capital gains are taxed at a maximum rate of 28% for individuals.[6]

- If you should accumulate more than $250,000 — $150,000 for professional and certain personal service firms — in after-tax earnings in your corporation, including the 70% of dividends that the corporation doesn't pay income tax on, and invest part of those earnings in liquid, nonbusiness investment assets like stocks, you may be inviting an IRS audit and a potential penalty tax for unreasonably accumulating earnings and profits in the corporation.[7] See the discussion of the accumulated earnings tax in Section 8.9.

- If too much of your corporation's income is in the form of dividends and other passive types of investment income, the corporation may be classified as a personal holding company for tax purposes, and this can have drastic tax consequences, as outlined in Section 8.9.[8] As long as more than 40% of your corporation's gross income is from sales of goods and services, however, as a general rule, you should not have to be concerned about personal holding company taxes.[9]

- Putting your personal assets that are not needed in the business into your corporation will subject those assets to the risk of the business. That is, anything you put into the corporation will be subject to the claims of the corporation's creditors if it goes bankrupt. If you put all of your assets into the corporation, you will in effect have given up the benefits of limited liability.

- If your corporation borrows money to invest in or carry stock investments, the 70% dividend exclusion will be reduced in part by the interest paid on the borrowed funds.[10]

Your accountant will probably be the best person to consult for determining how and whether you can use a corporation to reduce taxes on your business profits.

8.3 Retirement Plans and Other Fringe Benefits

One advantage of being your own boss, either as a sole proprietor, a partner, or a shareholder of a closely held corporation, is the opportunity to set up a Keogh plan or corporate retirement plan. In a C corporation, you can also obtain insurance and other important fringe benefits as an officer and employee of the corporation on a tax-favored basis. Some of the ways you can benefit from using retirement plans and other tax-favored fringe benefits are outlined in this section.

There are four main types of tax-favored retirement plans:

Tax Advantages of Retirement Plans

- Qualified retirement plans, a broad category that includes corporate pension and profit-sharing plans, as well as Keogh pension and profit-sharing plans of unincorporated businesses;
- Savings incentive match plans for employees (SIMPLE), which can be set up by small employers;
- Simplified employee pension (SEP) plans for any type of business, incorporated or not; and
- Individual retirement accounts (IRAs), which may be set up by any individual who has earned income, including an employee.

The primary tax advantages of all types of tax-qualified retirement plans are:

- Amounts contributed, up to certain limits, are deductible from the income of the corporation or individual taxpayer.[11] This deduction can be as much as 25% of the individual's compensation for the year (not counting the plan contribution) or $30,000, whichever is less. Even larger contributions can be made by so-called defined benefit plans.
- Contributed funds can be invested by pension or profit-sharing plans on a tax-free basis.[12] The qualified retirement trust that is usually set up to hold the retirement funds is exempt from state and federal income taxes on its income or capital gains from investments in stocks, bonds, savings accounts, precious metals, real estate, and other passive investments. Before 1998, IRAs or individually directed retirement plans generally could not invest in precious metals, other than gold and silver coins minted by the United States and coins issued under state law. However, beginning in 1998, they may also hold certain platinum coins and gold, silver, or platinum bullion.[13]
- When trust funds are paid out to you at retirement, you may be in a lower tax bracket than when you made the contributions to the plan. Thus, not only do you get to defer payment of any tax on amounts contributed to the plan until you retire, but the tax you finally pay at retirement is apt to be at a lower rate than you would have paid when you were working.

See Section 9.14 regarding a new type of pension plan created under the Small Business Job Protection Act of 1996.

Qualified Retirement Plans

Corporate and noncorporate Keogh retirement plans are almost identical under the tax law in all major respects, except for the ability to borrow one's retirement funds from the plan, which will be subject to an excise or penalty tax in the case of a Keogh. It does not pay to incorporate your business just for pension and profit-sharing plan purposes. If you decide to establish a retirement plan, you should consider several practical points before reaching a decision.

Model Corporate and Keogh Plans

If you are setting up a qualified corporate or Keogh retirement plan, it is possible to obtain canned prototype plans from banks if you allow them to act as trustee — or from insurance companies if you buy their insurance or managed fund accounts through the plan. These plans usually have variable terms that can be tailored somewhat to suit your needs, unless you want to do something out of the ordinary, such as allow each participant to direct the investment of his or her portion of the plan's funds. Other institutions, such as stockbrokerages and mutual funds, also offer model qualified plans.

Customized Retirement Plans

Even if you do need something unusual that requires a customized retirement plan for your corporation, you will probably find it more cost effective to have a benefit consulting firm draw up the plan for you. This way, your attorney would only be involved in reviewing the plan and obtaining approval of the plan from the IRS. Typically, benefit consultants or pension consultants will charge only a fraction of what a law firm would charge to draw up the plan, and the larger benefit consulting firms are generally quite competent. Most of their fees come from helping you administer the plan under ERISA after it is set up — a service you will need anyway.

Section 401(k) Plans

An increasingly popular form of qualified retirement plan is the Section 401(k) plan. This type of plan generally permits employees to elect to have a percentage of their salary — with various limitations — deducted from their paychecks, free of income tax, and deposited on their behalf in a profit-sharing-type plan. In many cases, as an additional incentive to employees to make such tax-favored savings, you, as an employer, may provide some degree of matching contribution to the plan on behalf of the employee. For example, a typical situation would be where you contribute $0.50 (50 cents) for every dollar the employee elects to have withheld from his or her pay. Your tax-deductible contribution is placed in the 401(k) plan and is tax-free to the employee.

Simplified Employee Pension (SEP) Plans

Simplified employee pension (SEP) plans can be set up by corporations, partnerships, or sole proprietorships. SEPs have gotten very little use since they were created by Congress several years ago; however, they now offer most of the attractive features of typical Keogh and corporate plans with virtually no administrative costs. This is in contrast to a Keogh or corporate plan that may cost up to $2,000 or $3,000 a year to maintain for only five or ten employees.

A SEP plan is basically a glorified individual retirement account (IRA), but it is one where as an employer, you contribute to each employee's IRA account an amount of up to 15% of an employee's compensation with a maximum of $30,000 — actually $24,000, as a practical matter.

The amount contributed is not taxed to the employee and can be invested in any type of IRA account the employee chooses. Participants can still contribute up to $2,000 a year to their SEP/IRA or to another IRA plan. SEP participants with taxable income in excess of $30,000 (single) or $50,000 (married filing jointly), however, will have their IRA deductions reduced or eliminated.

The main drawback of a SEP is that it is not possible for an employer to make contributions that do not "vest" immediately. Thus, an employee covered by a SEP will not forfeit any portion of his or her account under a SEP upon leaving your employment. Even so, a SEP strongly merits consideration as an alternative to Keogh or corporate retirement plans, due to its relative simplicity.

Model SEP or Keogh Plans from Financial Institutions

If you are setting up a SEP plan for yourself, or a Keogh plan, consider obtaining a "canned" plan from a bank, savings and loan, insurance company, stockbrokerage, or mutual fund. Usually, these preapproved plans will be suitable for you unless you have a significant number of employees to cover under your Keogh, in which case, you probably should be incorporated anyway. The great advantages of getting a canned SEP or Keogh plan from a financial institution are cost and simplicity. Most such institutions will charge you only $10–$25 to adopt their plan.

By contrast, hiring a lawyer or benefit consultant to draw up a customized SEP or Keogh plan for you could cost anywhere from a few hundred to a few thousand dollars in fees. In addition, since the pension laws seem to be rewritten every time Congress meets, you may find yourself paying hundreds or even thousands of dollars each year to your attorney or benefit consultant to revise or amend a custom-designed plan, just to keep it in compliance with the never-ending changes in the tax and other laws affecting pension plans.

SIMPLE Retirement Plans

The Small Business Job Protection Act of 1996 created a new type of retirement plan, called SIMPLE (savings incentive match plan for employees). These can be set up as either SIMPLE IRAs or SIMPLE 401(k) plans, and are available for small employers who had 100 or fewer employees who earned at least $5,000 in compensation for the preceding year. Under a SIMPLE plan, an eligible employee can elect to contribute a percentage of his or her compensation to the plan, up to a dollar limit of $6,000 a year.

The IRS has released a model SIMPLE plan that an employer may use in combination with SIMPLE IRAs to create a SIMPLE retirement plan. It can be adopted by using new IRS *Form 5305-SIMPLE*, which also contains a model notification to eligible employees (which an employer may also use, to meet SIMPLE plan notice requirements), plus a model salary reduction agreement.

The form is not to be filed with the IRS, but is to be kept on file by the sponsoring employer. A plan will be considered to be established when the form is completed and signed by the employer and the designated bank or other financial institution which will hold the IRA assets. If your plan is to allow employees to choose the financial institutions for their SIMPLE IRAs, you will not be able to use the IRS standard form, but will need to draw up your own plan, which is also permitted. To use the IRS standard form, all assets under the plan must be held by a single financial institution.

Individual Retirement Accounts

IRAs are of limited interest to most business owners, since the maximum annual contribution to an IRA is $2,000 a year for each spouse. The former limit on deductions to $250 for a nonworking spouse has been repealed by 1996 tax law changes. Even these small deductions may not be available if you are a participant in a Keogh or corporate retirement plan and your adjusted gross income is more than $60,000 — $40,000 if you are a single person (1998 limits).

New tax legislation has created a new "Super IRA," called a Roth IRA, beginning in 1998. Non-deductible contributions of up to $2,000 a year may be made to a Roth IRA, and if not paid out for five years (and other distribution requirements are met), all withdrawals from the Roth IRA can eventually be made free of federal income tax.

Various Nonretirement Fringe Benefit Plans

The federal tax laws are replete with a whole host of tax-favored employee fringe benefits, which are characterized as being deductible to you and nontaxable to the employee. If your business is organized as a C corporation, you, as an employee of the corporation, receive the same favorable treatment as other employees for health insurance, medical reimbursement, disability insurance, and group-term life insurance. If not a C corporation, these payments will either be nondeductible by the employer, or in some cases, will be taxable to you, as the recipient, if deductible by the employer. Some of the more common and important nontaxable fringes are discussed below.

Medical Insurance Plans

The corporation that maintains a medical insurance plan, such as Blue Cross or a prepaid health care plan, is permitted to deduct the premiums it pays to the insurer. In addition, the employee is not required to include either the cost of the premiums or the benefits provided by the insurer in his or her taxable income, as a general rule.[14]

Self-Insured Medical Reimbursement Plans

A corporation can set up a plan where the corporation directly reimburses employees for medical expenses or even for expenses such as dental care, orthodontic work, and prescription eyeglasses or contact lenses.[15] If the plan satisfies tax law requirements prohibiting discrimination in favor of highly paid employees, the reimbursements paid can be deducted by the corporation and are not taxable to the recipients.[16]

These plans are often set up in addition to medical insurance plans, either to cover deductibles that the insurance does not pay or to cover particular types of medical or dental costs that the insurance plan does not cover. The costs of cosmetic surgery are no longer deductible as medical expenses, and cannot be covered in a medical reimbursement plan.

Starting in 1997, on a limited basis, the tax law permits creation of medical savings accounts (MSAs), into which an individual may contribute tax-deductible amounts each year. This money can be used to pay non-covered medical costs, such as for paying the deductible (non-covered) amounts under medical insurance policies.

MSAs are only allowed for self-employed persons or the employees of small firms with 50 or fewer employees. In the case of employees, contributions to MSAs by the employer will not be taxable income to the employee, provided the MSA is not offered as a part of a "cafeteria plan." Any contributions that are not used to pay medical expenses can be invested, and will eventually come back to the person who owns the MSA.

Participation in an MSA is conditioned upon your having coverage under a high deductible health plan, one that has the following minimum deductibles and out-of-pocket expense limitations:

- Individual coverage. The minimum deductible must be at least $1,500, the maximum $2,250; the maximum out-of-pocket limitation is $3,000.
- Family coverage. The minimum deductible must be at least $3,000, the maximum $4,500; and the maximum out-of-pocket limitation is $5,500.

(All of the above amounts will be indexed for inflation after 1998.)

Since one of the main remaining benefits of incorporating a business has been to be able to get a tax deduction for medical insurance and medical/dental expenses, there is now even less reason to incorporate, if you can achieve most of the same benefits of deductibility with an MSA.

Medical Savings Accounts (MSAs)

Payment by a corporation of disability insurance premiums is deductible by the corporation and is not taxed to the employees covered by the insurance — except in the case of certain shareholders of an S corporation.[17]

If an employee becomes disabled and receives disability benefits under a policy that the employer has paid the premiums for, the benefits will be included in the employee's income for tax purposes. On the other hand, if an individual, such as a sole proprietor or partner, has paid his or her own premiums for disability insurance, any disability benefits received are tax-free.[18]

Disability Insurance

Your corporation may set up a group-term life insurance plan and deduct the insurance premiums it pays on behalf of employees. As long as the life insurance coverage on an employee does not exceed $50,000 under the plan during the taxable year, the employee does not have to report the premiums you pay for that coverage as taxable income on his or her personal income tax return.[19] Even if an employee's coverage exceeds $50,000, the amount the employee must include in taxable income from the additional insurance premiums paid by you for the excess coverage is sometimes considerably less than the premium actually paid and deducted.

Group-Term Life Insurance

The tax law also provides exclusions, for both income and employment tax (FICA and FUTA) purposes, for a number of "working condition fringes"

Section 132 Excludable Fringe Benefits

under Section 132 of the Internal Revenue Code. These exclusions generally apply to any employee of your business, whether or not incorporated, except as noted:

- No-additional-cost services provided to an employee. These services consist of benefits such as free airline, rail, or bus transportation provided by companies in those industries; rooms for hotel employees; or free phone service for telephone company employees.
- Employee discounts. Service companies can provide their services to employees at up to a 20% discount. For companies selling goods, the discount may not exceed the employer's gross profit percentage multiplied by the usual selling price of the item to customers.
- Working condition fringes. These fringe benefits are tax-free, up to the amounts that would have been deductible if paid by the employee. Benefits include such items as a company car or plane used for business purposes; subscriptions to trade or professional publications; on-the-job training; business travel; and others.
- Qualified transportation fringes. These benefits include employer-provided transit passes and commuter transportation worth up to $65 a month and parking provided to employees worth up to $165 a month. Parking fringes are not available to self-employed individuals.
- Minor fringes. These benefits are items that are considered to be too minimal to justify the administrative costs for them, such as using the company's copier machine or having a secretary type a personal letter.
- On-premises athletic facilities. Providing and operating facilities such as gyms, pools, tennis courts, or golf courses on the business premises, for employees, their spouses, and dependents is a nontaxable fringe benefit.[20]

Meals on Premises

If meals are provided on-premises to employees, for your convenience as the employer, the value of these meals is usually not taxable to the employee for income tax purposes.[21] You or your corporation, however, can deduct 50% of the cost of furnishing on-premise meals.

Educational Assistance Plans

You may pay educational expenses on behalf of an employee — free of employment taxes or income tax to the employee — if the purpose of such education meets one of the two following tests: 1) the education maintains or improves skills required by the job, and 2) the education meets requirements set by you or applicable laws, where such requirements are imposed as a condition of the retention of employment or rate of compensation.

You may also set up tax-qualified educational assistance plans to provide other — not necessarily job-related — educational benefits for employees, in amounts up to $5,250 a year per employee.[22] To qualify, the plan must be in writing, disclosed to employees, and no more than 5% of benefits paid under the plan can go to 5% owners of the firm or their spouses or dependents. While this exclusion expired on June 1, 1997, the Taxpayer Relief Act of 1997 reinstated it retroactively, and made it permanent. Payments for graduate level courses do not qualify for the exclusion.

Dependent care plans are one of the most popular and rapidly growing types of employee fringe benefit plans in recent years, providing up to $5,000 a year of dependent care benefits for children or elderly dependents per employee. Not more than 25% of benefits provided, however, can be on behalf of 5% owners of the employer company, and other technical nondiscrimination rules also apply.[23]

Dependent Care Plans

Companies have devised, or Congress has provided, a number of different stock option plans with various tax advantages, all of which are designed to encourage employees to acquire a proprietary stake in the companies they work for. Major types of such plans include:

Stock Option Plans

- Nonqualified stock options. In this plan, you usually grant favored employees options to acquire stock of the company at a bargain price during a period of several years. Such an option is usually not a taxable event; although, the excess of the value over the option price of the stock received, when the option is eventually exercised, is then taxed as ordinary compensation income in most cases — unless the stock is restricted or forfeitable.
- Incentive stock options (ISOs). ISOs are options granted under a plan that meets IRS requirements, where the term of the option is limited and the option price is not less than the value of the stock at the day the option is granted. That is, with an ISO, there is no bargain element built into the option. If the stock is worth $20 a share the day the option is granted to the employee, the option must be at an exercise price of no less than $20. Thus, the employee will not stand to profit from exercising the option unless the value of the stock subsequently rises to above $20 a share — which is good incentive for the employee to help make the company as profitable as possible. If certain requirements are met, the employee does not recognize taxable income when he or she exercises an ISO and may qualify for subsequent capital gains treatment if the stock received from exercise of the option is sold at a gain.[24]
- Employee stock purchase plans. Under a tax-qualified employee stock purchase plan, a company may allow employees to purchase its stock, directly from the company, for up to a 15% discount from the fair market value of the stock. The employee is not taxed when exercising the right to purchase stock under such a plan and may receive capital gain treatment when the stock is eventually sold at a gain.[25]

In the last few years another nonretirement fringe benefit plan — the flexible spending plan or flex plan — has become another increasingly popular type of tax-favored employee benefit. Each of the three flex plans below are designed to permit employees to choose how much to spend on a tax-free basis for various employee benefits, such as health care or dependent care. Flex plans are for employees only and cannot cover sole proprietors, partners in a partnership, or 2% shareholders in an S corporation.

Flexible Spending Plans

Premium-Conversion Accounts

Premium-conversion accounts are the simplest kind of flex account. They are primarily set up to allow employees to pay for their share of health, disability, or group-term life insurance premiums with untaxed dollars by deducting specified amounts out of their regular paychecks to pay for such coverage. The amounts the employees agree to have withheld from their salaries or wages to pay such insurance premiums are excluded from their taxable income, but deductible by the corporation or unincorporated employer. Such plans, in effect, convert part of wages directly into insurance payments, without having the government first remove a slice for taxes. Premium-conversion accounts are practical for even the smallest companies with only one or two employees.

Flexible Reimbursement Accounts

Flexible reimbursement accounts are accounts where an employee may agree to contribute a specified amount to each year and draw on the account to pay for health care expenses not covered by the company. Health care expenses could include medical insurance deductibles, vision care, dental coverage, and dependent care expenses for as much as $5,000 per year.

Here is how these accounts work: Before the start of each year, the employees must estimate their medical and dependent care costs for the coming year that they want paid out of their accounts. The amount designated by an employee is withheld from his or her paycheck during the year (tax-free). As expenses are incurred during the year for health and dependent care, the employee submits requests for reimbursement out of the account to the plan administrator, up to the specified maximum. Employers may choose to supplement or match amounts employees choose to have withheld from their pay, as an additional tax-free benefit to the employee.

Flexible reimbursement accounts may stand alone, or may be combined with premium-conversion accounts. They are feasible for fairly small employers as well; although administrative costs may tend to be greater than for premium-conversion accounts.

Cafeteria Plans

Cafeteria plans are more complex and are rarely adopted by companies with fewer than 50 employees. Under a cafeteria plan, a company gives employees a menu of benefit choices, provides a fixed number of tax-free dollars per employee each year, and allows the employees to each select or buy the particular benefits desired, such as:

- 401(k) contributions;
- Health insurance;
- Life insurance;
- Disability insurance;
- Vision or dental care, or both; and
- Vacation time.

If the costs of the benefits selected exceeds the dollar amount provided by you, the employee may fund the balance with salary reduction amounts through premium-conversion or reimbursement accounts, or both, also on an untaxed basis.

Under flex plans, the golden rule is "use it or lose it." Any amount in an employee's account that is not used by the employee during the year is forfeited, and reverts back to you at the end of the year. Flex plans are required to meet nondiscrimination tests to ensure that highly compensated employees do not receive a disproportionate share of the benefits provided.[26] For more information on flex plans, contact:

Employers Council on Flexible Compensation
927 15th Street NW, Suite 1000
Washington, DC 20005
(202) 659-4300

8.4 Sheltering Profits on Export Sales

Many small and large American businesses have an unfortunate tendency to look at the United States as their only market and to ignore the vast potential markets for their products or services that lie outside the borders of this country. One way in which Congress has taken constructive steps to encourage more exports and to make American goods and services more competitive in foreign markets is to provide a form of indirect tax subsidy to American firms that export.

While this export subsidy has not succeeded in stemming the unfavorable trend in the balance of trade the United States has experienced in recent years, it does provide a very attractive tax benefit for U.S. companies that export. If your business is one of the many small firms that does sell its goods or services overseas, you may be able to qualify for this tax incentive by setting up either a Domestic International Sales Corporation (DISC) or a Foreign Sales Corporation (FSC).

In general, a DISC will allow you to accumulate profits earned from export sales in a specially treated corporation, free of U.S. taxes until you eventually choose to distribute the deferred income. An FSC will allow you to accumulate such income, whether or not distributed, free (in part) of U.S. corporate taxes. For an FSC, the exempt foreign trade income will not even be taxed when paid out as a dividend if the shareholder is a corporation.[27] For small companies, DISCs may often be much simpler to operate and preferable to the FSCs, at least for the first few years of operation.

Here is a brief summary of DISC and FSC tax benefits.

- If your business will be engaged or is engaged in selling goods or services abroad, consult your tax adviser as to the advisability of establishing a DISC or FSC to shelter a large portion of your export profits.
- Both DISCs and FSCs are extremely complex entities to establish and administer, although a DISC will probably be much less of a headache

for a small business to operate than an FSC. In either case, you will need to hire some very sophisticated accounting talent, so unless you earn some fairly substantial export profits, the administrative costs of having a DISC or FSC may well exceed any tax savings you will generate.

▪ State tax treatment of DISCs and FSCs is discussed in Section 11.8.

8.5 Planning for Withdrawal of Corporate Funds with Minimum Tax Cost

Because of the many tax and other advantages of operating a corporation, there is a good chance you will choose, either initially or later on, to incorporate your business. If you do, and your business becomes profitable to the extent that it has significant profits even after paying you the largest salary that can be justified as "reasonable compensation," you will eventually be faced with the problem of how to remove the accumulated profits from the corporation without excessive tax costs.

If the corporation simply pays dividends to you, this activity will normally be a tax disaster because the dividends you receive will probably be taxable to you as ordinary income at federal income tax rates up to 39.6% or somewhat more. This will result in double taxation since the corporation will have already paid tax on the money it distributes to you as dividends. If both you and the corporation are in the maximum tax brackets, the result can be an effective tax rate of approximately 60% (a combination of federal corporate and individual taxes) on the income that is paid out as dividends. This rate can even be higher if there are also state income taxes. Fortunately, you have several tax-saving options for getting the money out of the corporation.

Personal Loans from the Corporation

First, your corporation can often serve as a bank for your short-term financial needs; however, if you continually borrow from your corporation, the IRS can in some cases treat the loans as dividends to you, which is just what you want to avoid. Or, if your corporation has an accumulated earnings problem, as described in Section 8.9, the existence of loans to shareholders can make it very difficult to argue that the corporation is accumulating earnings for the reasonable needs of the business. So, while a loan from your corporation can be a very good way to tap its funds on a temporary basis, it is not a long-term solution.

If you do borrow, you should normally pay interest if the loan is greater than $10,000. The interest rate should not be less than the applicable federal rate established by the IRS.[28] This rate is announced by the IRS each month of the year for transactions that occur during the following month.

Preliminary Structuring

Besides using your corporation as a source of personal loans, you can structure your corporation so it gives you more potential flexibility in getting money out for yourself, or family members, at no tax cost or, at worst, as only partially taxable. Some of these structural approaches can also make it possible to keep a significant amount of the value of the corporation's stock out of your taxable estate, which will help reduce estate tax and inheritance tax. Discuss the structuring of your corporation with your tax adviser before you form the corporation. Three strategies you might explore are putting stock in the names of your children or spouse, giving stock to your children as gifts, and using debt capitalization.

When the corporation is formed, consider putting a substantial part of the stock in the name of your spouse or children, or both. Later, when or if the business has prospered and the stock has become valuable, it may be possible to bail out a large chunk of the corporation's accumulated profits at a child's lower tax rates by having the corporation redeem (purchase) all of the stock of your spouse or child.

Putting Stock in Names of Spouse and Children

The redemption will usually be treated as a sale for a capital gain if your spouse or child agrees to notify the IRS if he or she reacquires any interest in the corporation within ten years after the redemption.[29] Working as an employee of the corporation would be an "interest" that would prevent the spouse or child from receiving favorable capital gains treatment. So if you want your son or daughter to work for you in the business, do not count on being able to redeem his or her stock as a capital gain.

Because capital gains are taxed at lower rates than ordinary income, it is very desirable to have a stock redemption qualify for capital gains treatment. Also part of the money received will be a nontaxable recovery of the shareholder's tax basis in the stock that is being redeemed. This is usually not the case if the redemption payment is treated as an ordinary income dividend.

Such redemption of stock as a capital gain could even be made on an installment basis.[30] For example, if your daughter had all her stock redeemed by the corporation for $150,000, the corporation could pay the $150,000 price, plus interest, in 15 annual installments of $10,000 each, so that your daughter would not have a "bunching" of all the capital gain on the sale in one tax year. Instead, the capital gains tax would be spread over a 15-year period, and the corporation should be able to deduct interest paid on the note held by the daughter.

Unfortunately, this tactic does not work as well in community property states if you attempt to redeem your spouse's stock. Under the community property laws, half of your stock will generally be treated as owned by your spouse. This makes it difficult to completely terminate his or her interest, unless all of the stock that is community property is first split in half between you by agreement, so that you each own your shares as separate property.

Constraints in Community Property States

Even in that case, your spouse may be considered to have reacquired a community property interest in your separately owned stock if you continue to work for the corporation and the value of the stock increases on account of your efforts. Thus, if you live in a community property state, you probably should not count on trying to redeem your spouse's interest in the corporation as a capital gain. The states that have community property laws are Arizona, California, Idaho, Louisiana, Nevada, New Mexico, Texas, Washington, and Wisconsin.

Gifts of Stock to Children

Even if the corporation never redeems your children's stock, it is useful to put some of the stock in their names when you form the corporation — especially at a time when a gift to them of the stock will be subject to little or no gift tax because of its low value. When you die many years later, the stock owned by your children may then be very valuable and will not be included in your estate in most instances, which could save your children a great deal in estate and inheritance taxes. The federal gift tax laws now permit you to make gifts worth up to $10,000 per child per year free of federal gift tax. If you are married, you and your spouse can jointly make gifts of up to $20,000 per year per child; however, you may be subject to state gift taxes in some states.

Debt Capitalization Pitfall

Until the Revenue Reconciliation Act of 1989 was passed, it was considered astute tax planning — when setting up a new corporation — to capitalize the company with both equity capital (stock) and debt capital (an interest-bearing note from the corporation to you). The benefit of using debt capital was that when the corporation repaid the debt to the stockholder later, it was a way for the stockholder to get money out of the corporation with little or no tax liability. However, such a tactic can now be a tax trap if you transfer property that has appreciated in value to the corporation in exchange for debt. Under the 1989 law, any notes or other debt capital you take back from the corporation will cause you to be immediately taxable on appreciated assets (land, equipment, etc.) that you transfer to the corporation in return for the stock and debt instruments.

Debt Capitalization Still Can Be Advantageous

If, however, the only asset you are putting in the corporation to start it up is, for example, cash, or property that has not appreciated in value, you will not be affected by the 1989 tax law change mentioned in the preceding paragraph. As an illustration, if you plan to put $10,000 in the corporation to get the business started, you might take back stock for $5,000 and a $5,000 note when the corporation is set up, rather than having the corporation issue you stock for the whole $10,000. While the note is outstanding, you will be able to siphon off some funds from the corporation as interest on the note, which the corporation can deduct. By contrast, if the corporation distributed profits to you as dividends on its stock, it would result in double taxation of those profits, since, unlike interest, the corporation cannot deduct dividends it pays.

More importantly, when the note becomes due, the corporation will repay you the $5,000 principal of the note; if things have been handled properly, you should pay no tax on that $5,000. In contrast, if the corporation attempted to return part of your investment in the stock, whatever you received would probably be fully taxable to you as a dividend, even if you surrendered some of your stock in a redemption. Lending the corporation part of its start-up capital allows you to withdraw part of your investment without paying tax.

Thus, there are considerable advantages in partially capitalizing your corporation with debt in the form of a note or notes that you will hold from the corporation. You will need competent tax advice before you do so, however, since there are hundreds of court cases that have tried to define when debt instruments will be considered debt and when they will be considered stock. For example, if you capitalize your corporation with more than $3 of debt for each $1 of stock — say a $6,000 note and $2,000 of stock — the note (debt) may be treated as though it were stock for tax purposes. Thus, if the corporation paid you interest or principal on the note, whatever payments you received would be treated as dividends to you, and the corporation's deduction for the interest payments would be disallowed. So tread very lightly in lending money to your corporation. See Section 8.9 for more on the distinction between debt and equity for tax purposes.

Post-Incorporation Planning

Whether or not you take advantage of the above planning suggestions at the time you incorporate, there are a number of other ways you can get cash out of your corporation at a low tax cost.

Leasing to the Corporation

Instead of putting your own money into the corporation so it can buy property it needs, keep the money outside the corporation, and buy the property yourself and lease it all at a reasonable rental to the corporation. This way, you will be able to directly obtain the tax depreciation and other benefits of owning the property. At the same time, by keeping the property out of the corporation, you will be putting less of your assets at risk in the business, especially if the corporation goes broke. Also, if the leased property is real estate, it will probably appreciate in value.

You can personally and directly benefit from that appreciation, including the increased rent you will be able to charge the corporation as inflation continues. Furthermore, if you have used straight-line depreciation and sell the property at a gain, all of the gain will be capital gain. By contrast, if the corporation sells real property at a gain, 20% of the straight-line depreciation is recaptured as ordinary income.[31] Although a corporation's capital gains are currently taxed at the same rate as ordinary income, Congress restored preferential tax rates for individuals' capital gains in 1990, and it may do the same for corporations in the future.

Structuring S Corporation Loans

If you have losses from your S corporation, you can only deduct these losses on your individual income tax return up to the total amount you have invested in its stock, plus what you have loaned to the corporation. Keeping that in mind, you will want to avoid the tragic situation of two unfortunate taxpayers, as seen in the *Uri* case.[32] In this tax case, two taxpayers had set up an S corporation, each investing $10,000 in its stock. The S corporation then took out a $210,000 SBA loan from a bank, which the two shareholders personally guaranteed. When the corporation racked up more than $180,000 in tax losses in three years, the stockholders were only allowed to deduct the $10,000 cost of their stock, since they had only guaranteed the loan, rather than making loans directly to the corporation. Had they merely structured the loan a little differently, by borrowing the money from the bank individually, and then relending it to the corporation, the S corporation's losses would probably have been fully deductible by the two owners. As it was, they had to file bankruptcy.

A shareholder who guarantees a loan to an S corporation can easily fall into a major tax trap, as the taxpayers in the *Uri* case found out — the hard way. Ironically, both of the taxpayers in *Uri* were partners in a CPA firm, who should have known better. To avoid this result, either borrow the funds and relend them to your S corporation, or look for other creative approaches to structuring an S corporation's financing, with the assistance and counsel of an experienced tax adviser.

Careful tax planning and structuring is an absolute necessity when setting up financing for an S corporation. Don't fall into the *Uri* trap!

Trusts for Your Children

You could make a gift of business property — or the funds to buy it — to a trust and have a bank or other independent trustee negotiate a reasonable lease of the property to the business, with the rental income going to the trust for distribution to your children. Upon the trust's termination, or earlier, such as when your children reach specified ages, the property and accumulated income can be distributed to the children. Or, if a child does not live until age 21, the property and accumulated income can revert to you at his or her death.

This can be a useful way of taking cash out of the corporation for the benefit of your children, who have lower tax brackets; however, since the IRS regularly attempts to attack these types of arrangements, you should go into this only with the help of an astute tax adviser. Be aware that the Tax Reform Act of 1986 eliminated nearly all the tax advantages of trusts for children under 14 years of age.

DISC Deferrals

Consider setting up a DISC corporation if your corporation has foreign sales. You can then hold the DISC stock yourself or give it to your children. This will not only enable you to indefinitely defer federal income taxes on part of the profits from export sales, it will also, in effect, allow you or your children to siphon off part of the profits on export sales — dividends paid by the DISC — in a manner that allows your corporation to deduct those dividends, thereby avoiding double taxation.

Benefit Plans

Consider adopting corporate pension or profit-sharing plans and various corporate fringe benefit plans. These types of benefit plans, in appropriate circumstances, can provide deferred retirement benefits or current insurance benefits to you tax-free — or on a tax-deferred basis, in the case of retirement plans — while reducing the corporation's current taxable income. See the discussion of these kinds of employee benefit plans in Section 8.3.

8.6 Deducting Expenses Related to Your Business

One major advantage of operating your own business is the opportunity it may give you to deduct the costs of certain activities or luxuries as business expenses. These deductions can prove very helpful in reducing your taxes; keep them in mind when developing your tax-saving strategies. Some of the tax benefits, however, that were available in the past — such as costs of attending foreign conventions [33] and treating part of your home as a business office [34] — have been severely curtailed, and there are strict recordkeeping requirements for others. [35] These two deductions and several others are discussed below.

Deductions for attending foreign conventions are now completely disallowed, unless you can show that:

Foreign Convention Expenses

- It is just as reasonable for the convention to be held abroad as it would be to hold it in North America; and
- The meeting is directly related to your trade or business.

If these two requirements are met, you must then meet the general requirements for traveling outside the United States. Deductions for conventions or seminars on cruise ships are limited to $2,000, and other travel by "luxury water transportation" is deductible only up to certain per diem amounts. [36]

If you use part of your residence for business purposes, you may be able to deduct part of your office-in-the-home expenses, but the rules are rather stringent. The general rule is that office-in-the-home expenses are not deductible for tax purposes, unless you meet a number of very technical requirements.

Office-in-the-Home Expenses

There are several types of situations under which you may be able to claim deductions for part of your rent or expenses related to ownership of your residence, as well as other occupancy expenses, despite the home-office deduction limitations.

If you use part of your residence exclusively for business purposes and on a regular basis, you may be able to claim office-in-the-home deductions if you also qualify under one of these tests: [37]

Exclusive-Use Tests

- You use a portion of your home as your principal place of business.
- You use your home as a place to meet clients, customers, or patients.
- Your home office is a separate structure that is not attached to your house or living quarters.

The ability to treat a home office as your "principal place of business" has been sharply limited by the U.S. Supreme Court's 1993 decision in the *Soliman* case. Under this holding, even if your home office is your "only" office, it won't qualify if it is not also your "most important" place of work. In *Soliman*, the Supreme Court disallowed home-office deductions of a physician who had no office other than a room in his home, where he kept his business records and made business-related phone calls. Most of his actual work was done at various hospitals where he performed services as an anesthesiologist.

However, beginning in 1999, a 1997 tax law amendment will go into effect, overruling the decision in the *Soliman* case. Under these new rules, your "principal place of business" will include a home office that is used only for administrative or management activities of the business, if there is no other fixed location where you conduct such activities.

Nonexclusive Uses that Qualify

Two special exceptions are made where part of a home is regularly, but not exclusively, used for business purposes.

- Storage of inventory. A wholesaler or retailer who uses part of a home to store inventory that·is being held for sale; if the dwelling unit is the taxpayer's sole fixed location of the trade or business; or
- Day care facility. Part of the home is used for day care of children, physically and mentally disabled persons, or individuals age 65 or older.

If you can show that a portion of your residence qualifies as a home office, you have cleared the first hurdle. But note that even if you don't meet any of the above requirements, these rules will not disallow your deductions that are otherwise allowed for tax purposes, such as interest on your home mortgage, real estate taxes, or casualty losses from damage to your residence.

Also, business expenses that are not home-related, such as business supplies, cost of goods sold, wages paid to business employees, and other such operating expenses, are not affected by the limitation on home office-related deductions.

If the business use of your home qualifies under one of the above tests, then you may be able to deduct part of the home office expenses that are allocable to the portion of your home that is used in your business, in addition to home mortgage interest, property taxes, and casualty losses.

For example, if 15% of your home is used exclusively and regularly as your principal place of business, you could possibly deduct up to 15% of your occupancy costs, such as gas, electricity, insurance, repairs, and similar expenses, as well as 15% of your rent or depreciation expense on 15% of the tax basis of your house. The IRS and the tax court don't agree on the deductibility of certain other types of expenses, such as lawn care.

Deductions Limited to Income

Note, however, that the amount of qualifying home office expense you can actually deduct for the year is limited to the gross income from your home business, reduced by regular operating expenses (wages, supplies, etc.) and an allocable portion (15% in the above example) of your mortgage interest, property taxes, and casualty loss deductions. If you still have net business income after taking those deductions, then you may deduct the allocable portion of your home office expenses, up to the amount of such net income.

Any portion of your home office expenses that isn't deducted due to the income limit in one year can be carried over to future years until usable, if ever. Thus, it pays to keep track of any such disallowed expenses, in case your home-based business becomes more profitable in the future, and you are then able to deduct the carried-over expenses from earlier years.

Your federal individual return, *Schedule C*, no longer asks you whether expenses for business use of a home are being deducted. Instead, you must determine a tentative profit or loss on *Schedule C*, without taking into account home use expenses.

Home office expenses are now computed separately on *Form 8829*. On this form, you must compute the amount of deductible expenses for business use of the home, which (if any) can then be deducted from the net *Schedule C* income. This will make it impossible, or at least illegal, for taxpayers filing *Schedule C* to simply bury the home office expenses in with other business expenses.

Potential Tax Trap of Office-Home Expenses

The downside of taking home office deductions is a potential tax bite when you sell your home. For example, if 15% of your home has been used for business and you sell your home for a gain, you may have to pay tax on 15% of the gain, even though sale of a residence is now generally tax free, on gains up to $500,000 (or $250,000 for a single person). Thus, a few hundred dollars of home office deductions now, could later result in many thousands of dollars of tax on the "business" part of your house if you sell it for a gain a few years down the road. For more information on the deductibility of home-office expenses, obtain IRS *Publication 587, Business Use of Your Home*.

Travel, Entertainment, and Meal Expenses

Business travel expenses, entertainment of your clients or customers, and business-related meals are deductible, but you can only deduct 50% of qualifying business meals and entertainment. Consequently, this 50% rule considerably complicates recordkeeping for these types of expenses.

For instance, if you stay in a hotel on a business trip and charge your meals to your room, you are required to separately break out your meal expenses for tax purposes because your meal expenses are only 50% deductible.

If you are an employee of your business, the 50% disallowance of meal and entertainment expenses does not apply to you individually if your company reimburses you for the expenses; it applies only at the company level.

Detailed Records Required

To claim any of these kinds of deductions, you must keep daily, detailed records of such expenditures, including bills, receipts, and the following information for each expense:

- The relationship of the expenditure to the business;
- The time when the expense was incurred;

- Where the money was spent, and to whom it was paid;
- The amount of the expenditure; and
- The identities of the persons involved, including persons entertained.[38]

The law requires that taxpayers keep "adequate records or ... sufficient evidence corroborating the taxpayer's own statement."[39] It is strongly recommended that you pick up a daily expense record book or diary and enter all expenses for travel, meals, and entertainment you think should be deductible. Include the above information for each item. Documentary evidence is not required to substantiate travel and entertainment expense items of less than $75 ($25 before October 1995) except for the cost of lodging while away from home.[40]

Not All Entertainment Expenses Deductible

Not all expenses for entertaining clients or customers will be deductible, even if you keep meticulous records. As a general rule, your records must show that you were engaged in a substantial and bona fide business discussion during or immediately before or after the entertainment.[41] Expenses of entertaining people just to create a good impression on them, in the hope they might send some business your way in the future, are classified as goodwill entertainment, and you cannot deduct them for tax purposes.

Quiet business meals with clients or potential customers — where no business is discussed — are not deductible. For more information on business-related expenses, contact your local IRS office and request *Publication 463, Travel, Entertainment, and Gift Expenses.*

Automobile Expenses

If you use an automobile more than 50% of the time for business purposes, you will generally be able to deduct a percentage of the costs of owning and operating the car if you can substantiate the business mileage. The expenses of using the car for commuting to and from work and for personal travel are not deductible.[42]

For example, if your business purchases a new car for your use as a business car, and 80% of the mileage on the car can be shown to be for business trips, and only 20% for commuting to work and other personal use, you should be able to deduct 80% of the gas, oil, insurance, and maintenance costs relating to the car. You can also depreciate the cost of the car, less 20% for personal use.

Rules are even more drastic for any automobile, airplane, boat, or computer not kept in your place of business if you can't establish a business-use percentage in excess of 50%. Automobile depreciation is stretched out over at least six years, straight-line: 10% the first year; 20% a year thereafter, for four years; and 10% the final year. For boats, planes, or computers, it can be stretched out for longer periods.[43] There are also strict dollar limits on maximum annual depreciation deductions for so-called luxury automobiles costing more than about $15,000. For luxury automobiles, the maximum annual depreciation deduction allowed is limited to the amounts below.[44]

Luxury Automobile Depreciation

1997 Acquisitions	**1995 and 1996 Acquisitions**
$3,160 for the first year	$3,060 for the first year
$5,000 for the second year	$4,900 for the second year
$3,050 for the third year	$2,950 for the third year
$1,775 for each succeeding year	$1,775 for each succeeding year

These restrictions don't apply to business vehicles such as ambulances, hearses, taxis, delivery vans, or heavy trucks.[45]   **Exemptions**

If you drive an inexpensive economy car on business, it may be simpler   **Mileage Deduction**
and more advantageous to elect to deduct a flat $0.315 (31.5 cents) per mile for 1997[46] for your business mileage rather than keep records of your various kinds of automobile expenses. If you use this method, you can still deduct tolls and parking incurred on business trips.If you drive an expensive car, you will probably get much larger tax deductions by reporting your actual operating expenses, plus depreciation, than by electing the mileage allowance. Be sure to keep an accurate record of your business mileage so you can substantiate the car was used for business purposes.

Form 4562 of your annual tax return requires you to answer a number of detailed questions if you claim an automobile deduction.

Remember, when projecting your start-up losses, you can't immediately   **Start-up Losses Must Be**
deduct preopening expenses; instead, you must capitalize those costs and   **Capitalized, Not Deducted**
write them off (straight-line) over 60 months.[47] For example, if you are starting a restaurant and are paying salaries to a manager and to employees being trained before the day the restaurant opens for business, you might well think those expenses are immediately deductible. Not so! All such preopening expenses must be capitalized, and you can't begin to amortize them until opening day.

8.7 Choosing the Best Taxable Year for a Corporation

If your business is an S corporation or is considered a personal service corporation, you will generally have no choice but to operate on a calendar-year basis, and you can skip over the following discussion of how to select a taxable year. If, however, your business is incorporated and is neither an S corporation or a personal service corporation in which the services performed are "substantially performed" by owner/employees,[48] you will have an opportunity to choose any tax fiscal-year period you desire during your initial year of operation as a corporation. There are significant tax deferral and savings opportunities in selecting the right year end.

Unfortunately, in some cases, it will be necessary to be able to project with some accuracy how much your corporation will earn or lose each month for several months to a year ahead. If you expect to have start-up losses and show an overall net profit for your first year as an incorporated business, one good rule is to cut off your first taxable year at the end of the month in which you first get back to breakeven for the year-to-date.

For example, assume your first tax year starts on January 1, 1998, and you show a cumulative tax loss of $20,000 at the end of June. You then have taxable income of $10,000 a month in July, August, and September, and expect profits to continue. If you chose June 30 as your tax year end, you would have a $20,000 loss for your first tax period ending June 30, 1998. For federal income tax purposes, it is no problem, since you can carry over the loss and use it to offset $20,000 of taxable income during the next tax year. Some states, however, do not allow a carryover of losses.

Another approach would be to choose an August 31 year end, so that you would show no taxable income for your first year, assuming the corporation continued to net $10,000 a month.

If you do not mind paying some tax earlier, it might pay, in the above example, to wait until the end of October, November, or even December to cut off the first tax year. This would enable the corporation to isolate $20,000 to $40,000 or so of profit in a tax period subject to low federal corporate income tax rates.

If you do so, however, you are making an assumption that the corporation will be in a higher tax bracket in the following year, which cannot be known with any certainty. In addition, the existence of tax credits would somewhat complicate the simple picture portrayed above. Obviously, your accountant can help you decide which tax year will produce the best result.

Benefits of Adopting January 31 Year End

Another planning approach in adopting a year end, which may sometimes conflict with the above strategy, is to adopt a January 31 year end. If you structure your employment contract with your corporation so that you receive a substantial part of your compensation in January each year, you can, in effect, defer the bonus to your following tax year, while the corporation can deduct it — if paid in January — for its fiscal year ending just after the bonus is paid. Naturally, the corporation will be required to withhold income tax from your bonus, but at reduced rates, compared to regular monthly salary payments. Federal income tax withholding on bonuses is at a flat rate of only 28%.

Seasonal Businesses

If you have a seasonal business, you may want to defer taxes by selecting a tax year that ends just before your most profitable season begins. For example, if you are in the business of selling Christmas tree ornaments and do most of your business from October through December each year, you might choose a September 30 tax year end.

Remember, though, that tax considerations are not the only factors to take into account in choosing a fiscal year. If taking an annual inventory is a major task, consider adopting a year end that occurs when inventory is at a low ebb and when business is slow, if possible. You may also find that you will get somewhat quicker and better service from your CPA firm for work such as annual tax returns and audits if you pick a fiscal year that ends several months before or after December. Most CPAs are at their busiest during their annual tax season from about February to May, preparing 1040s and doing audits for their many clients who have December year ends.

8.8 Selecting Tax Accounting Methods

Choosing tax accounting methods for your business may seem like a dull, uninteresting chore, something of interest to accountants only. However, the whole point of choosing the best tax accounting method for your situation is to maximize your cash flow, a goal which should be close to the heart of every business owner. In effect, the name of the game in choosing a favorable (and permissible) tax accounting method is to defer income to some time in the future, or else to accelerate tax deductions, taking them now, rather than later. By doing either, you will reduce your tax liability this year, and defer it to next year, or to an even later date, in some instances.

Rely on your tax accountant's advice when choosing which tax accounting methods you should adopt in your business. This section is provided for your information in case you are not sure whether your accountant has recommended the method that will produce the best results for you.

The two overall tax accounting methods most commonly used are the cash method and the accrual method. There are, however, other special overall methods, plus a number of special kinds of accounting elections a business can make with regard to particular items, such as installment sales, inventory valuations, and deduction of accrued vacation pay.

Cash Method

The cash receipts and disbursements method of accounting, called the cash method, is the simplest accounting method in use. Under this method, you include income only as it is actually or constructively received.

Likewise, you only become entitled to deductions when you actually pay expenses — except for certain special items like depreciation or amortization of certain kinds of expenditures — rather than when you receive bills for the expenses. Thus, you usually do not have to report your year-end accounts receivable in income for the year and cannot deduct your year-end accounts payable. This will normally allow you to defer some taxable income each year if your year-end receivables are larger than accounts payable and other accrued but unpaid expenses. Obviously, this gives you some flexibility, too, if you want to pay off a number of payables at year end to reduce your taxable income for the current year.

The cash method is used by most individual taxpayers and by businesses in the real estate, financial, and service fields, where inventories of goods are not material factors in producing income. Businesses with significant inventories, such as manufacturers and wholesale or retail firms, are usually required to use an accrual method of tax accounting.[49] In some cases, however, it is possible even for those businesses to use a hybrid accounting method — accounting for income and the cost of goods sold on an accrual method — while using the cash method to report selling expenses and administrative expenses.

The Tax Reform Act of 1986 disallowed use of the cash method for C corporations — regular corporations — and for partnerships that have C corporations as partners. One exception is for small firms with average gross receipts of five million dollars or less during the three preceding years.[50] Another exception is made for larger firms in the farming business and for certain employee-owned qualified personal service corporations in fields such as law, medicine, accounting, architecture, or consulting.

Sole proprietorships, S corporations, and partnerships with no C corporation partners are not affected by these restrictions, unless they are considered tax shelters, and may remain on the cash method if that is a permissible accounting method for their particular type of business. Firms that are forbidden from using the cash method must adopt the more complex accrual method of accounting.

Accrual Method

As noted above, most large corporations and businesses with significant inventories are required to report income on the accrual method of accounting for tax purposes. This method requires you to report income when income is earned rather than when you receive it. Similarly, expenses can be deducted when all events have occurred that fix the amount and the fact of your business' liability for a particular expense, even if it is paid in a subsequent tax year. However, if economic performance required of the other party does not occur until a subsequent tax year, you may not be able to deduct an accrued expense until economic performance occurs.

For example, if you sign a contract with your accountant in 1997 to prepare your tax return in 1998, "economic performance" does not occur until 1998, and you may be unable to accrue the deduction in 1997, unless you meet several requirements, such as recurring expenses or performance occurs within a reasonable time after the end of the tax year.[51]

Even though the accrual method may not be required for your business, you may find it preferable to use if most or all of your income is from cash sales and you pay a large part of your expenses on a delayed credit basis. In this case, you would have few, if any, receivables at year end but might have substantial accrued payables you could deduct in the current year without having to actually make payment before year end.

Accrual of bonuses to employees, in an incorporated business, is a good example of a deduction that can be accelerated by a business using the accrual method. But expenses owed to you or a related owner of the business can't be deducted until actually paid.[52]

If your business is engaged in heavy construction work on a long-term contract basis, it may be difficult to tell in advance whether a particular contract will result in a profit or loss since many unforeseen difficulties may arise. The tax regulations recognize this problem and allow such contractors to use special methods of accounting, which may delay the time when profit or loss is recognized on a long-term contract. They are:

Special Accounting Methods Long-Term Contracts

- The percentage of completion method; and
- The completed contract method.[53]

The Tax Reform Act of 1986, however, and subsequent legislation has eliminated the use of the completed contract method of accounting for most large companies, except for certain ship contracts and for some home construction and other residential building contractors. Fortunately, small businesses, whose average annual gross receipts for the three preceding years do not exceed ten million dollars, are still allowed to use completed contract accounting for tax purposes, at least for contracts that are estimated to take no more than two years to complete.[54] Even those completed contract method deferrals that survive the new restrictions are now mostly considered tax preference items under the alternative minimum tax rules.[55] In other words, heads you lose, tails the tax collector wins.

If your business makes casual or occasional sales of personal property — other than merchandise held for sale — or makes sales of real estate it owns, the profit on any such sale can, in general, be reported on the installment basis as and when payments are received, rather than in the year of sale.[56] The installment method of reporting, however, is not available for "dealers," such as retailers, in personal or real property, except for certain dealers in real property. This is an election that sellers of residential lots or time-shares may make to use the installment method. The catch is that the dealer making this election must agree to pay interest on any tax that is deferred by using installment reporting.[57]

Installment Sales

In the case of nondealer sales of property for more than $150,000, if the total face amount of all installment notes exceeds five million dollars for the year, at the end of the year, the seller must pay interest on the deferred tax liability.[58] Sales of personal-use property or of farm property, for any amount, are exempt from the interest-on-deferred-tax provisions.[59]

If you maintain substantial inventories, discuss with your accountant the pros and cons of using the last-in-first-out (LIFO) method of valuing year-end inventories, versus the more common and simpler first-in-first-out (FIFO) method.[60]

Inventory Valuation Methods

FIFO Method

Under the FIFO method, the cost of ending inventory is calculated under the assumption that the first items of inventory bought were the first ones to be sold, so that only the most recently purchased items are assumed to be left in inventory at the end of each year. This usually means the highest-cost items, in times of inflation. For example, if a company turns all its inventory over every three months, FIFO assumes, in effect, that the inventory remaining on hand at December 31 was all bought in the last three months of the year, rather than at some earlier date when prices may have been lower.

Most companies use the FIFO method because:

- FIFO is much simpler to use in terms of maintaining accounting records;
- When prices of goods are generally rising, FIFO has the effect of making a company's net income appear to be greater than if the more conservative LIFO method were used — but it also tends to inflate the amount of a company's taxable income; and
- Their accountants never mention to them that there is an alternative method (LIFO) of inventory accounting that can be used.

LIFO Method

In contrast to FIFO, the LIFO method assumes that the items in your ending inventory are the first or oldest ones that were acquired. Thus, under LIFO, ending inventory values for many of the items of inventory will be based on what that item cost in the very first year in which the business began using the LIFO method. The difference in inventory valuation can be dramatic if, for example, a business using LIFO for ten years was paying $10 each ten years earlier for the widgets it keeps in inventory versus a current price of $75 per widget. Under LIFO, the widgets would still be carried on the accounting records at a cost of $10 apiece versus $75 under FIFO.

Accordingly, the difference in inventory cost, or $65 per widget in the above example — called the LIFO reserve — would be the amount of taxable income per widget that the company has deferred over the ten years. Thus, for a company with large amounts of capital invested in inventories, it is easy to see how LIFO can result in a huge tax saving.

At present, using the LIFO method is extremely complex, and the tax savings may in some cases be offset by increased accounting fees incurred and additional management time spent in attempting to comply with the LIFO tax regulations. The tax requirements for using LIFO, however, are somewhat relaxed for those small businesses with less than five million dollars a year in sales.[61]

Choosing LIFO or FIFO

Any firm with inventories may elect to use either FIFO or LIFO. If a firm is already using FIFO, it may be able to change over to LIFO if a number of technical requirements set by the IRS are met. Or, a company using LIFO may also change over to FIFO. Note, however, that if a firm uses LIFO and changes to FIFO for some reason, it will usually have to pay a large amount of tax when it recaptures the LIFO reserve described above, at the time of the changeover. Any such changes in inventory accounting methods should not be attempted without the assistance of a competent tax adviser. If your C corporation already uses LIFO inventory accounting and elects S corporation status, your corporation will be required to pay tax, in four annual installments, on the LIFO reserve at the time of the changeover to an S corporation.[62]

Uniform Capitalization Rules

Regardless of whether a company uses LIFO or FIFO for inventory accounting, it generally must allocate a wide range of its indirect costs to inventory, rather than simply deducting them as expenses, under the IRS's uniform capitalization rules. The practical effect of this is these indirect costs that have been absorbed into the cost of inventory on hand at the end of the tax year do not get deducted currently for tax purposes. Manufacturing and processing operations of any size are subject to these complex capitalization rules. The uniform capitalization rules do not apply to a wholesale or retail business in any year when the company's annual gross receipts for the preceding three years have averaged ten million dollars or less.[63]

Vacation Pay Accrual Method

If you accrue employees' vacation pay for internal business purposes, you normally can only deduct your liability for these accruals when an employee actually uses his or her vacation pay. The only exception is for accrual-basis taxpayers, where vacation pay is vested at the end of a tax year and paid within two and a half months afterwards.

8.9 Tax Problems Unique to Corporations

While this book has outlined some of the many tax and other advantages inherent in operating a corporation, you need to be aware of a number of traps in the tax law if you go overboard in trying to take advantage of the tax benefits bestowed on corporations.

As is emphasized in this chapter, the most basic goal in corporate tax planning for many high-income individuals is to leave as much profit in the corporation as possible so it can be taxed at the relatively low corporate tax rates and later withdrawn tax-free or at capital gains rates, such as by selling or having the corporation redeem the stock or by liquidating the corporation.

The government's role is to prevent the taxpayer from reaching these goals except where the corporation has good business reasons — as opposed to the individual's tax and investment reasons — for virtually everything it does. In attempting to plug up all the possible loopholes taxpayers might use to take advantage of low corporate rates, the tax law contains a whole array of penalties for corporations that:

- Unreasonably accumulate earnings;[64]
- Are used as "incorporated pocketbooks" for holding personal investments;[65] or
- Are capitalized too heavily with debt.[66]

These and other operating problems of corporations under the tax law are briefly outlined below to give you a sense of what the limits are and how far you can go in using corporate tax advantages. None of these problems are significant concerns for S corporations.

Penalty Tax on Accumulated Earnings

The accumulated earnings tax potentially applies to almost every corporation that accumulates more than $250,000[67] in after-tax profits (with certain adjustments).[68] This is the case unless the corporation can demonstrate that it needs to retain the profits for use in its business operations.[69]

Your corporation can accumulate up to $250,000 — $150,000 for professional and certain personal service firms — in earnings without having to be concerned about this penalty tax.[70] If additional accumulations cannot be justified as being made for the "reasonable needs of the business," however, the corporation will be faced with the choice of paying out the excess earnings as dividends or paying the accumulated earnings tax. The tax is imposed at the rate of 39.6% on the improperly accumulated earnings.[71] Since this is a tax that is imposed in addition to the corporate income tax, it is one you probably do not ever want to be forced to pay.

As long as you are able to keep plowing profits back into your business; buying more facilities, equipment, and inventory; and maintaining needed working capital, you will not have much cause for worry about the accumulated earnings tax. If, however, you reach a point where the corporation has more liquid funds than it needs, and you are beginning to look for places to invest the surplus cash, like real estate or the stock market, that should serve as a signal to you that there may be a potential accumulated earnings problem. In that case, you will need some good tax advice as to what you can do to protect the corporation from imposition of the penalty tax.

Justifiable Accumulations

Fortunately, a number of acceptable reasons can justify accumulating funds that are not currently being used in the corporation's business. Some of the more important ones are listed below.

- You can set up a reserve to redeem enough of the stock of a shareholder (yourself, for example) who dies, in order to enable the individual's estate to pay certain expenses related to his or her death — such as estate and inheritance taxes, funeral expenses, and expenses of administering the estate.[72] This reserve can only be created by the corporation after the death of a shareholder and before the repurchase of the shareholder's stock.
- It is reasonable for you to create a fund to allow for a bona fide plan to replace facilities or expand the business, including the acquisition of another business.[73]

- You can also create a reasonable reserve fund to pay potential uninsured product liability claims.[74]
- Accumulating funds to retire indebtedness, created in connection with the business of the corporation, can be considered a justifiable accumulation.[75]
- You can set up a defined benefit pension plan with an initial "past service liability" to be funded over a number of years.

A number of ways also exist to reduce the accumulated earnings without paying them out as dividends. For example, one way would be to redeem part of the stock of the corporation, such as the stock of one of your children. This will not only reduce accumulated earnings, but it will also reduce the amount of excess cash not needed in the business.

Another useful approach is to have the corporation purchase real estate that it might currently be leasing. This can sometimes be particularly advantageous where you are the landlord who is leasing the property to the corporation, as suggested in Section 8.5. Technically, this tactic will not reduce the corporation's accumulated earnings, but it will use up excess cash that would otherwise raise questions by IRS auditors.

Another effective solution, if you have an accumulated earnings problem, is to convert your C corporation to an S corporation if that is possible. S corporations are not subject to the accumulated earnings tax because all their earnings are deemed to be distributed to shareholders.

Penalty Tax on Personal Holding Company Income

If a closely held corporation gets a large proportion of its gross income, usually 60% or more, in the form of personal holding company income,[76] such as dividends, interest, rents, and royalties, it will generally be considered a personal holding company for tax purposes.[77] Other kinds of income that are considered personal holding company income include:

- Income of a service business if it is received from someone who has the right under a contract to designate the particular individual who is to perform the contracted services.[78] For example, if a professional actor sets up a corporation, any income paid to the the corporation from his or her services will be personal holding company income if the movie studio has the right to name the actor who must perform the services. The corporation itself must retain the right to designate which employee will perform the services in order to avoid tax treatment of the income as personal holding company income. This rule makes it hard for a pro athlete or entertainer who incorporates to avoid personal holding company status.
- Payments a corporation receives from a 25% shareholder for use of its property is also personal holding company income.[79] This rule puts a damper on schemes such as having your corporation buy a yacht and charter it to you.

As a rule, if a corporation comes within the definition of a personal holding company, the tax law imposes a 39.6% penalty tax on any personal holding company income not distributed as a dividend.[80]

Most actively conducted small businesses will not need to be very concerned about being treated as personal holding companies since they will seldom get 60% or more of their gross income from passive sources like dividends and interest. The kind of small business most likely to have a personal holding company problem is the incorporated personal service business — when the corporation enters into contracts and agrees to provide the services of an employee who is a major shareholder.

The best way to avoid this problem is to specify in the contract that the corporation reserves the right to designate the person who will provide the services. You will need to consult your tax adviser, however, before entering into any such personal service contract since the tax rules in this area are quite subtle and the tax penalty is very heavy if the income under the personal service contract is considered to be personal holding company income.

Another type of operating company that frequently encounters personal holding company tax problems is the developer of computer software that generates much of its income from software licensing agreements. While the tax law provides a special exemption from the personal holding company provisions for corporations actively engaged in the computer software business, the terms of this exception are quite technical and many software firms will only be able to qualify for this relief with very careful planning.[81]

Possible Treatment of Corporate Debt as Stock

As discussed in Section 8.5, there are two significant advantages to putting part of your investment in an incorporated business into the corporation in the form of debt, rather than all of it in exchange for stock. These advantages are:

- The interest paid to you is normally deductible by the corporation, unlike dividends paid on its stock.
- Repayment of the money you loaned to the corporation allows you to take part of your investment out of the corporation tax-free.

Because the use of debt in structuring a closely held corporation is so advantageous, Congress has taken steps to limit the extent to which you can use debt to capitalize a corporation and still enjoy these advantages.[82]

Over the last two decades, the IRS has proposed several sets of new and complex regulations as to when loans to a corporation by its shareholders will be treated as equivalent to an investment in its stock — in which case interest payments will not be deductible by the corporation and principal payments would be taxable to the recipient.

Debt-Equity Distinction

These regulations have raised such a storm of protest each time they have been proposed that the IRS finally withdrew them. So, to determine what constitutes debt and stock, guidelines are used from hundreds of different court decisions. Nevertheless, you can follow a few generally accepted ground rules to avoid having corporate debt reclassified by the IRS as equity or stock:

- The loan should not have any equity-type features, such as interest or payments, pegged to the corporation's income.
- The loan should be made at a reasonable interest rate, such as the rate at which the IRS imputes interest between related parties.
- The corporation's total debts — other than trade accounts payable — should not be more than about three times its net worth.
- The loan should be documented by a written note and should have a specified maturity date. All interest and principal payments on the note should be made on time.

If you follow each of the above rules, you will generally avoid the problem of having debt reclassified as stock. If you fail to comply with one or more of those rules when lending money to your corporation, the loan may be treated as a stock investment. This can be a serious tax trap if, when the loan is to be repaid, you are unaware that the repayment to you may constitute taxable income.

Double Taxation of Corporate Income

The most basic tax problem resulting from incorporating a business is the possibility of double taxation of the business income if it is paid out as dividends. For example, if a C corporation has any profit after payment of salaries and other expenses, it must pay tax on those profits. Then, if those profits left after taxes are distributed to stockholders as dividends, the stockholders must also pay tax on the dividends they receive. Fortunately, the problem of double taxation is generally quite manageable and most small incorporated businesses never pay dividends. The owners normally are also the officers of the corporation and can take enough income out in the form of salary and fringe benefits to live on, usually leaving some profit in the corporation to be plowed back into the business.

Also, as outlined briefly in Section 8.5, there are a number of better ways to get the accumulated profits out of the corporation than by paying dividends.

Unreasonable Compensation

If you own an incorporated business or own a portion of its stock and are actively involved in operating the business, you will be an employee of the corporation and will draw a salary. Drawing a large salary from the corporation may enable you to withdraw much of the profits of the business without any problem of double taxation since the corporation can deduct reasonable compensation it pays to you as your salary.[83]

Thus, taking salary out of the corporation is preferable to taking money out in the form of dividends, since the corporation cannot deduct dividends it pays. The salary you receive, if reasonable, is deductible by the corporation; however, the key word here is reasonable. If you try to take too much income out of the corporation as salary, including bonuses and fringe benefits like pension and profit-sharing contributions, the IRS may try to treat part of your salary as unreasonable compensation.

If you are fortunate enough to be worried about the one-million-dollar limitation on executive compensation that went into effect in 1994, you can relax. That limitation will only apply to executives of publicly held corporations. So unless your company has gone public, you don't need to be concerned about this limitation.[84]

There are no hard and fast rules as to how much compensation is reasonable, but if you are taking no more than the officers in similar businesses of the same size are paid, you should not have any problem establishing that your compensation from the corporation is reasonable under the circumstances.

If, however, the IRS does succeed in treating part of your compensation as excessive, there will be two serious tax consequences:

- The deduction by the corporation for the unreasonable portion of your salary will be disallowed.
- Part of your salary will be reclassified as dividend income, and thus pension and profit-sharing plan contributions based on that salary may not be fully deductible, which could even result in disqualification of your pension or profit-sharing plan.

8.10 Estate Planning in Connection with Your Business

As the owner of part or all of even a moderately successful business, you may find that after a few years, the value of your business accounts for a very large portion of your personal net worth. As such, your business will probably be the most important single asset you have to be concerned with for estate planning purposes, both during your lifetime and at the time of your death.

No attempt will be made here to go into the intricacies of the estate-planning possibilities that may be available to you; instead, the fundamental approaches you need to be aware of are outlined below. Discuss how to relate these concepts to your own situation with your tax adviser and attorney.

Income Splitting

A useful method of reducing lifetime income taxes is to split the taxable income from your business between two or more persons or entities. Usually a corporation, particularly an S corporation, is a useful vehicle for doing this; you can split income between you and your children by giving them stock in the corporation. A corporation that has not elected S corporation treatment can also be used to split income between you and the corporation. See Section 8.2.

Reducing Estate and Gift Taxes

Often, the best time to remove potential wealth from your taxable estate at death is by giving your children part of the stock in your incorporated business when the business is formed — when the value of the stock is likely to be negligible. If you wait until the business has become a valuable and profitable enterprise, gifts of stock at that time may result in substantial taxable gifts for gift tax purposes, even though the tax cost of those gifts may not be felt until you die, in some cases. You can currently make gifts of up to $10,000 ($20,000 if married) per year to each of your children completely free of federal gift taxes.

Assuming that you want part of your stock in your incorporated business to pass to your children at your death, it obviously makes sense to give them a portion of the stock — but not enough to affect your control of the corporation — during your lifetime. By doing this, there will be little or no gift tax cost if it is done when the business is started. Thus, they will already own the stock when you die, and that valuable asset will have passed to them free of death taxes in most instances. In addition, as noted above, lifetime gifts of stock to your children may also save on income taxes.

Buy-Sell Agreements

If you have one or more partners or business associates who also own a part of the business, it is very important that you enter into a buy-sell agreement with them that spells out what happens if one of you dies, becomes disabled, or wants to sell his or her interest in the business.

Often, these agreements are funded by life insurance on the owners. So, for example, if you die, the business or the other owners will collect the life insurance proceeds and use those funds to buy out your interest in the business. Otherwise, your surviving family members might find it very difficult to sell the interest in the business they inherit from you, except at a give-away price.

Many small business owners ignore the need for buy-sell agreements or, like having a will drawn up, they keep putting it off. When one of the partners or shareholders dies, the survivors may have a problem in raising enough cash to pay the death taxes. This is only one of the problems that may arise when there is no buy-sell agreement.

The few hundred dollars you may spend in legal fees to have a buy-sell agreement with your business partners or associates drawn up is probably one of the best investments you and your associates will ever make.

Unlimited Estate Tax Marital Deduction

Thanks to the estate tax unlimited marital deduction, enacted by Congress in 1982, any assets you leave to your spouse are treated as a deduction from the amount of your estate that is subject to federal estate tax.[85] Thus, if you leave all of your assets to your spouse when you die, it is generally possible to avoid all federal estate tax at that time. However, those assets will increase the size of your surviving spouse's estate later, when he or she also dies, thus pyramiding the estate tax on the second spouse's death. Keep in mind that estate tax rates go up as the size of a taxable estate increases.

Since not all state inheritance tax laws permit an unlimited marital deduction, it can create inheritance tax problems in those states if you leave too much property to your spouse. Refer to Section 11.8 for details regarding this state's marital deduction rules under its inheritance tax laws.

Setting Up a Trust

If you are married, and if you and your spouse have a combined net worth of more than $600,000, you may be able to save as much as several hundred thousand dollars of estate tax by having wills drawn up that provide for creation of a "bypass trust" (or "credit shelter trust") for the other spouse when one of you dies.

No tax will be saved, or need be paid, on the first death; however, up to $600,000 can be left in trust (still tax-free) at that time for the survivor, instead of passing everything under the unlimited marital deduction to the surviving spouse. This $600,000 amount — plus any investment growth — will be entirely excluded from the estate of the other spouse later, when he or she dies.

Because the federal estate tax often takes close to 50% of the net estate on the death of the second spouse, having set aside $600,000 in a trust — plus any appreciation on that amount — at the first death will quite clearly result in a very large estate tax savings, thus greatly increasing the after-tax amount you can leave to your children.

For a relatively small expenditure in legal fees to draw up such wills and trust, this is one of the most easily attainable, and yet most substantial tax benefits you will ever be able to achieve, with almost no downside — except that you won't be around to see your heirs enjoy it.

8.11 Work Opportunity

For many years, the tax law has provided tax credits to employers of up to 40% of the first $6,000 in wages per employee, for hiring individuals from certain targeted groups of economically disadvantaged people.[86]

New legislation has reinstated this credit and extended it to June 30, 1998. Employers who claim this credit have to forego a tax deduction for wages, equal to the amount of the credit claimed.[87] Even so, the net effect is still a very substantial tax subsidy to employers for hiring employees from any of the targeted categories. Consult your tax adviser as to what provisions of this law have been reinstated.

Empowerment Zone Credit

A new employment credit has been enacted, for certain businesses deriving at least 80% of their gross income from within designated urban and rural "empowerment zones" and meeting other requirements. The new credit for qualified wages paid to residents of the zone is 20% of the first $15,000 of wages paid to each such employee each year, or a maximum credit of up to $3,000 per employee.[88] Unlike the work opportunity credit, the new credit is not limited to wages paid to the employee in the first year of employment; however, the employee must work for at least 90 days to qualify.

8.12 Hiring a Spouse as an Employee

If you run an unincorporated business and your spouse works with or for you, there are three ways your spouse can be treated for tax purposes:

- As an employee;
- As a partner in the firm; or
- As an unpaid employee in a family business.

Social Security Tax

Congress, by enacting the Omnibus Budget Reconciliation Act of 1987, ended the exemption from Social Security (FICA) taxes for wages paid to a spouse, parent, or minor child — with the exception of a child under 18 years of age. There are, however, still some advantages to having your spouse be a paid employee of your proprietorship, as described below.

Medical Insurance

You can deduct any medical insurance premiums that you pay for employees, but you can only deduct a limited portion of your own medical insurance premiums. If your spouse works for you, however, you can put your spouse on the payroll and provide a medical expense reimbursement plan or medical insurance for your spouse and his or her family — which includes you — you can then deduct the payments or premiums in full since your spouse is an employee.[89] See Section 11.8 regarding state tax exemptions and other implications of hiring a spouse as an employee.

8.13 How to Save on Unemployment Taxes

The unemployment tax rate you pay as an employer is one of the few taxes where you have some control over the rate you pay. The state maintains a reserve account for each employer, in which it monitors the unemployment taxes you pay in and the unemployment benefits it pays out to your former employees. The more benefits the state pays to your former employees, the higher your individual company's tax rate will be and vice versa. So it pays for you to have as few former employees as possible who are collecting unemployment benefits, since these are charged to your reserve account.

To succeed in keeping down the unemployment claims charged to your account, you need to challenge any former employees' claims that appear to be unjustified. Often, you will be surprised to learn that an employee you had fired for stealing or who had quit on you has filed for benefits and has lied about his or her reasons for leaving. In general, an ex-employee can't collect unemployment from you if he or she left your employment for one of these reasons:

- Refusal to work;
- Voluntarily quitting;

- Inability to continue work due to illness or injury; or
- Misconduct, such as theft, not showing up for work, or the like.

Reducing Claims

An employee who leaves your employ for virtually any other reason, such as being fired for incompetence, can generally collect benefits, which will cost you money by raising your unemployment tax rate. Here are some tips on how you can keep down the number of unemployment claims filed against your account.

- When you are hiring, be aware of the cost you may have if you lay off these people in the future. You may hire a number of new employees for an expansion or new project with the view that if things don't work out as planned, you will simply lay them off and cancel the project with no further cost. Count the cost. Remember that if you do have to lay them off, you may pay a much higher unemployment tax rate for several years.

- Document in writing your reasons for firing an employee, such as for theft, insubordination, absence, or intoxication on the job. This will buttress your argument that the fired employee is not entitled to benefits if he or she should file a claim.

- Be aware that if you change an employee's hours of work and he or she quits as a result, it will be considered involuntary dismissal and the employee will probably be eligible for benefits. So it pays to have a written agreement signed by the employee to work any shift or hours that are required, if needed. Then, if the employee quits, it will not be due to a change in job conditions in the eyes of the law.

- If you decide to fire someone for misconduct, do it on the spot. If you keep them on at your convenience until you find a replacement, it will not usually be considered a discharge for misconduct, and the fired employee will most likely be eligible for benefits.

- If new employees do not work out, consider firing them before they have worked three months. In most states, a person has to work for you at least three months before they can earn unemployment benefits that are chargeable to your reserve account.

In general, it pays to keep a close eye on your employer reserve account and be aware of who is filing benefit claims that will cost you money. Contest any claims that you feel are not legitimate.

Endnotes

1. I.R.C. § 1366(e).
2. I.R.C. § 1(g).
3. I.R.C. § 243(a).
4. I.R.C. §§ 301 and 302(d).
5. I.R.C. § 331.
6. I.R.C. § 1(h).
7. I.R.C. § 531.
8. I.R.C. § 542.
9. I.R.C. § 542(a)(1).
10. I.R.C. § 246A.
11. I.R.C. §§ 219 and 404(a).
12. I.R.C. § 501(a).
13. I.R.C. § 408(m).
14. I.R.C. §§ 105–106.
15. I.R.C. § 105(b).
16. I.R.C. § 105.
17. I.R.C. § 106.
18. I.R.C. § 104(a)(3).
19. I.R.C. § 79(a).
20. I.R.C. § 132.
21. I.R.C. § 119.
22. I.R.C. § 127.
23. I.R.C. § 129.
24. I.R.C. § 422.
25. I.R.C. § 423.
26. I.R.C. § 125.
27. I.R.C. § 245(c)(1).
28. I.R.C. § 7872.
29. I.R.C. § 302(c)(2) permits the complete termination of the interest of a family member in a corporation by means of a stock redemption to qualify for capital gains treatment, if certain conditions are met.
30. I.R.C. § 453(g).
31. I.R.C. § 291(a).
32. *Lawrence R. Uri, Jr.,* P-H Memo TC 1989-58 (1989).
33. I.R.C. § 274(h).
34. I.R.C. § 280A.
35. I.R.C. § 274(d).
36. I.R.C. §§ 274(m)(1) and 274(h)(2).
37. I.R.C. § 280A(c)(1).
38. I.R.C. § 274(d).
39. I.R.C. § 274(d), as amended by Pub. L. No. 99-44.
40. Treas. Regs. § 1.274-5T(c)(2)(iii); Notice 95-50, 1995-42 I.R.B. 8.
41. I.R.C. § 274(a)(1)(A).
42. I.R.C. § 262; Treas. Regs. § 1.212-1(f).
43. I.R.C. § 280F(b)(2).
44. I.R.C. § 280F(a)(1).
45. I.R.C. § 280F(d)(5)(B).
46. Rev. Proc. 96-63, 1996-53 I.R.B. 46.
47. I.R.C. § 195.
48. I.R.C. § 441(i).
49. Treas. Regs. § 1.446-1(c)(2)(i).
50. I.R.C. § 448.
51. I.R.C. § 461(h).
52. I.R.C. § 267(a)(2).
53. Treas. Regs. § 1.451-3.
54. I.R.C. § 460.
55. I.R.C. § 56(a)(3).
56. I.R.C. § 453(b).
57. I.R.C. §§ 453(1)(2)(B) and 453(1)(3).
58. I.R.C. § 453A(b).
59. I.R.C. § 453A(b)(3).
60. I.R.C. § 472.
61. I.R.C. § 474.
62. I.R.C. § 1363(d).
63. I.R.C. § 263A(b)(2)(B).
64. I.R.C. § 531.
65. I.R.C. § 541.
66. I.R.C. § 385.
67. I.R.C. § 535(c)(2).
68. I.R.C. § 535(a) and (b).
69. I.R.C. § 537(a).
70. I.R.C. § 535(c)(2).
71. I.R.C. § 531.
72. I.R.C. § 537(a)(2).
73. Treas. Regs. §§ 1.537-1(b)(1) and 1.537-2(b)(2).
74. I.R.C. § 537(b)(4).
75. Treas. Regs. § 1.537-2(b)(3).
76. As defined in I.R.C. § 543.
77. I.R.C. § 542.
78. I.R.C. § 543(a)(7).
79. I.R.C. § 543(a)(6).
80. I.R.C. § 541.
81. I.R.C. § 543(d).
82. I.R.C. § 385.
83. I.R.C. § 162(a)(1).
84. I.R.C. § 162(m).
85. I.R.C. § 2056.
86. I.R.C. § 51.
87. I.R.C. § 280C(a).
88. I.R.C. §§ 1396–1397D.
89. Rev. Rul. 71-588, 1971-2 C.B. 91.

Notes

Chapter 9

Miscellaneous Business Pointers

Money is not the root of all evil. The lack of money is the root of all evil.

— Reverend Ike

9.1 General Considerations

This chapter contains helpful information on a variety of topics of interest to many small businesses, ranging from basic information on accounting, auditing, cash-flow management, and sources of financing, to useful tax and business tips and a comprehensive discussion of the very wide range of environmental laws that may affect your business. Also covered are other matters you may have to consider, such as consumer credit laws, the pros and cons of using independent contractors, key areas of pending legislation, and developing legal and economic trends that may have an impact on you in the near future.

9.2 Accounting — Some Basics

Accounting Systems

Maintaining good accounting records is a must for any small business. Without accurate and up-to-date records, you will be operating your business without vitally important information. Meaningful financial statements can only be prepared if the underlying records of transactions are accurate and current.

It may help to think of your accounting system as being like an airplane's radar system. If you are not getting current and correct feedback from either system, you will not have enough time to react to prevent a potential crash.

Single-Entry Method

While most schools and colleges teach only the double-entry method of bookkeeping, which provides a series of checks and balances in recording income and expenditures, some small business owners use a single-entry method of accounting.

If you are not knowledgeable about double-entry bookkeeping and handle most of the funds directly yourself, you may find that a single-entry system is acceptable for your needs and much simpler to use. The single-entry method is only slightly more involved than keeping a checkbook record of cash income and disbursements and usually consists of three basic records:

- A daily cash receipts summary. This summary may come from a cash register tape or sales slips. It will not only give you a total of your daily cash receipts, but it will break down your sales by product, by salesperson, or by store, depending on how much detail you need.
- A monthly cash receipts summary. This is simply a monthly summary of the daily cash receipts.
- A monthly cash disbursements report. This is a report on expenses and other payments, such as debt repayments, purchases of capital assets, or distributions of profits.

A number of simplified write-it-once systems for all different kinds of businesses are available at office supply stores.

Double-Entry Method

While a single-entry system is easy to use, it is not a complete accounting system because it focuses mainly on profit and loss and does not provide a balance sheet. For all but the very smallest of businesses, a single-entry accounting system is likely to be inadequate. Even if your business is very small, but expects to grow, it is usually advisable to start out with a full set of books, using the double-entry method.

You can avoid many future problems if you get a CPA to help you set up the accounting system for your business. He or she will tailor a chart of accounts to your specific needs and build in internal controls to record all transactions and to reduce the possibilities of employee theft or embezzlement that might go undetected with a poorly designed system.

Accounting Software

If you use a personal computer in your business, you can buy any number of general ledger accounting software packages if your accounting needs are fairly straightforward and if you have a reasonable understanding of how double-entry accounting works. For a very small business, adequate software packages are available for less than $100.

Most of the better and more user-friendly accounting software programs tend to insulate you from the need to understand the niceties of double-entry accounting. However, it will still be helpful to you in understanding your accounting system if you have at least some grasp of how double-entry accounting works. Spending a few hours with an introductory textbook on basic accounting, long enough to get an overview of how double-entry accounting works, will be time well spent for the small business owner who would like to understand more of what is going on "under the hood."

Accounting Firm Services

If you are going to use an outside accounting firm to prepare financial statements, they can provide three different levels of service — compilations, reviews, and audits.

Compilations

Most financial statements prepared for small businesses are compilations because they are far less expensive than an audit or review. In a compilation, the outside accountant has no obligation to do any investigation unless something looks suspicious or misleading. Generally, all an accountant is required to do in preparing compilation statements is to take the financial data you give him or her and present it in a manner that conforms with generally accepted accounting principles (GAAP). In a compilation, the accountant expresses no opinion on the accuracy of the information presented. The accountant is simply taking what you gave him or her and putting it in a proper financial statement format. It is important for you to remember that regardless of what type of assurance your accountant expresses, you are ultimately the one responsible for ensuring your financial statements are prepared accurately.

Reviews

A review involves some limited analysis or testing of the financial records, but the certified public accountant (CPA) expresses only a very limited opinion as to the accuracy of the information in the financial statements. A review is somewhat less expensive than an audit, but more expensive than a compilation. Most small businesses hire a CPA firm to do a review only if their bankers or other lenders or financial backers insist on a review rather than a compilation.

Audits

An audit is invariably the most involved and most expensive level of service in connection with financial statements. An accounting firm that audits financial statements must not only verify that your financial statements are presented fairly and in accordance with GAAP, but it also checks and verifies some or all of the accounts to satisfy itself that they are real. To verify accounts, an accounting firm can request confirmations of bank accounts or receivable and payable account balances from banks, customers, and vendors to uncover possible errors or fraud in recordkeeping. Because audits are relatively expensive, many small businesses elect to have review or compilation statements done; however, lenders or bonding companies often insist that you have a certified audit.

Depreciation

The Tax Reform Act of 1986 effectively repealed the highly favorable accelerated cost recovery system (ACRS) tax depreciation system that was in force from 1981 until the end of 1986. In January 1987, taxpayers learned to live with another whole new complex system of depreciation.

Unfortunately, it is still necessary to know the former ACRS rules for assets acquired during the 1981–86 period, as well as the old depreciation rules for items acquired before 1981, to compute current depreciation on those assets.

The Modified ACRS System

The modified ACRS (MACRS) law from 1986 does not provide depreciation tables, unlike the previous ACRS system. Instead, all assets (with a few special exceptions) placed in service after 1986 are assigned to 3-, 5-, 7-, 10-, 15-, or 20-year recovery period categories, except for real estate, which must be depreciated over 39 years — 27.5 years for residential rental property.[1]

Under the MACRS system, most personal property is depreciated under the 200% declining balance method over a specified number of years — called a recovery period. The only exceptions are for 15- or 20-year property, for which the 150% declining balance method is used. Real estate may only be depreciated under the straight-line method.

Assets other than real estate are mostly assigned to the various recovery periods that vary from industry to industry and are far too voluminous and technical to reproduce in a book of this nature. MACRS, however, specifically assigns some types of assets to recovery classes. For example, autos and light trucks are five-year property. The MACRS provisions have also reduced the maximum annual depreciation deductions on luxury automobiles as discussed in Section 8.6.

One small ray of sunshine in the MACRS tax depreciation nightmare is a recent liberalization of the former $10,000 first-year expending election for tangible personal property. In 1993 this $10,000 limit was increased to $17,500, and 1996 tax legislation will gradually increase this deduction to $25,000 over a period of years. You may elect to expense the cost of furniture and equipment in the year such assets are placed in service, subject to the above dollar limits.[2] For example, if the only depreciable items you buy in 1998 are $15,000 of office equipment, you may be able to deduct the full $15,000 in 1998. Note, however, that this special deduction is not allowed to the extent that it would create a loss for your trade(s) or business(es) for the year. Also, the deduction is phased out if you acquire more than $200,000 of eligible property during the tax year.

Internal Accounting Controls

Poor internal accounting controls and recordkeeping procedures are a weakness for many small business owners. Lax procedures are frequently to blame when a secretary or bookkeeper departs for Brazil with thousands of dollars of stolen or embezzled funds belonging to his or her employer. Ideally, you would consult a good accountant to set up and review your internal financial controls; however, that will cost you a good deal of money, so before you do so, you may want to do your own review of your internal controls, using the checklist located at the end of this chapter.

9.3 Cash-Flow Management

Cash flow is the lifeblood of any business organization; yet, small business operators are often so concerned with other matters, they don't pay attention to managing their cash resources properly. Good cash management can make a significant contribution to the competitiveness and profitability of your business.

Poor cash management is one of the main causes of business failures, particularly among smaller firms, since a cash shortage due to poor planning can set off a chain reaction of disastrous consequences, even in a profitable business.

Cash-flow management has two aspects: 1) projecting future cash flow, and 2) controlling and maximizing the cash available from operations at all times.

Projecting Cash Flow

Perhaps the most important part of cash-flow management is accurately projecting your business' near- and long-term cash needs and making your business decisions reflect those needs. Often, to project what your sales will be in coming months, it will be necessary to rely on what has happened in the past — what percentage will be credit sales and when your receivables are likely to be collected.

Similarly, you have to estimate and project what you will have to pay out in the way of payroll, rent, taxes, servicing debts, purchasing inventory, and paying off existing payables, plus extraordinary outlays you can anticipate.

The purpose of making these detailed projections of expected cash inflows and outflows is to point out any future cash shortages or deficits, so you can take steps in advance to prevent such occurrences. For example, if your projections indicated you were going to experience a severe cash crunch in about three months, you might take any of a number of steps to avert it, such as:

- Seeking to raise new capital;
- Borrowing money;
- Liquidating some of your inventory by cutting prices; or
- Cutting back on planned expenditures.

If you have a computer, microcomputer models are available to assist you with preparing projections of cash flows. If you don't own a computer, your accountant may have models available to assist you.

Controlling and Maximizing Cash Flow

If you are able to increase available cash by speeding up collections, delaying payments, or by other means, you can use the extra cash to reduce your borrowing — thus saving interest expenses — or you can invest the surplus cash to earn interest. Either way, improving your cash flow should increase your net earnings and should also help you avert cash shortages.

Here are some basic ways to improve your business' cash flow.

- Bill your customers promptly. The later they receive the bill, the later you will usually collect for a particular sale.

- If you know that certain large customers must receive bills by certain days of the month so you can get paid in that month, try to bill them before those deadlines.

- Deposit your cash receipts daily if possible.

- Keep close tabs on credit customers. Send them past due notices as soon as payments become overdue.

- If you can do so without hurting business, add late charges to overdue accounts.

- Never pay bills until just before they become due, unless you will receive a worthwhile discount for quick payment.

- Try to keep inventories as lean as possible. Even if you occasionally lose a small sale because you are temporarily out of an item, you should be far ahead of the game by substantially reducing the amount of cash you have tied up in inventory.

- Look for items in your inventory that are moving slowly or not at all. Consider slashing the price on those articles to convert them to cash and also to reduce the cost of storing them or having them take up valuable shelf space.

- Consider leasing equipment items instead of buying because this will usually require a smaller cash outlay.

- Do not pay more on your estimated income taxes than you have to. You may qualify — without incurring interest charges or late payment penalties — under one or more exceptions that will allow you to delay paying much of your tax for the year until the tax return is due. If you realize that you have already overpaid your corporate estimated tax for the year, there is a procedure for obtaining a refund before the time when you can file a return [3]

- If your business has a net operating loss for tax purposes that can be carried back to prior years, a procedure exists for filing a claim for a quick refund of the prior years' taxes. File it as early as you can because the IRS no longer pays interest on these refunds.

- Instead of keeping all your business cash in a local bank account, consider putting a significant portion of your cash in an out-of-town money market type of fund that pays interest and allows you to write checks against the account. Since you continue to earn interest on funds on deposit until the checks clear, consider using a fund in a distant part of the country, so that it will take longer for your checks to clear when you make payments to local firms.

9.4 Protecting Your Assets

Starting a new business is almost always a risky proposition, and if the business fails, you may be forced into bankruptcy and could lose everything except what the bankruptcy laws allow you to keep. This is one reason why many small businesses incorporate at the outset, since a corporation will generally limit your liability to business creditors to the amount you invest in the corporation, plus any loans to the corporation you guarantee.

Accordingly, if you incorporate, be cautious about committing too much of your personal assets to the business. For example, instead of putting a building or piece of land you own into the corporation, it may be better — and may save income and property taxes — for you to keep the property and lease it to the corporation.

Even if you incorporate, the leases or bank loans you need to guarantee on behalf of the corporation could still wipe out your personal assets if the business folds. Thus, it often makes sense to have your corporation set up a tax-qualified pension or profit-sharing plan and to have it contribute as much as possible to the plan on your behalf. Not only does this provide substantial tax savings and deferral, but the law in most states will in many cases protect your account under such a plan from your creditors or the corporation's creditors.

So, if you can build up a significant retirement fund in your corporation's pension plan, you have at least some degree of assurance that the failure of the business or a disastrous lawsuit will not touch that nest egg. In a divorce, however, your spouse may be able to claim his or her share of the pension plan account.

9.5 Protecting Trade Names and Trademarks

If you intend to use some type of distinctive trade name for your business or trademark for your product or in advertising your services, consider taking steps to protect the use of the name or mark by registering it under state or federal law, or both. When considering your trade name or trademark, it may be necessary to perform a search, which can be expensive, to determine whether someone else has already registered the same or a very similar name or symbol. You do not want to open yourself up to a lawsuit for infringement. Since not every trade name can be registered, you will need to consult a trademark attorney if you are interested in protecting a particular name used by your business.

Federal registration of a name confers a number of significant benefits to registering your trade name or trademark, including:

Advantages to Trade Name or Trademark Registration

- Nationwide notice to others of your exclusive right to use the name or mark.

- Prima facie evidence of the validity of the registration and your exclusive right to use the mark throughout the country.

- With certain exceptions, registration gives you an unquestionable right to use the name or mark.

- If you can prove in court that someone violated your rights under the Trademark Act of 1946, you will be entitled to recover their profits and any damages to you from its use.[4]

- The right to sue in federal court for trademark infringement, regardless of the amount at stake and whether or not there is diversity of citizenship — that is, regardless of whether you and the defendant operate in the same or different states.

- The right to have customs officials halt importation of counterfeit goods using your trademark.

Federal registration is permitted only if you will use the trade name or trademark in more than one state.

9.6 Section 1244 Stock

If you invest directly in a small corporation by transferring money or property (other than securities) to the corporation in exchange for its common stock — or preferred stock, if issued after July 18, 1984 — the stock will usually qualify as Section 1244 stock.[5] If it does, and the stock later becomes worthless or you sell it at a loss, Section 1244 of the Internal Revenue Code permits you to deduct up to $50,000 of your loss — $100,000 for a couple filing a joint return — as an ordinary deduction instead of as a capital loss for that year. This can be very important, since you can fully deduct an ordinary loss from your taxable income, while capital losses can only be used to offset capital gains if you have any, or $3,000 of ordinary income per year until your capital losses are used up.[6]

The $50,000 or $100,000 limit on the amount of loss that can qualify for ordinary loss treatment is an annual limitation.

Any stock issued by a small business corporation will generally qualify as Section 1244 stock unless the corporation obtained half or more of its gross receipts from passive kinds of income, such as interest, dividends, and the like, in the five years before your loss is incurred.[7] A corporation qualifies as a small business corporation if the total invested in its stock is one million dollars or less.[8]

If the stock issued by your corporation meets the requirements of Section 1244, it will automatically qualify for ordinary loss treatment, up to the first one million dollars of stock issued. You should be aware, however, that capital contributions you make, where no stock is received by you for such money, will not qualify for ordinary loss treatment.[9]

See Section 11.9 as to whether state law also provides favorable tax treatment for losses on stock in a small business corporation.

9.7 U.S. Small Business Administration and Other Government Loans

If you need to borrow money for your business and cannot obtain regular bank financing, don't overlook the possibility of obtaining a loan through the U.S. Small Business Administration (SBA). Many small business owners are under the impression that it is virtually impossible to obtain an SBA loan unless a member of a minority group; this is not the case. Although the SBA does make special efforts to provide financing for minority-owned businesses, only a relatively small percentage of SBA loans are made to minority firms. Furthermore, a very high percentage of applications for SBA loans are approved often within three to six weeks, when applications are properly submitted.

SBA Loan Programs

The SBA, an agency of the U.S. government, guarantees intermediate and long-term loans to small firms, and to a limited extent, also makes direct loans to some small businesses. The SBA is not allowed to grant such financial assistance unless the borrower is unable to obtain private-sector financing on reasonable terms. The SBA does not compete with banks or other lenders; instead, it works with private lenders to assure availability of capital to potentially profitable small firms. Contrary to what you may have heard on late-night television infomercials, the SBA does not have a grant program for starting a small business.

For your business to qualify for SBA financial assistance, it must come within the current definition of a small business. In general, these are the types of small businesses eligible for SBA financing:

- Manufacturers with a maximum of 500 to 1,500 employees, depending upon the industry in which the applicant is engaged;
- Retailers with less than $3.5 million in annual sales — up to $13.5 million for some types of retailers;
- Wholesaling firms with 100 or fewer employees;
- General construction firms, whose annual sales have averaged less than $9.5 million for the last three fiscal years; lower limits apply to various special trade construction firms;
- Service firms with annual receipts not in excess of $3.5 to $14.5 million, depending on the industry; and
- Other definitions apply for businesses engaged in activities, such as agriculture and transportation.

Private lenders that are eligible to make SBA-guaranteed loans or participate in SBA financing packages include banks, savings and loans, and certain other lenders. The SBA has several types of loan programs for small businesses, the largest of which is the 7(a) Loan Program.

Guaranteed Loans

Most SBA financing actually consists of loans by banks or other lenders that are guaranteed by the SBA. This enables the small business to obtain such loans at reasonable interest rates because the bank's risk is largely eliminated. SBA-guaranteed loans are tied to the bank prime rate, as published in *The Wall Street Journal*, at a rate of 2.25% above prime rate for loans of less than seven years, or 2.75% above prime for loans of seven or more years. The SBA charges lenders a 2.0% guarantee fee on the portion of a loan that is guaranteed. Lenders are allowed to charge this fee to the borrower.

The SBA has recently adopted an alternate standard for the 7(a) Loan Program, under which a prospective borrower that does not qualify as a small business under the various standards listed above, may now qualify as such if its net worth is no more than six million dollars and if it had annual after-tax net income of two million dollars or less in each of the two preceding years. As the borrower, you put up a reasonable amount of equity or collateral. These loans are usually secured by fixed assets, real estate, and inventory and are limited in term to seven years for working capital loans or ten years for purchasing fixed assets. Construction loans can be for as long as 25 years.

Under this program, the bank or other private lender deals with the SBA, and you deal with the bank, not the SBA. You will, however, need to do the following when you apply for such a loan or any other SBA financing:

- Define the amount you need to borrow and the purposes for which the funds will be used.
- Describe the collateral you will offer as security.
- Determine, through your bank, that a conventional loan is not available.
- Prepare current financial statements, preferably with your accountant's assistance. These would include, at a minimum, a relatively current balance sheet and an income statement for the previous full year and for the current year up to the date of the balance sheet.
- Prepare personal financial statements of the owners, partners, or stockholders owning more than 20% of the stock of the company.

Direct Loans

If you are unable to obtain sufficient conventional financing or SBA-guaranteed loan funds, it may be possible, in rare instances, to obtain a direct loan from the SBA. When made, these direct loans are usually offered on a participation basis with a bank or other lender, where the bank oversees the loan payments and loan servicing on behalf of itself and the SBA. In recent years, the SBA has largely ceased making direct loans because it has had only occasional and minimal amounts available.

Even when it does occasionally have funds to lend, there are always far more qualified applicants than funds to lend to them. Consequently, you will have very little chance of obtaining such a direct loan.

In 1992, however, the SBA began, as part of its direct loan program, to make "microloans" at slightly below-market interest rates to veterans, business owners with disabilities, and persons desiring to start companies in economically depressed areas. These loans, ranging from as little as $100 to a maximum of only $25,000, are intended to help very small businesses, particularly those run by minorities, women, and low-income people, who generally have a difficult time raising capital. As such, microloans are designed to empower people, such as single mothers, disabled individuals, and public housing tenants, to become self-employed and self-supporting.

The SBA's microloans are modeled after microloan programs that have been operated for a number of years by nonprofit agencies in the United States and in a number of Third World countries, generally with great success. For the smallest microloans — often only a few hundred dollars — no collateral is generally required, only a good character reference or a good reputation in the community.

The SBA microloan program is generally run in cooperation with local nonprofit organizations. To find an SBA microlender, contact an SBA district office or:

SBA Answer Desk
(800) 827-5722

New legislation frequently adds to and modifies the number and scope of SBA loan programs. Other programs include:

Other SBA Programs

- Seasonal lines of credit;
- Economic opportunity loans for entrepreneurs who are physically disabled or members of a minority group;
- Short-term contract loan guarantees;
- Energy loans to small firms to install, sell, service, develop, or manufacture solar energy or energy-saving devices; and
- Disaster recovery loans to firms harmed by natural disasters.

Since the nature, scope, and availability of funds under these numerous programs are constantly changing, consult your bank or local SBA offices if you think your firm may qualify under one of these special financial assistance programs.

The Economic Development Administration (EDA) of the U.S. Department of Commerce makes direct loans and offers loan guarantees to businesses in areas with low family incomes or areas suffering from high unemployment. The purpose of these loans is to promote creation or retention of jobs for the residents living in these areas.

U.S. Department of Commerce

To qualify for this financing, your business must be located in an EDA redevelopment area and you need to demonstrate that the venture will directly benefit local residents and will not create local over-capacity for the industry in question. Application for EDA loan assistance is a long and complex process, taking much longer for processing than typical SBA loans.

Rural Economic and Community Development Service

The Rural Economic and Community Development Service (RECDS), formerly the Farmers Home Administration, can perhaps be thought of as an SBA for rural areas. It offers insured and guaranteed loans to develop business and industry in nonurban areas with populations of under 50,000. Like the SBA program, RECDS loan guarantees are for up to 90% of the total amount of the loan and are made for up to 30 years for financing real estate acquisition, 15 years for machinery and equipment, and 7 years for working capital. RECDS loan guarantees are not available for agricultural production.

Unlike SBA loan guarantees, there is no dollar limit on these loan guarantees, nor does the RECDS make direct loans. Applicants for RECDS loan guarantees must not only have adequate collateral and good business histories, they must also demonstrate that the project will have a favorable economic impact and will create new jobs in the area — not merely shifting business activity and jobs from one area to another. Preference is given:

- To businesses that are expanding rather than transferring into an area;
- To projects in open country areas or towns with populations of under 25,000; and
- To business owners who are military veterans.

Other Federal Loan Programs

Other major federal loan programs are provided through the Federal Land Bank Association, Production Credit Association, and the Federal Intermediate Credit Bank. These organizations offer loans to businesses that provide services to farmers. These loans can be for purchasing land and equipment and for obtaining start-up working capital.

SBICs and SSBICs

In addition to direct loans and guarantees from government agencies, don't overlook possible loans or equity financing from Small Business Investment Companies (SBICs) and Specialized Enterprise Small Business Investment Companies (SSBICs). Both are licensed and regulated by the SBA to provide equity capital, long-term loans, and management assistance to small businesses.

SBIC and SSBIC loans are usually subordinated to loans from other creditors and are typically made for five- to seven-year terms. Both types of investment companies are privately owned and thus tend to favor loans to established companies with significant net worth rather than new business start ups.

You may have to give up a large part of the equity in your business if you obtain SBIC financing. An SBIC is not permitted to control a company (50% or greater ownership) it lends to, but typically an SBIC lender will insist on debt that is convertible into common stock, warrants, and options, which may give it up to 49% ownership in your company. An SBIC will also want seats on your board of directors, will impose controls and restrictions on the way your business operates, and may insist upon salary limits for the principal owners. SBIC financing does not come without a price.

SSBICs serve only those small firms that are owned by members of economically or socially disadvantaged minority groups.

Business development corporations are local development companies (LDCs) and certified development companies (CDCs) organized by local residents to promote economic development in their particular communities. These entities do not make working capital loans or loans to purchase free-standing equipment. Instead, LDCs or CDCs will arrange for SBA-guaranteed bank loans and sale of SBA-guaranteed debentures for up to 90% financing for 25 years for land acquisition, building construction, or renovation and purchase of fixed assets, such as machinery and equipment. For information on what state business loan programs may be available in this state, refer to Section 11.9.

Business Development Corporations

9.8 Mail Order Sales and Telemarketing

The lifestyles of many U.S. families in the nineties have changed to embrace a new contentment with staying at home. These families spend their leisure entertaining at home, watching the latest movies at home, and getting their information from Internet links to cyberspace. More and more workers telecommute via computer instead of going to the office. These lifestyle changes have breathed new life into home-based businesses and self-directed success, which in turn, have created a boom in mail order and telemarketing sales.

The increased activity in these industries has also gained the attention of the government and brought about more careful regulation. If your business engages in mail order sales or telemarketing, acquaint yourself with the most recent regulations in this section.

If your business involves selling goods by mail order, become familiar with Rule 435.1, a regulation issued by the Federal Trade Commission (FTC).[10] This federal regulation requires any business soliciting mail order sales to be prepared to ship the merchandise within 30 days after an order

Mail Order Sales

is received, unless it has clearly stated in its solicitation that orders will not be shipped for a longer period. Otherwise, the solicitation will be considered as an unfair and deceptive trade practice. In addition, if you receive an order and for some reason you cannot ship it within 30 days, or the period stated in your solicitation, you must:

- Immediately notify the customer and offer to either cancel the order and receive a refund or consent to the delay in shipment;
- Indicate when you will be able to ship or that you do not know when you will be able to ship the order; and
- Provide other required information to the customer, which will vary in content depending upon when you expect to be able to ship.

The coverage of Rule 435.1 extends to all orders you receive, including those received by modem, fax, or telephone, in addition to those received by mail. Rule 435.1 is fairly complex and difficult to understand, but you need to understand and be familiar with it if you sell goods by mail order. For a free guide on this FTC rule, contact the FTC at the number listed below and request *A Business Guide to the Federal Trade Commission's Mail Order Rule.*

Federal Trade Commission
(202) 326-2222

If you are going into the mail order business and want a single source of information on state and federal mail order laws, obtain the *Mail Order Legal Guide*, by Erwin J. Keup, from your book source or:

The Oasis Press
(800) 228-2275

State Sales and Use Taxes

If you sell across state lines to customers in states where you have no offices, employees, or other presence, the sale is usually not subject to sales tax in either state, since it is an interstate sale; however, technically, such sales are subject to use tax in the customer's state. A use tax is sort of a shadow of the sales tax and, in most states, applies where the sales tax does not.

The U.S. Supreme Court and other courts generally have not supported attempts of the various states to force out-of-state retailers to collect use tax on mail order or other sales made to residents of the taxing state, so that most mail order firms tend to treat such interstate sales as being tax-free, or tell the customers that it is up to them to report the purchase and pay the use tax, which they rarely do.

Unfortunately, in the last few years, many states have enacted new and broader sales and use tax laws. Many of these laws require out-of-state retailers, who advertise in the local media or send substantial amounts of direct mail or catalog solicitations into the state, to register as retailers subject to sales or use tax in the state and to treat such direct sales as taxable.

The U.S. Supreme Court ruled that these aggressive new sales tax laws are unconstitutional in the 1992 case of *Quill Corporation v. North Dakota*. It appears most of the broad new mail order sales and use tax laws — which have been adopted in some 34 states and are targeted to hit out-of-state mail order firms — may be invalid. While this is good news for mail order retailers, the bad news is the court also indicated in its decision that Congress could, if it chose to do so, constitutionally enact legislation that would permit the states to require use tax collection on mail order and similar sales by out-of-state retailers.

Sales-Use Tax Bill

In fact, just such a bill, inaptly named the "Consumer and Main Street Protection Act," has twice been introduced in the U.S. Senate by Senator Dale Bumpers (D) of Arkansas. This bill, if enacted, would grant states the right to enact laws requiring out-of-state sellers of tangible personal property to collect and remit state and local sales-use taxes if the following requirements were met:

- The seller is subject to the personal jurisdiction of the taxing state;
- The tangible personal property has a final destination in the state in question;
- The seller's gross receipts from sales of such property in the twelve months ending September 30 of the calendar year before the year of the sale exceeded $100,000 in the taxing state or three million dollars in the United States as a whole; and
- The taxing state collects and administers all of the local sales-use taxes imposed on behalf of its local jurisdictions, such as cities and counties.

Where a state has nonuniform local sales tax rates, the proposed legislation would give the seller the choice of either collecting tax at the appropriate rate in each local jurisdiction, or collecting tax at a flat statewide rate, based on an average rate determined by the state, rounded to the nearest 0.25%. Each state passing such a law would have to maintain a toll-free help line, which small mail order sellers could call at any time to determine the appropriate sales tax rate for sales to residents of that state.

Thus, if this or another federal law authorizing such use tax collections is enacted, it seems likely it will provide some exemption for smaller retailers and a simplified, statewide tax rate and payment method for sellers who have only minimal sales in each of a number of states. Otherwise, most small mail order sellers would instantly be forced out of business without such an exemption, due to the impossible complexity and enormous cost of filing sales or use tax returns for every state and local taxing district where a sale is made.

Telemarketing Rules

If your business is engaged in telemarketing, you will need to keep one hand on the telephone, and one eye on the Code of Federal Regulations. Effective January 1, 1996, a new set of Federal Trade Commission regulations went into effect under the Telemarketing and Consumer Fraud and Abuse Prevention Act, imposing stringent restrictions on telemarketing companies and how and when they can "reach out and touch" potential customers.[11] These new rules are primarily designed to reign in fraudulent phone scamsters.

The new standards require, among other things, that anyone who makes telemarketing calls to consumers must:

- Inform the consumer that the call is a sales call;
- Inform the consumer if the seller has a "no refunds" sales policy;
- Describe the nature of the goods or services that are being sold;
- Tell the consumer, if a prize is involved, what the odds are of winning and that they don't have to buy something in order to win;
- Make such calls only between the hours of 8:00 A.M. and 9:00 P.M.; and
- Make no further calls to a consumer who has asked not to be called again.

The new rules also impose extensive recordkeeping of contacts made, items sold, and other details of any telemarketing program that is covered. In general, these rules do not apply to calls initiated by the consumer, such as calls in response to publicity or advertising of the seller.

Penalties for violating these standards include fines of up to $10,000 per violation and reimbursement of consumers for any losses they have incurred.

9.9 Environmental Laws Affecting Your Business

As the world becomes more crowded and as the damaging effects of two centuries of unrestrained industrial development become more apparent on the environment, political attempts to remedy these problems, particularly the problems of pollution and toxic emissions, have resulted in a flood of legislation, regulations, and litigation involving environmental matters. While this is probably all to the good in the larger sense, some of the immediate effects of these new environmental restrictions have been to create another whole layer of complex and often conflicting government regulations on business, plus a virtual minefield of legal exposure for companies of all sizes.

For small businesses — most of which do not have in-house legal staffs and can hardly afford the large legal fees needed for professional guidance through this maze of regulations — the effect of the growing body of environmental laws is especially harsh. Small businesses are also disproportionately affected by the heavy costs of complying with various mandated emissions requirements, which often require large capital expenditures for sophisticated new pollution control equipment.

While this section cannot do much more than scratch the surface of the environmental law exposure and increased operational complexities most businesses are going to face, the discussion below explains some of the main problem areas you need to be at least passingly familiar with. This section also provides a capsule description of the major areas of federal environmental law that may currently apply to your business or which may apply at some time in the future.

Perhaps the most pervasive of the environmental laws, with the most devastating potential consequences for the unwary, are the environmental clean-up laws, and the legal liability these laws attach to real estate that has been contaminated by hazardous substances. The main laws that apply in this area are the Comprehensive Environmental Response, Compensation and Liability Act[12] (CERCLA or the Superfund law) and the Resource Conservation and Recovery Act (RCRA).[13]

Environmental Clean-up Laws

CERCLA and RCRA apply to virtually every real estate transaction. While RCRA applies primarily to currently generated hazardous waste, including limits on creation of waste and requirements for disposing of it, CERCLA is more focused on cleaning up hazardous substances that have been spilled or dumped in the past.

CERCLA deals with all kinds of pollution: air, surface water, groundwater, and soil. It covers virtually every type of hazardous substance, as defined under CERCLA, the Clean Water Act, the Clean Air Act, or the Toxic Substances Control Act. There are, however, major exceptions for petroleum and certain petroleum derivatives. The main thrust of CERCLA is to impose liability on private owners of property to clean up hazardous wastes they have created. CERCLA would also apply to owners of inherited property if the property in question was already contaminated when it was acquired.

CERCLA Liability

In short, even though you were not responsible for creating a contamination problem, if you acquire real estate that is already contaminated — and it later becomes apparent there has been a spill or dumping that requires an environmental cleanup, possibly at astronomical cost — you are liable for the costs of the cleanup if you are the current owner. You can't simply walk away from the property and let the government take it in lieu of paying the clean-up costs.

Once the owner, you are the responsible party and may be held liable for costs that exceed the value of the property many times over. You may even become liable somewhere down the road if you sell a business — an existing corporation, for instance — that has formerly owned contaminated property. The government could eventually institute environmental proceedings against the current property owner, who then sues all the prior legal owners of the property, including you, for indemnity or reimbursement.

Of course, you may be able to sue the prior owner or anyone in the chain of prior owners for indemnification if they are still in existence and can be found. However, since that is a pretty slim thread upon which to hang your financial survival, you need to take precautions up front, before acquiring any real property, to protect yourself from possible environmental liability for cleanup under CERCLA.

The following are some things you can and should do to reduce your risk in any real estate or existing business acquisition.

- Exercise considerable diligence concerning the current condition and past uses of any real estate involved in a transaction. Also, if buying an existing corporation, you need to find out what properties it owned in the past and be concerned whether any such properties may have been contaminated by hazardous substances.

- Be particularly wary of any sites that have been used as gas stations, landfill areas, locations of dry cleaners, chemical or other industrial production processes, battery production, recycling, or metal plating. Be extremely cautious if the site contains underground storage tanks.

- Consider retaining an environmental audit firm to do detailed site inspections and evaluations to determine if there may be a contamination problem.

- In a business or real estate purchase agreement, require written representations and warranties about the site from the seller and include provisions under which he or she will indemnify you if there is a problem. Be mindful of the seller's financial viability, in case you are forced to seek indemnity from him or her. A promise isn't worth the paper it is written on if the seller doesn't have the wherewithal to make good on it.

Even though under the Superfund law there is an innocent purchaser defense, you must be able to demonstrate that you made appropriate inquiry before acquiring the property to determine any pre-existing contamination problem. There is little guidance in the law at this point as to what constitutes an appropriate inquiry, so perhaps you should not expect to escape liability under that rule. The best defense is to avoid purchasing property that is contaminated by taking the steps outlined above. Even if these steps fail to discover a lurking environmental problem, at least you will have a much stronger argument to make under the innocent purchaser defense if you have done a due-diligence survey and had an environmental audit performed by a reputable firm.

RCRA Requirements

RCRA contains a comprehensive set of rules for managing hazardous wastes, including petroleum-based substances, and regulating those who generate hazardous wastes, transport them, and store, treat, or dispose of them. Penalties for violations include fines of up to $25,000 a day, plus imprisonment.

One important focus of RCRA is on underground storage tanks (USTs), many of which are known to be leaking gasoline or other contaminants into the surrounding soil and groundwater. Under RCRA, much of the regulation of USTs is left to state governments. Thus, under federal regulations, the owner of a UST must notify the state of the tank's existence, including tanks that were taken out of service after January 1, 1974.[14]

New USTs must satisfy federal performance standards, which generally require that they be constructed of fiberglass-reinforced plastic or steel that is cathodically protected from corrosion.[15] Furthermore, all existing USTs must be upgraded to federal standards by December 22, 1998,[16] which will result in some major expenditures for many small businesses, such as service stations.

Community Right-To-Know Notification

Under the provisions of the Emergency Planning and Community Right-To-Know Act (EPCRA), you must report any hazardous materials your business uses or stores to state and local emergency planning agencies and your local fire department.[17] This is a very broad requirement, one that may even apply to unlikely culprits, such as white collar office employers who store quantities of toner for copying machines on their business premises.

The law also requires that you have an emergency plan in the event of a release of any hazardous substance.

If subject to EPCRA, you must also file regular release reports to the EPA or state environmental agencies, even if the report is for a substance for which you have a permit to release. Government agencies use this data to keep track of annual emissions.

Clean Water Act

Under the Clean Water Act, the federal Environmental Protection Agency (EPA) and individual states are the watchdogs of water pollution standards.[18] The law also allows private citizens to sue to enforce the act. Penalties for violations can be as high as $50,000 a day, and even negligent but unintentional violations can result in imprisonment. For certain existing facilities, this law provides for a system of EPA permits for discharging certain amounts of water pollutants.

Wetlands Development

Portions of the Clean Water Act require that all proposed development activities, which involve the dredging or filling of wetlands, obtain permits from the U.S. Army Corps of Engineers.[19] Thus, before you acquire real property that you plan to develop in any way, you need to do a careful survey to determine if the property lies within an area that is considered to be a wetland. Otherwise, you may end up with a piece of property that is undevelopable and can hardly be sold at all, even for a huge loss.

This has been a trap for more than one unwitting buyer of land in wetlands districts, since wetlands include much more than swamps and marshes. Many dry-looking parcels may also fall within the regulatory definition. Furthermore, be aware that many states have adopted wetlands restrictions, which may require you to also obtain state development permits.

Clean Air Act

The Clean Air Act of 1970 was substantially revised and strengthened by the Clean Air Act of 1990 amendments.[20] The new requirements are being phased in over a number of years. Under the provisions of the 1990 act, businesses are affected by controls on three types of air pollution.

- Primary urban pollution. The EPA already has set standards for six primary pollutants that are generally discharged in large quantities by a wide variety of sources in urban and other areas of the country. The six pollutants are ground level ozone (smog), carbon monoxide, particulate matter, nitrogen dioxide, sulfur dioxide, and lead. These pollutants are generally not thought to be carcinogenic, but they do give rise to other serious health risks. Control measures for ground level ozone will have particularly significant effects on many small businesses, as the 1990 amendments go into effect.

- Toxic air pollutants. These include chemicals that are known to cause, or that are suspected of causing, cancer and other serious health effects, such as birth defects and gene mutations. The amended act requires the EPA to set toxic air pollution standards for specific industry activities. A number of these standards are applicable to many small businesses.

- Ozone depleters. The third type of air pollutant regulated by the Clean Air Act includes the emissions of substances that deplete the upper (stratospheric) ozone layer, which exposes the life on earth to harmful ultraviolet radiation. Facilities that repair and maintain air conditioning equipment are a major source for these emissions, and are thus subject to some of the most extensive regulations.

Under the 1990 amendments to the Clean Air Act, much of the responsibility for administering the act is vested in state governments. Each state program must include three components: 1) appointment of a state small business ombudsman; 2) establishment of a comprehensive small business assistance program, helping small businesses deal with specific technical, administrative, and compliance problems; and 3) appointment of a seven-member state compliance advisory panel.

The types of businesses likely to be affected by one or more of the air pollution control programs under the 1990 Clean Air Act include:

Agricultural chemical applicators	Laboratories
Asphalt manufacturers	Lawnmower repair shops
Asphalt applicators	Lumber mills
Auto body shops	Metal finishers
Bakeries	Newspapers
Distilleries	Pest control operators
Dry cleaners	Photo finishing laboratories
Foundries	Printing shops
Furniture manufacturers	Refrigerator/air conditioning service and
Furniture repairs	repair
Gasoline service stations	Tar paving applicators
General contractors	Textile mills
Hospitals	Wood finishers

For help and additional information on the Clean Air Act requirements that may apply to your business, contact the state environmental agency in your state or local EPA office. You may also obtain assistance from the EPA Small Business Ombudsman:

Asbestos and Small Business Ombudsman
U.S. Environmental Protection Agency
401 M Street, SW (M.C. 1230-C)
Washington, DC 20460
(703) 305-5938 (from Washington, D.C. and Virginia)
(800) 368-5888 (National Hotline)

Toxic Substances Control Act

If your business is one that engages in the manufacturing, processing, or distribution of chemical substances, you may be required under the federal Toxic Substances Control Act (TSCA) to report certain information to the EPA regarding the chemical substances and mixtures you use.[21]

The TSCA requires manufacturers to give a 90-day notification before producing a new chemical substance and, in some cases, for older chemicals. The EPA may require safety testing before approval of such a chemical. The TSCA also has extensive recordkeeping rules regarding use and disposal of toxic chemicals.

There are severe penalties for failing to make the required reports to the EPA, including civil and criminal penalties of $25,000 and up, plus up to a year's imprisonment for each violation. Each day the violation continues is considered a separate violation for purposes of the fines levied under the TSCA.

Pesticide Regulations

The Federal Insecticide, Fungicide, and Rodenticide Act (FIFRA), which amends FEPCA (the Federal Environmental Pesticides Control Act of 1972), regulates both the manufacture and distribution of pesticides.[22]

Environmental Impact Statements

The National Environmental Policy Act of 1969 (NEPA) requires an environmental impact statement (EIS) to be prepared with respect to major federal actions that significantly affect the quality of the human environment.[23] While this would not, at first impression, seem to directly affect you, as a small business owner, the EIS requirement also applies in any situation where a federal agency approves some action by other persons, such as a private company.

In addition, many states have adopted similar EIS requirements; for instance, when a local planning board approves a real estate development, an EIS may be required under state law, if not federal.

Asbestos Regulation

As lung disease, cancer, and other health risks attributed to the exposure to asbestos have come to light, a number of state and federal laws have been enacted to deal with this problem. In addition, huge numbers of individual damage suits for alleged harm to individuals, who were exposed to asbestos in the workplace and elsewhere, have resulted in enormous judgments against many companies, even forcing a giant building materials firm, Johns-Manville Corporation, into Chapter 11 bankruptcy to protect itself from a host of asbestos-related lawsuits.

Federal amendments to the TSCA and the Asbestos Hazard Emergency Response Act of 1986 (AHERA) have given the EPA power to issue regulations regarding asbestos in school buildings. In addition, Occupational Safety and Health Administration (OSHA) regulations have been issued to limit asbestos exposure in the workplace and to set construction standards regarding use of asbestos.[24]

Noise Control

Both OSHA and the EPA have issued regulations on noise emission standards, ranging from aircraft noise to protections of workers from hearing impairment in the workplace.

9.10 Consumer Credit Laws and Regulations

Many of the largest and most successful companies in America have gotten where they are, in part, by providing consumer credit to persons who buy their products. Classic examples would include such giant companies as Sears and General Motors, although countless smaller companies have also found that financing their customers' purchases can be a major boon to sales and that the interest earned on such credit can also become an important profit center in its own right.

The definition of consumer credit does not refer to the practice of allowing a client or customer to charge it and pay you at the end of the month, which is largely unregulated by the government. Instead, the following discussion deals with the situation where your business extends credit and charges interest during the period over which the loan amount (or amount financed) is being paid off by the customer.

The three main areas of the law regulating the extension of consumer credit, which affects nearly all businesses that grant such credit, are the federal Equal Credit Opportunity Act, the federal Truth-in-Lending Act, and state laws that prohibit usury.

Equal Credit Opportunity Act

If your business is engaged in providing consumer credit, you will most likely be subject to the provisions of the federal Equal Credit Opportunity Act (ECOA).[25] In general, the ECOA prohibits discrimination in credit transactions on the basis of race, color, religion, national origin, sex, age, or marital status.

The basic principle of this law is that each person applying for credit must be considered as an individual. This means, primarily, that there are very strict limits regarding what you may ask about marital status and about the spouse of the applicant. You may ask about marital status, but only to determine what rights and remedies you might have as a creditor — such as in a community property state — to refuse an applicant's credit.

The ECOA also forbids discrimination in providing credit because some or all of the applicant's income derives from public assistance programs, or because a person exercised a right, in good faith, under the Consumer Credit Protection Act.

Truth-in-Lending Act

If your business activities involve lending money or selling to consumers on credit terms, you may have to comply with the federal Truth-in-Lending Act and state laws such as those that prohibit the charging of usurious interest rates on loans or other credit transactions.[26] Regulations under the Truth-in-Lending Simplification and Reform Act provide that a business is not subject to the truth-in-lending rules unless it extended consumer credit at least 25 times in either the previous year or the current calendar year.[27]

The rules regarding the Truth-in-Lending Act are far too complex to cover satisfactorily in a book of this nature; it can only alert you to the possibility that you may be required to comply with those rules and give you some sense of what will be required if the rules do apply to you. If you plan to extend credit to consumers — other than sending out bills requesting payment in full, without interest charge, after you have provided goods or services — you need to consult an attorney experienced in this area. Fortunately, legislation has considerably simplified the truth-in-lending rules, and the Federal Reserve Board has published model disclosure statements and billing rights statements that can be used to satisfy the requirements of the truth-in-lending regulations.

Cash Discount Act

The Cash Discount Act permits sellers to offer a discount of any amount to customers who pay in cash or by check without running afoul of the truth-in-lending rules. The discount, in this case, has to be clearly disclosed and made available to all customers.[28] In the past, if you offered more than a 5% cash discount, you were considered to be imposing a finance charge on credit customers and had to give them all the required truth-in-lending disclosures.

Usury Laws

See Section 11.9 for a brief description of how this state's usury laws may apply to your business.

9.11 Employee or Independent Contractor?

As was pointed out in Section 5.2, hiring independent contractors rather than employees to work in your business has some major advantages. Not only do you gain considerable payroll tax savings by retaining independent contractors, but you have far fewer administrative headaches.

Unfortunately, just because you hire someone and you agree that he or she will be an independent contractor, it does not necessarily make it so for tax and legal purposes. So before you hire anyone to work for you as an independent contractor, you need to take a hard look at whether the IRS or a court of law would consider that person to be your employee rather than an independent contractor.

While the IRS uses a 20-factor test to evaluate whether a person is or is not an employee, a few major warning flags will indicate to you whether the person is your employee, as opposed to being a contractor. These include:

- The person works mostly or only for your firm — that is, the person is not like a lawyer, for example, who has a number of clients besides you that he or she works for.
- The worker is subject to your control, and you have the right to direct how the work is done, not just to demand a particular result.
- The person works in your office or establishment and does not have his or her own place of business, business cards, or business name.
- The kind of work the person does for you is normally done by employees, such as secretarial work.
- The person is not a licensed professional of any type.

Unless you are quite clear that the work relationship will not be considered that of employer/employee, be very careful about hiring someone as a so-called independent contractor. The consequences of being wrong can be severe. Here are just a few of the things that can happen if your independent contractor is determined to be an employee:

- You are liable for not only the employer payroll taxes you failed to pay, but also for a portion of the employee taxes you failed to withhold, for example, income taxes and FICA tax.
- If you treat someone as an independent contractor, report payments of $600 or more a year to that person on IRS *Form 1099-MISC*. If you do, and the IRS later determines the person was really an employee, the back taxes you are liable for are limited to the employer payroll taxes, 20% of the employee's FICA tax you failed to withhold, and income tax withholding equal to only 1.5% of the wages you paid the person. If you do not file *Form 1099-MISC* and the person is reclassified as an employee, you are liable for 40% of the employee's FICA tax and income tax withholding equal to 3% of the wages — twice as much as if you would have filed *Form 1099-MISC*. Furthermore, there is a $100 penalty for failure to file *Form 1099-MISC*, and you will owe interest on the taxes due. It is no longer a bargain to "borrow" from the IRS. You may also be assessed other penalties if you did not have a reasonable basis for treating the person as a nonemployee and may be liable for up to 100% of the employee's FICA and income tax that you failed to withhold.

- If the person is hurt on the job and you have not provided workers' compensation insurance coverage, you will be liable for extensive legal damages.

- If your business has a qualified retirement plan and you have not contributed to the plan on behalf of the person because he or she was not thought to be an employee at the time, the retirement plan could be disqualified for tax purposes for failing to cover the employee in question.

Thus, do not get stampeded into the independent contractor game by your friends and business associates who tell you how simple it is to avoid all those payroll taxes.

The above discussion of independent contractors summarizes federal rules only. Many states take an even more restrictive view than the IRS on the employee versus independent contractor issue.

You can take a number of steps to strengthen your case for someone who works for you to be treated as an independent contractor. Obviously, not all of the items listed below will necessarily be feasible in every case. Furthermore, a number of these steps, if implemented, may require some significant changes in the way you do business. But if you can follow most of the suggestions below with regard to a given worker, you will improve your odds against having the IRS reclassify that worker as an employee.

Independent Contractor Treatment Tips

- Have a written agreement, signed by both parties, that makes it clear the company doesn't have the right to control the methods or procedures for the worker to accomplish the work contracted for. Include language in the agreement that states it is the worker's obligation to pay income and self-employment taxes on amounts earned, and that he or she will receive a *Form 1099* reflecting amounts earned if the amount earned is $600 or more.

- Try to avoid setting working hours by hour or week. It would be all right to specify starting and completion dates for the work.

- Make it clear that if additional workers are needed to help, the contractor will hire and pay them.

- The arrangement should make it clear that the contractor is not limited to working exclusively for you, but is free to take on other work from other customers.

- Compensation should be based on what work is performed rather than the time spent to do it. This may require careful estimates so that the worker is fairly paid, not overpaid, for the work done.

- Avoid providing office space to the contractor on a regular basis.

- Let the workers be responsible for their own training if that is possible.

- Each worker should be advised, in writing, to provide for their own liability, workers' compensation, health, and disability insurance coverage.

- Costs such as meals, transportation, and clothing should be built into the contract price of the job, rather than being billed directly to your account.

- It should be clear in your agreement with the worker that he or she can't be fired and can't quit. The worker's job is to fulfill a given work contract.
- Don't give the worker other work to fill in during down time. This may mean, of course, that you will have to pay the worker somewhat more for the work done than you otherwise would if you wish to keep him or her happy.
- Don't pay bonuses to a person you treat as an independent contractor.

Other Alternatives

Hiring individuals as your own employees or treating them as independent contractors may sometimes pose a difficult choice. Fortunately, you have other available options. You could hire temporary employees from a temporary help agency or lease employees from an employee leasing company. An increasing number of companies are using these two worthwhile alternatives.

Hiring "Temps"

Hiring "temps" is usually quite straightforward, at least for many kinds of positions, but it may cost you a bit more than straight hiring. A temporary help agency has to charge you enough to make a profit, as well as pay for any benefits it provides to the temps, who are the agency's employees — not yours. One benefit to you, other than the simplicity of having someone else handle payroll, benefits, workers' compensation, and other costs of retaining such workers, is that you can send temporary workers home the moment you no longer need them, with no adverse consequences.

Of even greater importance to many companies is the opportunity to try out temps and offer permanent jobs to those whose performance they like. In effect, you get to test out individuals for as long as you wish, before deciding if you want to offer them employment as your own employee, not the agency's, which is exactly what many temps are seeking.

Leasing Employees

Employee leasing is a bit more complicated, because in many cases, you do the hiring. In some cases, you may even transfer your existing staff over to the payroll of the leasing company, which then leases them back to you for a fee equal to the salaries, taxes, and benefits paid by the leasing company, plus its markup percentage.

Leasing tends to be more of a long-term solution than hiring temps. Do your homework when checking out the reputation and background of any leasing company you will be dealing with. A number of leasing companies have gone broke or absconded with the payroll taxes withheld from employees' salaries, frequently leaving the firms that leased from them holding the bag. While there are many reputable leasing firms, they tend not to be as large and well known as the major temp firms, such as Kelly Services, Manpower, and other well-established firms in the industry.

Similar to hiring temps, leasing can be a major time- and energy-saving convenience. For example, if you lease all of your employees, you may be freed up to do what you do best, such as selling, rather than spending much of your time bogged down with personnel management, payroll, benefits, and other employee-related paperwork. You may also actually save money on your costs for workers, particularly if the leasing company is large and has been able to negotiate much less expensive, pooled rates for health insurance or workers' compensation than you could as a small employer.

Thus, leasing can offer substantial advantages to small companies, and usually avoids the problems and risks involved in seeking to treat workers as independent contractors, where such status is somewhat questionable. Be sure you deal with a reputable, established, financially responsible employee leasing company.

9.12 Whether You Should Incorporate Outside Your State

For most small businesses, there is little reason to consider incorporating your business under the laws of some state other than where you live. In fact, there are a few good reasons why you should not incorporate in a different state.

- Your corporation may have to pay a qualification fee to transact business in your home state as a foreign corporation. See Section 11.2 on this point.

- If your attorney is a local lawyer, he or she is likely to be much less familiar with the corporate laws of some other state than those of your state. Thus, your attorney is likely to either charge you more for corporate law advice if he or she has to research the law of an unfamiliar jurisdiction or give you less accurate advice than he or she could about your state's corporate laws.

- In many states, your corporation will have to pay some sort of minimum annual franchise tax or capital tax to the state of incorporation, even if you do no business there.

Don't believe the newspaper ads that tell you to incorporate in wonderful, tax-free Nevada or some other state and avoid your state's corporation income or franchise taxes. It doesn't work. If your corporation does business in your state, it pays the same taxes on its taxable income regardless of whether it is incorporated in your state, Nevada, or in the Grand Duchy of Luxembourg.

Perhaps the only valid reason why you might want to incorporate elsewhere would be to take advantage of some particular provision or flexibility available under the corporate laws of a particular state. If you own all the stock of your company, it is unlikely you would ever need to take advantage of any such provisions, which are usually more important where different groups are struggling for control of a corporation's board of directors or the like.

9.13 Foreign Investment in U.S. Businesses

Under the Foreign Direct Investment and International Financial Data Improvements Act of 1990, foreign individuals owning or acquiring 10% or more voting interest in U.S. businesses, including interests in U.S. real estate, must report certain information, including annual financial and operating data, to the U.S. Department of Commerce. Failure to file can result in civil penalties of $2,500 to $25,000.[29] For more information on this law, write to:

Bureau of Economic Analysis
U.S. Department of Commerce
1441 L Street, NW
Washington, DC 20005
(202) 606-5577

9.14 Emerging Trends and Issues

Today, businesses of every size and type are being buffeted by the ever-accelerating rate of change in the business, economic, social, and political environment in which they must operate. Part of the reason is that Congress, along with 50 state legislatures and countless government agencies, spews out reams of new laws and regulations all year long, in ever greater volume. As Benjamin Franklin once put it, "No man is safe in his bed when the Congress is in session."

To blame all of the disorienting changes that are occurring on lawmakers, however, is unfair since it seems that life in general is becoming more complex and unpredictable by the day. Accordingly, this section attempts to provide you with a brief overview of developing and current trends in the business environment.

An Aging Population

More and more employers are beginning to offer long-term care insurance (nursing home care). According to a recent study by Hewitt Associates, 27% of surveyed employers are planning to offer long term care insurance within the next three years. In 1995, only 10% of employers surveyed did so, up from 6% in 1992.

As the U.S. population becomes older — persons over age 85 are currently the fastest-growing segment of the elderly population — it is expected that long-term care insurance will become an increasingly popular employee fringe benefit, particularly if Congress changes the tax law to bestow the same tax treatment on these benefits as is currently allowed for health insurance.

A whole range of businesses that cater to the aging population will experience increasing demand for their goods and services in the coming years, particularly in the medical and nursing home industries. For example, intense cost pressures on Medicare and Medicaid are already giving a huge boost to home health service providers, which furnish less costly alternatives to residential care, hospitals, or nursing homes for many older citizens.

Increase in Women-Owned Businesses

Census Bureau figures show that in 1992, the most recent year for which statistics are available, women owned 6.4 million businesses in America — about one-third of the companies in the nation. These women-owned businesses generated total revenues of some $1.6 trillion and provided employment for 13.2 million people.

Interestingly, during the 1987–92 period, the women-owned businesses grew by 43%, almost double the rate of growth for all small and medium-sized companies. A report by the Interagency Committee on Women's Business Enterprise, a group established by President Clinton, has updated the census numbers, stating that the number of women-owned businesses had grown to 7.7 million by 1994.

The agency's report also notes that women business owners still face the same problems as in the past — limited access to capital, scarcity of training and technical assistance, and difficulty in competing for federal procurement contracts. However, the report also revealed that many women are overcoming these obstacles, and that not only are women-owned businesses proliferating, but that many new firms are in nontraditional areas. For example, the number of women-owned construction companies increased by 95% in the 1987–92 period.

Electronic Data Interchange

Is electronic data interchange in your future? You have fully computerized your business, and have finally created a company Web site on the Internet .... You have just finished qualifying for the European Market's ISO-9000 quality standards requirements .... You are up to speed now on bar coding all your products to keep your domestic retailing customers happy .... What next?

Electronic Data Exchange (EDI) is the next technical hurdle your small business is likely to have to face, just to be able to continue to deal with large customers. Pioneered by large companies like Wal-Mart, EDI is filtering down to smaller companies now.

Briefly described, EDI is computer-to-computer exchange of business information — such as inventory data between retailers or wholesalers and their suppliers, in its classic form — between trading partners. It allows firms that do business on an ongoing basis with each other to eliminate the costly and time-wasting processes of generating and mailing paper documents, which must then be re-keyed into the recipient's computer system. Transferring such information, which is in many cases very time-sensitive, by modem not only avoids mail delays and costs, but tends to sharply reduce the errors that can result from having to retype the information to input it into the computers of the receiving entity. Some experts estimate that more than 75% of the information printed from a vendor's computer has to be re-entered manually in the purchaser's computer when EDI is not being used.

What allows EDI data swapping to work effectively is a number of "transaction sets" (designated X12) created by the American National Standards Institute (ANSI), for such common business documents as purchase orders and invoices. Using the X12 transaction sets, and in most cases relying on third-party value added networks (VANs), it is now possible for otherwise incompatible computer systems to communicate seamlessly.

The downside in this otherwise cheery picture is that many big vendors are requiring even the smallest suppliers to set up EDI links if they want to do business with the large firms. In addition, more and more government agencies that contract with small businesses are requiring bidders to have EDI capability to be considered for government contracts, except for the very smallest dollar amounts. Thus, if you aren't up to speed on EDI, you may be out of contention for most government contracting purposes now or in the very near future, as well as being unable to deal with many commercial firms that require EDI.

This trend is spreading rapidly across the country, so if your firm is a supplier to large customers, you may soon have to gear up your operation for EDI, or lose those customers. For most small suppliers, this will mean signing up with a VAN that can act as the intermediary between the supplier and its large customer. Relatively affordable EDI software packages are also available now that can make the transition to this way of doing business relatively painless.

Recommendation: Do your homework and get geared up for EDI now. Otherwise, you may soon be caught in a tight situation, when a major customer announces one day that it will henceforth require EDI links with all its suppliers. Many Small Business Administration (SBA) offices are now offering seminars on how to go about setting up your business on EDI. For assistance or to find out where you can attend a seminar on EDI, contact your local SBA office, SCORE chapter, or the nearest Small Business Development Center. See Section 11.10.

Age Discrimination Law Expanded

The definition of age discrimination has been expanded and clarified by a recent decision of the U.S. Supreme Court on April 1, 1996, in the case of *O'Connor v. Consolidated Coin Caterers Corp.* In this unanimous decision, the court held that although the age discrimination law applies to all workers of at least 40 years of age, such discrimination includes firing a 56-year-old and replacing that worker with a 40-year-old, even though both workers were within the protected class. Until this Supreme Court decision, many employers had felt it was safe to dismiss an over-40 employee if they replaced him or her with another over-40 employee.

The court has ruled that the relative ages of employees are what must be considered, not whether or not both are members of the protected class. By the same token, the decision suggests to some commentators that replacing a 40-year-old (protected) with a 38-year-old (non-protected) may not necessarily be considered age discrimination now, where there is such a minor age difference.

EPA Self-Evaluation Policy

Effective January 1, 1996, the Environmental Protection Agency (EPA) has adopted a revolutionary new "self-evaluation policy" for environmental monitoring and regulation. The new policy encourages industry to self-police itself — companies that do so can reduce civil penalties for violations and can usually eliminate criminal penalties entirely. Essentially, the new policy allows you to audit your own facility.

If you find environmental law violations, you must report them in ten days, and must then act to correct the problems found. In the past, strict liability standards applied, and violations of EPA standards were punished without regard to knowledge or intention of the violator. While strict liability is still generally the rule, the new policy allows for a major reduction of penalties for those violators who detect their own violations and immediately come forward to report them. Previously, the harsh civil and criminal penalties gave violators an incentive to conceal their pollution violations rather than come forward and take cleanup actions.

State Taxation of Nonresidents' Pensions

A new federal law now generally prohibits states from taxing the pension income of former residents who have moved to other states.[30] In recent years, certain states, such as California and New York, have been very aggressive in pursuing former residents who retired and moved to low-tax jurisdictions — such as Florida, Nevada, or Arizona — taking the position that since they earned their pensions while working in California or New York, that receipt of such pensions should be taxable in the state where earned, regardless of their residence. However, such states did not hesitate to take an inconsistent position by taxing the pensions of retirees who moved into their state, after having earned their pensions elsewhere. The new law will make retirement plans even more attractive now if you do business in a high-tax state, but plan to move to greener pastures upon retirement.

Civil Rights Law Changes

Major changes are occurring in the civil rights laws as a consequence of the political power shift that has occurred in Washington. In addition, a recent (June 12, 1995) U.S. Supreme Court decision has called the entire affirmative action program into question. This decision, which may represent a major change in the Supreme Court's interpretation of civil rights laws, held that employment decisions based on race or color, including racial quotas or affirmative action programs, while they are not discriminatory per se, will from now on be subject to close scrutiny as being potentially discriminatory.

In direct contrast, during the same week as the above Supreme Court decision, a bipartisan "non-discrimination in employment" bill was introduced in Congress, which would forbid any kind of discrimination based on sexual orientation, the one form of discrimination that is still legally permissible under federal law. Some states and local governments, however, already forbid such discrimination in the workplace.

Telecommuting

One of the most predictable trends, already well under way, is the growth of telecommuting. More and more people work out of their homes, communicating with their clients or employers by use of personal computers, modems, faxes, or multiple phone lines. Already, some employers, like certain government agencies in Washington, D.C., are taking an intermediate step by setting up satellite telecommuting offices in suburban areas. By going to these nearby offices, equipped with computer workstations, many workers can avoid long and arduous commutes to downtown offices by piping their work product electronically to the main office. Recent surveys by Link Resources Corporation, a research and consulting firm, show that telecommuting and working at home have become a huge factor in our economy almost overnight. Their studies indicate that company employees and others who work at home part- or full-time increased to 43.2 million (37 million households) in 1994. This number is again expected to increase to at least 60 million by 1998 — out of a total workforce of 125 million Americans. This is a change in the workplace of monumental proportions from only a few years ago, when relatively few people worked out of their homes.

Not all the consequences of increased telecommuting are positive. Some unforeseen side effects are already beginning to surface, such as rising workers' compensation costs for employers who have substantial numbers of employees working at home. Apparently, employees who injure themselves at home tend to claim in many cases that such injuries are work-related, and therefore compensable under the workers' compensation system. In addition, injuries sustained while commuting are also more likely to be compensable whenever workers are constantly taking work back and forth between the office and home. As a result, workers' compensation insurers have already begun to raise their rates for telecommuting employees. Don't overlook this potential expense when analyzing the costs and benefits of having more of your workforce telecommute.

Recent Tax Law Changes

The President has just signed the Taxpayer Relief Act of 1997, which makes many tax law changes. The key business provisions of this new legislation are summarized below.

Income Tax Provisions

Under the Taxpayer Relief Act of 1997 income tax changes in the new law include:

- A reduction in the maximum capital gains rate, to a maximum of 20% — 10% for low bracket individuals — on assets held more than 18 months has been approved.

- Individuals of any age may now sell their personal residences and pay no tax on gains of up to $500,000, if married and filing jointly, or $250,000 for single taxpayers. This may spawn a whole new home "fixer-upper" industry.

- The self-employed health insurance deduction will eventually increase to 100% of the amount paid, rather than 80%, by the year 2007.

- The expired R&D tax credit and the employee education plan benefit exclusion from taxable income have both been reinstated, along with an increase to the work opportunity credit.

- A new "welfare-to-work" credit of up to $8,500 per employee has been enacted for employers who hire persons formerly receiving AFDC benefits.

- Software exports can now qualify for tax benefits under the foreign sales corporation tax subsidy rules.

- Individuals are now required to make estimated tax payments only if the estimated tax liability is at least $1,000 — formerly $500.

- Small corporations — those with average gross receipts of less than $5 million a year for 3 previous years — will be exempted from the corporate alternative minimum tax.

Pension Law Changes

Recent legislation adopted which enhances retirement planning includes the following benefits:

- ERISA reporting requirements to the U.S. Department of Labor have been simplified, by repealing requirements to file plan descriptions, summary plan descriptions, and summaries of material plan modifications.

- New "Roth IRAs" are now permitted, allowing taxpayers to make nondeductible contributions and later, at retirement, take out totally tax-free withdrawals.

- 401(k) plans or "SIMPLE" plans with matching employer contributions are now permitted for self-employed persons, with the employer contribution not counted towards the $9,500 or $6,000 limit on annual employee contributions.

Estate Taxes

New estate tax provisions have been enacted that could affect you personally and as a business owner. The estate tax burden on family-owned businesses, where such a business constitutes more than 50% of the value of the estate, has been reduced. Additionally, the ceiling through which a taxable estate could pass free of tax will gradually increase from $600,000 to $1 million by the year 2006.

Excise Taxes

Additional benefits to the taxpayer recently adopted include:

- The airline passenger tax has been reduced to 7.5%, plus a $1.00 fee for each flight segment.

- The 15% excise taxes on annual pension distributions of over $150,000 or accumulations or lump sum distributions of over $750,000 have both been repealed.

Pending and Potential Law Changes

The surprising loss of both houses of Congress by the Democratic Party in 1994 and 1996, has returned Washington to gridlock once more, this time with a Republican Congress and a Democratic president. Despite promised revolutionary changes in environmental laws and reduction of taxes and government regulation, very little has happened since the Republicans took control of Congress, since President Clinton has successfully vetoed, or blunted under threat of veto, all significant Republican legislative proposals to date.

However, a number of legislative proposals are in the works that likely will be enacted in the next year or two. Many of these future law changes are sure to affect your business, for better or worse. Major new legislation to look for in the near future may include the ones discussed in this subsection.

Mandatory Health Care Coverage

Mandatory health care coverage was the biggest item on the entire legislative agenda in Congress in 1994, as the battle over what to do about the increasing inaccessibility of medical care to large segments of the population was fought out on Capitol Hill. While nothing passed in the 1994 legislative session, don't expect this issue to die. It may be dead with the current Republican majority in both houses of Congress, but it could be very much alive if the political pendulum swings back in the other direction, which history shows is quite possible.

There were a number of other legislative proposals that floated around Congress during 1993 and 1994, other than the dead-on-arrival Clinton health care plan. Most of these proposals, like the Clinton plan, offered a combination of:

- Requiring that most, or all employers, provide some level of medical coverage for their full-time employees; and
- Additional payroll taxes to finance the cost of government-provided health care for individuals outside of the workforce. In some of the proposals, the employer would be given a choice of paying a hefty tax for national health insurance, or else providing coverage for employees. Other proposals would require both, which could be a very difficult financial burden for many small businesses, even those that already provide medical insurance for their employees.

S Corporation Taxable Income

Another proposal that has surfaced in connection with the Clinton health care reform proposals is to tax the income of S corporation shareholders as self-employment income, as has long been the case with partners in partnerships.

This would close what has long been perceived as a loophole in the taxation of S corporations, by subjecting owners to self-employment tax on their share of the net taxable income of the S corporation — presumably with exceptions being made for rental income and interest income, which have never been considered self-employment income for owners of unincorporated businesses.

A proposed bill, the Consumer and Main Street Protection Act of 1995, is pending in Congress and would authorize states, for the first time, to enact legislation requiring out-of-state sellers to collect sales or use tax on interstate sales for goods shipped to residents of the state in question. For details, see the discussion of this proposed legislation in Section 9.8.

Consumer and Main Street Protection Act

The Clinton administration supported a striker replacement law in Congress in 1994, which was defeated by seven votes in the U.S. Senate. The intent of this proposed law was to overturn a 1938 Supreme Court decision that allows employers to fire workers who go on strike over economic issues, such as wages.

Striker Replacement Law

Although the bill was defeated in 1994 even with both Congress and the White House under Democratic control, and is almost certain not to be enacted by Congress with the Republicans in the majority, it will definitely be back on the front burner again if the Democrats regain control of Congress in the 1998 elections.

In the meantime, in March 1995, the Clinton administration, realizing that there was no hope of getting striker replacement legislation through a Republican Congress, attempted an end run around Congress by issuing an Executive Order that puts a limited striker replacement ban in effect. The Executive Order prohibited the use of striker replacements by federal contractors. However, the Supreme Court has struck down the Executive Order as unconstitutional.

Listed and discussed below are some other legal trends and new or pending legislation you should know about for future reference. This information provides possible tips on issues that may affect your business.

Other Legal and Business Trends

The IRS has recently initiated a new compliance program to identify self-employed individuals who report one income number to the IRS and a different (usually higher) number to a mortgage lender when applying for a mortgage loan. Under this new program, the mortgage company simply fills out a short form with your name, Social Security number, and the adjusted gross income amount from the tax return that you have submitted to the lender as proof of your income level. The lender then faxes the completed form to the IRS and receives a response within 48 hours verifying your income level — or not.

Closer IRS Scrutiny of the Self-Employed

If there is a discrepancy between the tax return you filed with the IRS and the return you submitted to the lender, you not only will face severe problems in connection with getting your mortgage loan, but you will be facing a likely IRS audit as well. According to IRS officials, initial results of this program — being tested only in California for now — show discrepancies in about 13% of the cases. For anyone who might be thinking about submitting a "doctored" copy of a federal tax return to a lender, as part of a mortgage application, our advice, in a nutshell, is: Don't!

Video Display Terminals

Until recently, white-collar workplaces or offices generally created very little liability exposure for employers, with regard to hazardous working conditions. This, too, is beginning to change.

In recent years, there have been an increasing number of lawsuits filed by employees in connection with hazards of working long hours on computers; and the city of San Francisco has adopted an ordinance that provides regulatory safeguards for workers using video display terminals (VDTs) for four or more hours per shift. A number of other city and state governments around the nation are also considering similar laws or ordinances because the use of computers in the workplace is such a universal phenomenon and because a number of threats to employees' health have arisen in connection with the heavy use of computers.

These threats range from excessive exposure to radiation emitted by VDTs to carpal tunnel syndrome, a common and debilitating nerve entrapment disorder that can cause severe pain and weakness in the wrist. Carpal tunnel syndrome can result from too many hours spent typing on a computer keyboard — as well as from many other tasks requiring repetitive flexing and extensions of the wrist.

Laws regulating VDTs are likely to begin appearing all over the country in the near future, and offices that don't pay attention to ergonomics — the study of equipment design to reduce workplace injury — may well become sitting ducks for lawsuits or fines. While most legal claims by employees regarding VDT usage have been imposed on workers' compensation insurers thus far, employers may become directly liable:

- If they participate actively in the design of computer systems or workstations that allegedly caused the injury to an employee; or
- If new state legislation removes such claims from the workers' compensation system and places financial responsibility directly upon employers.

Helpful Organizations

Communicate your thoughts on government policy and pending legislation to groups such as the National Federation of Independent Business (NFIB), the U.S. Chamber of Commerce, your local chamber of commerce, or a trade association for your industry. It also can be helpful to call or write your senator, U.S. representative, or state legislator to voice your opinion in favor of or opposition to pending legislation or regulations that will affect your business.

Small business has been hit very hard by the government at all levels in recent years, and the more small business owners join and work together through helpful organizations, the better the chances of shaping the future. Listed below are some organizations you may be interested in joining or contacting for more information on legislation and new and emerging business trends.

National Association for the Self-Employed

Founded in 1981, the National Association for the Self-Employed (NASE) is an action-oriented, nonprofit association committed to assisting the self-employed with meeting the challenges of making their businesses successful. More than 300,000 members give NASE a powerful voice in Washington, D.C.

National Association for the Self-Employed
P.O. Box 612067
Dallas Airport, TX 75261-2067
(800) 232-NASE (Nationwide)
FAX (800) 551-4446

The National Business Association (NBA) is a nonprofit organization specifically designed and actively managed to assist the small business-person in achieving his or her professional and personal goals. The NBA offers an array of benefits and services that provide monetary discounts and other quality resources.

National Business Association *(margin heading)*

National Business Association
P.O. Box 700728
Dallas, TX 75370
(800) 456-0440 (Nationwide)
FAX (972) 960-9149

The National Federation of Independent Business (NFIB) is the nation's largest small business organization, with more than half a million business owner members. The NFIB has been America's small business advocate since 1943 and is dedicated to preserving free enterprise. As an NFIB member, you would receive:

National Federation of Independent Business *(margin heading)*

- *Independent Business*, the bimonthly national magazine for small business owners; and
- *State Reports*, a publication that covers legislation and trends in this state.

To find out more regarding this helpful organization and its publication, *Independent Business*, contact Membership Services.

National Federation of Independent Business
Attn: Membership Services
53 Century Boulevard
Nashville, TN 37214
(800) NFIB NOW (Nationwide)

The Small Business Service Bureau, Inc. (SBSB) is a national small business organization with more than 50,000 members. Founded in 1968, SBSB provides small business owners and self-employed individuals with money-saving group benefits and services, low-cost group insurance programs, management assistance, and legislative advocacy in all the states and Washington, D.C.

Small Business Service Bureau, Inc. *(margin heading)*

Small Business Service Bureau, Inc.
P.O. Box 15014
Worcester, MA 01615-0014
(508) 756-3513
(800) 222-5678 (Nationwide)

U.S. Chamber of Commerce

The U.S. Chamber of Commerce is interested in promoting and assisting small business around the country. Its publication, *Nation's Business*, is a helpful source of emerging trends and issues facing small business.

U.S. Chamber of Commerce
Washington, DC
(202) 463-5650 (*Nation's Business* magazine)
(202) 659-6000 (General information)

Endnotes

1. I.R.C. § 168.
2. I.R.C. § 179(b)(1).
3. I.R.C. § 6425.
4. 15 U.S.C. §§ 1051–1128.
5. I.R.C. § 1244(c). The Tax Reform Act of 1984 § 481(a).
6. I.R.C. § 1211(b).
7. I.R.C. § 1244(c)(1)(C).
8. I.R.C. § 1244(c)(3).
9. I.R.C. § 1244(d)(1)(B).
10. 16 C.F.R. § 435.1.
11. 15 U.S.C. §§ 6101–6108; 16 C.F.R. § 310.
12. 42 U.S.C.A. §§ 9601 *et seq.*
13. 42 U.S.C.A. §§ 6901 *et seq.*
14. 40 C.F.R. § 280.22(a) and (b).
15. 40 C.F.R. § 280.20.
16. 40 C.F.R. § 280.21.
17. 42 U.S.C. §§ 11001 *et seq.*
18. 33 U.S.C.A. §§ 1251–1376.
19. 33 U.S.C.A. § 1344(a) and Executive Order 11990.
20. 42 U.S.C.A. §§ 7401–7626.
21. 15 U.S.C.A. §§ 2601–2629.
22. 7 U.S.C.A. §§ 136 *et seq.*
23. 42 U.S.C.A. §§ 4321–4347.
24. 29 C.F.R. § 1926.1101.
25. 15 U.S.C. § 1691.
26. 15 U.S.C. §§ 1601 *et seq.*
27. 12 C.F.R. § 226.2(a)(17).
28. 12 C.F.R. § 226.4(c)(8).
29. 15 C.F.R. § 806.
30. 4 U.S.C. § 114.

Internal Accounting Controls Checklist

☐ The same person who handles your cash receipts should not be the same person who makes the bank deposits. Cash is too easily misappropriated. Don't tempt an employee by letting him or her handle both of these duties.

☐ The person who writes checks should not also sign them or have the authority to sign checks. A different person should sign checks.

☐ Whoever signs checks should only sign them when the bill that is being paid is presented at the same time. The check number should be written on the bill to avoid double payments or payments to a nonexistent vendor. When you sign the check, be sure you know what the bill is for.

☐ Consider using some type of mechanical check imprinting equipment for all checks that are written, as a further means of preventing unauthorized payments. Such machines keep a record of the amount of any checks written.

☐ Use only prenumbered checks and keep all of the cancelled or voided checks in your records. This will help make it readily apparent if any additional checks are written without your knowledge.

☐ Complete a monthly bank reconciliation yourself or have your outside accountant do it. Never let the person who writes checks do the reconciliation.

☐ Deposit your daily cash receipts in the bank each day. Do not let cash collections for one day get mingled with the next day's collections.

☐ Use prenumbered sets of sales checks, invoices, and receipts to keep control of payments made and received. Duplicates will be kept track of by the individuals making sales, or other transactions, and the master copy will enable you to make sure they account for all of their transactions.

☐ Use a petty cash fund and voucher system for stamps, small bills, and other small cash outlays. Do not use cash from the day's receipts to pay bills! Put a voucher or bill in the petty cash box each time money is taken out. When the fund is depleted, write a check to bring it back up to the maximum amount (say $50), and record all the vouchers at the time the check is cashed to replenish the fund.

☐ Maintain a master or control account for all of your accounts receivable, and reconcile it each month to the subsidiary accounts receivable. If someone is stealing money from customer payments, it will be easier to spot if the master and subsidiary accounts are reconciled regularly.

Notes

Chapter 10

Sources of Help and Information

If you're going to sin, sin against God, not the bureaucracy.
God will forgive you, but the bureaucracy won't.

— Admiral Hyman G. Rickover

10.1 General Considerations

Many government agencies and private organizations provide free or low-cost services and publications to small businesses in an effort to ease the burden of compliance with government regulations. Unfortunately, most small business owners find out about only a few of these sources and often only on a haphazard basis. This chapter summarizes many of the services, publications, and on-line resources you may want to know about as an owner or operator of a small business.

10.2 Professional Services

Select your accountant carefully. This is the one person outside your business who is most likely to be closely in touch with almost everything going on in your operation. Besides helping to set up your books and to establish systems for handling cash receipts and disbursements, a good accountant can provide a wealth of practical advice on a wide range of subjects that are important to your business, including planning for taxes, managing your money, obtaining financing, and evaluating business opportunities. Attorneys and bankers are often in a good position to recommend accountants.

Accountants

Attorneys

Unless you are starting out as a sole proprietor, you will usually need an attorney to prepare a partnership agreement or to set up a corporation. You will probably do well to consult an attorney anyway to make sure you are obtaining necessary licenses and permits or to help you obtain them in some cases. In most parts of the country, local bar associations have lawyer referral services that can put you in touch with attorneys in your area. In most cases, you will do better to ask an accountant or banker to recommend a good business lawyer. If you need highly specialized legal advice or representation, ask an attorney you know to recommend a specialist.

Bankers

Establish a good relationship with officers of the bank branch where you open an account for your business. While you may find it tough to borrow from your banker when you first go into business, he or she will be interested in keeping an eye on your business to see how it develops. It pays to cultivate the relationship to create a good impression before you want to apply for a business loan from the bank. Ask around before opening an account; find out if there is a bank in your area that is well known for lending to small businesses. Many of the large banks tend to be more interested in larger accounts, although different branch managers of the same bank may have very different ideas about working with small businesses. Your banker can be a useful source of free financial advice and a good connection when wanting to meet other business owners in your community.

Benefit Consultants

If you intend to establish a corporate pension or profit-sharing plan — or Keogh plan if you have a number of employees — you may want to seek out a benefit consulting firm and obtain its proposals as to the type of benefit plan you need and how it should be structured. Since many of these firms are primarily engaged in selling insurance products, such as life insurance, annuities, and investment contracts, designed for pension plans, the plan these firms design for you will almost invariably involve building in their products. Since an insured retirement plan may not necessarily make sense in your particular situation, ask your attorney or accountant to recommend a benefit consulting firm that does not have products to sell other than its consulting and plan administration services.

10.3 U.S. Small Business Administration and Other Helpful Agencies

The federal Small Business Administration (SBA) is one government agency that is genuinely helpful to small businesses. The SBA not only guarantees financing for many small businesses (see Section 9.7), it also provides a number of valuable services, including SCORE, Small Business Institutes, Business Information Centers, and telephone hotlines.

In addition, SBA offices perform a variety of seminars and workshops on topics of interest to people who are starting or operating small businesses. Here are some of the seminars offered by the SBA.

- *Building a Business Plan*
- *Starting a New Business*
- *Preparing the Loan Proposal*

Contact your local SBA office for more information on available seminars and workshops. If you would like to know more about the SBA's on-line service, *SBA On-Line*, refer to Section 10.12.

One service you might find helpful is the Service Corps of Retired Executives (SCORE). SCORE is a program in which retired executives with many years of business experience volunteer their services as consultants to small businesses and charge only for their out-of-pocket expenses.

SCORE

Small Business Institutes (SBIs) are located on more than 400 university campuses throughout the United States. Part of a cooperative program with the SBA, SBIs offer business assistance while furthering the education of college students. Students, supervised by faculty members, can provide your business with:

Small Business Institutes

- Alternatives and recommendations to business problems;
- Free confidential consulting;
- In-depth analysis of your firm's business situation; and
- Written and oral reports.

The Small Business Advancement National Center collects and disseminates demographic and statistical information on SBI programs nationwide. This information is used for planning, analyzing, and improving the SBI program.

Small Business Advancement National Center

In addition, the center is dedicated to providing small business owners, entrepreneurs, and educators with the necessary resources to further their efforts and goals. Some of the services the center provides include consulting, educating, and training current and potential small business owners, as well as serving as a clearinghouse for small business information and inquiries. The center also offers a computer on-line service that is discussed more in Section 10.12. For more information on the services of the center, contact:

Small Business Advancement National Center
College of Business
University of Central Arkansas
UCA P.O. Box 5018
Conway, AR 72035-0001
(501) 450-5300
FAX (501) 450-5360
Internet: http://www.sbacr.uca.edu

Business Information Centers

The U.S. Small Business Administration's Business Information Centers (BICs) provide a one-stop location where current and future small business owners can receive assistance and advice.

BICs combine the latest computer technology, hardware and software, an extensive small business reference library of books and publications, and current management video tapes to help entrepreneurs plan their business, expand an existing business, or venture into new business areas. The use of software for a variety of business applications offers clients of all types a means for addressing diverse needs.

In addition to the self-help hardware, software, and reference materials, BICs have on-site counseling provided by the Service Corps of Retired Executives (SCORE). Individuals who are in business or are interested in starting a business can use a BIC as often as they wish at no charge.

For prospective business owners, visits to a BIC may be frequent, as they do the basic research necessary to reach the decision to start their business. Existing business owners may use a BIC less frequently, but will find many resources aimed at business growth.

All BICs add new materials and resources throughout the year and as they become aware of special needs in their small business community. The BICs are also used to inform the public about new initiatives and programs offered by the SBA and to reach business owners who might not otherwise take advantage of SBA's programs and services. In addition, every BIC has access to *SBA On-Line*, the agency's national electronic bulletin board.

BICs are located in several large metropolitan areas, and many new BIC sites will open in 1997. To determine if there is an existing BIC in your state, refer to Section 11.10. To see if a BIC will be opening in your area, call your local SBA district office, or:

Office of Business Initiatives
(202) 205-6665

Telephone Hotlines

The SBA and several other government agencies maintain toll-free telephone hotline information services to assist businesses and taxpayers. Some of the more important ones to know about are listed below.

SBA Answer Desk

The SBA Answer Desk has a toll-free number to reach a small business information and referral service offered by the SBA, which you can call from anywhere in the continental United States, except Washington, D.C. For the number in D.C., check the local directory.

The telephone Answer Desk offers a wide range of prerecorded, informational messages, any of which you may access if you have a touch-tone phone.

SBA Answer Desk
(800) U-ASK-SBA or 827-5722

The IRS has an assistance program called Tele-Tax. The program allows you to call a toll-free number in your state to listen to prerecorded tax information that will answer many federal tax questions. Approximately 140 topics are available, including information on the Small Business Tax Education Program (STEP), business income, sole proprietorships, and the self-employment tax.

For more information on Tele-Tax, call the IRS's toll-free number to request *Publication 910, Guide to Free Tax Services*. This publication not only lists the many tax publications you can order, but it also lists the Tele-Tax phone numbers and topic numbers in your state. See Section 11.10 for this state's Tele-Tax number.

Internal Revenue Service

(800) 829-3676 (Nationwide)

Internal Revenue Service

The Trade Information Center and the Global Export Market Information Service provide a hotline where you can receive information about export promotion programs, regional market information, and international trade agreements through their automated fax retrieval system. You may also choose to speak with a trade specialist.

Trade Information Center
U.S. Department of Commerce

(800) USA-TRADE or 872-8723 (Nationwide)

Trade Information Center

Like certain Scandinavian countries, the Environmental Protection Agency (EPA) has a small business ombudsman who gives easier access to the EPA, helps you comply with EPA regulations, and makes sure you are treated fairly in any EPA disputes.

EPA Small Business Ombudsman

(703) 305-5938
(800) 368-5888 (Nationwide)

Environmental Protection Agency Ombudsman

If you want to find out what records the Social Security Administration (SSA) has on your earnings and your projected benefits at retirement age, you can file a simple form requesting a detailed printout of this information. This is something everyone should do once every few years because if the SSA has made a serious mistake in your earnings record, you have only a limited number of years in which you can contact them and have your record corrected.

To obtain the request form, call the SSA's toll-free number or write to the Social Security Administration for this form at the Consumer Information Center address below.

Social Security Administration

(800) 772-1213 (Nationwide)

Consumer Information Center
Department 72
Pueblo, CO 81009

Social Security Administration

10.4 Publications Regarding Small Business Operations

U.S. Small Business Administration

The U.S. Small Business Administration (SBA) has more than 50 helpful booklets and other publications on subjects of importance to new and existing small businesses. The SBA sells these publications for a nominal fee — usually about $0.50 (50 cents) to $1.00 each, and never more than $2.00.

For a list of publications, call the SBA Answer Desk or contact your nearest SBA office.

SBA Answer Desk
(800) U-ASK-SBA or 827-5722

You can also use the preaddressed post card in the back of this book to request a directory of SBA publications.

The Oasis Press

The publisher of this book, The Oasis Press, has a number of how-to business guides and software programs targeted toward small businesses. Some of the most recent titles published by The Oasis Press include:

- *The Business Environmental Handbook*. This comprehensive guide tells you how your company can be both environment-friendly and profitable ($19.95).
- *Business Owner's Guide to Accounting and Bookkeeping*. This helpful guide enables entrepreneurs, who have no accounting background, to do their own bookkeeping using either a manual or automated system ($19.95).
- *The Buyer's Guide to Business Insurance*. A step-by-step guide that gives you advice and tips for improving your business insurance costs, coverage, and service ($19.95). A companion software, *The Insurance Assistant*, is also available from the publisher.
- *Location, Location, Location: How to Select the Best Site for Your Business*. This clear and complete entrepreneurial guide clues you into finding the best business location, using secrets employed by some of the world's largest franchises ($19.95).
- *People Investment*. An up-to-date guide for staffing a business and avoiding today's legal hurdles ($19.95).
- *Power Marketing*. A comprehensive guide that details successful marketing strategies for your business ($19.95).
- *The Secrets to Buying and Selling a Business*. A guide designed to help both buyers and sellers in their quest to make the best deal possible ($24.95).
- *Start Your Business: A Beginner's Guide*. This newly updated guide is an ideal companion to this *Starting and Operating a Business in ...* book, helping you answer the essential questions regarding money matters, marketing, staffing, business plans, and other important start-up issues (2nd ed., $9.95). Companion software is also available.

Information on these and other related resources from The Oasis Press is provided at the back of this book or it can be obtained by calling:

The Oasis Press
(800) 228-2275 (Nationwide)

Here are some magazines that provide continuing information for businesses in general and small businesses in particular. There are also a number of specialized publications you may find helpful. Most of these publications can be located through your local library or newsstand.

Magazines

The Wall Street Journal
200 Liberty Street
New York, NY 10281
(212) 416-2000
(800) 568-7625 (Nationwide)

D&B Reports
299 Park Avenue
New York, NY 10171-0002
(212) 593-6723
(800) 362-2255 (Nationwide)

Success Magazine
P.O. Box 3038
Harlin, IA 51537
(212) 551-9500
(800) 234-7324 (Nationwide)

Entrepreneur
Business Start-Ups
Subscriber Service
125 Armstrong Road
Des Plaines, IL 60018
(800) 421-2300 (Nationwide)

Business Review
P.O. Box 777
Cypress, TX 77410
(713) 256-4100

Business Week
Subscriber Service
P.O. Box 506
Hightstown, NJ 08520
(800) 635-1200 (Nationwide)

Nation's Business
U.S. Chamber of Commerce
1615 H. Street, NW
Washington, DC 20062
(202) 463-5650

Inc.
Subscriber Service
P.O. Box 54129
Boulder, CO 80322-4129
(800) 234-0999 (Nationwide)

Small Business Opportunities
1115 Broadway, 8th Floor
New York, NY 10010-2803
(212) 807-7100

Home Office Computing
Subscriber Service
P.O. Box 53561
Boulder, CO 80322
(800) 678-0118 (Nationwide)

Some of the more important sources of statistical information that you will need if you do your own marketing research are:

Statistical Information

Title	Publisher
Publication Price List Titles on corporate relations, human resources, management, economic and business environments, and consumer research.	**Conference Board** 845 Third Avenue New York, NY 10022 (212) 759-0900
Encyclopedia of Business Information Sources, Ninth Edition Arranged by industry, this guide lists trade associations and major sources of statistical information.	**Gale Research, Inc.** 835 Penobscott Building Detroit, MI 48226 (313) 961-2242 (800) 877-4253 (Nationwide)

Title	Publisher
Survey of Buying Power *Sales and Marketing Management* magazine Comprehensive data on population, retail sales, and consumer buying income for states, counties, and cities.	**Bill Communications, Inc.** 355 Park Avenue South New York, NY 10010 (212) 592-6200
Survey of Current Business U.S. Department of Commerce's monthly survey of business trends and conditions.	**Superintendent of Documents** **U.S. Government Printing Office** Washington, DC 20402 (202) 512-1800

Securities and Exchange Commission

The Securities and Exchange Commission (SEC) Office of Small Business Policy publishes *Q & A: Small Business and the SEC*, which is a guide to special services, rules, regulations, and suggestions regarding a company's first public offering of stock. It is available from:

Office of Small Business Policy
Securities and Exchange Commission
450 Fifth Street, NW
Washington, DC 20549
(202) 942-4046 (Publications)
Internet: http://www.sec.gov

10.5 Do-It-Yourself Incorporation

If you want to form your own corporation and save several hundred dollars in legal fees, there are books that tell you how to do it and provide the forms you need; however, think carefully before you attempt to do this on your own.

In some cases, setting up a corporation is not that complicated, and if you follow precisely the instructions in a self-incorporation book — if one is available for your state — you should be able to do it properly. But you will have to spend many hours carefully figuring out and then doing all that is required. Your time might be worth much more than the money you would save in legal fees because you could concentrate more on getting the business off to a good start.

Check Section 11.10 to see if there is an incorporation book for your state.

Corporate Agents, Inc.

There are also companies that can assist in the incorporation process, providing a variety of incorporation kits and services. One such company, Corporate Agents, Inc., can help you form your corporation in any state for as little as $39 (plus state fees), depending on the state. Some examples of complete costs for other states are $115 for Delaware, $119 for Florida, $271 for New York, and $1,014 for California.

The fees cover all costs, including all state filing fees and recording costs, preparing and filing articles of incorporation, and the registered agent's service is free for the first six months. Also available for an additional cost are personalized corporate seals and stock certificates, minute books, stock transfer ledgers, and sample minutes and bylaws.

For more information on this company, you can send the preaddressed post card located at the back of this book or call Corporate Agents at the toll-free number below:

Corporate Agents, Inc.
1013 Centre Road
P.O. Box 1281
Wilmington, DE 19899
(800) 877-4224 (Nationwide)
FAX (302) 998-7078
Internet: http://www.corporate.com

10.6 Information Regarding Payroll Taxes and Withholding

Major offices of the IRS frequently put on seminars for new employers regarding payroll tax requirements. Call your local IRS office for information as to when such seminars will be held in your area. In addition, you may want to obtain *Circular E, Employer's Tax Guide,* and *Notice 109, Information About Depositing Employment and Excise Taxes.* Both can be obtained from the IRS office nearest you. In addition, the Matthew Bender Company publishes an excellent book called the *Payroll Tax Guide,* which covers almost every aspect of federal payroll tax returns.

Matthew Bender Company
(800) 223-1940 (Nationwide)
Internet: http://www.corporate.com

10.7 Other Useful Tax Publications

The publications below can also be obtained from your local IRS office:

Publication	Subject
Publication 334	*Tax Guide For Small Business Income and Other Federal Taxes*
Publication 349	*Federal Highway Use Taxes on Heavy Vehicles*
Publication 378	*Fuel Tax Credits and Refunds*
Publication 463	*Travel, Entertainment, and Gift Expenses*
Publication 510	*Federal Excise Taxes*

Publication	Subject
Publication 541	Tax Information on Partnerships
Publication 542	Tax Information on Corporations
Publication 544	Sales and Other Dispositions of Assets
Publication 552	Recordkeeping Requirements
Publication 583	Taxpayers Starting a Business
Publication 587	Business Use of Your Home
Publication 589	Tax Information on S Corporations
Publication 910	Guide to Free Tax Services
Publication 937	Business Reporting

To order these free tax publications or other tax forms, call:

Internal Revenue Service
(800) 829-3676 (Nationwide)

10.8 ERISA Compliance

If your business has a pension or profit-sharing plan and you wish to handle your own Employee Retirement Income Security Act (ERISA) filings for the plan, obtain a copy of Charles D. Spencer & Associates' publication, *5500 Annual Reports for Employee Benefit Plans*. This publication will help you prepare the necessary *Form 5500* series through its easy-to-understand, step-by-step instructions.

For ordering information, contact:

Charles D. Spencer & Associates, Inc.
250 South Wacker Drive, Suite 600
Chicago, ÍL 60606
(312) 993-7900

10.9 OSHA Compliance

The U.S. Occupational Safety and Health Administration (OSHA) provides a number of useful publications on OSHA requirements for small businesses. The most important, *Recordkeeping Guidelines for Occupational Injuries and Illness (O.M.B. No. 1220-0029)*, provides a useful summary of what records must be kept, who must keep them, and for how long.

OSHA offices can also provide you with a package or folder entitled, *Information from the Occupational Safety and Health Administration,* that includes the above publication, plus required posters and about a dozen other OSHA informational booklets and pamphlets.

See the pre-addressed post card at the back of the book for ordering booklets and required posters.

10.10 ADA Compliance

The Equal Employment Opportunity Commission (EEOC) publishes and makes available to employers a *Technical Assistance Manual of the Employment Provisions (Title I) of the ADA*. To obtain single copies of this manual, contact the EEOC Publications and Information Center.

In addition, the EEOC publishes a useful and comprehensive publication on all the discrimination laws that it enforces, such as civil rights, age discrimination, and equal pay. To obtain the publication that is entitled, *Laws Enforced by EEOC*, contact:

EEOC Publications and Information Center
P.O. Box 12549
Cincinnati, OH 45212-0549
(513) 489-8692
(800) 669-3362 (Nationwide)

To reach the EEOC directly to ask questions and obtain more information about ADA, contact:

Office of Communications and Legislative Affairs
Equal Employment Opportunity Commission
Room 9405
1801 L Street, NW
Washington, DC 20507
(202) 663-4900
(800) 669-3362 (Voice)
(800) 800-3302 (TDD)

10.11 Information on Franchising

Title and Author	Publisher
Franchise Bible: How to Buy a Franchise or Franchise Your Own Business Erwin J. Keup	**The Oasis Press** 300 North Valley Drive Grants Pass, OR 97526 (800) 228-2275 (Nationwide)
Miscellaneous titles on franchise topics. Write for a catalog.	**International Franchise Association** 1350 New York Avenue, NW, Suite 900 Washington, DC 20005

Title and Author	Publisher
Business Franchise Guide	CCH, Inc. 2300 Lake Cook Road Riverwoods, IL 60015 (843) 267-7000
Miscellaneous titles on franchise topics. Write or call for a catalog.	Pilot Books 127 Sterling Avenue P.O. Box 2102 Greenport, NY 11944 (516) 477-1094 (800) 79PILOT
Franchise Opportunities Handbook U.S. Department of Commerce	Superintendent of Documents U.S. Government Printing Office Washington, DC 20402 (202) 512-1800
Franchising in the U.S. Michael M. Coltman	Self-Counsel Press, Inc. 1704 North State Street Bellingham, WA 98225 (800) 663-3007 (Nationwide)
The Info Franchise Newsletter *The Franchise Annual*	Info Press 728 Center Street P.O. Box 550 Lewiston, NY 14092-0550 (716) 754-4669 Internet: http://infonews.com/franchise
Survey of Foreign Laws and Regulations *Affecting International Franchising* Compiled by the Franchising Committee of the Section of Antitrust Law of the American Bar Association	American Bar Association Attn: Publication Orders P.O. Box 10892 Chicago, IL 60610-0892 (312) 988-5522

10.12 Computer On-Line Services

With the recent explosion of interest in computer on-line information, a variety of services have become available that you can access with your personal computer, modem, and appropriate software. Much of this information can be accessed at no additional cost through the Internet. The Internet is a worldwide computer database established by the government and research agencies to allow mail and information sharing. It has grown to become a popular backbone of the recently promoted "information superhighway."

SBA On-Line

The U.S. Small Business Administration has set up a comprehensive Web site on the Internet, called SBA-Online. The site includes over 500 business "shareware" programs you can download at no charge and offers a wealth of small business information, including tips for starting, financing, and expanding a small business, at this Web address:

SBA On-Line
Internet: http://www.sbaonline.sba.gov

It includes links to other Web sites, including a nifty new "U.S. Business Advisor" site (http://www.business.gov) that includes information on almost every subject for anyone who has dealings with the government.

Small Business Advancement Electronic Resource

As discussed in Section 10.3, the Small Business Advancement National Center helps facilitate the SBA's Small Business Institute (SBI) program by providing a number of services. One of these helpful services is the *Small Business Advancement Electronic Resource*, which is an extensive electronic link among small business owners, entrepreneurs, the U.S. Small Business Administration, and its resource partners. Information can be accessed by personal computer and modem or through the Internet.

The electronic resource features:

- Downloadable research information on all aspects of small business and entrepreneurship, including articles from conference proceedings, industry profiles, and publications from other pertinent sources;
- A means for electronic consulting and training;
- On-line databases, including those for SBIs, Small Business Development Centers (SBDCs), foreign market research firms, and SBA offices; and
- A LISTSERV for you to exchange ideas and questions about small business and entrepreneurship through e-mail.

If you have any questions or would like help on any of the different formats available for access, call:

Small Business Advancement Electronic Resource
Small Business Advancement National Center
University of Central Arkansas
(501) 450-5377

Other Federal On-Line Services

In addition to *SBA On-Line* and the *Small Business Advancement Electronic Resource*, the federal government offers other on-line services that will prove helpful to starting and operating your business. The Internet is the primary source that provides much of this government information, but there are some other services available.

- *Thomas* (http://thomas.loc.gov). This Library of Congress service named after former President Thomas Jefferson provides full text versions of bills in Congress, both current and last year's; access to the Congressional Record; and other legislative summaries and continuous updates.
- The Library of Congress World Wide Web site (lcweb.loc.gov) provides additional general reference information.

- *Marvel* (http://marvel.loc.gov). Also a service from the Library of Congress, *Marvel* provides directory access to a wide variety of other government information, including quick connections to the House of Representatives and Senate Internet sites.
- *FedWorld* (http://www.fedworld.gov). This service from the U.S. Department of Commerce's National Technical Information Division is the central clearing site for Internet sites that are related to the federal government. It is a good place to start for locating and reviewing available information on a wide array of federal agencies and departments.
- *Policy.Net* (http://policy.net). A project of Issue Dynamics, Inc., *Policy.Net* provides tracking of federal policies and issues and congressional data via *CapWeb* web site, *Washington Telecom Newswire*, and other political campaign sources.
- IRS (http://www.irs.ustreas.gov/). The Internal Revenue Service now has a Web site from which you can download tax forms and instructions and obtain other tax information. You can download forms and other items to your computer and print them out later if you have the right software, such as the Adobe Acrobat reader.
- *Edgar* (http://www.sec.gov). The SEC (U.S. Securities and Exchange Commission) Web site contains corporate filings that have been submitted to the SEC under the securities laws, including 10Ks, 10Qs and other forms.
- The White House (http://www.whitehouse.gov). The Clinton Administration has set up this popular Internet site, which offers information on many areas of the executive branch of the federal government, among other things.
- U.S. Tax Code (http://www.fourmilab.ch/ustax/ustax.html). If you are a lawyer or a CPA or other fearless soul, and want to go directly to the source to do your own tax research, you can search the federal Internal Revenue Code on the Web at this site. Be careful, however, as the tax code you will be viewing at this site is only updated to 1994.

State On-Line Services

In addition, state agencies across the country are also discovering that the Internet is an effective place for distribution of information. Almost every state has some form of Internet presence, and more sites are developing every month. This information can be provided from state agencies, universities, and corporations. Although the quality and quantity of state information varies widely between sites, this information can be valuable to businesses that need information updated rapidly and at a significantly lower cost than is usually found in traditional print mediums. State information providers include:

- The Library of Congress. The federal sites listed above provide state-by-state breakdowns of data.
- *Yahoo* (http://www.yahoo.com/regional/u_s_states). A good starting place to keep updated on state on-line resources is a service called *Yahoo*, originally from Stanford University. This service segments state information and provides links to other sources.

- The National Association of State Information Resource Executives (http://www.nasire.org). This clearinghouse for Internet topics on state government information is an excellent resource, especially if you are looking for information on a state-by-state basis.
- *CityNet* (http://www.city.net). This service provides specific information on individual cities in the United States, as well as worldwide.
- Other agencies. Every state has a department of commerce or business development agency eager to attract business and technology to its state. In addition, your local chamber of commerce should be able to provide you with information on any Internet activity, service providers, or groups in your region with helpful resources.

For more information on potential state on-line services, refer to Section 11.10.

Many commercial on-line services are available that have sections for businesses. Many of these sections provide access to articles from magazines or other sources. Sometimes a slight, additional fee per service or topic is charged.

Some of the more important and useful nongovernmental Internet sites include the following:

- *SmallbizNet* (http://www.lowe.org/smbiznet/books/index.htm). Probably the best site for general business information on the Internet, created by the Edward Lowe Foundation, a private philanthropic organization. It contains a vast number of business resources, and you can order whole books or for a modest fee, pick a subject and use their "fax-on-demand" service to fax specific information back to you on the subjects you select for a nominal charge. *SmallbizNet* contains the entire PSI Research/Oasis Press Successful Business Library, including the *Starting and Operating a Business in ...* series of books for all 50 states and D.C. (including this book).
- **WWW Virtual Library (http://www.w3.org/). Be sure to add this site to your Web sites hot list! It contains a collection of lists of sites kept by various parties throughout the world, on almost any conceivable subject area. You can link directly to any of those sites, including business-related ones, for lists of useful sites on the topics of your choice. It is like an index of indexes, and a great place to start your research on any subject.**
- *UCSD Library* (http://www.ucsd.edu). The University of California at San Diego library makes available a reference shelf with much information that can be useful to businesses. Its various menu options include dictionaries, encyclopedias, and a facility for linking to the United Nations to get the United Nations Currency Exchange Rates.
- *BizWeb* (http://www.bizweb.com) and the *Commercial Sites Index* (http://www.directory.net). These addresses are two key sites for locating companies that are on the Net. *BizWeb* is sort of a "yellow pages" listing of companies, arranged by category, but also includes a handy

Other Commercial On-Line Services

search engine. *Commercial Sites Index* lists thousands of companies that have set up a home page on the Net.

- *Women on the Web.* (http://www.womweb.com/index.html). This is probably the best Web site for women in business, and is the home page for *Working Women*, *Working Mother*, and *Ms.* magazines. It contains an extensive database of articles on subjects such as best companies for working mothers, the best women-owned businesses, and the hottest careers for women. You simply identify your criteria, such as salary range, access to child care, and percentage of women employees, and the database will create a package of information customized to your tastes and particular interests.

- *Copyright Website.* (http://www.benedict.com) This site contains helpful information and advice on how to copyright your writing or other creative works, including a special emphasis on copyright laws as they apply to Web publishing.

If you have memberships on *America Online*, *Compuserve*, *Prodigy*, or the *Microsoft Network*, contact some or all of the following sites:

- *America Online.* Go to the area on AOL known as the Entrepreneur Zone, which provides a number of business information services and content providers, such as business magazines. Keyword: ezone

- *Compuserve.* The Working from Home Forum contains a wide range of downloadable software, and you can interact with other home-based entrepreneurs to exchange ideas and information. Go: work

- *Prodigy.* On the Prodigy service, the main business bulletin board and discussion group area is the Entrepreneur Exchange. Jump: entrepreneur exchange

- *Microsoft Network.* The business information publishing giant, Commerce Clearing House (CCH), now maintains an area on the MSN called the CCH Business Owner's Toolkit, which offers a wide range of basic information on business laws and taxes. Go word: CCH

On-Line Incorporation or Formation of a Limited Liability Company

If you wish to set up a corporation or a limited liability company without using an attorney, there are a number of on-line companies that can help you with the necessary paperwork:

American Incorporators, Ltd
http://internet.village.com/business/
  inc/liability.html

J&S Resources
http://pw2.netcom.com/~js4info/
  LLCIL.html

BizTech
http://www.biztechs.com

Registered Agents, Ltd.
http://www.regagents.com/llcadv.html

Business Filings Incorporated
http://www.bizfilings.com

The Company Corporation
http://www.service.com/tcc/home.html

Corporate Agents, Inc.
http://www.corporate.com/js/home.html

T.L.M. Corporate Agents, Inc.
http://www.delcorp.com/cllcfrm.htm

State Laws & Related Resources

Part IV ▆▆▆▆▆

Notes to North Carolina State Chapter

What's New

This update of the North Carolina state chapter features new information and additions in several areas. The list below will help you locate the most significant changes by chapter–section number.

- Rates for corporate income surtaxes were decreased in 1994 – 11.2
- A limited liability company act was enacted – 11.2
- Computer software was declared exempt from property taxes – 11.4
- The intangible property tax was repealed – 11.4
- Inventories were declared exempt from property taxes – 11.4
- Minimum wage changes due to federal legislation – 11.5
- More information on state tax incentives is provided – 11.8
- More helpful resources are listed – 11.10

If changes have occurred since publication of this update, contact this office for assistance or referral to the appropriate agency.

Business/Industry Development Division
North Carolina Department of Commerce
301 North Wilmington
P.O. Box 29571
Raleigh, NC 27626-0571
(919) 733-4151
FAX (919) 733-9299
Internet: http://www.commerce.state.nc.us

About the Author

The state author of *Starting and Operating a Business in North Carolina* is James E. Scott.

Mr. Scott is a tax senior manager in the Raleigh, North Carolina office of the accounting firm of Ernst & Young. He has more than 10 years experience advising closely held corporations. Mr. Scott is a member of Ernst & Young's State and Local Tax (SALT) Group who, through Ernst & Young's national SALT network, represents Carolinas-based companies in all facets of state and local taxation.

Mr. Scott is a certified public accountant, who graduated from the University of North Carolina at Chapel Hill.

Acknowledgments

Mr. Scott would like to acknowledge Patrick Carney, senior manager, Mark Inman, senior tax consultant, and Jeff Meigs, senior tax consultant for their assistance in researching this chapter.

Chapter 11

State Laws and Taxes

11.1 Introduction

North Carolina continues to be an excellent state in which to start or operate a business. The state's business climate offers a strong labor environment, a central market location and extensive transportation network, some of the lowest costs in the nation for starting or operating a business, and an excellent support network for small businesses.

With a population of nearly 6.8 million — the 10th largest in the nation — North Carolina offers the largest manufacturing work force in the country. Some 500,000 workers are available for recruitment at any given time.[1] North Carolina workers are also noted for a high rate of productivity that can be attributed to the excellent work ethic of the people and the skill levels available. This strong labor environment is supported by the state's system of 58 community colleges, which offers free customized skills training to new and expanding businesses through its Industrial Training Program.

In addition, North Carolina has a right-to-work law that promotes good will between management and labor, low workers' compensation insurance rates with high benefits, and one of the nation's lowest unemployment rates.[2]

Labor Environment

The state's excellent market location and transportation network make the state an ideal business and distribution center. North Carolina's central east coast location puts businesses within a 700-mile radius of more

Market Location and Transportation

than 150 million U.S. and Canadian consumers, 64 of the nation's largest metropolitan areas, 61% of the U.S. industrial base, and 20 of the 27 states with at least $20 billion in retail sales.[3]

In addition to easy access to major markets, North Carolina provides an extensive transportation network of air, truck, rail, and port facilities. This includes:

- A 78,000-mile highway system;
- Two international airports and two domestic major airline hubs;
- A 4,000-mile rail network that is in the middle of a 27,000 mile network serving 22 states and Canada; and
- Two deep-water seaports that are also foreign trade zones.

Low Business Costs

North Carolina prides itself in keeping costs for businesses low. The state offers some of the lowest costs in the nation for labor, construction, and utilities. Combined state and local taxes are also among the lowest in the nation because of a requirement in the state constitution to keep the budget balanced. This, as well as the fact that the overall cost of living is well below the national average, gives North Carolina the "better business climate" that has attracted businesses to the state.[4]

State Support

Businesses in North Carolina can also expect the cooperation and assistance of many state agencies and offices, which are more than happy to answer questions regarding business requirements and laws for the Tar Heel State. Many of these state offices are listed throughout this chapter, following the section describing the information the office covers.

Since this book was written to provide you the basics for starting or operating a business in North Carolina, use the phone numbers mentioned whenever you need more information or details specific to your concern. If any phone numbers have changed — which does happen — use the government section of your local telephone directory or call your local operator. Many of the offices listed are based in the state capital. If you reside outside the state capital and do not want to make a long distance phone call, check the government listings of your local phone book. There may be a local office in your city. Many of the major offices you need to contact are also listed in Section 11.10 for easy reference.

The state of North Carolina also provides for free many booklets and guides to assist people starting or operating a business. These materials are listed whenever possible throughout this state section. If you request these publications, you should note that quantities may be limited. State agencies usually print only a certain quantity, based on their budgets.

As highlighted above, North Carolina has a lot to offer to anyone wishing to start, relocate, or operate a business in the state. The following sections will deal with the state-related aspects of general areas covered in the first ten chapters of this book.

11.2 Choosing the Legal Form of the Business

One of the first decisions you must make when starting your new business is to choose which legal form of business organization you will adopt. The three basic forms of business organization are the sole proprietorship, the partnership, and the corporation. Another legal form, the limited liability company, is also available in North Carolina. General considerations for choosing a legal form of business are located in sections 2.1–2.6. More state-specific considerations for North Carolina are discussed below. Other requirements, such as business name registration, taxes, wage-hour, and labor laws, are discussed in sections 11.4–11.7.

Sole Proprietorships

A sole proprietorship is a business that is owned by one person. Because there are no formal legal requirements for setting up a sole proprietorship, you will find it relatively simple to form and operate. A sole proprietorship offers you greater personal control of your business, fewer tax requirements and filings than other forms of business, and all the profits or losses. You will be personally liable, however, for all your business' debts and obligations, as discussed in Section 2.2.

Similar to federal tax law, as an owner of a sole proprietorship in North Carolina, your business earnings or losses will be subject to income taxes and you report them on *Schedule C* of your personal individual income tax returns.

For additional information on sole proprietorship taxes and requirements, refer to sections 11.4 and 11.5.

Partnerships

Any two or more individuals or entities who agree to contribute money, labor, property, or skill to a business and who agree to share in its profits, losses, and management are considered to have a partnership.

General Partnerships

As a partner in a general partnership, you have the right to share in management and have unlimited personal liability for the partnership's debts, taxes, and other obligations. Partnership agreements are not required by law, but it is sound business practice for you and your partner(s) to draw up a partnership agreement that, at a minimum, outlines basic business issues. Consider consulting an attorney when writing your partnership agreement.

As a general partnership, your company itself is not subject to an income tax; however, it is required to report income and expenses of the partnership on federal and state information returns. The state return, *Form D-403*, must be filed on or before the 15th day of the fourth month after the close of the taxable year.

In addition, you and your partner(s) are required to report your share of the partnership's profit or loss on your personal individual income tax returns, the same as sole proprietors. If any of the partners are nonresidents, your partnership must pay the tax based on individual rates for its nonresident partners' distributive share of partnership income.

Partnerships in North Carolina are also subject to an intangibles tax, which is described in more detail in Section 11.4.

Limited Partnerships

A limited partnership can be formed between two or more individuals, partnerships, corporations, or other entities. In this type of partnership, limited partners have limited liability and are only liable for the amount of their investment in the partnership. In exchange for this limited liability, limited partners cannot participate in the day-to-day management of the business. That responsibility is left to the general partners who have unlimited liability. A limited partnership must always have at least one general partner and one limited partner. In addition, there must be a written limited partnership agreement.

The North Carolina Revised Uniform Limited Partnership Act (RULPA) has several substantive differences from the federal RULPA. For example, the provisions for foreign limited partnerships differ substantially from the federal RULPA, with the North Carolina foreign corporation law serving as a model for the changes; in addition, the North Carolina act defines partnership interest as including income, gain, loss, deductions, and credits. This change brings the North Carolina act into conformity with the current Internal Revenue Code.

North Carolina limited partnerships are required to:

- File a *Certificate of Limited Partnership* with the secretary of state and record a certified copy in the office of the register of deeds in the county in which the partnership's registered office is located;
- Reserve a name with the secretary of state's office for 90 days; and
- Keep the names, addresses, and contributions of the limited partners at the registered office of the limited partnership.[5] This information, however, is not required to be included on the *Certificate of Limited Partnership*.

Foreign limited partnerships — those formed under the laws of a state other than North Carolina — are required to file an application for certificate of authority with the North Carolina secretary of state's office.

Corporations

A corporation is a more complicated form of business because it is considered a distinct legal entity and has a legal status or existence separate from you, the incorporator or owner. One of the main advantages to incorporating your business is that you are not personally liable for the corporation's debts, as long as you comply with all the necessary corporate formalities and recordkeeping requirements. To learn more about corporate formalities, obtain a copy of *The Essential Corporation Handbook* by Carl Sniffen from your local bookstore or through The Oasis Press.

If you are considering incorporating your business, consult an attorney to be sure you know what your responsibilities are and to better understand your options. To form a corporation, you will need to know how to file articles of incorporation, what types of taxes to expect, and how to comply with state securities laws.

A brief overview of some of these issues is presented below. Other requirements are discussed in sections 11.4 and 11.5. Keep in mind you will need to research more details once you make your decision to incorporate. One office that can help you with state requirements is:

Corporations Division
North Carolina Secretary of State
300 North Salisbury Street
Raleigh, NC 27611
(919) 733-4201

Domestic Corporations

If yours is a domestic corporation — incorporated in North Carolina — you will need to file articles of incorporation with the secretary of state's office. The fee for filing is $100.

As a corporation in North Carolina, you will also need to register your business name as discussed in Section 11.4.

Foreign Corporations

If your business is incorporated in another state and you seek to do business in North Carolina as a foreign corporation, your corporation is required to file an application for certificate of authority or existence or claim exemption from this requirement with the secretary of state's office.[6] The filing fee for a certificate of authority is $200.

S Corporations

North Carolina recognizes S corporations, and as a general rule, affords them the same tax treatment as is afforded to S corporations under federal law.

If your corporation elects S corporation status for federal income tax purposes, your company must file North Carolina S corporation tax returns on *Form CD-401S*.[7] Each shareholder must also include on his or her individual income tax return his or her pro rata share of the S corporation's net income or net loss, to the extent it is apportioned or allocated to North Carolina. The S corporation, however, must pay franchise taxes the same as regular corporations.

For more specific information on S corporation taxation in North Carolina, ask the Forms Division of the North Carolina Department of Revenue for a copy of the *Franchise Tax and Corporate Income Tax* rules booklet. For information on the federal treatment of S corporations, see Section 2.5.

Annual Reports

Once your corporation has completed its initial filings and registered for a business account number, you will have to remember to file its annual report. The annual report must be filed with the North Carolina Secretary of Revenue. The fee is $10. Failure to file this report or pay fees and taxes could result in your corporation's charter being revoked or suspended.

Corporate Taxation

In addition to federal taxes affecting corporations, as discussed in Section 2.4, North Carolina corporations are subject to a state corporation income tax and a franchise tax.

Income Tax

The state's corporation income tax is assessed on all corporations — excluding S corporations — doing business in North Carolina and is based on the portion of its income which is allocated and apportioned to the state at a flat rate.[8] The rate, which was 7.75% in 1997, is reduced to 7.25% in 1998 and will continue to decrease each of the next two years to 7.0% in 1999 and to 6.9% in 2000.

For income apportionment of a business operating in more than one state, North Carolina uses a four-factor formula of property, payroll, and twice sales.[9] Nonbusiness income is allocated in North Carolina based on the situs of the property or the domicile of the company.[10]

Any corporation doing business in North Carolina, or any corporation qualified to do business in North Carolina, is required to file a state income tax return regardless of whether it has net income allocated or apportioned to North Carolina.

Franchise Tax

In addition to net income, a franchise tax is levied on the largest of:

- The amount of capital stock, surplus, and undivided profits apportionable to the state;
- Fifty-five percent of the appraised value of property in North Carolina, plus the value of intangible property subject to taxation; or
- The net tax value of real and tangible personal property in North Carolina, less any debt incurred to purchase North Carolina real property.

The tax is $1.50 per $1,000, or $35.00, whichever is greater.[11]

The North Carolina annual income and franchise tax return is due on or before the 15th day of the third month following the close of the corporation's taxable year. A separate state extension is required if more than $500 of franchise and income tax is due. Payment of the tax balance is due for the extension to be valid.[12]

Help and Information

The North Carolina Department of Commerce produces a very good summary of corporate taxes in the state. To obtain the publication, *State and Local Taxes*, contact:

North Carolina Department of Commerce
(919) 733-4151

If you need more specific information, the *Franchise Tax and Corporate Income Tax* rules and bulletins booklet covers major areas of the laws. To request this booklet or to ask questions regarding your particular tax situation, contact:

Corporate Income and Franchise Tax Division
North Carolina Department of Revenue
(919) 733-3166

State Securities Laws

When your newly formed corporation issues shares of its stock to you or to any other shareholders, you must be very careful to comply with both federal and state securities laws. Otherwise, you could be a target for lawsuits from disgruntled investors in your corporation or even criminal prosecution.

In the case of the typical small corporation start up, you will probably be able to qualify for exemption from registering with the Securities and Exchange Commission (SEC), under federal laws, as described in Section 4.12. For more information about state registration of stock, exemptions, and state securities (or blue sky) laws in general, consult your attorney.

Limited Liability Companies

North Carolina offers you a fourth and relatively new legal form of business organization: the limited liability company (LLC). An LLC, as described in Section 2.6, is not a corporation or a partnership, yet it combines the corporate characteristic of limited liability for owners with partnership-type taxation. Advantages of selecting LLC status, as compared to other legal forms, include:

- Pass-through tax treatment — In North Carolina, an LLC is subject to taxation as a partnership if it is classified as a partnership for federal income tax purposes. It can also be classified as a corporation if it is classified as such for federal income tax purposes. If classified as a corporation, the LLC is not subject to the franchise tax. If treated as a partnership, taxable income or loss of an LLC "passes through" to you, as one of the owners. Thus, if your business expects to generate taxable losses for some time, your ability to pass through those losses to offset your taxable income from other sources could be an important reason to select LLC status.

  On the other hand, if your business generates large profits, LLC status will prevent the possible double taxation that can occur when a regular corporation distributes some of its profits to the owners as dividends. When losses or substantial profits are generated, an LLC can provide tax advantages. In intermediate situations, a regular corporation will probably remain a good choice since it can be used as a separate taxpayer to split taxable income between the firm and its owners.

- Limited liability — Like a corporation, an LLC limits your personal liability to the amount you have invested or promised to invest. Unlike a general partnership, you are not liable for the debts of the business beyond that initial investment.

- No maximum limitations on number or type of owners — Although an LLC must have a minimum of two owners, an LLC does not have to meet the numerous S corporation requirements — such as no more than 75 shareholders and no corporations or partnerships or certain other entities or persons allowed as shareholders.

- Simpler to operate than S corporations — While LLCs are in many ways equivalent to S corporations, they are much simpler to maintain and operate from a tax-compliance and tax-planning perspective. The tax requirements for S corporations are notorious for their complexities and numerous pitfalls which can inadvertently result in loss of S corporation tax status or unpleasant tax surprises.

- Active management participation — Like general partnerships, LLCs may permit all owners to participate in day-to-day management of the business.

The District of Columbia and all 50 states have adopted limited liability company legislation. While your firm, if set up in the form of an LLC, will have limited liability under North Carolina law, and presumably under the law of other states, many questions are still unanswered about how LLCs will be treated from state to state.

If your firm will be doing business in other states that have not adopted LLC laws, it is unclear at this time whether other states will respect the limited liability provisions of North Carolina's LLC law. It is also not clear whether other states will treat your LLC as a partnership for tax purposes, although it seems likely that most other states will as long as the Internal Revenue Service does. To determine whether the advantages of operating as an LLC — if you will be doing business in other states — will outweigh the potential legal and tax risks, consult with your tax attorney and accountant.

The fee for filing North Carolina articles of organization for domestic limited liability companies is $100; the fee for filing an application for a certificate of authority for foreign LLCs is $200. An annual report with a $200 filing fee is also required.

For more information on LLCs in North Carolina, contact the secretary of state's office.

11.3 Buying an Existing Business — State Legal Requirements

Buying a business is always a significant undertaking, and as a prospective purchaser, you must investigate the business being acquired as thoroughly as possible to avoid hidden liabilities and pitfalls. Be sure your investigation includes:

- A review of business books and records, including tax returns, payroll records, current receivables and payables, and minute books;

- A physical inventory of all furniture, fixtures, equipment, stock, and tangible personal or real property being acquired;
- A review of the status of any leases, contracts, or pending litigation;
- A search to determine if the seller has any overdue taxes, such as unemployment tax, owed to the state or federal governments;
- A review of all intangible property rights, such as patent, trade or service marks, and copyrights; and
- Discussions with customers and suppliers of the business.

In many instances, you or the seller may want to keep the potential sale confidential, so your discussions with customers and suppliers may be limited. Any purchasing agreement should contain a detailed set of representations and warranties concerning the business being acquired. You may also wish to consider using an escrow or set-off provisions to provide recourse in the event a hidden liability is discovered after closing.

Do not purchase an existing business without the assistance of an attorney. For more information on buying a business, refer to Chapter 3. Important new environmental laws you need to be aware of when purchasing an existing business are discussed in Section 9.9.

Bulk Sale Law

Although most states have repealed their bulk sale law, North Carolina's law is still in effect. When a business sells all or substantially all of its assets or enters into a major transaction that is not part of its ordinary business activities, the bulk sale law is used to protect the rights of creditors, such as suppliers and others, who have advanced goods or money to a business and have not yet been paid.

Like most other states that still have such a law, North Carolina's bulk sale law follows the general requirements outlined in the Uniform Commercial Code (UCC). This law is of particular importance to you, because as purchaser of an existing business, you are required to perform certain duties under this law to ensure that the rights of the seller's creditors are protected. To comply with this law, both you and the seller have certain responsibilities.

- The seller must furnish you with a list of the names and correct addresses of all his or her creditors and those claiming to be creditors.
- You and the seller must prepare a list of all items of property to be transferred.
- You must notify each creditor in advance, by certified mail or in person, that a transfer is about to occur.[14]
- You must keep the property list on file and make it available to the public for at least six months.

Once you have complied with the state requirements above, the burden shifts to the seller's creditors to take some action to protect their rights. Compliance will also protect you from later claims against the assets you have purchased.[15] If you fail to comply with these provisions, it could cause you major financial hardship. To be sure you meet the requirements of the bulk sales law, consult with your attorney.

Recorded Security Interests

Before closing a deal, it is important for you to know if there are any security interests or liens against any of the assets of the business that would interfere with your receiving clear title to any part of it. To protect yourself, have your attorney thoroughly research county, state, and federal records before you finalize your agreement to acquire the property.

Of course, if the transaction involves a purchase of real property, you should also have a title search performed to find out if the seller has good title and if there are any recorded deeds of trust or other claims against the property that the seller has not disclosed to you. You also want to make sure that the title grants you adequate means of access to the property.

Unemployment Tax Experience Rating

A company's unemployment tax experience rate determines the amount that must be contributed to the state unemployment insurance fund. If the seller has earned a better state unemployment tax experience rating than you would receive as a new employer, you may wish to explore the option of taking over the seller's rate when you acquire all or part of the business.

Succeeding to the seller/employer's experience rating involves a transfer of the reserve account.[16] The North Carolina Employment Security Commission (ESC) administers the unemployment insurance program in North Carolina and will determine the eligibility to transfer the reserve.[17] Upon notification, the transfer is usually automatic if the business purchase is a total acquisition.

The local ESC offices will provide you with forms and information. See the telephone book for a local address and phone number or contact:

North Carolina Employment Security Commission
P.O. Box 25903
Raleigh, NC 27611-5903
(919) 733-3098

Unemployment Tax Release

In addition to investigating your seller's tax experience rating when you purchase an existing business, look into its history of activity with unemployment taxes. You will want to be sure that the seller has made all the required unemployment reports and payments; otherwise, you may be held liable for any unpaid taxes. To avoid becoming liable for any unpaid unemployment taxes owed to the state by the seller, require that the seller obtain an unemployment tax release from the North Carolina Employment Security Commission.

This release will either assure you that no unpaid or overdue unemployment taxes are owed, or it will inform you of the amount of any such tax that you are required to withhold from the purchase price. If there is any unpaid tax, failure to withhold the tax from the purchase price will make you liable to the state for that amount. For more information on unemployment tax experience ratings, taxes, and contributions, contact the North Carolina Employment Security Commission.

Sales Tax Release

Like the unemployment tax release, you will want to be sure the seller provides you with a sales tax release before closing the deal. This will protect you from being liable for the prior owner's sales tax obligations.

In North Carolina, a final return of sales tax due must be filed within 30 days of the date a business is sold or transferred.[18] Until the taxes are paid, you are required to withhold sufficient purchase money to satisfy the unpaid taxes.[19]

Upon written request by the seller, the North Carolina Department of Revenue will furnish a transcript of the account to the seller. This will provide information about whether returns have been filed and amounts paid. This information can be requested in writing from:

Sales and Use Tax Division
North Carolina Department of Revenue
P.O. Box 25000
Raleigh, NC 27640
(919) 733-3661

The Sales and Use Tax Division will not certify that the account of the seller is accurate in the amounts of taxes paid except after an audit of the seller's business records.

Payroll Tax Obligations

When you purchase a business, you will need to complete and file an application for a withholding number on *Form AS/RP1*.[20] Every new employer is required to obtain a new number because the seller's withholding account will not be passed on to the new employer.

To avoid becoming liable for any unpaid withholding taxes owed to the state by the seller, you will need to require that the seller obtain a transcript for his or her account. This transcript will indicate whether all withholdings have in fact been paid. If any such taxes are still owed to the state, the transcript will inform you of the amount you will need to withhold from the purchase price. In fact, your purchase contract should include language allowing you to withhold from the purchase price any taxes owed to the state. Although not required by the state, this is a sound planning practice. For more information, contact:

Administrative Officer
Withholding Section
North Carolina Department of Revenue
P.O. Box 25000
Raleigh, NC 27640
(919) 733-4626

Change in Real Estate Ownership

If the business you purchase owns real property in North Carolina, report the change in ownership to the county tax assessor.

Environmental Warranties

Today, many purchasers of businesses are being held liable for the environmental problems created by their predecessors. There are many federal and state laws and regulations regarding the environment you must consider. Environmental laws pertain to air, water, storage of hazardous materials — including some very common household-type products — waste disposal, underground storage tanks, and other matters. Clean-up costs can sometimes exceed the cost of the property acquired.

As a result, you may want to consider an environmental audit of the property before you buy it. The audit would test the soil and water of any real estate being acquired to determine the environmental condition of the property. The purchase agreement should contain detailed representations and warranties of the seller stating that:

- The seller has not violated any environmental law or regulation; and
- The seller will reimburse you against any cost or liability imposed for environmental matters occurring before the acquisition.

For additional information about environmental issues, refer to Section 9.9. and 11.9.

11.4 State Requirements that Apply to Nearly All New Businesses

Regardless of the legal form of business organization you choose, your business will be required to comply with a number of state requirements, such as obtaining business licenses, paying various taxes, and registering your fictitious business name.

Local requirements, taxes, and restrictions also may apply to your business. Like state requirements and taxes, local requirements can change every year. Before starting your business, contact the appropriate state or local government agencies to make sure your business complies with state and local laws. This section introduces you to several basic state requirements and offers further information on what you need to do.

Business Licenses and Permits

If you start a business in North Carolina, you will probably need at least one license from the state and others from the city or county in which you conduct business. To find out what type of local license you may need, contact your city hall or county clerk's office. As stated in sections 4.3 and 9.9, make sure your business also conforms to local zoning laws, building codes, health and environmental requirements, and fire and police regulations by obtaining the necessary permits.

The state also requires business operating licenses, which include privilege, retail, and wholesale licenses. The licensing system in North Carolina is very broad. Fortunately, there is a central information agency — the North Carolina Business License Information Office — you can contact for assistance.

Business License Information Office
North Carolina Department of the Secretary of State
110 South Blount Street
Raleigh, NC 27611
(919) 733-0641
(800) 228-8443 (in North Carolina)

Your business may also require state licenses based on your occupation, as discussed in Section 4.4. For a detailed listing of occupations and businesses that require state licenses, refer to Section 11.6.

Estimated Income Taxes

One of the most surprising concepts to new entrepreneurs is that, as a business owner, you will have to estimate how much money you will make before you make it. Then several times each year, you must pay taxes on the amount you have estimated.

No matter which business form you choose, filing and paying North Carolina estimated taxes must now become part of your regular agenda. If you don't have the money to pay estimated income taxes, get your accountant's advice on whether you should get a loan to cover the tax when due or pay underpayment penalties to the government after the end of the year. Note that any state tax penalties you pay — unlike the state tax itself — will not be allowed as a deduction on your federal tax return.

Individual

If your business is a sole proprietorship or partnership, you must report the business income — whether it is actually distributed to you or not — on your personal tax return. If you are just starting your business, contact your state income tax office to get estimated tax forms. To be sure you handle the estimating, filing, and paying correctly, consult your accountant.

After your first year of paying estimated taxes to the state, you will probably automatically receive forms to use in future years, but even if the forms don't come, you are still responsible for filing and paying on time.

The rules for estimated tax payments for individuals are similar to federal requirements. As in the case of federal estimates, North Carolina individual estimated tax vouchers, *Form NC-40*, are due for a particular calendar year on April 15, June 15, September 15, and January 15 (of the following year). Any remaining unpaid personal income tax is due on April 15 of the following year with the North Carolina personal income tax return, *Form D-400*. For more details on federal estimated taxes, see Section 4.6.

Corporate

If your business is a corporation and your tax liability is more than $500, you are required to pay 90% of your estimated income tax liability by installment. Tax payments are due in four installments, based on this schedule:

Estimated Tax Payment Schedule for Corporations

1st Payment – Due on the 15th day of the fourth month of the fiscal year (April 15 for calendar-year corporations).

2nd Payment – Due on the 15th day of the sixth month of the fiscal year (June 15 for calendar-year corporations).

3rd Payment – Due on the 15th day of the ninth month of the fiscal year (September 15 for calendar-year corporations).

4th Payment – Due on the 15th day of the twelfth month of the fiscal year (December 15 for calendar-year corporations).

If your business expects to pay less than $500, estimated payments can be made but are not required by law. For more information, contact:

Corporate, Excise, and Insurance Tax Division
North Carolina Department of Revenue
P.O. Box 25000
Raleigh, NC 27640-0055
(919) 733-3166

Sales and Use Taxes

If your business is involved in retail sales, you are required to collect tax for the state on all sales or rentals of tangible personal property (not real estate).

Resale

Sales of tangible personal property within the state are subject to sales tax unless the property was purchased for resale. Wholesalers and retailers are exempt from tax on their purchases of goods for the purpose of resale if:

- The transactions are supported by a *Certificate of Resale, Form E590*; or
- Other evidence adequately supports the fact that the property is being purchased for resale.

Labor charges for repairs or installation that are separately stated by vendors in their records and on invoices are exempt; however, services offered by a retail dry cleaner or laundry are subject to the sales tax.

Use Tax

Use tax is intended to tax the use of all property purchased outside the state — where North Carolina sales tax has not been collected — but actually used within North Carolina. Use tax also applies to items that were exempt from sales tax when purchased — such as items bought for resale — that you end up using instead of reselling.

Rates

The sales tax is levied and imposed upon the retailer, and it is the intent of the law that it be passed on to the purchaser. All sales or rentals of tangible personal property are taxed at 1% to 4%, unless they are specifically exempt by statute. Sales subject to the state 4% rate — other than sales of taxable utility services — are also subject to a local rate of 2%. The sale of motor vehicles is exempt from sales tax. These sales, however, are subject to a 3% highway use tax up to a $1,500 maximum.

Sales of the items listed below are taxed at a 3% rate, subject to a maximum tax of $1,500:

- Aircraft
- Railway locomotives or railway cars
- Boats

The following are taxed at a rate of 1% with a maximum tax of $80 per article:

- Sales of farm machines and machinery;
- Sales of mill machines and machinery, including parts and accessories;
- Sales of telephone equipment to telephone companies;
- Sales of certain machinery to commercial laundries and freezer locker plants;
- Sales of broadcasting equipment to radio and television stations; and
- Sales of machinery used by publishers and printers.

Exemptions

Here are examples of items exempt from taxation.

- Inventories of wholesalers, retailers, and manufacturers;
- Farm products in their original or unmanufactured state that are sold by the producer in the capacity as producer;
- Holy bibles and public school books on the adopted list, the selling price of which is fixed by state contract;
- Gasoline on which the gallonage tax has been paid;
- The first $1,500 of all funeral expenses, including gross receipts from tangible personal property furnished and services rendered by funeral directors, morticians, and undertakers, or by monument and memorial stone dealers; and
- Custom software.

Sales subject to the state 1% and 2% tax limitations and sales of taxable utility services subject to the state 3% rate are not subject to the local option sales tax.

Sales Tax Identification Number

With a limited number of exceptions, every business that will sell tangible personal property, such as merchandise, to customers must obtain a sales tax identification number.

To obtain this number, you must complete *Form E-504, Application for Sales and Use Tax Registration and Annual Wholesale License*, which is available from the Sales and Use Tax Division. The filing fee is $15. A sample of this form is provided for your review at the back of this book.

If you are a merchant, you can also use *Form E-504* to apply for a merchant's annual wholesale license, which requires payment of an annual $25 fee. As a merchant, you must also apply for a merchant's certificate of registration, which requires a one-time $15 fee. The applications for the wholesale license are due on the first of July of each year. If yours is a new business, you must file your applications before starting your business.[21]

After you receive your sales tax identification number, the secretary of revenue will send you the appropriate reporting forms and schedules. Sales and use tax reports are due monthly, unless the sales tax liability is consistently less than $50 per month. In that case, sales tax may be reported and paid quarterly.[22] Quarterly filing status must be requested and authorized by the North Carolina Department of Revenue. If you are consistently liable for at least $20,000 per month in sales and use taxes, you must file returns on a semi-monthly basis.

Recordkeeping

Whether you are a retail merchant, wholesale merchant, or customer, you must keep adequate and complete records to determine the amount of sales and use tax for which you may be liable. Records are required to be kept for at least three years. The secretary of revenue has the discretion to sustain or waive penalties for failure to follow the law and file returns.[23] For clarification of the sales and use tax law as it applies to your business, contact:

Sales and Use Tax Division
North Carolina Department of Revenue
(919) 733-3661

Property Taxes

Property taxes are assessed on a per-county basis. The value is determined by the county tax supervisor. Property taxes are based on assessments as of January 1. The taxes are due September 1, but may be paid at par as late as January 5 of the following year. Listings are due to the county by January 31 of each year.

Exemptions

Property tax exemptions include:

- Computer software (as of Jan. 1, 1994);
- Manufacturer's inventories and inventories of retail and wholesale merchants — tangible personal property held for sale and not manufactured, processed, or produced by the merchant;
- Property imported from a foreign country and stored — for the first year only — at a terminal while awaiting further shipment;
- "Bill and hold" goods manufactured in North Carolina and held by the manufacturer for shipment to a nonresident customer;
- Motor vehicle chassis in transit;
- Nuclear materials;[24] and
- Certain recycling and pollution control equipment if certified by the state.

The North Carolina taxes intangible personal property tax was repealed as of January 1995. Unless otherwise exempted, individuals, partnerships, and corporations, were required to file an intangibles tax return each year.

Intangible Property

An assumed, fictitious, or trade name is any name used in the course of business that does not include the full legal name of all the owners of the business. If your business goes by any name other than your own real name, your business is operating under an assumed name. An assumed name might also suggest the existence of additional owners by using such words as "company," "associates," or "group."

Fictitious or Assumed Business Name

If you operate a sole proprietorship or a partnership and use your own true name in the business name, you probably do not have to register the name. If you don't use your own true name, you need to file your assumed name certificate in the register of deeds' office for each county in which you conduct business under the assumed name. The same is true of a limited partnership operating under a name other than that filed in the secretary of state's office.

If your business is a corporation, you can reserve your corporate name for 120 days with the secretary of state. A filing fee of $10 per document is charged.

Although being the first to register a certain name probably keeps any other business in your industry from using that name in your state, it is not a universal guarantee. If name protection is critical to your business — especially if you will be marketing in more than one state — it is best to discuss your situation with an attorney who specializes in this area of law.

To register your business name in North Carolina, contact the Office of the Register of Deeds for forms and specifics on how to complete the procedure. A registration fee is required.

Trademarks and Service Marks

The term "trademark" refer to any word, name, symbol, or device used by a company to distinguish its goods from those of another company. A service mark is used to identify and distinguish services as opposed to goods. Although not required, you can register your trade mark or service mark with the secretary of state's office. State registration is also not considered as public notice of ownership. Registration is for a term of 10 years. The filing fee is $50.

Checklist of State Requirements

To summarize, you will have many decisions to make when starting a new business. One decision is the type of business to undertake. The specific business you choose may be subject to registration, licensing, taxes, or other requirements that apply only to your particular product, service, or activity.

Another important decision your new business faces concerns location. Counties and cities have different property tax rates, and this may provide an incentive to locate in a certain area. A third decision that confronts your new business is which legal form you will choose. Are the advantages of incorporation greater than the disadvantages caused by corporate taxes and additional recordkeeping and paperwork?

Most businesses, regardless of type, location, or form, will be subject to the taxes and requirements discussed in this chapter. It will be your responsibility as a new business owner to understand and comply with all the regulations and reporting requirements that apply to your business.

This checklist summarizes the main requirements that you will need to satisfy to start a business in North Carolina whether or not you have employees. If you have employees, the following section describes additional requirements for your business.

Requirements	Proprietorships	Partnerships	Corporations	LLOs
Local occupational licenses	X	X	X	X
State operating licenses	X	X	X	X
State sales tax identification number	X	X	X	X
Merchants annual wholesale license	X	X	X	X
Local property tax forms	X	X	X	X
Assumed name certificate	X	X	X	X
Corporate income tax			X*	

Requirements	Proprietorships	Partnerships	Corporations	LLCs
Franchise tax			X	
Partnership tax		X	X**	X
Sales and use tax	X	X	X	X
Intangibles property tax	X	X	X	X
Individual income tax	X	X		X
Annual Reports			X	X

  * Except S corporations
** S corporations only

11.5 Additional Requirements for Businesses with Employees

Once you hire an employee to work in your business, you take on several additional responsibilities. In North Carolina, you will need to withhold certain payroll taxes, obtain workers' compensation insurance, comply with safety and health regulations, and know your rights and those of your employees under various labor laws. This section discusses these requirements in further detail and recommends publications and assistance programs offered by various agencies. General considerations and federal requirements are covered in Chapter 5.

Withholding Taxes

As an employer, you are responsible for withholding a portion of an employee's gross compensation to cover his or her North Carolina income tax liability. Withholding occurs at the time wages are paid. In addition to making payments, you must file withholding tax returns.

A withholding identification number is required. To obtain this number, your business must complete *Form NC-1, Application for Withholding Identification Number* and file it with the North Carolina Department of Revenue. If you change from one form of doing business to another, you will have to apply for a new withholding identification number.

Withholding Methods

The two primary methods used for withholding North Carolina income tax are:

- The wage bracket tables,[25] which can be obtained from the North Carolina Department of Revenue. These tables are for weekly, biweekly, semimonthly, and monthly pay periods.
- The annualized percentage method,[26] which uses a graduated rate schedule based on projected taxable income — gross pay less the standard deduction and personal exemptions.

The cumulative year-to-date method and approximation plan are two other methods that may be used in determining the amount of income tax to withhold.[27] Prior permission is not required for using either of these two methods; however, any alternative method is subject to review by the secretary of revenue.[28]

In addition, you may use any other method or formula to determine the amount of tax required to be withheld if the amount is substantially the same as the amount determined by using the wage bracket tables or the annualized percentage method.[29]

Currently, there are no other state taxes required to be withheld from wages. In addition, no city or county taxes must be withheld.

Reports and Payments

If you withhold less than an average of $500 per month, you must file quarterly reports on *Form NC-5*. This form and payment of the tax withheld must be filed by the last day of the month following the end of each calendar quarter.[30]

If you are required to withhold an average of at least $500 but less than $2,000 per month, you must file monthly reports on *Form NC-5M*. This form and the payment of the tax due must be filed by the 15th day of the following month. The exception is the report and payment for the month of December, which are due on January 31.[31]

If you average $2,000 or more of withholding each month, your reports and payments are due at the same time as the federal reports and payments. North Carolina, however, does not require next day deposit on withholding of $100,000 or more. If you are a new employer who falls into this category, contact the North Carolina Department of Revenue for details.

Help and Information

If you have specific questions regarding withholding tax, obtain a copy of *NC-30, Income Tax Withholding Tables and Instructions for Employers* or contact:

Individual Income Withholding Tax Section
North Carolina Department of Revenue
P.O. Box 25000
Raleigh, NC 27640
(919) 733-4626
(800) 222-9965 (in North Carolina)

State Unemployment Tax

If your business employs one or more individuals in each of 20 weeks during any calendar year or if your payroll amounts to $1,500 in any calendar quarter, you will be responsible for paying unemployment tax. These payments or contributions provide unemployment compensation for workers who become involuntarily unemployed. Any employer subject to the Federal Unemployment Tax Act (FUTA) is automatically subject to the North Carolina tax.[32]

The tax is imposed on your employees' covered wages, but it is illegal to deduct this tax from their wages. You, as the employer, are responsible for paying the state unemployment tax.

If you are the owner of a sole proprietorship or a partner in a partnership, you do not have to pay unemployment tax for yourself since you are not considered an employee of the business.

Employees and services exempt from the North Carolina unemployment tax include:

Exemptions

- Railroad employees;
- Services covered by the federal unemployment system;
- Services by a minister or member of a religious order;
- Services for a rehabilitation, work-relief, or work-training program;
- Services by a student for a college or university in which he or she is enrolled;
- Services by a student in a work-study program;
- Services for certain hospitals by a patient of that hospital;
- Services for a non-American vessel or aircraft;
- Services of an individual in the employ of his or her child or spouse, or a child under the age of 21 who is employed by his or her parent, or a partnership consisting only of the child's parents;
- Newsboys or newsgirls who sell newspapers on the street or from house to house;
- Casual labor which is not in the course of one's trade or business; and
- Services for certain tax exempt organizations — if the remuneration is less than $50.[33]

When you become an employer, you must file *Form NCUI 604-15, Employer Status Report to Determine Liability under the N.C. Employment Security Law*, with the Employment Security Commission (ESC). Quarterly contribution reports must be filed with the ESC on *Form NCUI-101*, which is due by the last day of the month following the calendar quarter. Payment of the tax should accompany the report.[34]

If you have any questions regarding unemployment insurance, contact:

North Carolina Employment Security Commission
P.O. Box 25903
Raleigh, NC 27611
(919) 733-3098

The rate at which you will have to pay unemployment tax is called an unemployment tax experience rating. This rate is based on the amount of unemployment benefits paid to your former employees as it relates to the total wages your company has paid over a period of years. For example, the more former employees who claim benefits, the higher your experience rating. Conversely, the fewer former employees claiming benefits, the lower your rate.

Tax Experience Rating

To find out how you can save on unemployment taxes, see Section 11.8.

If you are a new employer, you will be assigned by the state a standard rate of 2.25% during the first three years. This rate may increase or decrease over the course of time, depending in large part on your unemployment experience history. If you are purchasing a business and you would like to take over the previous employer's rate, see Section 11.3.

Workers' Compensation Insurance

Workers' compensation insurance is a state-mandated insurance requirement for most companies with three or more employees. While, as the owner of a sole proprietorship or a partner in a partnership, you do not have to obtain workers' compensation for yourself, you are required to provide it for your employees. It provides wage loss and medical benefits to employees injured on the job and it protects you from legal action for damages for injuries suffered by your employees.[35]

Be aware that neither general liability nor health and accident insurance can properly substitute for workers' compensation insurance. Jobs that are not covered by the workers' compensation act include casual employees, farm labor, and domestic employees.

If you are covered by the act, you must prove your compliance to the North Carolina Industrial Commission by obtaining standard workers' compensation insurance from an insurance company. You may also self-insure your business, if certain requirements are met.

It is your responsibility to provide workers' compensation insurance, and as such, it is illegal to charge employees for this insurance. You are also required to post a notice to employees stating that they are covered by the provisions of the North Carolina Workers' Compensation Act. This notice must be posted in a prominent location at your place of business.

Help and Information

The North Carolina Industrial Commission publishes several helpful booklets and brochures you may be interested in obtaining. The publications listed below range in price from free to $10 and require prepayment for processing.

- *Bulletin: Information About the NC Workers' Compensation Act*
- *Workers' Compensation Rules and Regulations of the Industrial Commission*
- *Workers' Compensation Act Annotated*
- *Workers' Compensation Fee Schedule*

For further information or to order any of the above publications, contact:

North Carolina Industrial Commission
430 North Salisbury Street
Raleigh, NC 27611
(919) 733-4820

Safety and Health Regulations

As an employer in North Carolina, you will have to comply with state and federal job safety laws designed to prevent injuries resulting from unsafe or unhealthy working conditions. Health and safety protection is provided to workers under the Occupational Safety and Health Act of North Carolina. This act was initiated in response to Section 18 of the federal Occupational Safety and Health Act (OSHA) of 1970 which allows states to develop a state plan for administration of OSHA standards. The state plan must show that state administration is at least as effective as direct federal administration and meets the state plan requirements outlined in Section 18.

The North Carolina Department of Labor has been designated by the occupational safety and health act of North Carolina to administer the state plan and enforce the act.

The act spells out the rights and obligations of both employers and employees and establishes penalties and procedures to be followed. Every employer is covered by the state's occupational safety and health act, except those employers covered by the federal Mine Safety and Health Act and certain others with employees covered by federal safety and health laws. The Mine Safety and Health Act of North Carolina issues rules and regulations for employees of mines, quarries, and sand and gravel operations.

On-Site Inspections

The Occupational Safety and Health Act provides for periodic on-site inspections. Be aware that your employees have the right to request an inspection of your workplace if they believe you are not providing a safe and healthful place of employment.

Assistance and Information

If you need more specific information regarding the North Carolina Occupational Safety and Health Act and what is specifically required for your particular business, contact the Division of Occupational Safety and Health. This office also offers free consultation services to North Carolina employers who need assistance with their safety and health programs.

Division of Occupational Safety and Health
North Carolina Department of Labor
413 North Salisbury Street
Raleigh, NC 27603
(919) 733-3900

Wage-Hour Laws and Labor Standards

Before hiring your employees, you need to know about the wage-hour laws and labor standards that will affect your business.

In North Carolina, you must notify your employees at the time of hiring of your company's policy for and rate of pay and the day and place of payment of wages. Pay periods may be daily, weekly, biweekly, semi-monthly, or monthly.[36] Deductions, other than those required or authorized by law, may only be made after you obtain a written authorization from your employee. Employees who are terminated must be paid all wages due on or before the next regular payday.[37] It is also wise to maintain an accurate record of each employee's earnings and hours worked.

You will also have to notify your employees at the time of hiring of your policies on vacation time and sick leave. This information, and comparable matters, must be made available to your employees in writing or through posted notices.[38] If you make any changes to any of your policies, you must inform your employees in writing of those changes before the changes take affect. If you need help in writing your company policies, consider obtaining a copy of The Oasis Press' *A Company Policy and Personnel Workbook*, listed in back of this book.

Other employee-related issues are discussed in general below. Federal requirements are discussed in Section 5.7. If you need more specific information on state labor laws and requirements, contact:

Wage and Hour Division
North Carolina Department of Labor
413 North Salisbury Street
Raleigh, NC 27603
(919) 733-2152

Minimum Wage

North Carolina's minimum wage law requires employees to be paid at least $5.15 per hour, the same as the federal minimum wage. Employees of day care, hospitals, schools, and businesses with a gross revenue of over $500,000 are automatically subject to the federal minimum wage which is currently $5.15 an hour. Businesses with less than $500,000 gross revenue follow state minimum wage. The minimum wage for full-time students, learners, apprentices, or messengers is 90 percent of state rate rounded to the lowest nickel.[39] The commissioner of labor may also establish a lower minimum wage in certain cases to prevent the curtailment of opportunity of employment.[40]

Equal Pay

Federal and state equal opportunity statutes require equal pay for men and women performing similar services. Failure to do so can result in a claim based on wage or sex discrimination.

Overtime Pay

North Carolina's overtime pay law requires that all employees be paid at a rate of one and one-half times their regular rate for all hours worked in excess of 40 hours per work week.[41] Seasonal amusement and recreational workers must be paid the overtime rate for time in excess of 45 hours per week.

Child Labor

Like most states, North Carolina regulates the employment of children. If you intend to hire children in your business, check with the North Carolina Department of Labor to find out what specific restrictions and exemptions there are relating to acceptable occupations and conditions and to allowable hours of employment. Refer also to Section 5.7 for a discussion of federal laws that apply to the employment of minors. In general, a youth employment certificate is required from the North Carolina Department of Labor before hiring a minor. No youth under age 16 may be employed except for those occupations permitted under the federal Fair Labor

Standards Act. Those youths may not be employed on the premises of an establishment selling alcoholic beverages for on-premises consumption. No one under age 18 may be employed in occupations considered hazardous by the U.S. Department of Labor, or declared detrimental by the commissioner of labor.[42]

Breaks, Holidays, and Sick Leave

Most employers allow employees breaks for meals and rest. Generally, employees also receive at least seven paid holidays a year and are granted sick leave, which is paid time off for an employee who is temporarily incapacitated.

Family Leave

More companies today are voluntarily providing family or parental leave or a combination of both for their employees. Family/parental leave generally allows employees several weeks of paid or unpaid leaves of absence for family or medical purposes, such as:

- The birth or adoption of a child; or
- A serious health condition of the employee, spouse, child, or parent.

Closely related to family leave is maternity leave, which typically allows pregnant employees up to twelve weeks of paid or unpaid leave during pregnancy or following the birth of the child, or both. The employee is usually returned to her previous job or a comparable one at equal pay, benefits, and seniority. If your company does not currently have a family/medical leave policy, you may want to establish one now that the mandatory federal Family and Medical Leave Law became effective August 1993. This law, signed in February 1993 by President Clinton, affects companies with 50 or more employees.

Right-to-Work

In about half of the states, right-to-work laws have been enacted to guarantee that no person may be denied employment for refusing to join a union. Many also prohibit mandatory payment of union dues by non-union workers in order to retain employment. North Carolina has a right-to-work law, which makes it an attractive place to locate companies that prefer to have a nonunionized workforce.

Anti-Discrimination

Section 5.8 provides you with a detailed discussion of the federal anti-discrimination laws you need to follow when hiring and employing your staff. In addition to the federal laws, the North Carolina Equal Employment Practices Act[43] forbids discrimination in employment practices based on race, religion, color, national origin, age, sex, or handicap.[44] This act covers all employers who regularly employ 15 or more persons. In addition, the North Carolina Handicapped Persons Protection Act makes it illegal to discriminate in employment practices against any person on the basis of a physical or mental impairment.[45]

Independent Contractors

If you have only occasional needs for particular skills or services, you might want to use independent contractors, rather than hire more employees. When you have work performed by independent contractors, you have fewer governmental regulations and taxes to deal with and you can disengage the relationship when the contract is completed.

It is critical that you don't unknowingly misclassify, as independent contractors, individuals who should be treated as employees — you could be held liable for back taxes and penalties. As discussed in sections 5.2 and 9.11, it is sometimes difficult to determine whether an individual qualifies as an independent contractor. As a general rule, if your company is the individual's only customer or client, the government will probably maintain that the person is your employee and expect your firm to withhold taxes and comply with other employer regulations.

Although the criteria are not precisely defined, contractors have the freedom to choose what work they will do and when, where, and how it will be done. Contractors maintain a separate business location and usually furnish their own tools and supplies. Contractors report income to the IRS on *Schedule C* or *Schedule F* and the IRS compares it to the *Form 1099*s it receives from you and the contractors' other clients.

Depending on their industry and size of business, contractors also provide their own licenses, permits, performance bonds, insurance, advertising, business cards, and stationery. Contractors can hire and fire their own employees and subcontractors.

To avoid the ramifications of a wrong determination, consult your tax accountant or attorney before using an independent contractor.

11.6 State Licenses

As noted in Chapter 6, many businesses and professions are required to obtain licenses before engaging in business. State governments have traditionally licensed professionals, such as doctors, lawyers, and accountants. To further protect consumers, North Carolina has expanded the list to include other occupations.

No central licensing board exists in North Carolina. Each professional board operates as an independent unit within the parameters of the federal and North Carolina constitutions. The state of North Carolina as well as its cities and counties issue licenses or permits to practice a trade, business, or profession. In addition to a regulatory license or licenses, a revenue license or licenses may be required by the state and local governmental agencies.

Since North Carolina's licensing requirements are numerous and, depending on your type of business, can require contacting several government licensing agencies, the Business License Information Office (BLIO) was created to assist North Carolina businesses. This office has a Master

License Application Program that will help you determine what licenses you need. The BLIO also offers:

- Consultants who, over the phone or in person, provide whatever help is necessary to guide you through the licensing process; and
- Customized information packets, including application forms and instructions.

The BLIO charges no fees for their services and any sized business is welcome to contact their office. For more information, contact:

Business License Information Office
North Carolina Secretary of State
110 South Blount Street
Raleigh, NC 27601
(919) 733-0641
(800) 228-8443 (in North Carolina)

Businesses Requiring Licenses

Listed below are a number of occupations that do require licenses in North Carolina. If your particular business or occupation is not listed below, check with the BLIO to find out if you need a license or if there are any other requirements.

Airline companies	Dry cleaners	Motor vehicle salespersons
Auctioneers	Electricians	Nursery operators
Bakeries	Employment agencies	Nursing home owners
Boiler inspectors	Florists	Pawnbrokers
Business agents	General repairpersons	Private investigators
Cashers of checks	Investment advisers	Retail beer sales
Cemeteries	Landscape architects	Retail wine sales
Cesspool cleaners	Manufacturers	Retail liquor sales
Clockmakers	Masseurs	Taxi or bus drivers
Coin-operated machines	Mechanics	Warehouses
Dairypersons	Merchants	Wholesale merchants
Drugstores	Motel operators	Wrecker services

Professions Requiring Licenses

Listed below are some of the occupations and professions regulated in North Carolina and the licensing boards and agencies that regulate them.

Accountants	NC Board of CPA Examiners
Architects	NC Board of Architecture
Bankers	NC State Banking Commission
Barbers	State Board of Barber Examiners
Chiropractors	State Board of Chiropractic Examiners
Contractors	NC Licensing Board for Contractors
Cosmetologists	NC Board of Cosmetology Examiners
Dentists	NC Board of Dental Examiners

Professions Requiring Licenses (continued)

Doctors	Board of Medical Examiners of the State of NC
Educators	NC Department of Public Instruction
Electricians	NC Board of Examiners of Electrical Contractors
Engineers	NC Board of Registration for Engineers and Land Surveyors
Funeral directors	NC State Board of Mortuary Science
Insurance brokers	NC Department of Insurance
Lawyers	NC Board of Law Examiners
Librarians	NC Public Librarian Certification Commission
Nurses	NC Board of Nursing
Opticians	NC State Board of Opticians
Optometrists	NC State Board of Examiners in Optometry
Osteopathic surgeons	State Board of Osteopathic Examination and Registration
Pest controllers	NC Department of Agriculture
Plumbers	NC Board of Examiners of Plumbing, Heating, and Fire Sprinkler Contractors
Pharmacists	NC State Board of Pharmacy
Physical therapists	NC State Committee of Physical Therapy Examiners
Podiatrists	State Board of Podiatry Examiners
Psychologists	NC Board of Examiners of Practicing Psychologists
Realtors	NC Real Estate Commission
Veterinarians	NC Veterinary Medical Board

11.7 State Excise Taxes

North Carolina imposes a number of excise taxes and certain license fees. Some excise taxes are imposed on the production, importation, use, or sale of certain goods. Others are imposed on services and certain types of businesses. Excise taxes that may apply to your business are listed below. Refer to Chapter 7 for information on federal excise taxes. If you need additional information on state excise taxes, contact:

License & Excise Tax Division
North Carolina Department of Revenue
P.O. Box 25000
Raleigh, NC 27640
(919) 733-3673

Alcoholic Beverages

An excise tax is levied on the sale of malt beverages, unfortified wine, and fortified wine. The tax is payable by the resident wholesaler or importer who first handles the beverages in the state. An excise tax is levied on the retail price of liquor sold in Alcohol and Beverage Control (ABC) stores and is payable by the local ABC board. Excise tax reports are due monthly by the 15th day of the following month.[46]

The excise tax is based on the following rates:[47]

Type of Beverage	Tax Rate
Beer	$0.48387 per barrel holding more than 7.75 gallons
Beer	$0.53376 per barrel holding less than 7.75 gallons
Fortified wine	$0.24 per liter
Unfortified wine	$0.21 per liter
Liquor	28% of case cost, bailment, and local board markup

Various state licenses are required in addition to the ABC permits.[48] Alcoholic beverages are sold only where authorized by local election. The ABC board provides the following publications for your information. Since the publications range in price, contact the Alcohol Beverage Control Commission for current price information.

- *ABC Rules*
- *ABC Laws*

  North Carolina Alcohol Beverage Control Commission
  P.O. Box 26687
  Raleigh, NC 27611-6687
  (919) 779-0700

Tobacco Products

North Carolina levies a cigarette tax of $0.0025 (one-quarter of one cent) per cigarette or $0.05 (five cents) per package of 20 cigarettes on all distributors.[49] Tobacco products other than cigarettes are subject to a tax at the rate of 2% of cost.

No tax is levied on manufacturers shipping to distributors or on out-of-state shipments. The tax is paid by purchasing stamps, which the distributors are required to affix to each package of cigarettes.[50] Reports are due by the 20th day of each month, reporting the activity for the preceding month.

In addition to the taxes, distributors are required to obtain licenses from the secretary of revenue. The license fee is $25.[51]

Gasoline and Special Fuels

If you sell, distribute, purchase, produce, refine, or manufacture any type of fuel used in motor vehicles in North Carolina, you are subject to a motor fuels tax. All gasoline or petroleum products purchased in North Carolina and kerosene used for heating are also subject to inspection fees. In addition, motor carriers are liable for road taxes.

Reports are due monthly to the secretary of revenue from distributors and suppliers. The tax is due with the return.[52] Motor carriers are required to file reports quarterly.

Wholesale fuel distributors pay an additional annual license tax determined on a graduated rate based on the number of pumps owned or leased.

Motor Vehicle Registration

Registration fees are charged based on passenger capacity for passenger vehicles and on the weight of the vehicle for common carrier vehicles. All commercial and noncommercial motor vehicles — except certain farm vehicles and vehicles owned by the U.S. government — must be registered with the state of North Carolina. No returns are due.

To register a vehicle in North Carolina, you must pay one or all of the fees listed below, depending on your situation.

- Five dollars for the title fee;
- Twenty dollars for the private passenger license plate fee; and
- The license fee for trucks, which is based on the gross weight of the truck.[53]

The fees are paid annually at the time the vehicle is registered. At the time of registration, proof of insurance and personal property tax listing must be shown.

Insurance Companies

Insurance companies and self-users of workers' compensation are subject to an insurance tax.[54] This tax is levied in place of franchise and income and intangibles taxes. The tax is imposed on the gross premiums of policies written on the lives of North Carolina residents and property located in North Carolina.[55] The rates used to compute this tax are:[56]

- 2.5% on amounts collected on annuities, plus an additional amount on all other insurance contracts issued by insurers; and
- An additional 1.33% on the amounts collected on fire and lightning coverage.

The tax on hospital, medical, and dental service corporations is 0.5%.

Annual reports of gross premiums for the preceding calendar year are required to be filed, along with the tax payment, with the commissioner of insurance. The returns are due on varying dates depending on the type of insurance. Reports for workers' compensation are due on April 1, other insurance on March 15, and firemen's relief 50 days after December 31.

In addition, all insurance companies are required to have a license to operate in North Carolina. A certificate of registration must be purchased annually from the commissioner of insurance.[57] For more information, contact:

North Carolina Department of Insurance
Dobbs Building
430 North Salisbury Street
Raleigh, NC 27611
(919) 733-2032

Real Estate Transfers

A property transfer tax is imposed on all instruments that transfer an interest in North Carolina real estate, except for transfer by the following means:

- Operation of law
- Lease
- Will
- Gift
- Merger or consolidation
- Instruments of indebtedness [58]

Also exempt are transfers for no consideration or transfers by governmental units. The tax rate is $1.00 per $500 or fractional part of value. [59] The tax is paid by the seller to the county register of deeds. [60]

Chain Stores

If you own more than one wholesale or retail store, you will have to pay a tax of $65 per additional store. [61] Automobile dealerships, stores of nonprofit organizations, and bakery thrift stores are exempt. The tax is due annually on July 1. No returns are required. [62]

Soft Drinks

An excise tax is imposed on the sale, use, and distribution of all soft drink products in North Carolina. [63] The rate of tax is $0.01 (one cent) for each bottle of soft drink. Soft drink syrup is taxed at the rate of $1.00 per gallon or $0.008 (four-fifths of one cent) per ounce or fractional part thereof. Soft drink powders are taxed at $0.01 (one cent) per ounce or fractional part thereof. [64] Fountain drinks are also taxed accordingly.

Wholesale dealers or distributors liable for the tax may pay an alternate rate of $0.72 (72 cents) per gross for the first 15,000 bottles and $0.01 (one cent) per bottle thereafter. In addition, wholesalers and distributors are allowed a 4% discount.

In lieu of the reporting methods available, the tax is paid when stamps or crowns are purchased from the secretary of revenue. The stamps or crowns must be affixed to the soft drink containers. Returns are due on the 15th of each month for the preceding month.

All distributors and dealers must have a soft drink license for each place of business. The license fee is $25 for distributors and wholesalers and $5 for retailers. [65]

Other Taxes

In addition to the major excise taxes discussed above, North Carolina also imposes taxes on:

- Highway use
- White goods (major appliances) disposal
- Occupancy

For more information, contact the License and Excise Tax Division.

11.8 Planning for Tax Savings in a Business — State Tax Laws

As discussed in Chapter 8, there are effective legal ways to reduce your taxes. This section continues that discussion and provides you with state specifics on those tax strategies that can help you in your business. Before implementing any of the following tax-saving tips, be sure to consult your tax adviser or accountant.

Unemployment Tax Savings

Your best strategy for reducing the unemployment tax your company pays is to plan and hire carefully, so you have minimal layoffs. Over time, this will lower your unemployment tax rating. An effective way to pre-screen employees and to test your long-term need for a new position is to use a temporary help agency as a source for workers at all skill levels.

If you operate your business as a sole proprietorship, there are some minor tax advantages in hiring certain family members as employees in your business. In North Carolina, any wages your sole proprietorship pays to your spouse, or children under 21 years of age, are exempt from state unemployment tax.

Keep in mind, however, that because you don't pay unemployment tax for them, they are not eligible to collect benefits if you fire or lay them off. Also, if your child is employed by your corporation or by a partnership which has other partners, your child is not considered to be employed by you, and therefore, not exempt from unemployment tax. If, however, your child works for your sole proprietorship, he or she is considered to be employed by you and is exempt.

Another advantage of operating a sole proprietorship is that you are not considered an employee of your business; therefore, you do not have to pay any unemployment tax on your wages. Of course, once you hire additional employees, you will be responsible for paying unemployment tax as well as other payroll taxes on their wages.

State Tax Credits and Incentives

North Carolina provides a wide array of tax credits and incentives for businesses. If your company seeks to relocate to North Carolina, contact the North Carolina Department of Commerce below and ask for the booklet describing financial incentives and advantages. This publication lists many of the programs available in the state.

If you need additional information, contact:

Commerce Finance Center
Business/Industry Development Division
North Carolina Department of Commerce
(919) 733-5297

Job Training

Some of the financial incentives and advantages that may apply to you are listed below.

North Carolina's nationally acclaimed community college system offers free, customized skills training to new and expanding industries. An industrial training specialist will help to plan the most effective use of 58 technical college campuses, available public or private buildings and equipment, convenient curriculum courses, and training supervisors. The state will also provide use of facilities for training. If a company's skills or standards are unique, the state will hire that company's employees to do the training.

Jobs Creation Tax Credit

If your company creates full-time jobs in one of North Carolina's designated economically-distressed counties, your company may be eligible for a tax credit of $2,800 per job created above a threshold of nine. This credit is taken ratably over a four-year period and can offset up to 50 percent of your firm's annual North Carolina income tax after other credits, if any.

Manufacturer's Incentive Tax Formula

North Carolina offers an income tax allocation formula which can cut taxable income by up to 25 percent. The system of allocation offers a break to corporations interested in taking advantage of North Carolina's low land and labor costs without penalizing them for not making a high percentage of their sales in North Carolina.

Industrial Building Renovation

If you relocate to one of North Carolina's less developed counties you could receive funds to repair or renovate "basic" or existing buildings for use as manufacturing and industrial operations. Your company can receive $2,400 per job created, up to a maximum of $250,000, for repair, renovation, or equipping a structure for industrial use.[66]

No repayment is required in cases where funds are used to provide a utility service to the building and the improvement is then owned by the local government. When the money is used to benefit a private entity for improvements — such as the installation of air-conditioning or equipment — the funds are to be recovered, or paid back, with a maximum interest rate of 2 percent. Terms can provide for unusual cash flow expectations or for credit collateral subordination.

Job Screening and Tax Credit

If your company plans to relocate to North Carolina, the North Carolina Employment Security Commission can screen, test, and recommend job applicants for you. All you need to do is provide the agency with a list of job openings and the requirements for each position.

The ESC then matches its applicants with job positions and will refer these people to your company by setting up appointments for interviews, sending resumes, or any other method of referral which your company chooses. If an ESC referral is released from a job for poor performance within 100 days of employment, your company can request noncharging for unemployment insurance.

If your company hires people in any of several hard-to-employ categories, such as economically disadvantaged youth or vocational rehabilitation clients, your company may also receive a 40 percent tax credit that is available on the first $6,000 in wages paid in the first year of employment.

Estate Planning and Marital Deduction

Estate planning for your business and personal assets is easier for married couples because of the unlimited marital deduction for federal estate tax purposes, as discussed in Chapter 8, which postpones all federal estate tax until the death of the surviving spouse.

In North Carolina, a similar rule generally applies for state death tax purposes because the state estate tax also allows an unlimited marital deduction for assets left to surviving spouses; thus, simplifying overall estate planning.

Sheltering Profits on Export Sales

If your company does significant export business, you may want to form a separate Domestic International Sales Corporation (DISC) or Foreign Sales Corporation (FSC) to take advantage of the federal export incentives described in Section 8.4. You should keep in mind, however, that North Carolina does not grant any special tax benefits for DISCs.[67]

Dividends Received Deduction

If your corporation owns stock in another corporation, your company may qualify for a dividends received deduction which could reduce the income tax it has to pay on the dividends it receives. To find out if your corporation can take advantage of the federal dividends received deduction, or similar state deduction, consult with your accountant.

North Carolina allows a dividends received deduction for corporations limited to $15,000.[68] The portion of dividends that is deductible corresponds to the North Carolina allocation percentage of the corporation. No deduction is allowed for dividends received from a corporation that does not file a North Carolina tax return. The North Carolina Department of Revenue compiles a list each year showing the percentage of dividends that are taxable for all major corporations.[69]

Contribution Deduction

Charitable contributions are deductible by corporations. The deduction, however, is limited to 5% of net income computed before the contribution deduction. Contributions to the state of North Carolina, its political subdivisions, or to educational institutions located in North Carolina are not subject to this limitation.[70]

Net Economic Loss

In North Carolina, a loss deduction is allowed for state income tax purposes. This deduction, however, must be a net *economic* loss rather than a net operating loss. A net economic loss is the amount by which allowable deductions, other than prior years losses, exceed income from all sources in the year including any income not taxable.[71] In North Carolina, this loss can only be carried forward for a period of five years, subject to certain limitations.

More specific information on computing a net operating loss is explained in the *North Carolina Franchise Tax and Corporate Income Tax* rules booklet.

Local government and private organizations also offer a variety of incentive programs. Local communities, for example, may offer incentives for:

Local and Private Incentives

- Water and sewer services at no cost;
- Electric and gas lines services;
- Solid waste and garbage;
- Professional development/relocation services;
- Road improvements;
- Rail sidings improvements; and
- Pollution control equipment.

Groups of local businesses and professional people may also assist businesses who are interested in relocating to their area. Contact the Commerce Finance Center for more information.

11.9 Miscellaneous Business Pointers

This section provides general business information on such topics as financial assistance, usury laws, and emerging trends in North Carolina. Refer to Chapter 9 for information on federal assistance programs and other basic business pointers.

A wide variety of financial incentive programs are available in North Carolina for new or expanding businesses.

State Business Loan Programs

The industrial revenue bond (IRB), a form of long-term, low-interest financing, continues to be a productive means of financing a facility that will have a measurable economic impact on the community. The low interest rate is made possible because the interest earned by the purchaser is exempt from income taxes. Because the bond debt is secured by the firm's credit or its bank's credit and is not guaranteed by either the county or state, the company issuing these bonds must have a strong financial position relative to the amount borrowed.

Industrial Revenue Bonds (IRBs)

Industrial firms may finance projects related to product manufacturing (including new or expanded plants), distribution centers, or research and development facilities necessary to the manufacturing process. Generally, capital projects with investments under $10 million can be financed in full. Prospective clients should be familiar with statutory safe guards associated with this program. For more information, contact the Commerce Finance Center.

Taxable Industrial Development Bonds

If your company does not qualify for financing that is exempt from federal taxes, your firm may be eligible for a Taxable Industrial Development Bond (TIDB) from North Carolina bond authorities. The income on the debt obligation of an TIDB is exempt from state income taxes.

Financial institutions in the state offer placement of the debt for borrowers who seek the exemption. Alternatively, financial institutions offer placement of completely taxable bonds issued directly by companies without the involvement of bond authorities. Both kinds of securities, as well as conventional bank financing, avoid the limitations imposed by federal revenue bond law on project size and nature and on debt terms. For more information, contact the Commerce Finance Center.

North Carolina Biotechnology Center

The North Carolina Biotechnology Center was established in 1981 to ensure that North Carolina gains long-term economic benefits from the development of the biotechnology industry. The Center's Economic Development Division provides economic assistance in the form of two loan programs.

The Economic Development Finance Program provides up to $250,000 for 18 months of support for research and development activities. Any North Carolina-based biotechnology company may apply. The Small Business Innovation Research (SBIR) Matching Fund Program provides up to $50,000 for research and development activities that refine Phase I SBIR research results and initiate work on Phase II project objectives. Any North Carolina-based biotechnology company that receives a Phase I SBIR award, completes the Phase I project, and intends to submit a Phase II proposal may apply.

Significant presence must be maintained by the company in North Carolina for at least five years from the date a proposal for either program is funded. Proposals are accepted on the first business day of each month.

For more information, contact:

Economic Development Office
North Carolina Biotechnology Center
P.O. Box 13547
15 T.W. Alexander Drive
Research Triangle Park, NC 27709
(919) 541-9366

Small Business Investment Companies

A Small Business Investment Company (SBIC) is a privately owned and operated company that has been licensed by the U.S. Small Business Administration (SBA) to provide equity capital and long-term loans to small firms. Often, an SBIC also provides management assistance to the companies it finances.

SBICs invest in all types of manufacturing and service industries and a wide variety of other businesses, including construction, retail, and wholesale concerns. Many investment companies seek out small businesses that offer new products or services because these small businesses usually have the growth potential that is attractive to SBICs.

For more information on SBICs in the state, contact:

U.S. Small Business Administration
200 North College Street
Charlotte, NC 28202
(704) 344-6563

Usury Laws

Usury laws define the maximum amount of interest that may be charged on a credit transaction, such as a promissory note or other instrument, that requires the payment of interest.

When extending credit, the legal rate of interest in North Carolina is 8%;[72] however, parties may agree in writing for an amount in excess of this rate.[73] The maximum allowable contract rates vary according to the amount lent and the type of contract.[74] North Carolina has a number of usury statutes that regulate the amount of interest on a loan. For example, mortgages, revolving charge accounts, and retail installment contracts are regulated. For more information on state usury laws, contact your accountant or banker.

Environmental Regulations

If your business will have any impact on the surrounding environment, such as erecting a new building or renovating an existing structure, contact the U.S. Environmental Protection Agency (EPA) to make sure you meet its requirements. Inquiries regarding specific state permits should be directed to:

Environmental Specialist
Business/Industry Development Division
North Carolina Department of Commerce
301 North Wilmington
Raleigh, NC 27626-0571
(919) 733-4151

Emerging Trends and Issues

If you would like to keep abreast of emerging trends and issues that will affect your business, consider joining the National Federation of Independent Business (NFIB). The NFIB is this nation's largest organization representing the interests of small business owners.

Through NFIB, you will learn more about pending state and federal legislation, regulations, and taxes that will affect you and, more importantly, you will be able to speak out on these issues through NFIB's state and national lobbying efforts. As an NFIB member, you would receive:

- *Independent Business (IB)*, the bimonthly national magazine for small business owners; and
- *State Reports*, that specifically cover issues in North Carolina.

For more information on NFIB, contact:

National Federation of Independent Business
Attn: Membership Services
53 Century Boulevard
Nashville, TN 37214
(800) NFIB NOW (634-2669)

11.10 State Sources of Help and Information

Throughout the state, you will be able to find many public and private agencies and organizations that can assist you with your business. For your convenience, many of these sources of help and information are listed below.

Do-It-Yourself Incorporation

You can incorporate your business on your own in North Carolina, but if you have an existing partnership or sole proprietorship that you want to convert to a corporation, see your accountant first. Important tax consequences may influence the way you transfer assets and structure the corporation.

Your tax accountant, attorney, or secretary of state's office may also be able to refer you to a do-it-yourself incorporation book that can assist you through the incorporation process, providing state-specific information, ready-to-use forms, and stock certificates.

One such book is *Incorporating In North Carolina Without A Lawyer*. Published by Consumer Publishing, Inc., this $24.95 book is updated monthly by the author, W. Dean Brown. To order this book, contact:

The Oasis Press
(800) 228-2275

The Corporations Division of the North Carolina Secretary of State's office can also send you a packet of incorporation information which includes the publication, *North Carolina Business Corporation Guidelines*. Since quantities may be limited, check for availability.

State Agency Assistance

For your specific questions regarding state laws, regulations, taxes, incentives, and other state-specific issues, these state agencies and offices can be very helpful.

One-Stop or Business Assistance Center

The North Carolina Small Business and Technology Development Center (SBTDC) can answer general questions on starting or expanding a small business, refer you to the proper agency or agencies if you need more information, or provide you with a packet of free information on starting a business in the state. To request this information, contact the office below or mail the preaddressed post card provided at the back of this book.

Small Business and Technology Development Center
North Carolina Department of Commerce
333 Fayetteville Street Mall, Suite 1150
Raleigh, NC 27601-1742
(919) 715-7272
FAX ((919) 715-7777
Internet: http://www.commerce.state.nc.us

Tax or Revenue Office

If you have any questions regarding state taxes, contact the North Carolina Department of Revenue. This department can also send you *Income Tax Withholding Tables and Instructions for Employers*, a booklet that provides instructions and information on employer/employee issues and charts for computing withholding on the various pay periods.

North Carolina Department of Revenue
P.O. Box 25000
Raleigh, NC 27640
(919) 733-3991 (Taxpayer assistance)
(800) 222-9965 (in North Carolina)
(919) 733-3166 (Income tax)
(919) 733-4147 (Intangible tax)
(919) 733-3661 (Sales and use tax)
(919) 733-4626 (Withholding tax)

Secretary of State

The Corporations Division of the North Carolina Secretary of State's office can answer your questions regarding corporations, limited liability companies, choosing business names, trademarks and service marks, business licensing, and securities offerings. This division also distributes a free publication, *North Carolina Business Corporation Guidelines*, that covers most of the areas above. To request the booklet (when available) or to call for more information, call:

Corporations Division
North Carolina Secretary of State
300 North Salisbury Street
Raleigh, NC 27611
(919) 733-4201

Business Licenses

For information on state business licenses and help through the licensing process, contact:

Business License Information Office
North Carolina Secretary of State
301 West Jones Street
Raleigh, NC 27603
(919) 733-0641
(800) 228-8443 (in North Carolina)

Labor/Industrial Relations

For information regarding labor laws and health and safety regulations, contact:

North Carolina Department of Labor
(919) 733-7166 (General inquiries)
(919) 733-2152 (Wage and hour)
(919) 733-3900 (Employee health and safety)

Federal Agency Assistance

The federal agencies described in Chapter 10 also have regional and local offices in North Carolina.

U.S. Small Business Administration

The SBA publishes pamphlets and books covering the myriad aspects of business and provides limited financing for qualified borrowers. A U.S. Small Business Administration (SBA) office is also located in Charlotte.

U.S. Small Business Administration
200 North College Street
Charlotte, NC 28202
(704) 344-6563

Service Corps of Retired Executives

Sponsored by the SBA, the Service Corps of Retired Executives (SCORE) is an association of retired businesspeople in your area who provide counseling. To find the nearest chapter, write or call SCORE at the U.S. Small Business Administration office above.

Small Business Institute

The Small Business Institute (SBI) program is a joint effort of the SBA and North Carolina universities. As part of their course work, senior-level college students, under the direction of faculty members, provide management consulting, market surveys, and other assistance for small business owners. To learn more about this program, contact the SBA office above.

Internal Revenue Service

To ask questions or request forms from the Internal Revenue Service, you can call the toll-free information number below. You can also hear pre-recorded tax information from the IRS Tele-Tax number. The codes and topics that may be of interest to you include:

- 101 – IRS help available
- 103 – Small Business Tax Education Program
- 309 – Business use of home
- 310 – Business use of car
- 311   Business travel expense
- 312 – Business entertainment expenses
- 352 – Self-employment tax
- 455 – Forms and publications – How to order

For a complete list of codes, contact the IRS forms and publications number and request *Publication 910, Guide to Free Tax Services.*

Internal Revenue Service
(800) 424-1040 (State office)
(800) 829-1040 (Questions)
(800) 829-3676 (Forms and publications)
(800) 829-4477 (Tele-Tax)

Local Sources

Most communities throughout the state provide additional resources that can be invaluable to your business whether you are currently operating, just starting, or relocating a business.

Public Libraries

Your local public library offers a wealth of useful information. You can locate answers to a number of business-related questions in the reference section. Statistics available on your industry and your competition can contribute to your market research and business plan. In the periodical section, you will find publications that can provide information on emerging trends and issues in the business world. Telephone and specialized directories, available in libraries, can help you locate hard-to-find suppliers, potential buyers, associations, and organizations.

Many of the larger libraries also offer a reference assistance section. If a library in your area has this service, you may even be able to call the reference librarian for the information you need. Specialized, private, or college libraries may be available in your area, as well. To find a library near you, look in the Yellow Pages or under the government section of your phone directory.

Small Business Center Network

Fifty of the fifty-eight colleges in the community college system currently operate a small business center. The centers provide the following services:

- Information on starting a new business or developing an existing business;
- Counseling and referral services; and
- Short-term training sessions for small businesses at little or no cost.

For help or information about a local center, contact:

Small Business Center Network
North Carolina Community College System
200 West Jones Street
Raleigh, NC 27603-1337
(919) 733-7051

Chambers of Commerce

Local chambers of commerce can provide information about the living and business environment of the area you've chosen for your business. To locate the nearest chamber of commerce or obtain a listing of local offices, contact:

North Carolina Citizens for Business and Industry Inc.
225 Hillsborough Street, Suite 460
Raleigh, NC 27602
(919) 828-0758

State Business Publications

Trade and business journals can keep you up-to-date on business-related activities and issues in North Carolina. Those publications are listed below for your information.

The Business Journal
128 South Tryon, Suite 2250
Charlotte, NC 28202-5003
(704) 347-2340

Business North Carolina
5435 Seventy-Seven Center Drive, Suite 50
Charlotte, NC 28217
(704) 523-6987

Carolina Business
P.O. Box 12006
New Bern, NC 28561
(919) 633-5106

North Carolina
225 Hillsborough Street, Suite 460
P.O. Box 2508
Raleigh, NC 27603-1760
(919) 828-0758

Triangle Business Journal
P.O. Box 95143
Raleigh, NC 27625
(919) 878-0010

Newspapers can also be helpful. To find the newspapers in your area, contact:

The North Carolina Press Association, Inc.
4101 Lake Boone Trail, Suite 201
Raleigh, NC 27607-6518
(919) 787-7443

Small Business and Technology Development Centers

A primary source of business assistance in North Carolina comes from the 15 Small Business and Technology Development Centers (SBTDCs) located throughout the state. State SBTDCs provide managerial and technical assistance in the form of:

- In-depth, one-on-one confidential counseling — assessing the feasibility of a business idea, preparing a business plan, finding sources of capital, developing marketing strategies, and managing operations and human resources.
- Specialized market development assistance — government procurement, international business development, and new product or technology development.

The SBTDCs also offer *New Business Start-up Kits* free when requested. If you feel your business would benefit from this program and would like to request a kit or seek assistance from an SBTDC, use the list below to locate an SBTDC nearest you. A handy post card is also located in back of the book for requesting more information.

SBTDC: Headquarters
333 Fayetteville Street Mall, Suite 1150
Raleigh, NC 27601
(919) 715-7272
FAX (919) 715-7777

SBTDC: Central Carolina Region
608 Airport Road, Suite B
CB #1280 UNC-CH
Chapel Hill, NC 27514
(919) 962-0389
FAX (919) 962-3291

SBTDC: Cape Fear Region
FSU Continuing Education Center
P.O. Box 1334
Fayetteville, NC 28302
(910) 486-1727
FAX (910) 486-1949

SBTDC: Capital Region
North Carolina State University SBTDC
800 1/2 South Salisbury Street
Raleigh, NC 27601
(919) 715-0520
FAX (919) 715-0518

SBTDC: Eastern Region
300 East First Street, Willis Building
East Carolina University
Greenville, NC 27858-4353
(919) 757-6157
FAX (919) 757-6992

SBTDC: Northwestern Region
Walker College of Business
Appalachian State University
Boone, NC 28608
(704) 262-2492
FAX (704) 262-2027

SBTDC: Northern Piedmont Region
Winston-Salem State University
P.O. Box 13025
Winston-Salem, NC 27110
(910) 750-2030
FAX (910) 750-2031

SBTDC: Northeastern Piedmont Region
NC A&T University/CH Moore Agricultural
Research Center
P.O. Box D-22
Greensboro, NC 27411
(910) 334-7005
FAX (910) 334-7073

SBTDC: Southeastern Region
UNC Wilmington, Westside Hall
601 South College Road
Wilmington, NC 28403
(910) 395-3744
FAX (910) 350-3990

SBTDC: Southern Piedmont Region
The Ben Craig Center
8701 Mallard Creek Road
Charlotte, NC 28262
(704) 548-1090
FAX (704) 548-9050

SBTDC: Western Region
Center for Improving Mountain Living,
 WCU
Cullowhee, NC 28723
(704) 227-7492
FAX (704) 227-7422

SBTDC: Catawba Valley Region
514 Highway 321 NW, Suite A
Hickory, NC 28601
(704) 345-1110
FAX (704) 326-9117

Endnotes

1. "North Carolina — Where Business Receives a Warm Welcome," *Business Week* (advertisement), Fall, 1993.

2. "The 10 Best Reasons For Locating in North Carolina," Business/Industry Development Division.

3. "North Carolina — Where Business Receives a Warm Welcome," *Business Week* (advertisement), Fall, 1993.

4. "North Carolina — Thinking the World of Business," *Fortune* (advertisement), March 9, 1992.

5. *N.C. Legal Aspects,* N.C. Business/Industry Development Division, 1988.

6. *N.C. Legal Aspects For Business,* N.C. Business/Industry Development Division, 1993.

7. *Franchise Tax and Corporate Income Tax,* 1992 ed., North Carolina Department of Revenue.

8. *State Tax Reporter* ¶¶ 10-905, 10-910, and 10-925, Commerce Clearing House, Inc.

9. *Franchise Tax and Corporate Income Tax,* 1992 ed., North Carolina Department of Revenue.

10. N.C. GEN. STAT. § 105-130.4.

11. N.C. GEN. STAT. § 105-122.

12. *Franchise Tax and Corporate Income Tax,* 1987 ed., p. 84, North Carolina Department of Revenue.

13. N.C. GEN. STAT. § 25-6-102.

14. N.C. GEN. STAT. § 25-6-105.

15. N.C. GEN. STAT. § 25-6-104.

16. N.C. GEN. STAT. § 96-9(c)(4)a.

17. N.C. GEN. STAT. § 96-9(c)(4)b.

18. N.C. GEN. STAT. § 105-164.38.

19. Id.

20. *Payroll Management Guide* ¶ 7580, Commerce Clearing House, Inc.
21. N.C. GEN. STAT. § 105-112.
22. N.C. GEN. STAT. § 105-164.16.
23. N.C. GEN. STAT. § 105-237.
24. *State Tax Reporter* ¶ 2239, Commerce Clearing House, Inc.
25. N.C. GEN. STAT. § 105-163.2(b).
26. N.C. GEN. STAT. § 105-163.2(f).
27. Id.
28. Id.
29. Id.
30. N.C. GEN. STAT. § 105-163.6(a).
31. N.C. GEN. STAT. § 105-163.6(c).
32. N.C. GEN. STAT. § 96-8.
33. Id.
34. N.C. GEN. STAT. § 96-4, 96-9.
35. N.C. GEN. STAT. § 97.
36. N.C. GEN. STAT. § 95-25.6.
37. N.C. GEN. STAT. § 95-25.7.
38. N.C. GEN. STAT. § 95-25.13.
39. N.C. GEN. STAT. § 95-25.3(b).
40. N.C. GEN. STAT. § 95-25.3.
41. N.C. GEN. STAT. § 95-25.4.(a).
42. N.C. GEN. STAT. § 95-25.5.
43. N.C. GEN. STAT. § 143-422.1.
44. N.C. GEN. STAT. § 143-422.2.
45. N.C. GEN. STAT. § 168A.
46. N.C. GEN. STAT. § 105-113.83(b).
47. Id.
48. N.C. GEN. STAT. § 105-113.74.
49. N.C. GEN. STAT. § 105-113.5.
50. N.C. GEN. STAT. § 105-113.10.
51. N.C. GEN. STAT. § 105-113.12.
52. N.C. GEN. STAT. § 105-436.
53. *State Tax Reporter* ¶ 50, Commerce Clearing House, Inc.
54. N.C. GEN. STAT. § 105-228-3.
55. N.C. GEN. STAT. § 105-228-5.
56. Id.
57. N.C. GEN. STAT. § 105-228.4.
58. N.C. GEN. STAT. § 105-228.29.
59. N.C. GEN. STAT. § 105-228.30.
60. N.C. GEN. STAT. § 105-228.32.
61. N.C. GEN. STAT. § 105-98.
62. *State Tax Reporter* ¶ 53-695, Commerce Clearing House, Inc.
63. N.C. GEN. STAT. § 105-113.45.
64. Id.
65. *State Tax Reporter* ¶ 33-005, Commerce Clearing House, Inc.
66. *North Carolina Financial Incentives and Advantages,* Commerce Finance Center.
67. *State Tax Reporter* ¶ 10-105, Commerce Clearing House, Inc.
68. N.C. GEN. STAT. § 105-130.7.
69. *State Tax Reporter* ¶ 10-315, Commerce Clearing House, Inc.
70. N.C. GEN. STAT. § 105-139.9.
71. *Franchise Tax and Corporate Income Tax,* 1992 ed., pp. 69–70, North Carolina Department of Revenue.
72. N.C. GEN. STAT. § 24-1.
73. N.C. GEN. STAT. § 24-1.1.
74. N.C. GEN. STAT. § 24.

Index

Notes

Notes

Appendix

Checklist of Tax and Other Major Requirements for Nearly All Small Businesses

Requirement	None	1–4	5–10	11–14	15–19	20–99	100+	Section Reference
Federal estimated taxes	√	√	√	√	√	√	√	Sec. 4.6
Federal income tax returns	√	√	√	√	√	√	√	Sec. 4.12
Form SS-4, Application for Federal I.D. Number:								
Sole Proprietorships		√	√	√	√	√	√	Sec. 5.2
Partnerships	√	√	√	√	√	√	√	Sec. 5.2
Corporations	√	√	√	√	√	√	√	Sec. 5.2
Form 1099 returns	√	√	√	√	√	√	√	Sec. 4.7
Federal payroll tax returns		√	√	√	√	√	√	Sec. 5.2, 5.3
Provide and file W-2's to employees at year-end		√	√	√	√	√	√	Sec. 5.2
ERISA compliance:								
For unfunded or insured employees' welfare plan:								
Provide a Summary Plan Description to employees		√	√	√	√	√	√	Sec. 5.5
File a Summary Plan Description							√	Sec. 5.5
File *Form 5500, Annual Report*							√	Sec. 5.5
Provide a Summary Annual Report to employees							√	Sec. 5.5
File and provide to employees a Summary of Material Plan Modifications							√	Sec. 5.5
File a Terminal Report, if plan terminated							√	Sec. 5.5
For funded employee welfare plan:								
File and provide all items described in ERISA list		√	√	√	√	√	√	Sec. 5.5
For employees' pension or profit-sharing plan:								
Provide a Summary Plan Description to employees and file with U.S. Department of Labor		√	√	√	√	√	√	Sec. 5.5
File *Form 5500, Annual Report*							√	Sec. 5.5
File *Form 5500-C* or *Form 5500-R*		√	√	√	√	√	√	Sec. 5.5
Provide to employees and file a Summary of Material Modifications		√	√	√	√	√	√	Sec. 5.5
File a Terminal Report, if plan terminated		√	√	√	√	√	√	Sec. 5.5
Provide a Summary Annual Report to employees		√	√	√	√	√	√	Sec. 5.5
Bonding requirement for plan officials		√	√	√	√	√	√	Sec. 5.5
Federal Wage and Hour Laws and Regulations — coverage depends on nature of business and employee types not covered		√	√	√	√	√	√	Sec. 5.7

Checklist of Tax and Other Major Requirements for Nearly All Small Businesses (continued)

Requirement	None	1–4	5–10	11–14	15–19	20–99	100+	Section Reference
Federal Fair Employment Laws:								
Americans with Disabilities Act anti-discrimination rules					√*	√*	√	Sec. 5.8
Anti-discrimination laws regarding race, color, sex, etc.					√	√	√	Sec. 5.8, 11.5
Anti-discrimination laws regarding age						√	√	Sec. 5.8
Anti-discrimination laws regarding federal contracts		√	√	√	√	√	√	Sec. 5.8
Equal Pay Act for Women		√	√	√	√	√	√	Sec. 5.8
File *Form EEO-1*							√	Sec. 5.8
Post notice regarding discrimination: racial, sexual, etc.					√	√	√	Sec. 5.8
Post notice regarding age anti-discrimination laws						√	√	Sec. 5.8
Post other anti-discrimination notices by certain federal contractors		√	√	√	√	√	√	Sec. 5.8
Federal Family and Medical Leave Act						√**	√	Sec. 5.12
Post notice regarding family and medical leave						√**	√	Sec. 5.12
Immigration Laws:								
Complete *INS Form I-9* for each new hire		√	√	√	√	√	√	Sec. 5.9
OSHA Job Safety Regulations:								
Health and safety		√	√	√	√	√	√	Sec. 5.6, 11.5
Post *Job Safety and Health Notice*		√	√	√	√	√	√	Sec. 5.6
Post *Employee Rights Notice* regarding OSHA		√	√	√	√	√	√	Sec. 5.6
Record industrial injuries and illnesses				√	√	√	√	Sec. 5.6
Report job fatalities or multiple injuries to OSHA		√	√	√	√	√	√	Sec. 5.6
Federal and State Child Labor Laws		√	√	√	√	√	√	Sec. 5.7, 11.5
Local business licenses	√	√	√	√	√	√	√	Sec. 4.3, 11.4
Sales and use tax permit and returns, if selling tangible personal property	√	√	√	√	√	√	√	Sec. 11.4
Fictitious business name statement, if using fictitious business name	√	√	√	√	√	√	√	Sec. 11.4
North Carolina estimated taxes	√	√	√	√	√	√	√	Sec. 11.4
North Carolina income taxes	√	√	√	√	√	√	√	Sec. 11.2, 11.4
North Carolina Wage and Hour Laws and Regulations — most employees are covered, yet some types are not		√	√	√	√	√	√	Sec. 11.5
Workers' compensation insurance		√	√	√	√	√	√	Sec. 11.5
North Carolina Fair Employment Laws: General prohibition of discrimination		√	√	√	√	√	√	Sec. 11.5

* Applies to companies with 25 or more employees until July 26, 1994 when it will apply to companies with 15 or more employees.

** Only applies to companies with 50 or more employees.

Checklist of Official Government Posters and Notices Required to be Displayed by Businesses

Type of Poster or Notice	When required	Where to obtain
Local business license	Required to be obtained by nearly all businesses operating in a particular locality.	Local city hall or county courthouse
Sales tax permit	Required to be displayed at each place of business where tangible personal property is sold.	State tax office
OSHA poster regarding job safety and health	Required to be posted by all employers.	U.S. Department of Labor, Occupational Safety and Health Administration
U.S. Fair Labor Standards Act Federal Minimum Wage poster *(WH Publication 1088)*	Required to be posted by employers with employees whose wages and working conditions are subject to the U.S. Fair Labor Standards Act.	U.S. Department of Labor, Employment Standards Administration, Wage and Hour Division offices
Federal Equal Employment Opportunity poster	Required to be posted by all employers with 15 or more employees 20 weeks of a calendar year or with federal contracts or subcontracts of $10,000 or more.	Federal Equal Employment Opportunity Commission offices
Federal Age Discrimination poster	Required to be posted by all employers with 20 or more employees, 20 or more weeks in a calendar year.	U.S. Department of Labor, Wage and Hour Division offices
Federal Rehabilitation Act poster regarding hiring of disabled persons	Required to be posted by employers with federal contracts or subcontracts of $2,500 or more.	Assistant Secretary for Employment Standards, U.S. Department of Labor, Washington, D.C.
Poster regarding hiring of Vietnam-era veterans	Required to be posted by employers with federal contracts or subcontracts of $10,000 or more.	The government contracting officer on the federal contract
Employee Polygraph Protection Act notice	Required to be posted by most private employers.	U.S. Department of Labor, Wage and Hour Division offices

Notes

Application for Sales and Use Tax License: Sample

N. C. DEPARTMENT OF REVENUE
P. O. BOX 25000
RALEIGH, N. C. 27640

OFFICE USE ONLY

REGISTRATION APPLICATION
(SEE INSTRUCTIONS ON REVERSE)

AS/RP1(6–93)

SALES AND USE TAX AND / OR INCOME TAX WITHHOLDING

1. Are you applying for a Sales and Use Tax Number; an Income Tax Withholding Number; or both? _____

2. Type Ownership –   (   )–Individual Proprietorship   (   )–Partnership   (   )–Corporation   (   )–Other _____

3. _____   4. (   ) _____
           Trade Name   Daytime/Business Telephone Number

5. _____
           Name

6. Business Location in N. C. _____
    (Not P. O. Box)   Street   City   State   Zip   County

7. Mailing Address _____
    (If different from Line 6)   Street or P. O. Box   City   State   Zip

8   Federal Employer Identification No. _____   9. Individual Owner's Social Security No. _____

10. Complete for primary partners or corporate officers (President, Vice–President, Secretary, Treasurer):
    NAME   **TITLE**   **SOCIAL SECURITY NO.**   **ADDRESS**
    _____   _____   _____   _____
    _____   _____   _____   _____
    _____   _____   _____   _____

11. Is business located within city/town limit? _____ Yes or No   Number of locations in N. C. _____

12 Does the business have employees who are subject to withholding? _____ Yes or No
    First month/year wages paid in N. C. subject to withholding _____
    Check the amount of income tax you expect to withhold each month _____ less than $500, _____ $500–$2,000, _____ more than $2,000
    Are you a new employer for federal employment taxes? _____ Yes or No

13. Does the business have sales? _____ Yes or No   Enter first month/year of sales_____ and check the appropriate item below
    Retail (to users or consumers) _____ Wholesale (to registered merchants for resale)_____ Both retail and wholesale _____
    Description of type of sales _____
    Do you sell new tires? _____ Yes or No   Do you lease or rent motor vehicles? _____ Yes or No
    Anticipated monthly sales and use tax liability _____ less than $50 _____ $50 or more

14. Seasonal Business? _____ Yes or No   If Yes:
    Check months of sales

Jan	Feb	Mar	Apr	May	Jun	Jul	Aug	Sep	Oct	Nov	Dec

    Check months employees are paid

Jan	Feb	Mar	Apr	May	Jun	Jul	Aug	Sep	Oct	Nov	Dec

15. If this business was acquired, complete previous owner information

    _____   _____
         Previous Owner Name   Previous Trade or Business Name
    Previous Withholding Identification No. if known _____ Previous Sales Tax No. if known _____

16. State of incorporation (if other than N. C.)_____ Registered agent in N. C. _____
                                                              Name   Address

17. Check appropriate box(es) and <u>attach check</u> for total amount due.
    ☐ Merchants Certificate of Registration – $15.00
    ☐ Annual Wholesale License – $25.00
    ☐ User or Consumer Registration – No Fee
    ☐ Income Tax Withholding Registration – No Fee

    ENTER TOTAL AMOUNT DUE
    $

    Under penalties provided by law, I hereby affirm that to the best of my knowledge and belief this application is true and complete.

    _____   _____   _____
         Signature   Title   Date

Application for Sales and Use Tax License: Sample (continued)

GENERAL INFORMATION

INCOME TAX WITHHOLDING

North Carolina law requires withholding of income tax from salaries and wages of all residents regardless of where earned and from wages of non–residents for personal services performed in this State. Under the law, the tax must be withheld from each payment of wages, and the amount is considered to be held in trust until it is paid to the Department of Revenue. Due date requirements for reporting and paying the tax depend on the amount of tax withheld each month. Employers withholding less than $500 per month, report and pay the tax quarterly. Employers who average withholding at least $500 but less than $2,000 per month, report and pay monthly. Employers who average withholding $2,000 or more per month, make payments on the dates Federal deposits are required and file quarterly reports. For full details of North Carolina income tax withholding, see the Income Tax Withholding Table and Instructions for Employers (Form NC–30).

SALES AND USE TAX

Every person who is engaged in the business of selling at retail and/or renting or leasing taxable tangible personal property in this State or who operates a laundry, dry cleaning plant or similar business or a hotel, motel or similar business in this State is liable for a Merchants Certificate of Registration license and payment of a $15 fee.

> **IMPORTANT NOTICE** – Your license will allow you to issue a certificate of resale to obtain property for resale. A purchaser is liable for a $250 penalty for misuse of a certificate of resale. See the certificate for instructions on its proper use.

Every person who is engaged in business in this State and makes sales of tangible personal property in this State to registered merchants for resale is liable for an Annual Wholesale License and payment of a $25 fee in addition to the $15 fee for a Merchants Certificate of Registration license except; a. A manufacturer selling and shipping its manufactured products directly and exclusively from the place of manufacture; b. A firm outside this State which ships tangible personal property to its customers from a place outside this State exclusively.

Every person who buys taxable tangible personal property from out–of–state vendors for storage, use or consumption in North Carolina is required to obtain a Users or Consumers Use Tax Registration except: a. Persons registered for payment of sales tax; b. Persons who have paid their vendors all taxes due on their purchases for storage, use or consumption.

REGISTRATION APPLICATION INSTRUCTIONS

Most of the items on the application are self–explanatory and do not require any instructions. The following information is to assist you in completing certain items:

Item 3	Enter the "trading as" name by which your business is known to the public.
Item 5	If the business is a sole proprietorship, insert the name of the owner. If the business is a corporation, insert the legal name of the corporation. If the business is a partnership, do not complete Item 5, but list the partners' names in Item 10.
Item 6	Enter the address of the actual location of the business. Do not enter the home address of an individual owner or a salesman in North Carolina.
Item 8	Enter your Federal Employer's Identification Number. If the number has been applied for but not received, enter "applied for" and then furnish the number as soon as you receive it.
Item 9	Enter the Social Security Number of the owner of the business if the business is an individual proprietorship; otherwise, leave blank.
Items 12 & 13	Complete Items 12 and 13 if you are applying for both a Sales and Use Tax Number and an Income Tax Withholding Number. Complete Item 12 and omit Item 13 if applying for only an Income Tax Withholding Number. Complete Item 13 and omit Item 12 if applying for only a Sales and Use Tax Number.

Books that save you time & money.

An extensive summary of every imaginable tax break that is still available in today's "reform" tax environment. Deals with the various entities that the owner/manager may choose to operate a business. Identifies a wide assortment of tax deduction, fringe benefits, and tax deferrals. Includes a simplified checklist of recent tax law changes with an emphasis on tax breaks.

Top Tax Saving Ideas for Today's Small Business   *Pages: 320*
Paperback; $16.95   *ISBN: 1-55571-343-2*

Makes understanding the economics of your business simple. Explains the basic accounting principles that relate to any business. Step-by-step instructions for generating accounting statements and interpreting them, spotting errors, and recognizing warning signs. Discusses how creditors view financial statements.

Business Owners' Guide to Accounting and Bookkeeping   *Pages: 150*
Paperback $19.95   *ISBN: 1-55571-381-5*

Essential for the small business operator in search of capital, this helpful, hands-on guide simplifies the loan application process. *The Insider's Guide to Small Business Loans* is an easy-to-follow roadmap designed to help you cut through the red tape and show you how to prepare a successful loan application. Packed with helpful resources such as SBIC directories, SBA offices, microloan lenders, and a complete nationwide listing of certified and preferred lenders — plus more than a dozen invaluable worksheets and forms.

The Insider's Guide to Small Business Loans   *Pages: 230*
Paperback: $19.95   *ISBN: 1-55571-373-4*
Binder Edition: $29.95   *ISBN: 1-55571-378-5*

In today's cut-throat business world, businesses often disregard the importance of building lasting business relationships. This guide shows how business owners can slow down their feeding frenzy approach to business activities and build profitable and worthwhile relationships.

Friendship Marketing   *Pages: 200*
Paperback $18.95   *ISBN: 1-55571-399-8*

Books that save you time & money.

A compendium of real business opportunities, not just "how" new ventures which often have limited earning potential. Which Business? will help you define your skills and interests by exploring your dreams and how you think about business. The book profiles 24 business areas, reviewing how each got their start and the problems and successes that they have experienced.

Which Business? Help in Selecting Your New Venture   *Pages: 300*
Paperback $18.95   *ISBN: 1-55571-390-4*

Written for the business owner or manager who is not a personnel specialist. Explains what you must know to make your hiring decisions pay off for everyone. Learn more about the Americans With Disabilities Act (ADA), Medical and Family Leave, and more.

People Investment   *Pages: 210*
Paperback $19.95   *ISBN: 1-55571-161-8*
Binder Edition: $39.95   *ISBN: 1-55571-187-1*

Now you can find out what venture capitalists and bankers really want to see before they will fund a company. This book gives you their personal tips and insights. The Abrams Method of Flow-Through Financials breaks down the chore into easy-to-manage steps, so you can end up with a fundable proposal. Windows™ software is also available to accompany the book with all the tools needed to create your own business plan.

ALSO AVAILABLE AS A BOOK & DISK PACKAGE FOR WINDOWS™
Successful Business Plan: Secrets & Strategies   *Pages: 332*
Paperback: $27.95   *ISBN: 1-55571-194-4*
Binder Edition: $49.95   *ISBN: 1-55571-197-9*
Paperback & Disk Package $109.95

Over 200 reproducible forms for all types of business needs: personnel, employment, finance, production flow, operations, sales, marketing, order entry, and general administration. A time-saving, uniform, coordinated way to record and locate important business information.

Complete Book of Business Forms   *Pages: 234*
Paperback $19.95   *ISBN: 1-55571-107-3*
Binder Edition $39.95   *ISBN: 1-55571-103-0*

THE OASIS PRESS® ORDER FORM

Call, Mail, Email, or Fax Your Order to: PSI Research, 300 North Valley Drive, Grants Pass, OR 97526 USA
Email: psi2@magick.net   Website: http://www.psi-research.com
Order Phone USA & Canada: +1 800 228-2275   Inquiries & International Orders: +1 541 479-9464 Fax: +1 541 476-1479

TITLE	✔ BINDER	✔ PAPERBACK	QUANTITY	COST
Bottom Line Basics	❏ $39.95	❏ $19.95		
The Business Environmental Handbook	❏ $39.95	❏ $19.95		
Business Owner's Guide to Accounting & Bookkeeping		❏ $19.95		
Buyer's Guide to Business Insurance	❏ $39.95	❏ $19.95		
Collection Techniques for a Small Business	❏ $39.95	❏ $19.95		
A Company Policy and Personnel Workbook	❏ $49.95	❏ $29.95		
Company Relocation Handbook	❏ $39.95	❏ $19.95		
CompControl: The Secrets of Reducing Worker's Compensation Costs	❏ $39.95	❏ $19.95		
Complete Book of Business Forms		❏ $19.95		
Customer Engineering: Cutting Edge Selling Strategies	❏ $39.95	❏ $19.95		
Develop & Market Your Creative Ideas		❏ $15.95		
Doing Business in Russia		❏ $19.95		
Draw The Line: A Sexual Harassment Free Workplace		❏ $17.95		
The Essential Corporation Handbook		❏ $21.95		
The Essential Limited Liability Company Handbook	❏ $39.95	❏ $21.95		
Export Now: A Guide for Small Business	❏ $39.95	❏ $24.95		
Financial Management Techniques for Small Business	❏ $39.95	❏ $19.95		
Financing Your Small Business		❏ $19.95		
Franchise Bible: How to Buy a Franchise or Franchise Your Own Business	❏ $39.95	❏ $24.95		
Friendship Marketing: Growing Your Business by Cultivating Strategic Relationships		❏ $18.95		
Home Business Made Easy		❏ $19.95		
Incorporating Without A Lawyer (Available for 32 states) SPECIFY STATE:		❏ $24.95		
Joysticks, Blinking Lights and Thrills		❏ $18.95		
The Insider's Guide to Small Business Loans	❏ $29.95	❏ $19.95		
InstaCorp – Incorporate In Any State (Book & Software)		❏ $29.95		
Keeping Score: An Inside Look at Sports Marketing		❏ $18.95		
Know Your Market: How to Do Low-Cost Market Research	❏ $39.95	❏ $19.95		
Legal Expense Defense: How to Control Your Business' Legal Costs and Problems	❏ $39.95	❏ $19.95		
Location, Location, Location: How to Select the Best Site for Your Business		❏ $19.95		
Mail Order Legal Guide	❏ $45.00	❏ $29.95		
Managing People: A Practical Guide		❏ $21.95		
Marketing Mastery: Your Seven Step Guide to Success	❏ $39.95	❏ $19.95		
The Money Connection: Where and How to Apply for Business Loans and Venture Capital	❏ $39.95	❏ $24.95		
People Investment	❏ $39.95	❏ $19.95		
Power Marketing for Small Business	❏ $39.95	❏ $19.95		
Profit Power: 101 Pointers to Give Your Business a Competitive Edge		❏ $19.95		
Proposal Development: How to Respond and Win the Bid	❏ $39.95	❏ $21.95		
Raising Capital	❏ $39.95	❏ $19.95		
Retail in Detail: How to Start and Manage a Small Retail Business		❏ $15.95		
Secrets to Buying and Selling a Business		❏ $24.95		
Secure Your Future: Financial Planning at Any Age	❏ $39.95	❏ $19.95		
The Small Business Insider's Guide to Bankers		❏ $18.95		
Start Your Business (Available as a book and disk package – see back)		❏ $ 9.95 (without disk)		
Starting and Operating a Business in...series Includes FEDERAL section PLUS ONE STATE section	❏ $34.95	❏ $27.95		
PLEASE SPECIFY WHICH STATE(S) YOU WANT:				
STATE SECTION ONLY (BINDER NOT INCLUDED) SPECIFY STATE(S):	❏ $8.95			
FEDERAL SECTION ONLY (BINDER NOT INCLUDED)	❏ $12.95			
U.S. EDITION (FEDERAL SECTION – 50 STATES AND WASHINGTON DC IN 11-BINDER SET)	❏ $295.95			
Successful Business Plan: Secrets & Strategies	❏ $49.95	❏ $27.95		
Successful Network Marketing for The 21st Century		❏ $15.95		
Surviving and Prospering in a Business Partnership	❏ $39.95	❏ $19.95		
TargetSmart! Database Marketing for the Small Business		❏ $19.95		
Top Tax Saving Ideas for Today's Small Business		❏ $16.95		
Which Business? Help in Selecting Your New Venture		❏ $18.95		
Write Your Own Business Contracts	❏ $39.95	❏ $24.95		
BOOK SUB-TOTAL (FIGURE YOUR TOTAL AMOUNT ON THE OTHER SIDE)				

OASIS SOFTWARE   Please check Macintosh or 3-1/2" Disk for IBM-PC & Compatibles

TITLE	3-1/2" IBM Disk	Mac-OS	Price	QUANTITY	COST
California Corporation Formation Package ASCII Software	☐	☐	$ 39.95		
Company Policy & Personnel Software Text Files	☐	☐	$ 49.95		
Financial Management Techniques (Full Standalone)	☐		$ 99.95		
Financial Templates	☐	☐	$ 69.95		
The Insurance Assistant Software (Full Standalone)	☐		$ 29.95		
Start A Business (Full Standalone)	☐		$ 49.95		
Start Your Business (Software for Windows™)	☐		$ 19.95		
Successful Business Plan (Software for Windows™)	☐		$ 99.95		
Successful Business Plan Templates	☐	☐	$ 69.95		
The Survey Genie - Customer Edition (Full Standalone)	☐		$149.95		
The Survey Genie - Employee Edition (Full Standalone)	☐		$149.95		
SOFTWARE SUB-TOTAL					

BOOK & DISK PACKAGES   Please check whether you use Macintosh or 3-1/2" Disk for IBM-PC & Compatibles

TITLE	IBM-PC	Mac-OS	BINDER	PAPERBACK	QUANTITY	COST
The Buyer's Guide to Business Insurance w/ Insurance Assistant	☐		☐$ 59.95	☐$ 39.95		
California Corporation Formation Binder Book & ASCII Software	☐	☐	☐$ 69.95	☐$ 59.95		
Company Policy & Personnel Book & Software Text Files	☐	☐	☐$ 89.95	☐$ 69.95		
Financial Management Techniques Book & Software	☐		☐$ 129.95	☐$ 119.95		
Start Your Business Paperback & Software (Software for Windows™)	☐			☐$ 24.95		
Successful Business Plan Book & Software for Windows™	☐		☐$125.95	☐$109.95		
Successful Business Plan Book & Software Templates	☐	☐	☐$109.95	☐$ 89.95		
BOOK & DISK PACKAGE TOTAL						

AUDIO CASSETTES

TITLE	Price	QUANTITY	COST
Power Marketing Tools For Small Business	☐ $ 49.95		
The Secrets To Buying & Selling A Business	☐ $ 49.95		
AUDIO CASSETTE SUB-TOTAL			

OASIS SUCCESS KITS   Call for more information about these products

TITLE	Price	QUANTITY	COST
Start-Up Success Kit	☐ $ 39.95		
Business At Home Success Kit	☐ $ 39.95		
Financial Management Success Kit	☐ $ 44.95		
Personnel Success Kit	☐ $ 44.95		
Marketing Success Kit	☐ $ 44.95		
OASIS SUCCESS KITS TOTAL			

COMBINED SUB-TOTAL (FROM THIS SIDE)

SOLD TO: *Please give street address*

NAME:

Title:

Company:

Street Address:

City/State/Zip:

Daytime Phone: Email:

SHIP TO: *If different than above, please give alternate street address*

NAME:

Title:

Company:

Street Address:

City/State/Zip:

Daytime Phone:

YOUR GRAND TOTAL

SUB-TOTALS (from other side) $

SUB-TOTALS (from this side) $

SHIPPING (see chart below) $

TOTAL ORDER $

If your purchase is:	Shipping costs within the USA:
$0 - $25	$5.00
$25.01 - $50	$6.00
$50.01 - $100	$7.00
$100.01 - $175	$9.00
$175.01 - $250	$13.00
$250.01 - $500	$18.00
$500.01+	4% of total merchandise

PAYMENT INFORMATION: *Rush service is available, call for details. International and Canadian Orders: Please call for quote on shipping.*

☐ CHECK Enclosed payable to PSI Research   Charge: ☐ VISA   ☐ MASTERCARD   ☐ AMEX   ☐ DISCOVER

Card Number: Expires:

Signature: Name On Card:

s&o 01/98

Call toll free to order 1-800-228-2275 PSI Research 300 North Valley Drive, Grants Pass, OR 97526 FAX 541-476-1479

Use this form to register for an advance notification of updates, new books and software releases, plus special customer discounts!

Please answer these questions to let us know how our products are working for you, and what we could do to serve you better.

Starting & Operating a Business in _____

(PLEASE WRITE IN THE APPROPRIATE STATE NAME)

Rate this product's overall quality of information:
☐ Excellent
☐ Good
☐ Fair
☐ Poor

Rate the quality of printed materials:
☐ Excellent
☐ Good
☐ Fair
☐ Poor

Rate the format:
☐ Excellent
☐ Good
☐ Fair
☐ Poor

Did the product provide what you needed?
☐ Yes ☐ No

If not, what should be added?
_____
_____
_____
_____
_____
_____
_____
_____

This product is:
☐ Clear and easy to follow
☐ Too complicated
☐ Too elementary

Were the worksheets easy to use?
☐ Yes ☐ No ☐ N/A

Should we include?
☐ More worksheets
☐ Fewer worksheets
☐ No worksheets

How do you feel about the price?
☐ Lower than expected
☐ About right
☐ Too expensive

How many employees are in your company?
☐ Under 10 employees
☐ 10 - 50 employees
☐ 51 - 99 employees
☐ 100 - 250 employees
☐ Over 250 employees

How many people in the city your company is in?
☐ 50,000 - 100,000
☐ 100,000 - 500,000
☐ 500,000 - 1,000,000
☐ Over 1,000,000
☐ Rural (Under 50,000)

What is your type of business?
☐ Retail
☐ Service
☐ Government
☐ Manufacturing
☐ Distributor
☐ Education

What types of products or services do you sell?
_____
_____

What is your position in the company?
(please check one)
☐ Owner
☐ Administrative
☐ Sales/Marketing
☐ Finance
☐ Human Resources
☐ Production
☐ Operations
☐ Computer/MIS

How did you learn about this product?
☐ Recommended by a friend
☐ Used in a seminar or class
☐ Have used other PSI products
☐ Received a mailing
☐ Saw in bookstore
☐ Saw in library
☐ Saw review in:
  ☐ Newspaper
  ☐ Magazine
  ☐ Radio/TV

Where did you buy this product?
☐ Catalog
☐ Bookstore
☐ Office supply
☐ Consultant

Would you purchase other business tools from us?
☐ Yes ☐ No

If so, which products interest you?
☐ EXECARDS® Communications Cards
☐ Books for business
☐ Software

Would you recommend this product to a friend?
☐ Yes ☐ No

Do you use a personal computer?
☐ Yes ☐ No

If yes, which?
☐ Macintosh
☐ PC Compatible
☐ Other

Check all the ways you use computers?
☐ Word processing
☐ Accounting
☐ Spreadsheet
☐ Inventory
☐ Order processing
☐ Design/Graphics
☐ General Data Base
☐ Customer Information
☐ Scheduling
☐ Internet

May we call you to follow up on your comments?
☐ Yes ☐ No

May we add your name to our mailing list? ☐ Yes ☐ No

If you'd like us to send associates or friends a catalog, just list names and addresses on back.

Is there anything we should do to improve our products?
_____

Just fill in your name and address here, fold (see back) and mail.

Name _____
Title _____
Company _____
Phone _____
Address _____
City/State/Zip _____
Email Address (Home) _____ (Business) _____

s&o:01/98

If you have friends or associates who might appreciate receiving our catalogs, please list here. Thanks!

Name_____   Name_____

Title_____   Title_____

Company_____   Company_____

Phone_____   Phone_____

Address_____   Address_____

Address_____   Address_____

FOLD HERE FIRST

- -

‖‖‖‖

NO POSTAGE
NECESSARY
IF MAILED
IN THE
UNITED STATES

BUSINESS REPLY MAIL

FIRST CLASS MAIL PERMIT NO. 002 MERLIN, OREGON

POSTAGE WILL BE PAID BY ADDRESSEE

PSI Research
PO BOX 1414
Merlin OR 97532-9900

‖‖‖‖‖‖‖‖‖‖‖‖‖‖‖‖‖‖‖‖‖‖‖‖‖

- -

FOLD HERE SECOND, THEN TAPE TOGETHER

✂
Please cut
along this
vertical line,
fold twice,
tape together
and mail.